T0340205

# The Econometric Analysis of Network Data

# The Econometric Analysis of Network Data

Edited by

**Bryan Graham**
University of California, Berkeley
Berkeley, CA, United States

**Áureo de Paula**
University College London
London, United Kingdom

ELSEVIER

**ACADEMIC PRESS**
An imprint of Elsevier

Academic Press is an imprint of Elsevier
125 London Wall, London EC2Y 5AS, United Kingdom
525 B Street, Suite 1650, San Diego, CA 92101, United States
50 Hampshire Street, 5th Floor, Cambridge, MA 02139, United States
The Boulevard, Langford Lane, Kidlington, Oxford OX5 1GB, United Kingdom

**Library of Congress Cataloging-in-Publication Data**
A catalog record for this book is available from the Library of Congress

**British Library Cataloguing-in-Publication Data**
A catalogue record for this book is available from the British Library

ISBN: 978-0-12-811771-2

For information on all Academic Press publications
visit our website at https://www.elsevier.com/books-and-journals

*Publisher:* Candice Janco
*Acquisitions Editor:* Scott Bentley
*Editorial Project Manager:* Susan Ikeda
*Production Project Manager:* Swapna Srinivasan
*Designer:* Christian J. Bilbow

Typeset by VTeX

Working together
to grow libraries in
developing countries

www.elsevier.com • www.bookaid.org

# Contents

## 4. Testing for externalities in network formation using simulation

*Bryan S. Graham and Andrin Pelican*

## 5. Econometric analysis of bipartite networks

*Stéphane Bonhomme*

## 6. An empirical model for strategic network formation

*Nicholas Christakis, James Fowler, Guido W. Imbens, and Karthik Kalyanaraman*

## 7.  Econometric analysis of models with social interactions

*Brendan Kline and Elie Tamer*

## 8.  Many player asymptotics for large network formation problems

*Konrad Menzel*

# Preface

**Introduction**

Collectively, the chapters in this book—contributed by multiple authors—provide an introduction to the econometric analysis of network data. Whereas an established, albeit also rapidly developing, literature on network analysis exists in other fields, spanning many of the social sciences, physics and statistics, the contributions here focus on tools and applications related to the field of economics. While they build upon, and draw inspiration from, developments in other fields, many of them quintessentially relate to research in economics. Our aim here is not to be exhaustive, but to provide a gateway to some of the questions of interest to economists and recent methods for handling them. The topics include, for example, econometric models of network formation (both dyadic and game-theoretic), the econometrics of bipartite structures, as well as social interaction models, with outcomes mediated by networks.

**Target audience**

The target audience for this book is broad. We hope the book will be a useful reference for graduate students as well as more established researchers looking for an introduction to network data analysis from an econometric viewpoint. While the volume is not structured as a course textbook per se, it provides a nice mix of introductory and advanced material, such that it could serve as a useful organizing reference for a graduate course, or module, on the econometrics of networks.

**Acknowledgments**

This book is a team effort and we would like to thank the various contributors to this volume for their willingness to prepare chapters: Stephane Bonhomme, Nicholas Christakis, James Fowler, Guido Imbens, Kartik Kalyanaraman, Brendan Kline, Konrad Menzel, Andrin Pelican and Elie Tamer. We would also like to thank Susan Ikeda, who gently kept the editorial train on the tracks. Áureo de Paula thanks his close friends Christian Julliard and Albina Danilova, for always receiving him with a warm meal, good wine and wise advice whenever the going got tough in preparing this manuscript, and his family for always being present, even if far away. Bryan Graham thanks many students and colleagues for suffering through lectures and/or conversations based upon preliminary versions of some the material included here.

# List of contributors

**Stéphane Bonhomme**, University of Chicago, Chicago, IL, United States

**Nicholas Christakis**, Department of Sociology, Internal Medicine and Biomedical Engineering, Yale University, New Haven, CT, United States

**James Fowler**, Department of Political Science, University of California at San Diego, San Diego, CA, United States

**Bryan S. Graham**, Department of Economics, University of California - Berkeley, Berkeley, CA, United States
National Bureau of Economic Research, Cambridge, MA, United States

**Guido W. Imbens**, Department of Economics and Graduate School of Business, Stanford University, Stanford, CA, United States
NBER, Cambridge, MA, United States

**Karthik Kalyanaraman**, 64/1, Bengaluru, India

**Brendan Kline**, University of Texas at Austin, Austin, TX, United States

**Konrad Menzel**, New York University, New York, NY, United States

**Áureo de Paula**, University College London, CeMMAP, IFS and CEPR, London, United Kingdom

**Andrin Pelican**, Department of Economics, School of Economics and Political Science, University of St. Gallen, St. Gallen, Switzerland

**Elie Tamer**, Harvard University, Cambridge, MA, United States

# Chapter 1

# Introduction

## Bryan S. Graham[a] and Áureo de Paula[b]
[a]*Department of Economics, University of California - Berkeley, Berkeley, CA, United States,*
[b]*University College London, CeMMAP, IFS and CEPR, London, United Kingdom*

## Contents

In this chapter we provide the foundational vocabulary for discussing, describing and summarizing network data like that shown in Fig. 1.1. This figure depicts buyer–supplier relationships among publicly traded firms in the United States. Each dot (*node* or *vertex*) in the figure corresponds to a firm. If a firm, say, United Technologies Corporation, supplies inputs to another firm, say Boeing Corporation, then there exists a *directed edge* (also referred to as *link* or *tie*) ●—● from United Technologies to Boeing. The supplying firm (left node) is called the *tail* of the edge, while the buying firm (right node) is its *head*. The set of all such supplier–buyer relationships forms the graph $G(\mathcal{V}, \mathcal{E})$, a directed network or *digraph* defined on $N = |\mathcal{V}|$ vertices or agents (here publicly traded firms). The set $\mathcal{V} = \{1, \ldots, N\}$ includes all agents (firms) in the network and $\mathcal{E} \subseteq \mathcal{V} \times \mathcal{V}$ the set of all directed links (supplier–buyer relationships) among them.[1],[2] The number of nodes $N$ is sometimes referred to as the *order* of the digraph and $|\mathcal{E}|$, its *size*.[3]

---

[1] Here $\mathcal{U} \times \mathcal{V}$ denotes the Cartesian product of the set $\mathcal{U}$ and $\mathcal{V}$ (i.e., $\mathcal{U} \times \mathcal{V} = \{(u, v) : u \in \mathcal{U}, v \in \mathcal{V}\}$).
[2] The buyer-supplier network depicted in Fig. 1.1 was constructed using information on large customers disclosed by firms when filing with the United States Securities and Exchange Commission (SEC). Statement of Financial Accounting Standards (SFAS) regulation 131, in effect since 1998, requires firms to report sales to customers which account for 10 percent or more of all firm sales in a given year. Prior to 1998, SFAS regulation 14 imposed similar requirements. Firm-reported large customers are included in the Compustat – Capital IQ customer segments file. Cohen and Frazzini (2008) and Atalay et al. (2011) also construct Supplier–Buyer networks from Compustat data.
[3] In what follows, depending on the context, we will refer synonymously to (di)graphs or (directed) networks.

The Econometric Analysis of Network Data. https://doi.org/10.1016/B978-0-12-811771-2.00007-9

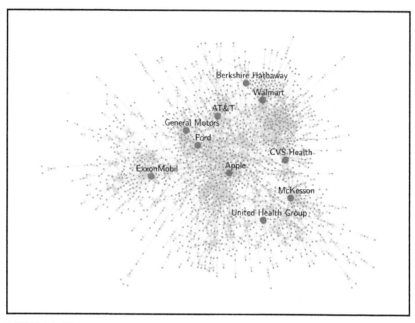

**FIGURE 1.1** US buyer–supplier production network, 2015. *Sources:* Compustat – Capital IQ and authors' calculations.

If $i$ directs an edges to $j$, and $j$ likewise directs and edge back to $i$, we say the link is *reciprocated*. In some settings links are automatically reciprocated, or naturally "directionless" (e.g., partnerships), in which case the network is undirected. This is the case, for instance, in Fafchamps and Lund (2003) which focuses on (reciprocal) risk-sharing relationships in the rural Phillipines. Links in such an undirected graph are represented as unordered pairs of nodes instead of ordered pairs as described previously. In what follows we will present results for both directed and undirected networks depending on a combination of our immediate pedagogical goals, the illustrating application, and the state of the literature. While analogs of methods and algorithms available for directed networks are typically available for undirected ones, and vice versa, this is not always the case.

Returning to the digraph discussed earlier, the US supplier–buyer network is extraordinarily complex. Its structure may have implications for regulation and industrial policy, the diffusion of technology, and even macroeconomic policy-making (e.g., Carvalho, 2014; Acemoglu et al., 2016). In order to study this network, and others like it, we first need to know how to summarize its essential features. In non-network settings, empirical research often begins by tabulating a variety of summary statistics (e.g., means, medians, standard deviations, correlations). How might a researcher similarly summarize a dataset of relationships among agents? We outline some answers to this question in what follows.

While Fig. 1.1 is interesting to look at, it is not especially useful for statistical analysis. For this purpose it is convenient to represent $G(\mathcal{V}, \mathcal{E})$ by its $N \times N$ *adjacency matrix* $\mathbf{D} = [D_{ij}]$ where

$$
D_{ij} = \begin{cases} 1, & (i, j) \in \mathcal{E}(G), \\ 0, & \text{otherwise.} \end{cases} \tag{1.1}
$$

Here $D_{ij} = 1$ if agent $i$ "sends" or "directs" a link to agent $j$ (and zero otherwise), while $D_{ji} = 1$ if agent $j$ directs a link to $i$. While the adjacency matrix for an undirected network will be symmetric as links are reciprocal, the adjacency matrix for a digraph need not (and typically will not) be symmetric. Self-links, or loops, are ruled-out here, though they may be allowed in different contexts, such that $D_{ii} = 0$ for all $i = 1, \ldots, N$. Econometric analysis of network data typically involves operations on the adjacency matrix as they allow one to focus on algebraic operations rather than graph-theoretic, combinatorial manipulations.[4] These matrices can also encode the strength of any links between a pair of nodes if this is available, like the traffic flow (edge) from one city (node) to another. A network with unweighted edges is typically referred to as a *simple graph* in the graph theory literature.

Once we define the basic objects of interest as graphs or adjacency matrices representing those, we can expand our discussion on probabilistic processes leading to observed social and economic networks. In other words, one can postulate a statistical model on the examined networks. Letting $\mathcal{G}$ be a particular set of graphs or networks, we can define a probability distribution over that particular set of graphs taken as a sample space. These probability models can be and usually are indexed by features or parameters related to the graphs in $\mathcal{G}$, like the number of vertices and/or other features. A collection of such models provides the basis for a statistical model. One of the early models, for example, imposes a uniform probability on the class of graphs with a given number of nodes, $N$, and a particular number of edges, $|\mathcal{E}|$, for $g \in \mathcal{G}$ (see Erdös and Rényi (1959) and Erdös and Rényi (1960)). Another basic, canonical random-graph model is one in which the edges between any two nodes follow an independent Bernoulli distribution with equal probability, say $p$. For a large enough number of nodes and sufficiently small probability of link formation $p$, the degree distribution approaches a Poisson distribution, and the model is consequently known as the Poisson random-graph model. This class of models appears in Gilbert (1959) and Erdös and Rényi (1960) and has since been studied extensively. While they

---

[4] There are other matrix representations for a network. For example, the *incidence* matrix will list vertices as rows and edges as columns. In digraphs, a node-edge entry in the incidence matrix is 1 if the node is the tail of the edge and $-1$ if it is the head. For undirected networks, the (unoriented) incidence matrix entry is 1 if the node in the row is part of the edge in that column. Such representations are related and informative about features of the network (e.g., via its eigenvalues and eigenvectors) and might be adequate for different purposes.

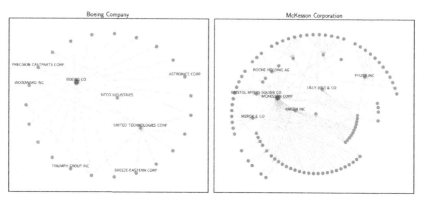

**FIGURE 1.2** Boeing and McKesson supply chains, 2015. *Sources:* Compustat – Capital IQ and authors' calculations.

fail to reproduce important dependencies observed in social and economic networks accurately, they form important antecedents for the ensuing discussion in this volume.

## Paths, distance and diameter

Imagine Fig. 1.1 is a map showing one way roads (edges) between cities (nodes). Under this analogy reciprocated links correspond to two way roads. If an individual can legally travel from city $i$ to $j$ along a sequence of one way roads (edges), we say there is a *walk* from $i$ to $j$. When the walk does not repeat any cities (nodes) along the way, it is called a *path* and when it does not repeat any edges, it is called a *trail*. If our traveler traverses $k$ edges on her trip, then we say the walk is of *length $k$*. Walks are directed in a digraph: it may be possible to go from $i$ to $j$, but not back from $j$ to $i$. If a walk runs from $i$ to $j$, but not from $j$ to $i$, we say $i$ and $j$ are *weakly connected*. If a walk runs in both directions, the two agents are *strongly connected*. In this case, a walk from city $i$ to $j$ and back that does not repeat any cities in between is a trail, in fact a *cycle*, but not a path. The shortest walk from $i$ to $j$ equals the *distance* from $i$ to $j$.

The left-hand panel of Fig. 1.2 shows Boeing's supply chain. Inspecting this figure we can see that there is a length 1 path from Precision Castparts Corporation to Boeing. There is also a length 2 path which runs through United Technologies Corporation. Precision Castparts is both a direct and indirect supplier to Boeing. The distance from Precision Castparts to Boeing is one. The distance from Breeze Eastern Corporation to Boeing is two. Note that there is no directed path from Boeing to Breeze Eastern; the distance from Boeing to Breeze Eastern is infinite.

We say a directed network is *weakly connected* if for any two agents, there is a directed path connecting them. The network is *strongly connected* if there is a directed path from both $i$ to $j$ and $j$ to $i$ for all pairs of agents $i$ and $j$.

Most real-world directed networks are not strongly connected, but many are weakly connected or, more precisely, contain a large *giant component* that is weakly connected. Fig. 1.1 actually does not show the full US buyer-supplier network, instead it just shows its largest weakly connected component (i.e., the maximum subset of nodes such that there is a directed path between all nodes in the subset). This weakly connected component includes over 80 percent all publicly traded firms in the United States. This indicates the substantial level of interconnectedness across the supply-chains of large firms in the United States economy. Such interconnectedness implies that shocks to just a few firms may affect the macroeconomy. Carvalho et al. (2016) show how the Great East Japan Earthquake of 2011, while directly impacting only a small fraction of Japanese firms, ultimately disrupted production in large portions of the Japanese and, to a lesser extent, global economies.

It turns out that we can count the number of $k$-length walks connecting two agents in a network, by inspecting powers of the adjacency matrix. Consider first the square of the adjacency matrix:

$$\mathbf{D}^2 = \begin{pmatrix} \sum_j D_{1j}D_{j1} & \sum_j D_{1j}D_{j2} & \cdots & \sum_j D_{1j}D_{jN} \\ \sum_j D_{2j}D_{j1} & \sum_j D_{2j}D_{j2} & & \sum_j D_{2j}D_{jN} \\ \vdots & & \ddots & \\ \sum_j D_{Nj}D_{j1} & \sum_j D_{Nj}D_{j2} & \cdots & \sum_j D_{Nj}D_{jN} \end{pmatrix}. \quad (1.2)$$

The $ij$th element of (1.2) coincides with the number of length two walks from agents $i$ to $j$. If $i$ links to $k$, and $k$ links to $j$, then there exists a length two walk from $i$ to $j$. The $ij$th element of (1.2) is a summation over all such length two walks. The diagonal elements of (1.2) equal the number of reciprocated ties to which agent $i$ is party. Observe that reciprocated links are equivalent to length two walks from an agent back to herself.

Calculating $\mathbf{D}^3$ yields

$$\mathbf{D}^3 = \begin{pmatrix} \sum_{j,k} D_{1j}D_{jk}D_{k1} & \sum_{j,k} D_{1j}D_{jk}D_{k2} & \cdots & \sum_{j,k} D_{1j}D_{jk}D_{kN} \\ \sum_{j,k} D_{2j}D_{jk}D_{k1} & \sum_{j,k} D_{2j}D_{jk}D_{k2} & & \\ \vdots & & \ddots & \\ \sum_{j,k} D_{Nj}D_{jk}D_{k1} & \sum_{j,k} D_{Nj}D_{jk}D_{k2} & \cdots & \sum_{j,k} D_{Nj}D_{jk}D_{kN} \end{pmatrix}$$

whose $ij$th element gives the number of walks of length 3 from $i$ to $j$. Note these walks may pass through a single agent twice. For example a length three path from $i$ to $j$ may involve walking from $i$ to $k$, then back to $i$ (via a reciprocated link), and then finally to $j$.

Proceeding inductively it is easy to show that the $ij$th element of $\mathbf{D}^k$ gives the number of walks of length $k$ from agent $i$ to agent $j$.

**Theorem 1.1.** *For a digraph $G$ with adjacency matrix $\mathbf{D}$ and $k$ a positive integer, the number of $k$-length walks from agents $i$ to $j$ coincides with the $ij$th element of $\mathbf{D}^k$.*

*Proof.* Let $D_{ij}^{(k)}$ denote the $ij$th element of $\mathbf{D}^k$. Begin by observing that $\mathbf{D}^0 = I_N$, correctly implying that the only zero length walks in the network are those from each agent to herself. Under the maintained hypothesis, $D_{ij}^{(k)}$ equals the number of $k$-length paths from $i$ to $j$. The number of $k+1$ length paths from $i$ to $j$ then equals

$$\sum_{k=1}^{N} D_{ik}^{(k)} D_{kj},$$

which equals the $ij$th element of $\mathbf{D}^{k+1}$. The claim follows by induction. $\quad\square$

We can also use powers of the adjacency matrix to calculate shortest path distances or "degrees of separation". Specifically,

$$M_{ij} = \min_{k \in \{1,2,3,\dots\}} \left\{ k : D_{ij}^{(k)} > 0 \right\} \tag{1.3}$$

equals the distance from $i$ to $j$ (if it is finite). For modestly-sized networks $M_{ij}$ can be calculated by taking successive powers of the adjacency matrix. If the network is strongly connected, we can compute the *average distance* as

$$\overline{M} = \frac{1}{N(N-1)} \sum_{i=1}^{N} \sum_{j \neq i} M_{ij}. \tag{1.4}$$

Since few directed networks are strongly connected, (1.4) is rarely finite. Consequently it can be insightful to first convert a directed network to an undirected one and then compute average distance as

$$\overline{M} = \binom{N}{2}^{-1} \sum_{i=1}^{N} \sum_{j < i} M_{ij}.$$

If the undirected network is not connected, then the average can be taken across dyads within its largest connected component.

The *diameter* of a network is the largest distance between any two agents in it. It will be finite if the network consists of a single strongly connected component (in which case all agents are "reachable" starting from any other agent) and infinite in weakly connected networks, or in those consisting of multiple strongly connected components (in which case there are no paths connecting some pairs of agents). As with average distance, it can sometimes be fruitful to first convert a directed network to an undirected one prior to computing is diameter.

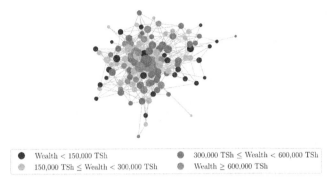

FIGURE 1.3 Nyakatoke risk-sharing network. *Sources:* De Weerdt (2004) and authors' calculations.

**TABLE 1.1** Frequency of degrees of separation in the Nyakatoke network.

|           | 1      | 2      | 3      | 4      | 5      |
|-----------|--------|--------|--------|--------|--------|
| Count     | 490    | 2666   | 3298   | 557    | 10     |
| Frequency | 0.0698 | 0.3797 | 0.4697 | 0.0793 | 0.0014 |

*Source:* De Weerdt (2004) and authors' calculations.

An illustration of these concepts is provided by the Nyakatoke risk-sharing network first studied by De Weerdt (2004). This network is depicted in Fig. 1.3, which plots risk-sharing links between households in the village of Nyakatoke, Tanzania. Households in Nyaktoke were asked about other individuals in the village they could "personally rely on for help". The network in Fig. 1.3 was constructed by placing an undirected edge between two households if a member in one reports being able to rely on help from a member in another, the opposite, or both.

The Nyakatoke network consists of a single giant component. Table 1.1 tabulates the frequency of shortest path lengths across all $\binom{119}{2} = 7,021$ dyads in the Nyakatoke network. The Nyakatoke network is, in many ways, prototypical of other small and medium-sized social and economic networks. First it is relatively *sparse*: only 490 out of 7,021 dyads in the Nyakatoke are directly connected (less than seven percent).[5] While only a small fraction of all possible links are present, shortest path lengths between any two nodes are small: over 85 percent of dyads are less that three degrees apart. The maximum distance between any two households, corresponding to the diameter of the network, is also small, equaling five.

The conjunction of sparseness and low diameter is common in social and economic networks and sometimes called the "small world phenomenon." This

---

[5] In statistical models of network formation investigated later, sparsity typically refers to the number of links, being $O_p(N^2)$, when $N$ is allowed to grow.

phrase was popularized by the social psychologist Stanley Milgram (1967) who argued, on the basis of computer simulations and real-world data collected through a series of postal experiments in the 1960s, that any two individuals in the United States are often connected through a short chain of acquaintances (e.g., "six degrees of separation").

Network sparseness and low diameter make the statistical analysis of network data challenging. Intuitively these two properties imply that there is little data and (perhaps) appreciable dependence across observations. Much of modern statistical analysis involves understanding what can be learned by averaging many independent pieces of data. Network statistical analysis often requires assessing what can be learned from small amounts of dependent data.

## Measuring homophily

A well-documented feature of many real-world social and economic networks is homophily: the tendency of agents to form links with others similar to themselves (e.g., McPherson et al., 2001; Pin and Rogers, 2016). Many types of social relationships occur more frequently between individuals with similar socio-demographic attributes (i.e., race, gender, social class; cf., Marsden, 1987). Homophily also extends beyond social links to economic ones. For example, Bengtsson and Hsu (2015) present evidence that co-ethnicity of investors and company founders is an important predictor of venture capital flows in the United States.[6]

The presence and magnitude of homophily and degree heterogeneity has implications for how information diffuses, the spread of epidemics, as well as the speed and precision of social learning (e.g., Pastor-Satorras and Vespignani, 2001; Jackson and Rogers, 2007; Golub and Jackson, 2012; Jackson and López-Pintado, 2013).[7]

In this section we consider the measurement of homophily in practice. For simplicity we focus on the *undirected* network case.

A measure of homophily captures the extent to which observed agent attributes $X_i$ and $X_j$ are more similar (in value) across agents who are linked ($D_{ij} = 1$) relative to those who are not ($D_{ij} = 0$); or relative to some benchmark model (e.g., a null model where agents match completely at random). In the statistical physics literature homophily is typically measured by what Newman (2010) calls the *modularity* of a network; this measure is now widely used in other fields as well. In the case of a binary attribute, network modularity is closely related to standard (and decades old) measures of residential segregation. As in the literature on the measurement of segregation, statistical measures of homophily are often presented as denizens of the sample data alone. That

---

[6] Another empirically robust example is assortative-matching by race among high schoolers in the United States (e.g. Currarini et al., 2009).

[7] Apicella et al. (2012) even study the relationship between homophily and the emergence of cooperation in hunter-gatherer societies.

is, without the context of a clear generative or population model (cf., Graham, 2018). The lack of such a generative model makes the interpretation and analysis of homophily measures difficult though connections with statistically-based models where ties form based on communities have been established (see Newman (2016)).

In this section we introduce some notation and use it to provide a simple probabilistic interpretation of network modularity. Our approach is guided (albeit rather indirectly) by graphon representations of probability distributions for exchangeable random graphs (e.g., Diaconis and Janson, 2008; Lovász, 2012; Bickel and Chen, 2009). Let $X_i \in \mathbb{X} \subset \mathbb{R}^1$ be some scalar-valued agent attribute and imagine that the link probability between $i$ and $j$ is guided by such attributes. Adapting the sample-based definition given by Newman (2010, p. 779), we define the *assortativity coefficient* or *normalized modularity* as

$$\rho_{\mathrm{AC}} = \frac{\mathbb{E}\left[X_i X_j \mid D_{ij} = 1\right] - \mathbb{E}\left[X_i \mid D_{ij} = 1\right]\mathbb{E}\left[X_j \mid D_{ij} = 1\right]}{\mathbb{E}\left[X_i^2 \mid D_{ij} = 1\right] - \mathbb{E}\left[X_i \mid D_{ij} = 1\right]^2}. \tag{1.5}$$

Eq. (1.5) is reminiscent of the definition of correlation between two random variables Goldberger (1991, p. 66). In fact (1.5), as we will demonstrate shortly, has such an interpretation, but, in the absence of additional structure, it is difficult to make much sense of the expected values present in (1.5).

We begin by establishing notation for the conditional probability of the event $D_{ij} = 1$ given that $X_i = x$ and $X_j = y$:

$$\omega(x, y) = \Pr\left(D_{ij} = 1 \mid X_i = x, X_j = y\right). \tag{1.6}$$

Integrating (1.6) over $x$ and $y$ gives, in a small abuse of notation, the marginal link probability

$$\rho = \int \omega(x, y) f_X(x) f_X(y) \, dx dy. \tag{1.7}$$

Finally, Bayes' law, together with (1.6) and (1.7), gives

$$f_{X_i, X_j \mid D_{ij}}(x, y \mid D_{ij} = 1) = \frac{\omega(x, y)\rho}{f_X(x) f_X(y)}, \tag{1.8}$$

which illustrates how linking behavior determines the conditional distribution of covariates across linked dyads and hence homophily. The elements in the numerator of (1.8) are features of the network formation process, while those entering the denominator are features of the population of agents. Both are familiar objects. The distribution (1.8) can be used to understand the expectations appearing in (1.5) above.

In the Nyakatoke network the assortativity coefficient takes a value of 0.073 for the logarithm of land and livestock wealth (converted into Tanzanian shillings) and 0.094 for age of household head in years.

## Measuring agent centrality

A natural question to ask, when viewing Fig. 1.1, is: which firms are most important or *central* in the US economy? It turns out that this is a classic question in network analysis, with a long history across several disciplines (e.g., Wasserman and Faust, 1994). Here we review a handful of centrality measures that economists undertaking network analysis have found especially useful.

Acemoglu et al. (2012) study how firm-level production shocks may cascade through the economy via supplier connections (cf., Carvalho, 2014). They argue that local shocks to certain 'key', or central, firms may have sizable aggregate effects. Ballester et al. (2006) develop a model of criminal behavior where a specific measure of centrality identifies those criminals in a network whose apprehension would lead to the greatest reductions in criminal activity. Kim et al. (2015) use various centrality measures to target a peer-spread public health intervention in Honduras (cf., Banerjee et al., 2013). In the wake of the 2007 to 2009 financial crisis, regulators have been interested in identifying financial institutions which are 'too connected to fail' (e.g., Battiston et al., 2012; Denbee et al., 2014). Measures of agent centrality feature in all of these research projects.

### Degree centrality

In a digraph, the *indegree* of agent $i$ coincides with the number of arcs directed toward her, while her *outdegree* equals the number of arcs she directs toward other agents. Arithmetically, the indegree of agent $i$ equals $D_{+i} = \sum_j D_{ji}$, while her outdegree equals $D_{i+} = \sum_j D_{ij}$ (here the '+' denotes summation over the replaced index). For an undirected network, the degree of a vertex is simply the number of edges incident with that node. The indegree *sequence* of the network, $\mathbf{D}_{+\bullet}$, equals the vector of column sums of the adjacency matrix (i.e., $\mathbf{D}_{+\bullet} = \mathbf{D}' \iota_N$). The *outdegree sequence*, $\mathbf{D}_{\bullet+}$, equals the vector of row sums of the adjacency matrix (i.e., $\mathbf{D}_{\bullet+} = \mathbf{D} \iota_N$). When the network is undirected, the *degree sequence* is given by the vector of column or row sums of the adjacency matrix, which are equal by symmetry of that matrix.

In sociology an agent's indegree is often called degree prestige (e.g., Wasserman and Faust, 1994, p. 202). Outdegree sequences are less well-studied, but can be important in economics. For example, the outdegree may be informative about agents who are well positioned to disperse information quickly (e.g., by sending 'news' to agents to which they have directed ties). In the context of production networks, the outdegree may help to identify critical input suppliers; firms whose output is used by many different downstream firms (e.g., Acemoglu et al., 2012).

Table 1.2 lists those firms with the largest number of suppliers according to the Compustat production network dataset (i.e., an indegree ranking). The list is populated by a mix of large retailers (Walmart, Home Depot and Target), healthcare and pharmaceutical firms (McKesson, Cardinal Health and AmerisourceBergen), as well automakers (Ford, General Motors), an energy

**TABLE 1.2** US firms with the most suppliers, 2015.

| Firm | Number of suppliers |
| --- | --- |
| Walmart Stores Inc. | 115 |
| Royal Dutch Shell plc | 48 |
| McKesson Corp. | 41 |
| Cardinal Health Inc. | 40 |
| Home Depot Inc. | 37 |
| AmerisourceBergen Corp. | 35 |
| Ford Motor Co. | 31 |
| General Motors Co. | 28 |
| Target Corp. | 26 |
| AT&T Inc. | 22 |
| Chevron Corp. | 22 |

*Notes:* List of top ten firms by indegree (number of suppliers) in the US economy in 2015. Note there is a tie for 10th place.
*Sources:* Compustat – Capital IQ and authors' calculations.

conglomerate (Shell), and a communications company (AT&T). As detailed by Carvalho (2014), the high indegree of the "Big Three" automakers, as well as the overlap among their suppliers, was used as an argument for the 2009 government rescue of General Motors and Chrysler.

Unfortunately the Compustat data is not helpful for ranking firms by outdegree, since most firms list (at most) their ten largest customers when filing with the SEC. This reporting rule artificially truncates firm outdegree at ten (cf., Atalay et al., 2011).

## Refinements of degree centrality

While degree-based centrality measures are simple to understand and compute, they have well-known limitations. Consider two firms, both with ten upstream suppliers. For one of those firms, each of its suppliers, itself has 10 suppliers further upstream, while the other firm's suppliers do not (e.g., they are just raw materials suppliers). Indegree centrality ranks these two firms identically, while intuition would suggest that the former firm is more central since its suppliers have higher indegree. Bonacich (1972), building on earlier work by Katz (1953), introduced a measure of centrality, called *eigenvector centrality*, designed to ameliorate this limitation of degree centrality.[8] In directed networks there are two variants of Bonacich's (1972) measure, respectively generalizing indegree and outdegree centrality. In what follows we first introduce various generaliza-

---

[8] The eigenvector centrality also appears in the independent work by Gould (1967) and is alternatively known as Gould's accessibility index in geography.

tions of indegree centrality before subsequently discussing how these measures may be adapted to generalize outdegree centrality.

The eigenvector centrality of an agent is recursively defined as a linear combination of the centralities of those who direct links toward her:

$$c_i^{EC}(\mathbf{D}) = \sum_j c_j^{EC}(\mathbf{D})D_{ji},$$

or, in matrix form, with $\mathbf{c}^{EC}(\mathbf{D}) = \left(c_1^{EC}(\mathbf{D}), \ldots, c_N^{EC}(\mathbf{D})\right)$,

$$\mathbf{c}^{EC}(\mathbf{D}) = \mathbf{c}^{EC}(\mathbf{D})\mathbf{D}. \tag{1.9}$$

Like other centrality measures, this is a self-referential measure: a vertex is central if it is connected to more central vertices. Inspection of (1.9) indicates that $\mathbf{c}^{EC}(\mathbf{D})$ is a row (or left) eigenvector of $\mathbf{D}$ associated with an eigenvalue 1. Therefore (1.9) only has a non-zero solution if 1 is an eigenvalue of the adjacency matrix. To ensure a non-zero solution Bonacich (1972) suggests replacing (1.9) with $\mathbf{c}^{EC}(\mathbf{D}, \phi) = \phi\mathbf{c}^{EC}(\mathbf{D}, \phi)\mathbf{D}$, where $\phi$ equals the inverse of the largest eigenvalue of $\mathbf{D}$.[9] An alternative approach, first suggested by Katz (1953), is to row-normalize the adjacency matrix. Define the *row-normalized* adjacency matrix as

$$\mathbf{G} = \mathrm{diag}\left\{\max\left(1, D_{1+}\right), \ldots, \max\left(1, D_{N+}\right)\right\}^{-1} \times \mathbf{D}. \tag{1.10}$$

Observe that the $i$th row of (1.10) sums to either zero (if agent $i$ has an outdegree of zero) or one (if agent $i$ has positive outdegree). If all agents have positive outdegree, then $\mathbf{G}$ will be a row-stochastic matrix. Replacing $\mathbf{D}$ with its row-normalized counterpart $\mathbf{G}$ in (1.9) yields

$$\mathbf{c}^K(\mathbf{D}) = \mathbf{c}^K(\mathbf{D})\mathbf{G}. \tag{1.11}$$

If $\mathbf{G}$ is row-stochastic, then $\mathbf{c}^K(\mathbf{D})$ corresponds to a stationary vector of a Markov chain with transition matrix $\mathbf{G}$. From the theory of Markov chains we know that if the matrix $\mathbf{G}$ is irreducible, then this stationary vector is unique. It turns out that irreducibility holds if, and only if, the network is strongly connected. Unfortunately, as noted earlier, few real-work social and economic networks are strongly connected (at least when edges are directed). This includes the production network depicted in Fig. 1.1. Indeed, not only does strong connectivity typically fail, but many directed networks have "dangling nodes"

---

[9] This gives $\mathbf{c}^{EC}(\mathbf{D}, \phi)$ as the solution to $\mathbf{c}^{EC}(\mathbf{D}, \phi)\left[\frac{1}{\phi}I_N - \mathbf{D}\right] = 0$, which corresponds the left eigenvector associated with the largest eigenvalue of $\mathbf{D}$. If the adjacency matrix is nonnegative and corresponds to a strongly connected network, a linear algebra result known as the Perron–Frobenius theorem guarantees that there is a dominant real eigenvalue corresponding to the one (up to normalization) eigenvector that can be taken to have positive entries. Its entries correspond to the eigenvector centrality.

(agents with zero indegree); $c_i^K(\mathbf{G})$ will equal zero for such agents. This will also be the case for all agents with incoming links solely from dangling nodes and so on.

## PageRank

The problem of dangling nodes, as well as the failure of strong connectivity, motivated Sergey Brin and Lawrence Page, at the time graduate students in computer science at Stanford University, to develop the PageRank centrality measure, now used by Google to rank web-search results (Brin and Page, 1998; Page et al., 1999). Brin and Page made two modifications to the basic Katz (1953) measure. First, they regularized the (row-normalized) adjacency matrix so that all rows, including those associated with dangling nodes, sum to one. Specifically, they introduced what is now called the *Google Matrix* $\mathbf{H} = \left[ H_{ij} \right]$ with elements

$$H_{ij} = \begin{cases} \phi G_{ij} + \frac{(1-\phi)}{N} & \text{if } D_{i+} > 0, \\ \frac{1}{N} & \text{otherwise.} \end{cases} \tag{1.12}$$

Observe that $\mathbf{H}$ is both row-stochastic and irreducible.

Second, as first suggested by Katz (1953) and Bonacich (1987), they endow each agent with a small amount of exogenous centrality:

$$\mathbf{c}^{\text{PR}}(\mathbf{D}, \phi) = \phi \mathbf{c}^{\text{PR}}(\mathbf{D}, \phi) \mathbf{H} + \left( \frac{1-\phi}{N} \right) \iota'_N. \tag{1.13}$$

Here $\iota_N$ denotes a $N \times 1$ vector of ones. A typical value for $\phi$, at least in web search, is 0.85.[10] For $|\phi| < 1$ the matrix $I_N - \phi\mathbf{H}$ is strictly (row) diagonally dominant ($I_N$ is the $N \times N$ identity matrix). By the Levy–Desplanques theorem (e.g., Horn and Johnson, 2013) it is therefore non-singular. Non-singularity of $(I_N - \phi\mathbf{H})$ allows us to solve for the PageRank vector as

$$\mathbf{c}^{\text{PR}}(\mathbf{D}, \phi) = \left( \frac{1-\phi}{N} \right) \iota'_N (I_N - \phi\mathbf{H})^{-1}. \tag{1.14}$$

To motivate the PageRank measure we can appeal to a random web surfer stochastic process. Imagine an individual surfing the web. With probability $\phi$ she moves to another page by choosing one of the outgoing links at her current location, each with equal probability. With probability $1 - \phi$ she instead chooses a page at random from the set of all pages. If the current page corresponds to a dangling node, she just chooses a page at random. Given the above process,

---

[10] This value is related to the magnitude of the second eigenvalue of the Google Matrix, the size of which determines the speed with which (1.13) may be iteratively solved for $\mathbf{c}^{\text{PR}}(\mathbf{D}, \phi)$. In modestly sized networks it is generally possible to set $\phi$ much closer to one.

**TABLE 1.3** Central buying firms in the US economy, 2015.

| Firm | Buyer's PageRank |
|------|------------------|
| Walmart Stores Inc. | 0.0272 |
| CVS Health Corp. | 0.0198 |
| Royal Dutch Shell plc | 0.0124 |
| AmerisourceBergen Corp. | 0.0094 |
| McKesson Corp. | 0.0086 |
| Cardinal Health Inc. | 0.0081 |
| Home Depot Inc. | 0.0060 |
| HP Inc. | 0.0056 |
| Express Scripts Holding Co. | 0.0050 |
| BP Plc. | 0.0047 |
| Apple Inc. | 0.0047 |
| Boeing Co. | 0.0047 |

*Notes:* List of ten most central firms in the US economy in 2015 according to PageRank ($\alpha = 0.95$). Note there is a three-way tie for 10th place.
*Sources:* Compustat – Capital IQ and authors' calculations.

$c_i^{PR}(\mathbf{D}, \phi)$ corresponds to the frequency with which our surfer visits page $i$ in equilibrium.[11]

Table 1.3 lists the top ten firms in the US economy according to the PageRank index. The list largely overlaps with the indegree ranking reported in Table 1.2, but there are also important differences. Specifically the aircraft manufacturer Boeing, and the computer companies Hewlett-Packard and Apple, enter the top 10; displacing the car manufacturers Ford and General Motors.

Some insight into why the relative rankings according to indegree and PageRank of, for example, Ford and Boeing, differ is provided by examining their respective supply chains. The *ancestors* of node $i$ consist of all nodes with a directed path from themselves to $i$. In the context of a supply chain ancestors of a firm include its direct suppliers, its supplier's suppliers and so on. Figs. 1.2 (left panel) and 1.4 (right panel) display the subgraphs induced by, respectively, Boeing and all its direct and indirect suppliers and those induced by Ford and all its direct and indirect suppliers. Ford's supply chain takes a traditional "vertical" form, with many firms delivering intermediate parts to Ford for final assembly into cars. Boeing's supply chain is more complicated; United Technologies di-

---

[11] If we use the series expansion

$$(I_N - \phi\mathbf{H})^{-1} = \sum_{k=0}^{\infty} \phi^k \mathbf{H}^k,$$

as well as the fact that $\mathbf{H}\iota_N = \iota_N$ (and hence that $\mathbf{H}^k\iota_N = \iota_N$ for $k \geq 1$) it is easy to verify that $\sum_{i=1}^{N} c_i^{PR} = \left(\frac{1-\phi}{N}\right)\iota_N'(I_N - \phi_0\mathbf{H})^{-1}\iota_N = 1$. Hence $\mathbf{c}^{PR}(\mathbf{D}, \phi)$ is a valid probability distribution.

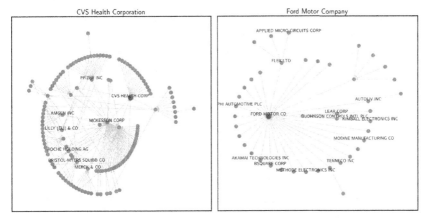

**FIGURE 1.4** Supply chain structure and PageRank. *Notes:* The left-hand figure displays the induced subdigraph associated with CVS and all its ancestor nodes (i.e., the CVS supply chain). The right-hand figure displays the corresponding Ford Motor Company supply chain. *Sources:* Compustat - Capital IQ and authors' calculations.

rectly supplies Boeing, while also being a large buyer of intermediate inputs. Furthermore the two firms share three suppliers in common. These features of Boeing's supply chain architecture drive its higher PageRank customer ranking compared to Ford.

## PageRank and the social multiplier

The concept of a social multiplier has been a key theme of empirical work on social interactions in economics since the publication of Manski (1993). It features in, for example, Brock and Durlauf (2001), Glaeser and Scheinkman (2001, 2003), Graham (2008), Graham et al. (2010), Angrist (2014) and Galeotti et al. (2017). In the presence of social multiplier effects, the full impact of an intervention exceeds the initial impact due to feedback effects across agents. When interactions occur on a non-trivial network, the magnitude of any multiplier effect will also depend upon exactly which agent is initially acted upon by the policy-maker. This is the intuition behind *social multiplier centrality*. In turns out that PageRank centrality shares a close connection with *social multiplier centrality*.

There are several ways to make the connection between PageRank and the social multiplier; the easiest involves introducing a simple quadratic complementarity game of the type recently surveyed by Jackson and Zenou (2015). Let $Y_i$ be some continuously-valued action chosen by agent $i = 1, \ldots, N$. Let **Y** be the $N \times 1$ vector of all agents' actions. Let, as before, $\iota_N$ be an $N \times 1$ vector of ones, and **G** be the row-normalized network adjacency matrix. Initially assume that this matrix is row-stochastic and irreducible (i.e., that the network is strongly connected).

Observe that

$$\mathbf{G}_i \mathbf{y} = \sum_{j \neq i} G_{ij} y_j \overset{def}{\equiv} \bar{y}_{n(i)}$$

equals the average action of player $i$'s direct peers (i.e. those players to whom she has directed a link) under the (perhaps hypothetical) action profile $\mathbf{y}$. Here $\mathbf{G}_i$ denotes the $i$th row of $\mathbf{G}$, $n(i)$ the index set $\{j : D_{ij} = 1, j \neq i\}$, and $\bar{y}_{n(i)}$ the average of $Y_j$ over these indices.

Following Blume et al. (2015), among others, assume that the utility agent $i$ receives from action profile $\mathbf{y}$ given the network structure is

$$u_i (\mathbf{y}; \mathbf{D}) = (\alpha_0 + U_i) y_i - \frac{1}{2} y_i^2 + \beta_0 \bar{y}_{n(i)} y_i$$

$$= (\alpha_0 + U_i) y_i - \frac{1}{2} y_i^2 + \beta_0 \mathbf{G}_i \mathbf{y} y_i \qquad (1.15)$$

with $0 < |\beta_0| < 1$ and $\mathbb{E}[U_i] = 0$. Here $U_i$ captures heterogeneity in agents' preferences for action.

The marginal utility associated with an increase in $y_i$ is increasing in the average action of one's peers, $\bar{y}_{n(i)}$. Specifically,

$$\frac{\partial^2 u_i (\mathbf{y}, \mathbf{D})}{\partial y_i \partial \bar{y}_{n(i)}} = \beta_0.$$

That is, if $\beta_0 > 0$, own- and peer-action are complements. In the terminology of Manski (1993), the magnitude of $\beta_0$ is an index for the strength of any *endogenous social interactions*.

Assume that the observed action $\mathbf{Y}$ corresponds to a Nash equilibrium where no agent can increase her utility by changing her action given the actions of all other agents in the network. Agents observe $\mathbf{D}$, the network structure, and $\mathbf{U}$, the $N \times 1$ vector of individual-level heterogeneity terms.

The first order condition for optimal behavior associated with (1.15) generates the following best response function:

$$y_i = \alpha_0 + \beta_0 \bar{y}_{n(i)} + U_i \qquad (1.16)$$

for $i = 1, \ldots, N$. Eq. (1.16) is a special case of what is called the linear-in-means model of social interactions (e.g., Brock and Durlauf, 2001). An agent's best reply varies with the average action of those to whom she is directly connected, $y$, as well as the unobserved own attribute, $U_i$ (which shifts the marginal utility of action across agents).

Eq. (1.16) defines an $N \times 1$ system of simultaneous equations. Since observed actions correspond to equilibrium values, the econometrician observes actions which satisfy (1.16). Writing the system defined by (1.16) in matrix form gives

$$\mathbf{Y} = \alpha_0 \iota_N + \beta_0 \mathbf{G} \mathbf{Y} + \mathbf{U}. \tag{1.17}$$

For $|\beta_0| < 1$, solving (1.17) for the equilibrium action vector, $\mathbf{Y}$, as a function of $\mathbf{D}$ and $\mathbf{U}$ alone, yields the reduced form

$$\mathbf{Y} = \alpha_0 \left( I_N - \beta_0 \mathbf{G} \right)^{-1} \iota_N + \left( I_N - \beta_0 \mathbf{G} \right)^{-1} \mathbf{U} \tag{1.18}$$

or, using a series expansion (see footnote 11),

$$\mathbf{Y} = \frac{\alpha_0}{1 - \beta_0} \iota_N + \left[ \sum_{k=0}^{\infty} \beta_0^k \mathbf{G}^k \right] \mathbf{U}. \tag{1.19}$$

Eq. (1.19) provides some insight into what various researchers have called the social multiplier. Consider a policy which increases the $i$th agent's value of $U_i$ by $\Delta$. We can conceptualize the full effect of this increase on the network's distribution of outcomes as occurring in "waves". In the initial wave only agent $i$'s outcome increases. The change in the entire action vector is therefore

$$\Delta \mathbf{e}_i,$$

where $\mathbf{e}_i$ is an $N$-vector with a one in its $i$th element and zeros elsewhere.

In the second wave all of agent $i$'s peers experience outcome increases. This is because their best reply actions change in response to the increase in agent $i$'s action in the initial wave. The action vector in wave two therefore changes by

$$\Delta \beta_0 \mathbf{G} \mathbf{e}_i.$$

In the third wave the outcomes of agent $i$'s friends' friends change (this may include a direct feedback effect back onto agent $i$ if some of her links are reciprocated). In wave three we get a further change in the action vector of

$$\Delta \beta_0^2 \mathbf{G}^2 \mathbf{e}_i.$$

In the $k$th wave we have a change in the action vector of

$$\Delta \beta_0^{k-1} \mathbf{G}^{k-1} \mathbf{e}_i.$$

Observing the pattern of geometric decay we see that the "long-run" or full effect of a $\Delta$ change in $U_i$ on the entire distribution of outcomes is given by

$$\Delta \left( I_N - \beta_0 \mathbf{G} \right)^{-1} \mathbf{e}_i. \tag{1.20}$$

Eq. (1.20) indicates the effect of perturbing $U_i$ by $\Delta$ on the equilibrium action vector coincides with the $i$th column of the matrix $\Delta \left( I_N - \beta_0 \mathbf{G} \right)^{-1}$. The total effect on aggregate action is therefore given by the sum of the $i$th column of this matrix. Hence the row vector

$$\mathbf{c}^{SM}(\mathbf{D}, \beta) = \iota'_N (I_N - \beta\mathbf{G})^{-1} \qquad (1.21)$$

equals a *social multiplier centrality* measure for each agent in the network. By construction this measure is greater than or equal to one for $\beta_0 \geq 0$. If $c_i^{SM}(\mathbf{D}, \beta) = 2$, then the effect of intervening to increase $U_i$ by $\Delta$ on the aggregate action $\sum_{i=1}^{N} Y_i$ is twice the initial direct effect of $\Delta$. Averaging over all agents we get

$$\frac{1}{N} \sum_{i=1}^{N} c_i^{SM}(\mathbf{D}, \beta) = \frac{1}{1 - \beta}$$

(again see footnote 11); this is the form of the social multiplier in the linear-in-means model as first formulated by Manski (1993) (cf., Glaeser and Scheinkman, 2001, 2003). In the presence of non-trivial network structure, the full effect of an intervention will, unlike in the model of Manski (1993), vary heterogeneously across agents. If we multiply the elements of (1.21) by $(1 - \beta)/N$ we recover the PageRank centrality measure of Brin and Page (1998).

Our analysis assumes that $\mathbf{G}$ is irreducible. In cases where it is not, replacing $\mathbf{G}$ in (1.21) with the Google matrix (1.12), with $\phi$ set equal to a value 'close to one', yields a centrality measure with approximately the same interpretation. In this case $\phi$ is a regularization parameter.

## Katz–Bonacich centrality

Closely related to both PageRank and social multiplier centrality, but older than either, is the Katz–Bonacich centrality measure (Bonacich, 1987; Bonacich and Lloyd, 2001). This measure also often arises in the context of quadratic complementarity games played on networks (Ballester et al., 2006; Calvó-Armengol et al., 2009; Jackson and Zenou, 2015). Katz–Bonacich centrality is increasing in the indegree of an agent, the indegree of those agents who direct link to her and so on, with weights discounted according to the degree of separation:

$$\mathbf{c}^{KB}(\mathbf{D}, \phi) = \phi\iota'_N\mathbf{D} + \phi^2\iota'_N\mathbf{D}^2 + \phi^3\iota'_N\mathbf{D}^3 + \cdots$$
$$= \left(\phi\iota'_N\mathbf{D}\right)\left(I_N + \phi\mathbf{D} + \phi^2\mathbf{D}^2 + \cdots\right)$$
$$= \left(\phi\iota'_N\mathbf{D}\right)\left[\sum_{k=0}^{\infty} \phi^k\mathbf{D}^k\right].$$

For $\phi < 1/\lambda_1$, with $\lambda_1$ the maximum eigenvalue of the adjacency matrix, the sequence in brackets converges so that the vector of Katz–Bonacich centralities equals

$$\mathbf{c}^{\mathrm{KB}}\left(\mathbf{D}, \phi\right) = \left(\phi \iota_N' \mathbf{D}\right)\left(I_N - \phi \mathbf{D}\right)^{-1}. \tag{1.22}$$

## Outdegree-based centrality measures

PageRank, social multiplier and Katz–Bonacich centrality, as introduced above, are all prestige-type measures: central nodes have links directed toward them by other central nodes and so on. In settings where the process of information diffusion or shock propagation is of central interest, outdegree-based measures may be of greater interest. For an empirical example in economics consider the work of Acemoglu et al. (2012) and Carvalho (2014). These papers study the macro effects of output shocks on downstream firms. They argue that shocks to firms that supply many firms (or supply a firm that itself supplies many firms) may have large aggregate effects.

For concreteness consider the Buyer–Supplier network depicted in Fig. 1.1. Replacing $\mathbf{D}$ with $\mathbf{D}'$ in (1.14) yields an outdegree-based variant of PageRank. While $\mathbf{c}^{\mathrm{PR}}\left(\mathbf{D}, \phi\right)$ will tend to rank large downstream firms with many suppliers as central, $\mathbf{c}^{\mathrm{PR}}\left(\mathbf{D}', \phi\right)$ will instead rank key upstream firms as central (i.e., suppliers with high outdegree, or suppliers-of-suppliers with high outdegree and so on).

A stochastic process interpretation of $\mathbf{c}^{\mathrm{PR}}\left(\mathbf{D}', \phi\right)$ may be helpful. Consider an input purchaser traversing our buyer-supplier network. During each period she makes, with probability $\phi$, an intermediate input purchase from one of the suppliers (predecessors) of the current firm; choosing one supplier at random. With probability $1 - \phi$ she makes a purchase completely at random from the set of *all* firms. She then moves *upstream* to the *selling* firm from which she made a purchase and repeats the purchasing process. If, during this process, she ends up at a firm with no suppliers (e.g., a raw materials company) she simply makes a purchase at random from the set of all firms. In equilibrium $c_i^{\mathrm{PR}}\left(\mathbf{D}', \phi\right)$ equals the fraction, out of all her intermediate input purchases, that come from firm $i$ (i.e., where firm $i$ is the selling or supplying firm). Hence if $c_i^{\mathrm{PR}}\left(\mathbf{D}', \phi\right)$ is large we might reasonably call firm $i$ an 'important' or a *central intermediate input supplier*.

The analogous stochastic process for $\mathbf{c}^{\mathrm{PR}}\left(\mathbf{D}, \phi\right)$, PageRank as initially introduced, involves a hypothetical saleswoman. During each period she sells her current firm's output, with probability $\phi$, to one of its buyers (successors). With probability $1 - \phi$ she sells to a random firm chosen from the set of all firms. She then moves *downstream* to the *buying* firm which made the purchase from her and repeats the sales process. If, during this process, she ends up at a firm with no buyers (e.g., a large retail firm that sells only to final consumers like Walmart) she makes a sale at random to a firm chosen from the set of all firms. In equilibrium $c_i^{\mathrm{PR}}\left(\mathbf{D}, \phi\right)$ equals the fraction of all intermediate input sales made to, or purchases made by, firm $i$. Hence if $c_i^{\mathrm{PR}}\left(\mathbf{D}, \phi\right)$ is large we might reasonably call firm $i$ an 'important' or a *central intermediate input buyer*.

The work of Acemoglu et al. (2012) and Carvalho (2014) focuses on the macroeconomic implications of productivity shocks to intermediate goods producers. In that context, $c_i^{\mathrm{PR}}(\mathbf{D'}, \phi)$, measures *supplier centrality*. Acemoglu et al. (2016) additionally explore the macroeconomic implications of firm-specific demand shocks. In that case, $c_i^{\mathrm{PR}}(\mathbf{D}, \phi)$, *buyer centrality*, plays a central role.

# References

Acemoglu, D., Akcigit, U., Kerr, W., 2016. Networks and the macroeconomy: an empirical exploration. NBER Macroeconomics Annual 31 (1), 273–335.

Acemoglu, D., Carvalho, V., Ozdaglar, A., Tahbaz-Salehi, A., 2012. The network origins of aggregate fluctuations. Econometrica 80 (5), 1977–2016.

Angrist, J., 2014. The perils of peer effects. Labour Economics 30, 98–108.

Apicella, C.L., Marlowe, F.W., Fowler, J.H., Christakis, N.A., 2012. Social networks and cooperation in hunter-gatherers. Nature 481 (7382), 497–501.

Atalay, E., Hortaçsu, A., Roberts, J., Syverson, C., 2011. Network structure of production. Proceedings of the National Academy of Sciences 108 (13), 5199–5202.

Ballester, C., Calvó-Armengol, A., Zenou, Y., 2006. Who's who in networks. wanted: The key player. Econometrica 74 (5), 1403–1417.

Banerjee, A., Chandrasekhar, A.G., Dulfo, E., Jackson, M.O., 2013. The diffusion of microfinance. Science 341 (6144), 363–370.

Battiston, S., Puliga, M., Kaushik, R., Tasca, P., Caldarelli, G., 2012. Debtrank: Too central to fail? financial networks, the fed and systemic risk. Scientific Reports 2 (541).

Bengtsson, O., Hsu, D.H., 2015. Ethnic matching in the u.s. venture capital market. Journal of Business Venturing 30 (2), 338–354.

Bickel, P.J., Chen, A., 2009. A nonparametric view of network models and Newman-Girvan and other modularities. Proceedings of the National Academy of Sciences 106 (50), 21068–21073.

Blume, L.E., Brock, W.A., Durlauf, S.N., Jayaraman, R., 2015. Linear social interaction models. Journal of Political Economy 123 (2), 444–496.

Bonacich, P., 1972. Factoring and weighting approaches to status scores and clique identification. Journal of Mathematical Sociology 2 (1), 113–120.

Bonacich, P., 1987. Power and centrality: A family of measures. American Journal of Sociology 92, 1170–1182.

Bonacich, P., Lloyd, P., 2001. Eigenvector-like measures of centrality for asymmetric relations. Social Networks 23 (3), 191–201.

Brin, S., Page, L., 1998. The anatomy of a large-scale hypertextual web search engine. Computer Networks 30 (1–7), 107–117.

Brock, W.A., Durlauf, S.N., 2001. Handbook of Econometrics. North-Holland, Amsterdam, pp. 3297–3380. volume 5, chapter Interactions-based models.

Calvó-Armengol, A., Patacchini, E., Zenou, Y., 2009. Peer effects and social networks in education. The Review of Economic Studies 76 (4), 1239–1267.

Carvalho, V., 2014. From micro to macro via production networks. Journal of Economic Perspectives 28 (4), 23–48.

Carvalho, V.M., Nirei, M., Saito, Y.K., Tahbaz-Salehi, A., 2016. Supply chain disruptions: evidence from the great east japan earthquake. Cambridge University.

Cohen, L., Frazzini, A., 2008. Economic links and predictable returns. Journal of Finance 63 (4), 1977–2011.

Currarini, S., Jackson, M., Pin, P., 2009. An economic model of friendship: homophily, minorities and segregation. Econometrica 70 (4), 1003–1045.

De Weerdt, J., 2004. Insurance Against Poverty, chapter Risk-sharing and endogenous network formation. Oxford University Press, Oxford, pp. 197–216.

Denbee, E., Julliard, C., Li, Y., Yuan, K., 2014. Network risk and key players: A structural analysis of interbank liquidity. LSE Working Paper.

Diaconis, P., Janson, S., 2008. Graph limits and exchangeable random graphs. Rendiconti di Matematica 28 (1), 33–61.

Erdös, P., Rényi, A., 1959. On random graphs. Publicationes Mathematicae Debrecen 6, 290–297.

Erdös, P., Rényi, A., 1960. On the evolution of random graphs. Publications of the Mathematical Institute of the Hungarian Academy of Sciences 86 (5), 17–61.

Fafchamps, M., Lund, S., 2003. Risk sharing networks in rural Philippines. Journal of Development Economics 71 (2), 261–287.

Galeotti, A., Golub, B., Goyal, S., 2017. Targeting Interventions in Networks. Technical Report arXiv:1710.06026.

Gilbert, E., 1959. Random graphs. Annals of Mathematical Statistics 30 (4), 1141–1144.

Glaeser, E.L., Scheinkman, J.A., 2001. Social Dynamics, chapter Measuring social interactions. The MIT Press, Cambridge, MA, pp. 83–132.

Glaeser, E.L., Scheinkman, J.A., 2003. Advances in Economics and Econometrics: Theory and Applications, Eighth World Congress, volume 1, chapter Non-market interactions. Cambridge University Press, Cambridge, pp. 339–369.

Goldberger, A.S., 1991. A Course in Econometrics. Harvard University Press, Cambridge, MA.

Golub, B., Jackson, M.O., 2012. How homophily affects the speed of learning and best-response dynamics. Quarterly Journal of Economics 127 (3), 1287–1338.

Gould, P., 1967. On the geographical interpretation of eigenvalues. Transactions of the Institute of British Geographers 42, 53–83.

Graham, B., 2008. Identifying social interactions through conditional variance restrictions. Econometrica 76 (3), 643–660.

Graham, B., 2018. Identifying and estimating neighborhood effects. Journal of Economic Literature 56 (2), 450–500.

Graham, B.S., Imbens, G.W., Ridder, G., 2010. Measuring the effects of segregation in the presence of social spillovers: a nonparametric approach. Working Paper 16499. NBER.

Horn, R.A., Johnson, C.R., 2013. Matrix Analysis, 2nd edition. Cambridge University Press, Cambridge.

Jackson, M.O., López-Pintado, D., 2013. Diffusion and contagion in networks with heterogeneous agents and homophily. Network Science 1 (1), 49–67.

Jackson, M.O., Rogers, B.W., 2007. Relating network structure to diffusion properties through stochastic dominance. B.E. Journal of Theoretical Economics 7 (1), 6 (Advances).

Jackson, M.O., Zenou, Y., 2015. Handbook of Game Theory, vol. 4. Amsterdam. chapter Games on networks, (pp. 95–163). North-Holland.

Katz, L., 1953. A new status index derived from sociometric analysis. Psychometrica 18 (1), 39–43.

Kim, D.A., Hwong, A.R., Stafford, D., Hughes, D.A., O'Malley, A.J., Fowler, J.H., Christakis, N.A., 2015. Social network targeting to maximise population behaviour change: a cluster randomised controlled trial. Lancet 386 (9989), 145–153.

Lovász, L., 2012. Large Networks and Graph Limits. American Mathematical Society Colloquium Publications., vol. 60. American Mathematical Society.

Manski, C.F., 1993. Identification of endogenous social effects: the reflection problem. Review of Economic Studies 60 (3), 531–542.

Marsden, P.V., 1987. Core discussion networks of Americans. American Sociological Review 52 (1), 122–131.

McPherson, M., Smith-Lovin, L., Cook, J.M., 2001. Birds of a feather: homophily in social networks. Annual Review of Sociology 27 (1), 415–444.

Milgram, S., 1967. The small-world problem. Psychology Today 1 (1), 61–67.

Newman, M.E.J., 2010. Networks: An Introduction. Oxford University Press, Oxford.

Newman, M.E.J., 2016. Community detection in networks: Modularity optimization and maximum likelihood are equivalent. Physical Review E 94 (5), 052315.

Page, L., Brin, S., Motwani, R., Winograd, T., 1999. The PageRank citation ranking: bringing order to the web. Technical report. Stanford University.

Pastor-Satorras, R., Vespignani, A., 2001. Epidemic spreading in scale-free networks. Physical Review Letters 86 (14), 3200–3203.

Pin, P., Rogers, B., 2016. The Oxford Handbook on the Economics of Networks. Oxford University Press, Oxford. chapter Stochastic network formation and homophily, (pp. 138–166).

Wasserman, S., Faust, K., 1994. Social Network Analysis: Methods and Applications. Cambridge University Press, Cambridge.

# Chapter 2

# Dyadic regression[☆]

## Bryan S. Graham[a,b]

[a]*Department of Economics, University of California - Berkeley, Berkeley, CA, United States,*
[b]*National Bureau of Economic Research, Cambridge, MA, United States*

## Contents

Let $Y_{ij}$ equal total exports from country $i$ to country $j$ as in Tinbergen (1962); here $i$ and $j$ are two of $N$ independent random draws from a common population. Let $W_i$ be a vector of country attributes and $R_{ij} = r\left(W_i, W_j\right)$ a vector of constructed dyad-specific attributes; $R_{ij}$ typically includes the logarithm of both exporter and importer gross domestic product (GDP), the physical distance between $i$ and $j$, and other variables (e.g., indicators for sharing a land border or belonging to a common customs union). The analyst, seeking to relate $Y_{ij}$ and $R_{ij}$, posits the relationship

$$Y_{ij} = \exp\left(R'_{ij}\theta_0\right) A_i B_j V_{ij}, \tag{2.1}$$

with $A_i$, $B_i$ and $V_{ij}$ mean one random variables and $\left\{\left(V_{ij}, V_{ji}\right)\right\}_{1\leq i \leq N-1, j>i}$ independent of $\{W_i, A_i, B_i\}_{i=1}^{N}$ and independently and identically distributed across the $\binom{N}{2} = \frac{1}{2}N(N-1)$ dyads. Here the $\{A_i\}_{i=1}^{N}$ and $\{B_i\}_{i=1}^{N}$ sequences correspond, respectively, to (unobserved) exporter and importer heterogeneity

---

[☆] This chapter is based upon lecture notes prepared for a series of short courses on the econometrics of networks. I thank Michael Jansson for several useful discussions and participants in short courses in Olso, Norway (September, 2017), Hejnice, Czechia (February 2018), St. Gallen, Switzerland (October 2018), Annweiler, Germany (July 2019) and Prague, Czechia (August 2019) for useful feedback. Portions of this material were also presented at an invited session of the 2018 LACEA/LAMES meetings in Guayaqil, Ecuador. All the usual disclaimers apply. Financial support from NSF grant SES #1851647 is gratefully acknowledged.

*The Econometric Analysis of Network Data.* https://doi.org/10.1016/B978-0-12-811771-2.00008-0

terms. These terms are sometimes referred to as "multilaterial resistance" terms by empirical trade economists. For example, a high $A_i$ might reflect an unmodeled export orientation of an economy or an undervalued currency. Similarly, a high $B_i$ might capture unmodeled tastes for consumption. Head and Mayer (2014) survey the gravity model of trade, including its theoretical foundations. Conditional on the exporter and importer effects we have

$$\mathbb{E}\left[ Y_{ij} \mid W_i, W_j, A_i, B_j \right] = \exp\left( R'_{ij}\theta_0 \right) A_i B_j.$$

If, additionally, $\mathbb{E}\left[ (A_i, B_i)' \mid W_i \right] = (1, 1)'$, such that $W_i$ does not covary with the exporter and importer "multilaterial resistance" terms,[1] then unconditional on $A_i$ and $B_j$ we have the *dyadic regression* function

$$\mathbb{E}\left[ Y_{ij} \mid W_i, W_j \right] = \exp\left( R'_{ij}\theta_0 \right). \tag{2.2}$$

Interpret (2.2) as follows: draw countries $i$ and $j$ independently at random and record their values of $W_i$ and $W_j$. Given this information set what is the mean square error (MSE) minimizing predictor of $Y_{ij}$? Eq. (2.2) gives a parametric form for this prediction/regression function. This chapter surveys methods of estimation of, and inference on, $\theta_0$.

Santos Silva and Tenreyro (2006) recommended estimating $\theta_0$ by maximizing a Poisson pseudo log-likelihood with a conditional mean function given by (2.2) (cf. Gourieroux et al., 1984). For inference they constructed standard errors using the sandwich formula of Huber (1967); implicitly assuming that the $\{Y_{ij}\}_{1 \le i, j \le N, i \ne j}$ are conditionally independent of one another given $\mathbf{W} = (W_1, \ldots, W_N)'$. In practice this conditional independence assumption, although routinely made in the empirical trade literature (e.g., Rose, 2004; Baldwin and Taglioni, 2007), is very unlikely to hold. Exports from, say, Japan to Korea likely covary with those from Japan to the United States. This follows because $A_i$—the Japan exporter effect—drives Japanese exports to both Korea and the United States. It is also possible that exports from Japan to Korea may covary with those from Korea to Thailand; perhaps because $A_j$ and $B_j$—the Korean exporter and importer effects—covary (as would be true if there exist common unobserved drivers of Korean exporting and importing behavior).[2]

Loosely following Fafchamps and Gubert (2007) I call the above patterns of dependence "dyadic dependence" or "dyadic clustering". Consider two pairs of

---

[1] If, for example, a subset of $\mathbb{W}$ is associated with membership in the World Trade Organization (WTO), then reasoning about this condition involves asking whether countries belonging to the WTO have a greater latent propensity to export or import? In what follows I entirely defer consideration of these questions and focus solely on the inferential issues raised by the network structure.

[2] Researchers also sometimes "cluster" on dyads (e.g., Santos Silva and Tenreyro, 2010); this assumes that the elements of $\{(Y_{ij}, Y_{ji})\}_{1 \le i \le N-1, j > i}$ are conditionally independent given covariates. While this allows for dependence between, say, exports from Japan to the United States and from the United States to Japan, it does not allow for dependence between, say, exports from Japan to the United States and from Japan to Canada.

dyads, say $\{i_1, i_2\}$ and $\{j_1, j_2\}$, if these dyads share an agent in common—for example $i_1 = j_1$—then $Y_{i_1 i_2}$ and $Y_{j_1 j_2}$ will covary. Failing to account for dependence of this type will, typically, result in standard errors which are too small and consequently more Type I errors in inference than is desired (e.g., Cameron and Miller, 2014; Aronow et al., 2017).

In this chapter I describe how to estimate and conduct inference on $\theta_0$ in a way that appropriately accounts for dependence across dyads sharing a unit in common. Section 2.1 outlines the population and sampling framework. Section 2.2 introduces a composite maximum likelihood estimator. Section 2.3 develops the asymptotic properties of this estimator and discusses variance estimation. Sections 2.4 presents a small empirical illustration.

Dyadic data, where outcomes reflecting pairwise interaction among sampled units are of primary interest, arise frequently in social science research. Such data play central roles in contemporary empirical trade and international relations research (see, respectively, Tinbergen (1962) and Oneal and Russett (1999)). They also feature in work on international financial flows (Portes and Rey, 2005), development economics (Fafchamps and Gubert, 2007), and anthropology (Apicella et al., 2012) among other fields. Despite their prominence in empirical work, the properties of extant methods of estimation and inference for dyadic regression models are not fully understood. Only recently have researchers begun to formally study these methods (e.g., Aronow et al., 2017; Menzel, 2017; Tabord-Meehan, 2018; Davezies et al., 2019). Some of the results presented in this chapter are novel, others, while having antecedents going back decades, are not widely known among empirical researchers. Section 2.5 ends the chapter with a discussion of further reading (including historically important references).

## 2.1 Population and sampling framework

Let $i \in \mathbb{N}$ index agents in some (infinite) population of interest. In what follows I will refer to agents as, equivalently, nodes, vertices, units and/or individuals. Let $W_i \in \mathbb{W} = \{w_1, \ldots, w_L\}$ be an observable attribute which partitions this population into $L = |\mathbb{W}|$ subpopulations or "types"; $\mathbb{N}(w) = \{i : W_i = w\}$ equals the index set associated with the subpopulation where $W_i = w$. While $L$ may be very large, the size of each subpopulation is assumed infinite. In practice $\mathbb{W}$ will typically enumerate different combinations of distinct agent-specific attributes (e.g., $W_i = w_1$ may correspond to former British colonies in the tropics with per capita GDP below \$3,000). Heuristically we can think of $\mathbb{W}$ as consisting of the support points of a multinomial approximation to a (possibly continuous) underlying covariate space as in Chamberlain (1987).

The indexing of agents within subpopulations homogeneous in $W_i$ is arbitrary; from the standpoint of the researcher all vertices of the same type are exchangeable. Similar exchangeability assumptions underlie most cross-sectional microeconometric procedures. For each (ordered) pair of agents—or *directed dyad*—there exists an outcome of interest $Y_{ij} \in \mathbb{Y} \subseteq \mathbb{R}$. The first subscript in $Y_{ij}$ indexes the directed dyads *ego*, or "sending" agent, while the second its *alter*, or "receiving" agent. The *adjacency matrix* $[Y_{ij}]_{i,j \in \mathbb{N}}$ collects all such outcomes into an (infinite) random array. Within-type exchangeability of agents implies a particular form of joint exchangeability of the adjacency matrix.

To describe this exchangeability condition let $\sigma_w : \mathbb{N} \to \mathbb{N}$ be any permutation of indices satisfying the restriction

$$\left[ W_{\sigma_w(i)} \right]_{i \in \mathbb{N}} = [W_i]_{i \in \mathbb{N}}. \tag{2.3}$$

Condition (2.3) restricts relabelings to occur among agents of the same type (i.e., *within* the index sets $\mathbb{N}(w)$, $w \in \mathbb{W}$). Following Crane and Towsner (2018) a network is *relatively exchangeable* with respect to $W$ (or $W$-exchangeable) if, for all permutations $\sigma_w$,

$$\left[ Y_{\sigma_w(i)\sigma_w(j)} \right]_{i,j \in \mathbb{N}} \overset{D}{=} \left[ Y_{ij} \right]_{i,j \in \mathbb{N}} \tag{2.4}$$

where $\overset{D}{=}$ denotes equality of distribution.

If we regard $[Y_{ij}]_{i,j \in \mathbb{N}}$ as a (weighted) directed network and $W_i$ as vertex $i$'s "color", then (2.4) is equivalent to the statement that all colored graph isomorphisms are equally probable. Since there is nothing in the researcher's information set which justifies attaching different probabilities to graphs which are isomorphic (as vertex colored graphs) any probability model for the adjacency matrix should satisfy (2.4). If $W_i$ encodes all the vertex information observed by the analyst, then $W$-exchangeability is a natural *a priori* modeling restriction.

Condition (2.4) allows for the invocation of very powerful de Finetti (1931) type representation results for random arrays. These results provide an "as if" (nonparametric) data generating process for the network adjacency matrix. This, in turn, facilitates various probabilistic calculations (e.g., computing expectations and variances) and gives (tractable) structure to the dependence across the elements of $[Y_{ij}]_{i,j \in \mathbb{N}}$.

Let $\alpha$, $\{U_i\}_{i \geq 1}$ and $\left\{ (V_{ij}, V_{ji}) \right\}_{i \geq 1, j > i}$ be i.i.d. random variables. We may normalize $\alpha$, $U_{ij}$ and $V_{ij}$ to be $\mathcal{U}[0, 1]$—uniform on the unit interval—without loss of generality. We do allow for within-dyad dependence across $V_{ij}$ and $V_{ji}$; the role such dependence will become apparent below. Next consider the random array $[Y_{ij}]_{i,j \in \mathbb{N}}$ generated according to the rule

$$Y_{ij} \overset{def}{=} \tilde{h} \left( \alpha, W_i, W_j, U_i, U_j, V_{ij} \right). \tag{2.5}$$

The data generating process (DGP) (2.5) has a number of useful features. First, any pair of outcomes, $Y_{i_1 i_2}$ and $Y_{j_1 j_2}$, sharing at least one index in common are dependent. This holds true even conditional on their types $W_{i_1}$, $W_{i_2}$, $W_{j_1}$ and

$W_{j_2}$. Second, if $Y_{i_1 i_2}$ and $Y_{j_1 j_2}$ share exactly one index in common, say $i_1 = j_2$, then they are independent if $U_{i_1} = U_{j_2}$, $U_{i_2}$ and $U_{j_1}$ are additionally conditioned on. Third, if they share both indices in common, as in $i_1 = j_2$ and $i_2 = j_1$, then there may be dependence even conditional on $U_{i_1} = U_{j_2}$ and $U_{i_2} = U_{j_1}$ due to the within-dyad dependence across $V_{i_1 i_2}$ and $V_{i_2 i_1}$. These patterns of structured dependence and conditional independence will be exploited below to derive the limit distribution of parametric dyadic regression coefficient estimates. Shalizi (2016) helpfully calls models like (2.5) conditionally independent dyad (CID) models (see also Chandrasekhar (2015)).

Crane and Towsner (2018), extending Aldous (1981) and Hoover (1979), show that, for any random array $\left[ Y_{ij} \right]_{i,j \in \mathbb{N}}$ satisfying (2.4), there exists another array $\left[ Y_{ij}^* \right]_{i,j \in \mathbb{N}}$, generated according to (2.5), such that

$$\left[ Y_{ij} \right]_{i,j \in \mathbb{N}} \stackrel{D}{=} \left[ Y_{ij}^* \right]_{i,j \in \mathbb{N}}. \tag{2.6}$$

Rule (2.5) can therefore be regarded as a nonparametric data generating process for $\left[ Y_{ij} \right]_{i,j \in \mathbb{N}}$. Eq. (2.6) implies that we may proceed 'as if' our $W$-exchangeable network was generated according to (2.5). In the spirit of Diaconis and Janson (2008) and Bickel and Chen (2009) and others, call $\bar{h}$ : $[0, 1] \times \mathbb{W}^2 \times [0, 1]^3 \to \mathbb{R}$ a *graphon*. Here $\alpha$ is an unidentifiable mixing parameter, analogous to the one appearing in de Finetti's (1931) classic representation result for exchangeable binary sequences. Since I will focus on inference which is conditional on the empirical distribution of the data, $\alpha$ can be safely ignored and I will write $h \left( W_i, W_j, U_i, U_j, V_{ij} \right) \stackrel{def}{=} \bar{h} \left( \alpha, W_i, W_j, U_i, U_j, V_{ij} \right)$ in what follows (cf., Bickel and Chen, 2009; Menzel, 2017).

The Crane and Towsner (2018) representation result implies that a very particular type of dependence structure is associated with $W$-exchangeability. Namely, as discussed earlier, $Y_{i_1 i_2}$ and $Y_{j_1 j_2}$ are (conditionally) independent when $\{i_1, i_2\}$ and $\{j_1, j_2\}$ share no indices in common and dependent when they do. This type of dependence structure, which is very much analogous to that which arises in the theory U-Statistics, is tractable and allows for the formulation of laws of large numbers and central limit theorems. The next few sections will show how to use this insight to develop asymptotic distribution theory for dyadic regression.

## Sampling assumption

I will regard $\left[ Y_{ij} \right]_{i,j \in \mathbb{N}}$ as an infinite random (weighted) graph, $G_\infty$, with nodes $\mathbb{N}$ and (weighted) edges given by the non-zero elements of $\left[ Y_{ij} \right]_{i,j \in \mathbb{N}}$. Let $\mathcal{V} = \{1, \ldots, N\}$ be a random sample of size $N$ from $\mathbb{N}$. Let $G_N = G_\infty [\mathcal{V}]$ be the subgraph indexed by $\mathcal{V}$. We assume that the observed network corresponds to the one induced by a random sample of agents from the larger (infinite) graph.

The sampling distribution of any statistic of $G_N$ is induced by this (perhaps hypothetical) random sampling of agents from $G_\infty$.

If $G_\infty$ is relatively exchangeable, then $G_N$ will we be too. We can thus proceed 'as if'

$$Y_{ij} = h\left(W_i, W_j, U_i, U_j, V_{ij}\right)$$

for $1 \leq i, j \leq N$. In what follows we assume that we observe $W_i$ for each sampled agent, and for each pair of sampled agents, we observe both $Y_{ij}$ and $Y_{ji}$. The presentation here rules out self loops (i.e., $Y_{ii} \equiv 0$); however, incorporating them is natural in some empirical settings and what follows can be adapted to handle them. Similarly the extension to undirected outcomes, where $Y_{ij} = Y_{ji}$, is straightforward.

## 2.2  Composite likelihood

Let $f_{Y_{12}|W_1,W_2}\left(Y_{12}|W_1, W_2; \theta\right)$ be a parametric family for the conditional density of $Y_{12}$ given $W_1$ and $W_2$. This family is chosen by the researcher. Let $l_{12}(\theta)$ denote the corresponding log-likelihood. As an example to help fix ideas, return to the variant of the gravity model of trade introduced in the introduction. Following Santos Silva and Tenreyro (2006) we set

$$l_{12}(\theta) = Y_{12}R'_{12}\theta - \exp\left(R'_{12}\theta\right),$$

which equals (up to a term not varying with $\theta$) the log likelihood of a Poisson random variable $Y_{12}$ with mean $\exp\left(R'_{12}\theta\right)$, and choose $\hat{\theta}$ to maximize

$$L_N(\theta) = \frac{1}{N}\frac{1}{N-1}\sum_i\sum_{j\neq i} l_{ij}(\theta). \tag{2.7}$$

The maximizer of (2.7) coincides with a maximum likelihood estimate based upon the assumption that $\left[Y_{ij}\right]_{1\leq i,j\leq N, i\neq j}$ are independent Poisson random variables conditional on $\mathbf{W} = (W_1, \ldots, W_N)'$.

In practice, trade flows are unlikely to be well-described by a Poisson distribution and independence of the summands in (2.7) is even less likely. As discussed earlier any two summands in (2.7) will be dependent if they share an index in common. The likelihood contribution associated with exports from Vanuatu to Fiji is not independent of that associated with exports from Fiji to Bangladesh. Dependencies of this type mean that proceeding 'as if' (2.7) is a correctly specified log-likelihood (or even an M-estimation criterion function) will lead to incorrect inference.

If there exists some $\theta_0$ such that $f_{Y_{12}|W_1,W_2}\left(Y_{12}|W_1, W_2; \theta_0\right)$ is the true density, then (2.5) corresponds to what is called a *composite* likelihood (e.g., Lindsey, 1988; Cox and Reid, 2004; Bellio and Varin, 2005). Because it does not correctly reflect the dependence structure across dyads, (2.5) is not a correctly specified log-likelihood function in the usual sense. If, however, the marginal density of $Y_{ij} | W_i, W_j$ is correctly specified, then $\hat{\theta}$ will generally be consistent for $\theta_0$. That is, we may have

$$f_{Y_{12} | W_1, W_2} (Y_{12} | W_1, W_2) = f_{Y_{12} | W_1, W_2} (Y_{12} | W_1, W_2; \theta_0)$$

for some $\theta_0 \in \Theta$ (i.e., the marginal likelihood is correctly specified), but it *is not* the case that, setting $\mathbf{Y} = [Y_{ij}]_{1 \leq i, j \leq N, i \neq j}$,

$$f_{\mathbf{Y} | \mathbf{W}} (\mathbf{Y} | \mathbf{W}) = \prod_{1 \leq i, j \leq N, i \neq j} f_{Y_{12} | W_1, W_2} (Y_{ij} | W_i, W_j; \theta_0),$$

due to dependence across dyads sharing agents in common (i.e., the joint likelihood is not correctly specified). A composite log-likelihood is constructed by summing together a collection of component log-likelihoods; each such component is a log-likelihood for a portion of the sample (in this case a single *directed* dyad) but, because the joint dependence structure may not be modeled appropriately, the summation of all these components may not be the correct log likelihood for the sample as a whole.

If the marginal likelihood is itself misspecified, then (2.5) corresponds to what might be called a pseudo-composite-log-likelihood; "pseudo" in the sense of Gourieroux et al. (1984) and "composite" in the sense of Lindsey (1988). In what follows I outline how to conduct inference on the probability limit of $\hat{\theta}$ (denoted by $\theta_0$ in all cases); the interpretation of this limit will, of course, depend on whether the pairwise likelihood is misspecified or not. In the context of the Santos Silva and Tenreyro (2006) gravity model example, if the true conditional mean equals $\exp\left(R'_{ij}\theta_0\right)$ for some $\theta_0 \in \Theta$, then $\hat{\theta}$ will be consistent for it (under regularity conditions). The key challenge is to characterize this estimate's sampling precision.

## 2.3 Limit distribution

To characterize the limit properties of $\hat{\theta}$ begin with a mean value expansion of the first order condition associated with the maximizer of (2.7). This yields, after some re-arrangement,

$$\sqrt{N}\left(\hat{\theta} - \theta_0\right) = \left[-H_N\left(\bar{\theta}\right)\right]^+ \sqrt{N} S_N\left(\theta_0\right)$$

with $\bar{\theta}$ a mean value between $\hat{\theta}$ and $\theta_0$ which may vary from row to row, the $+$ superscript denoting a Moore–Penrose inverse, and a "score" vector of

$$S_N\left(\theta\right) = \frac{1}{N} \frac{1}{N-1} \sum_i \sum_{j \neq i} s_{ij}\left(Z_{ij}, \theta\right) \tag{2.8}$$

with $s\left(Z_{ij}, \theta\right) = \partial l_{ij}\left(\theta\right)/\partial\theta$ for $Z_{ij} = \left(Y_{ij}, W_i', W_j'\right)'$ and $H_N(\theta) = \frac{1}{N}\frac{1}{N-1}\sum_i \sum_{j\neq i}\frac{\partial^2 l_{ij}(\theta)}{\partial\theta\partial\theta'}$. In what follows I will just assume that $H_N\left(\bar{\theta}\right) \xrightarrow{p} \Gamma_0$, with $\Gamma_0$ invertible (see Graham (2017) for a formal argument in a related setting and Eagleson and Weber (1978) and Davezies et al. (2019) for more general results).

If the Hessian matrix converges in probability to $\Gamma_0$, as assumed, then

$$\sqrt{N}\left(\hat{\theta} - \theta_0\right) = \Gamma_0^{-1}\sqrt{N}S_N\left(\theta_0\right) + o_p\,(1)$$

so that the asymptotic sampling properties of $\sqrt{N}\left(\hat{\theta} - \theta_0\right)$ will be driven by the behavior of $\sqrt{N}S_N\left(\theta_0\right)$. As pointed out by Fafchamps and Gubert (2007) and others, (2.8) is not a sum of independent random variables, hence the basic central limit theorem (CLT) cannot be (directly) applied.

My analysis of $\sqrt{N}S_N\left(\theta_0\right)$ borrows from the theory of U-Statistics (e.g., Ferguson, 2005; van der Vaart, 2000). To make these connections clear it is convenient to re-write $S_N\left(\theta_0\right)$ as

$$S_N\left(\theta\right) = \binom{N}{2}^{-1}\sum_{i<j}\left\{\frac{s\left(Z_{ij}, \theta\right) + s\left(Z_{ji}, \theta\right)}{2}\right\}$$

where $\sum_{i<j} \overset{def}{\equiv} \sum_{i=1}^{N-1}\sum_{j=i+1}^{N}$.

Let $s_{ij} \overset{def}{\equiv} s\left(Z_{ij}, \theta_0\right)$, $S_N = S_N\left(\theta_0\right)$ and $\bar{s}\left(w, u, w', u'\right) = \mathbb{E}[s_{12}|W_1 = w, U_1 = u, W_2 = w', U_2 = u']$; next decompose $S_N$ as follows:

$$S_N = U_N + V_N,$$

where $U_N$ equals the projection of $S_N$ onto $\mathbf{W} = [W_i]_{1\leq i\leq N}$ and $\mathbf{U} = [U_i]_{1\leq i\leq N}$:

$$U_N = \mathbb{E}[\,S_N|\mathbf{W}, \mathbf{U}] = \binom{N}{2}^{-1}\sum_{i<j}\frac{\bar{s}\left(W_i, U_i, W_j, U_j\right) + \bar{s}\left(W_j, U_j, W_i, U_i\right)}{2}$$

$$(2.9)$$

and $V_N = S_N - U_N$ is the corresponding projection error:

$$V_N = \binom{N}{2}^{-1}\sum_{i<j}\frac{[s(Z_{ij},\theta)-\bar{s}(W_i,U_i,W_j,U_j)]+[s(Z_{ji},\theta)-\bar{s}(W_j,U_j,W_i,U_i)]}{2}. \quad (2.10)$$

Observe that $U_N$ and $V_N$ are uncorrelated by construction. Furthermore $U_N$ is a U-statistic, albeit defined—partially – in terms of the latent variable $U_i$. Although we cannot numerically evaluate $U_N$, we can characterize is sampling properties as $N \to \infty$. In order to do so we further decompose $U_N$ into a Hájek projection and a second remainder term:

$$U_N = U_{1N} + U_{2N}$$

where, defining $\bar{s}_1^e(w, u) = \mathbb{E}[\bar{s}(w, u, W_1, U_1)]$ and $\bar{s}_1^a(w, u) = \mathbb{E}[\bar{s}(W_1, U_1, w, u)]$,

$$U_{1N} = \frac{2}{N} \sum_{i=1}^{N} \frac{\bar{s}_1^e(W_i, U_i) + \bar{s}_1^a(W_i, U_i)}{2},$$

$$U_{2N} = \binom{N}{2}^{-1} \sum_{i<j} \left\{ \frac{\bar{s}(W_i, U_i, W_j, U_j) + \bar{s}(W_j, U_j, W_i, U_i)}{2} \right.$$
$$\left. - \frac{\bar{s}_1^e(W_i, U_i) + \bar{s}_1^a(W_i, U_i)}{2} - \frac{\bar{s}_1^e(W_j, U_j) + \bar{s}_1^a(W_j, U_j)}{2} \right\}.$$

The superscript in $\bar{s}_1^e(W_i, U_i)$ stands for 'ego' since $\bar{s}_1^e(W_1, U_1) = \mathbb{E}[\bar{s}(W_1, U_1, W_2, U_2)|W_1, U_1]$ corresponds to the expected value of a (generic) dyad's contribution to the composite likelihood's score vector holding its ego's attributes fixed. Similarly the superscript in $\bar{s}_1^a(W_i, U_i)$ stands for 'alter', since it is her attributes being held fixed in that average.

Putting things together yields the score decomposition

$$S_N = \overbrace{\underbrace{U_{1N}}_{\text{(Second) Hájek Projection}} + \underbrace{U_{2N}}_{\text{(Second) Projection Error}}}^{\text{(First) Projection onto } \mathbf{W} \text{ and } \mathbf{U}} + \overbrace{V_N}^{\text{(First) Projection Error}}.$$

The limit distribution of $\sqrt{N}\left(\hat{\theta} - \theta_0\right)$ depends on the joint behavior of $U_{1N}$, $U_{2N}$ and $V_N$ as $N \to \infty$. A similar type of double projection argument was utilized by Graham (2017) to characterize the limit distribution of the Tetrad Logit estimator.[3] The analyses of Menzel (2017) and Graham et al. (2019) both utilize a similar decomposition.

### Variance calculation

In this section I first derive the sampling variance of $\sqrt{N}\left(\hat{\theta} - \theta_0\right)$ and then provide an interpretation of it. I begin by calculating the variance of $S_N$:

$$\mathbb{V}(S_N) = \mathbb{V}(U_{1N}) + \mathbb{V}(U_{2N}) + \mathbb{V}(V_N).$$

---

[3] It is also implicit in the analysis of Bickel et al. (2011).

Let

$$\Sigma_q = \mathbb{C}\left(\bar{s}\left(W_{i_1}, U_{i_1}, W_{i_2}, U_{i_2}\right) + \bar{s}\left(W_{i_2}, U_{i_2}, W_{i_1}, U_{i_1}\right),\right.$$
$$\left.\bar{s}\left(W_{j_1}, U_{j_1}, W_{j_2}, U_{j_2}\right) + \bar{s}\left(W_{j_2}, U_{j_2}, W_{j_1}, U_{j_1}\right)\right)$$

when the dyads $\{i_1, i_2\}$ and $\{j_1, j_2\}$ share $q = 0, 1, 2$ indices in common. A Hoeffding (1948) variance decomposition gives

$$\mathbb{V}\left(U_N\right) = \mathbb{V}\left(U_{1N}\right) + \mathbb{V}\left(U_{2N}\right)$$
$$\frac{4}{N}\Sigma_1 + \frac{2}{N\left(N-1\right)}\left(\Sigma_2 - \Sigma_1\right).$$

Direct calculation yields (see Appendix 2.A)

$$\Sigma_1 \overset{def}{=} \mathbb{V}\left(\frac{\bar{s}_1^e\left(W_1, U_1\right) + \bar{s}_1^a\left(W_1, U_1\right)}{2}\right) \tag{2.11}$$
$$= \frac{\Omega_{12,13} + 2\Omega_{12,31} + \Omega_{21,31}}{4}$$

with

$$\Omega_{i_1 i_2, j_1 j_2} = C\left(\bar{s}\left(W_{i_1}, U_{i_1}, W_{i_2}, U_{i_2}\right), \bar{s}\left(W_{j_1}, U_{j_1}, W_{j_2}, U_{j_2}\right)\right).$$

Similarly we have

$$\Sigma_2 = \mathbb{V}\left(\frac{\bar{s}\left(W_1, U_1, W_2, U_2\right) + \bar{s}\left(W_2, U_2, W_1, U_1\right)}{2}\right) \tag{2.12}$$
$$= \frac{\Omega_{12,12} + \Omega_{12,21}}{2}$$

and, in an abuse of notation, letting $\Sigma_3 \overset{def}{=} \mathbb{V}\left(\sqrt{\binom{N}{2}}V_N\right)$,

$$\Sigma_3 = \mathbb{E}\left[\frac{\Delta_{12,12}\left(W_1, U_1, W_2, U_2\right) + \Delta_{12,21}\left(W_1, U_1, W_2, U_2\right)}{2}\right] \tag{2.13}$$
$$= \frac{\bar{\Delta}_{12,12} + \bar{\Delta}_{12,21}}{2}$$

where

$$\Delta_{12,12}\left(W_1, U_1, W_2, U_2\right) = \mathbb{V}\left(s\left(Z_{12}, \theta\right) \middle| W_1, U_1, W_2, U_2\right),$$
$$\Delta_{12,21}\left(W_1, U_1, W_2, U_2\right) = \mathbb{E}\left[s\left(Z_{12}, \theta\right)s\left(Z_{21}, \theta\right)' \middle| W_1, U_1, W_2, U_2\right].$$

From (2.11), (2.12) and (2.13) we have, collecting terms, a variance of $S_N$ equal to

$$\mathbb{V}(S_N) = \mathbb{V}(U_{1N}) + \mathbb{V}(U_{2N}) + \mathbb{V}(V_N) \qquad (2.14)$$

$$\frac{4}{N}\Sigma_1 + \frac{2}{N(N-1)}(\Sigma_2 - 2\Sigma_1) + \frac{2}{N(N-1)}\Sigma_3$$

$$= \left(\Omega_{12,13} + 2\Omega_{12,31} + \Omega_{21,31}\right)\left(\frac{N-2}{N-1}\right)$$

$$+ \frac{1}{N-1}\left(\Omega_{12,12} + \bar{\Delta}_{12,12} + \Omega_{12,21} + \bar{\Delta}_{12,21}\right).$$

To understand (2.14) note that there are exactly $\binom{N}{2}\binom{2}{1}\binom{N-2}{1} = N(N-1)(N-2)$ pairs of dyads sharing one agent in common. Consequently, applying the variance operator to $S_N$ yields a total of $N(N-1)(N-2)$ non-zero covariance terms across the $\binom{N}{2}$ summands in $S_N$. It is these covariance terms which account for the leading term in (2.14). The second and third terms in (2.14) arise from the $\binom{N}{2}$ variances of the summands in $S_N$. Indeed, it is helpful to note that

$$\Sigma_2 = \mathbb{V}\left(\mathbb{E}\left[\frac{s(Z_{12},\theta) + s(Z_{21},\theta)}{2}\,\middle|\, W_1, U_1, W_2, U_2\right]\right),$$

$$\Sigma_3 = \mathbb{E}\left[\mathbb{V}\left(\frac{s(Z_{12},\theta) + s(Z_{21},\theta)}{2}\,\middle|\, W_1, U_1, W_2, U_2\right)\right],$$

and hence that

$$\mathbb{V}\left(\frac{s(Z_{12},\theta) + s(Z_{21},\theta)}{2}\right) = \Sigma_2 + \Sigma_3. \qquad (2.15)$$

Although it may be that $\Sigma_2 + \Sigma_3 \geq \Sigma_1$ (in a positive definite sense), the larger number of non-zero covariance terms generated by applying the variance operator to $S_N$ contributes more to its variability, than the smaller number of own variance terms. Inspecting (2.14) it is clear that the multiplying by $\sqrt{N}$ stabilizes the variance such that

$$\mathbb{V}\left(\sqrt{N}S_N\right) = 4\Sigma_1 + O\left(N^{-1}\right)$$

and hence

$$\mathbb{V}\left(\sqrt{N}\left(\hat{\theta} - \theta\right)\right) \to 4\left(\Gamma'\Sigma_1^{-1}\Gamma\right)^{-1}$$

as $N \to \infty$.

If a researcher uses standard software, for example a Poisson regression program, to maximize the composite log-likelihood (2.7) and then chooses to report robust Huber (1967) type standard errors, this corresponds to assuming that

$$\Omega_{12,13} = \Omega_{12,31} = \Omega_{21,31} = \Omega_{12,21} = \bar{\Delta}_{12,21} = 0.$$

This approach would ignore the dominant variance term and part of the higher order term too. If, instead, the researcher clustered her standard errors on dyads, as in, for example, Santos Silva and Tenreyro (2010), then this corresponds to assuming that

$$\Omega_{12,13} = \Omega_{12,31} = \Omega_{21,31} = 0$$

but allowing $\Omega_{12,21}$ and/or $\bar{\Delta}_{12,21}$ to differ from zero. This approach would still erroneously ignore the dominant variance term. In both cases reported confidence intervals are likely to undercover the true parameter; perhaps by a substantial margin. This is shown, by example, via Monte Carlo simulation below.

### Variance estimation

Graham (2020) provides a comprehensive discussion of variance estimation for dyadic regression. One approach to variance estimation he reviews shows that $\Sigma_1$ can be estimated by the analog covariance estimate

$$\hat{\Sigma}_1 = \frac{1}{4} \frac{2}{N(N-1)(N-1)} \sum_{i=1}^{N-2} \sum_{j=i+1}^{N-1} \sum_{k=j+1}^{N} \left\{ \left( \hat{s}_{ij} + \hat{s}_{ji} \right) \left( \hat{s}_{ik} + \hat{s}_{ki} \right)' \right.$$
$$\left. \left( \hat{s}_{ij} + \hat{s}_{ji} \right) \left( \hat{s}_{jk} + \hat{s}_{kj} \right)' + \left( \hat{s}_{ik} + \hat{s}_{ki} \right) \left( \hat{s}_{jk} + \hat{s}_{kj} \right)' \right\},$$

where the summation is over all triads in the sampled network. Each triad can itself be partitioned into three different pairs of dyads, each sharing an agent in common.

It turns out, as inspection of (2.15) suggests, it is easiest to estimate the sum of $\Sigma_2$ and $\Sigma_3$ jointly by

$$\widehat{\Sigma_2 + \Sigma_3} = \frac{1}{4} \frac{2}{N(N-1)} \sum_{i=1}^{N-1} \sum_{j=i+1}^{N} \left( \hat{s}_{ij} + \hat{s}_{ji} \right) \left( \hat{s}_{ij} + \hat{s}_{ji} \right)'.$$

The Jacobian matrix, $\Gamma_0$, may be estimated by $-H_N\left(\hat{\theta}\right)$, which is typically available as a by-product of estimation in most commercial software. Putting things together gives a variance estimate of

$$\hat{\mathbb{V}}\left( \sqrt{N} \left( \hat{\theta} - \theta_0 \right) \right) = \hat{\Gamma}^{-1} \left( 4\hat{\Sigma}_1 + \frac{2}{N-1} \left( \widehat{\Sigma_2 + \Sigma_3} - 2\hat{\Sigma}_1 \right) \right) \left( \hat{\Gamma}^{-1} \right)'.$$
$$(2.16)$$

Graham (2020) shows that (2.16) is numerically equivalent, up to a finite sample correction, to the variance estimator proposed by Fafchamps and Gubert (2007). This variance estimator includes estimates of asymptotically negligible terms. Although these terms are negligible when the sample is large enough, in practice they may be sizable in real world settings.

**Limit distribution**

The variance calculations outlined above imply that $\sqrt{N} S_N = \sqrt{N} U_{1N} + o_p(1)$ and hence that

$$\sqrt{N}\left(\hat{\theta} - \theta_0\right) = \Gamma_0^{-1}\sqrt{N} U_{1N} + o_p(1).$$

Since $U_{1N}$ is the sum of i.i.d. random variables a CLT gives

$$\sqrt{N}\left(\hat{\theta} - \theta_0\right) \xrightarrow{D} \mathcal{N}\left(0, 4\left(\Gamma_0' \Sigma_1^{-1} \Gamma_0\right)^{-1}\right), \qquad (2.17)$$

The variance expression, Eq. (2.14), indicates that inference based upon the limit distribution (2.17) would ignore higher order variance terms included in (2.16). In practice, as has been shown in other contexts, an approach to inference which incorporates estimates of these higher order variance terms may result in inference with better size properties (e.g., Graham et al., 2014; Cattaneo et al., 2014; Graham et al., 2019). In practice I suggest using the normal reference distribution, but with a variance estimated by (2.16), which includes asymptotically negligible terms which may nevertheless be large in real world samples.

## 2.4 Empirical illustration

This section provides an example of a dyadic regression analysis using the dataset constructed by João Santos Silva and Silvana Tenreyro (2006) in their widely-cited paper "The Log of Gravity". This dataset, which as of the Fall of 2019 was available for download at http://personal.lse.ac.uk/tenreyro/LGW. html, includes information on $N = 136$ countries, corresponding to 18,360 directed trading relationships. Here I present a simple specification which includes only the log of exporter and importer GDP, respectively `lyex` and `lyim`, as well as the log distance (`ldist`) between the two trading countries. Maximizing (2.7) yields a fitted regression function of

$$\hat{\mathbb{E}}\left[Y_{ij} \mid W_i, W_j\right] = \exp\left(\underset{(1.9382)}{-5.688} + \underset{(0.0750)}{0.9047} \; \texttt{lyex} + \underset{(0.0668)}{0.8941} \; \texttt{lyim}\right.$$
$$\left. + \underset{(0.0982)}{-0.5676} \; \texttt{ldist}\right).$$

Standard errors which cluster on dyads, but ignore dependence across dyads sharing a single agent in common, are reported in parentheses below the coefficient estimates. Specifically these standard errors coincide with square roots of the diagonal elements of

$$\frac{2}{N(N-1)} \hat{\Gamma}^{-1} \left( \widehat{\Sigma_2 + \Sigma_3} \right) \left( \hat{\Gamma}^{-1} \right)'. \tag{2.18}$$

The coefficient estimates and reported standard errors are unremarkable in the context of the empirical trade literature. I refer the reader to Santos Silva and Tenreyro (2006) or Head and Mayer (2014) for additional context.

If, instead, the Fafchamps and Gubert (2007) dyadic robust variance-covariance estimator is used to construct standard errors (see (2.16) earlier), I get

$$\hat{\mathbb{E}} \left[ Y_{ij} \mid W_i, W_j \right] = \exp \left( \begin{array}{cc} -5.688 \\ (3.6781) \end{array} + \begin{array}{cc} 0.9047 & \texttt{lyex} \\ (0.1319) \end{array} + \begin{array}{cc} 0.8941 & \texttt{lyim} \\ (0.1345) \end{array} \right.$$
$$\left. + \begin{array}{cc} -0.5676 & \texttt{ldist} \\ (0.2191) \end{array} \right).$$

Standard errors which account for dependence across dyads sharing an agent in common are approximately twice those which ignore such dependence.

## Monte Carlo experiment

Next I summarize the results of a small Monte Carlo experiment to illustrate the properties of inference methods based upon the different variance-covariance estimates described above. I set $N = 200$ and generate outcome data for all $N(N-1)$ ordered pairs of agents according to the outcome model:

$$Y_{ij} = \exp \left( \theta_1 R_{ij} + \theta_2 W_{2i} + \theta_2 W_{2j} \right) A_i A_j U_{ij}.$$

Here $A_i$, for $i = 1, ..., N$, is a sequence of i.i.d. log normal random variables, each with mean 1 and scale parameter $\sigma_A$; $U_{ij}$ for $i = 1, ..., n$ with $n = N(N-1)$ is also sequence of i.i.d. log normal random variables, each with mean 1 and scale parameter $\sigma$.

Each agent is uniformly at random assigned a location on the unit square, $(W_{1i}, W_{2i})$, $R_{ij} = \sqrt{\left( W_{1i} - W_{1j} \right)^2 + \left( W_{2i} - W_{2j} \right)^2}$ equals the distance between agents $i$ and $j$ on that square; $W_{3i}$ is a standard uniform random variable. I set $\theta_1 = -1$, $\theta_1 = -1/2$ and $\theta_3 = 1/2$. I set $\sigma = 1$ and $\sigma_A = 1/4$. This generates moderate, but meaningful, dependence across any two dyads sharing at least one agent in common.

Table 2.1 reports Monte Carlo estimates of confidence interval coverage (the nominal coverage of the intervals should be 0.95). These estimates are based

**TABLE 2.1** Coverage of different confidence intervals with dyadic data.

|            | i.i.d. | dyadic clustered |
|------------|--------|------------------|
| $\theta_1$ | 0.789  | 0.950            |
| $\theta_2$ | 0.520  | 0.942            |
| $\theta_3$ | 0.556  | 0.941            |

Notes: Actual coverage of nominal 0.95 confidence intervals. The data generating process is as described in the text. Coverage estimates are based upon 1,000 simulations. Intervals are Wald-type; constructed by taking the coefficient point estimate and adding and subtracting 1.96 times a standard error estimate. For the "i.i.d." column this standard error is based upon the assumption of independence across dyads (see Eq. (2.18)). In the "dyadic clustered" column standard errors which account for dependence across pairs of dyads sharing an agent in common are used (see Eq. (2.16)).

upon 1,000 simulated datasets. The coverage properties of two intervals are evaluated. The first is a Wald-based interval which uses standard errors constructed from (2.18). This corresponds to assuming independence across dyads or "clustering on dyads". Confidence intervals constructed in this way are routinely reported in, for example, the trade literature. The coverage of these intervals is presented in first column of Table 2.1. The second interval is based on the Fafchamps–Gubert variance estimate (see (2.16) above). The coverage of these intervals, which do take into account dependence across pairs of dyads sharing an agent in common, are reported in column two of the table.

In the experiment, the intervals which do not appropriately account fo dyadic clustering, drastically undercover the truth, whereas those based on the variance estimator outline above have actual coverage very close to 0.95. While there is no doubt additional work to be done on variance estimation and inference in the dyadic context, a preliminary suggestion is to report standard errors and confidence intervals based upon Eq. (2.16) of the previous section. These intervals perform well in the simulation experiment, while those which ignore dyadic dependence, are not recommended.

## 2.5 Further reading

Although the use of gravity models by economists dates back to Tinbergen (1962), discussions of how to account for cross dyad dependence when conducting inference have been rare. Kolaczyk (2009, Chapter 7), in his widely cited monograph on network statistics, discusses logistic regression with dyadic data. He notes that standard inference procedures are inappropriate due to the presence of dyadic dependence, but is unable to offer a solution due to the lack of formal results in the literature (available at that time).

Fafchamps and Gubert (2007) proposed a variance-covariance estimator which allows for dyadic dependence. Their estimator coincides with the bias-corrected one discussed in Graham (2020) and is the one recommended here. Additional versions (and analyses) of this estimator are provided by Cameron and Miller (2014) and Aronow et al. (2017). A special case of the Fafchamps and Gubert (2007) variance estimator actually appears in Holland and Leinhardt (1976) in the context of an analysis of subgraph estimation. Snijders and Borgatti (1999) suggested using the Jackknife for variance estimation of network statistics. Results in, for example, Callaert and Veraverbeke (1981) and the references therein, suggest that a modified version of this estimate is (almost) numerically equivalent to $\hat{\Sigma}_1$ defined above.

Aldous' (1981) representation result evidently inspired some work on LLNs and CLTs for so called dissociated random variables and exchangeable random arrays (e.g., Eagleson and Weber, 1978). The influence of this work on empirical practice appears to have been minimal. Bickel et al. (2011), evidently inspired by the variance calculations of Picard et al. (2008), but perhaps more accurately picking up where Holland and Leinhardt (1976) stopped (albeit inadvertently), present asymptotic normality results for subgraph counts. Network density, which corresponds to the mean $[N(N-1)]^{-1} \sum_{i \neq j} Y_{ij}$ when $Y_{ij}$ is binary, is the simplest example they consider and also prototypical for understanding regression. The limit theory sketched hear was novel at the time of drafting, but substantially related results—independently derived—appear in Menzel (2017) and Davezies et al. (2019). Both of these papers also present bootstrap procedures appropriate for network data. The Menzel (2017) paper focuses on the important problem of graphon degeneracy. This occurs when the graphon only weakly varies in $U_i$ and $U_j$; degeneracy effects rates of convergence and limit distributions. Graham et al. (2019) present results on kernel density estimation with dyadic data. Tabord-Meehan (2018) showed asymptotic normality of dyadic linear regression coefficients using a rather different approach.

## Appendix 2.A    Derivations

Eq. (2.11) of the main text is an implication of calculations like

$$
\mathbb{V}\left(\bar{s}_1^e(W_1, U_1)\right)
$$
$$
= \mathbb{E}\left[\mathbb{E}\left[\bar{s}(W_1, U_1, W_2, U_2)\mid W_1, U_1\right]\mathbb{E}\left[\bar{s}(W_1, U_1, W_2, U_2)\mid W_1, U_1\right]'\right]
$$
$$
= \mathbb{E}\left[\mathbb{E}\left[\bar{s}(W_1, U_1, W_2, U_2)\mid W_1, U_1\right]\mathbb{E}\left[\bar{s}(W_1, U_1, W_3, U_3)\mid W_1, U_1\right]'\right]
$$
$$
= \mathbb{E}\left[\mathbb{E}\left[\bar{s}(W_1, U_1, W_2, U_2)\,\bar{s}(W_1, U_1, W_3, U_3)'\mid W_1, U_1\right]\right]
$$
$$
= \mathbb{E}\left[\bar{s}(W_1, U_1, W_2, U_2)\,\bar{s}(W_1, U_1, W_3, U_3)'\right]
$$
$$
= \Omega_{12,13}.
$$

The second equality immediately above follows because $W_2, U_2 | W_1, U_1 \stackrel{D}{=} W_3, U_3 | W_1, U_1 \stackrel{D}{=} W_2, U_2$, the third by independence of $\bar{s}(W_1, U_1, W_2, U_2)$ and $\bar{s}(W_1, U_1, W_3, U_3)$ *conditional* on $W_1, U_1$, and the fourth by iterated expectations.

# References

Aldous, D.J., 1981. Representations for partially exchangeable arrays of random variables. Journal of Multivariate Analysis 11 (4), 581–598.

Apicella, C.L., Marlowe, F.W., Fowler, J.H., Christakis, N.A., 2012. Social networks and cooperation in hunter-gatherers. Nature 481 (7382), 497–501.

Aronow, P.M., Samii, C., Assenova, V.A., 2017. Cluster-robust variance estimation for dyadic data. Political Analysis 23 (4), 564–577.

Baldwin, R., Taglioni, D., 2007. Trade effects of the euro: a comparison of estimators. Journal of Economic Integration 22 (4), 780–818.

Bellio, R., Varin, C., 2005. A pairwise likelihood approach to generalized linear models with crossed random effects. Statistical Modelling 5 (3), 217–227.

Bickel, P.J., Chen, A., 2009. A nonparametric view of network models and Newman-Girvan and other modularities. Proceedings of the National Academy of Sciences 106 (50), 21068–21073.

Bickel, P.J., Chen, A., Levina, E., 2011. The method of moments and degree distributions for network models. The Annals of Statistics 39 (5), 2280–2301.

Callaert, H., Veraverbeke, N., 1981. The order of the normal approximation for a studentized u-statistic. The Annals of Statistics 9 (1), 194–200.

Cameron, A.C., Miller, D.L., 2014. Robust Inference for Dyadic Data. Technical report. University of California, Davis.

Cattaneo, M., Crump, R., Jansson, M., 2014. Small bandwidth asymptotics for density-weighted average derivatives. Econometric Theory 30 (1), 176–200.

Chamberlain, G., 1987. Asymptotic efficiency in estimation with conditional moment restrictions. Journal of Econometrics 34 (3), 305–334.

Chandrasekhar, A., 2015. Econometrics of network formation. In: Bramoullé, Y., Galeotti, A., Rogers, B. (Eds.), Oxford Handbook on the Economics of Networks. Oxford University Press.

Cox, D.R., Reid, N., 2004. A note on pseudolikelihood constructed from marginal densities. Biometrika 91 (3), 729–737.

Crane, H., Towsner, H., 2018. Relatively exchangeable structures. The Journal of Symbolic Logic 83 (2), 416–442.

Davezies, L., d'Haultfoeuille, X., Guyonvarch, Y., 2019. Empirical Process Results for Exchangeable Arrayes. Technical report, CREST-ENSAE.

de Finetti, B., 1931. Funzione caratteristica di un fenomeno aleatorio. Atti Della R. Academia Nazionale Dei Lincei, Serie 6. Memorie, Classe Di Scienze Fisiche, Mathematice E Naturali 4, 251–299.

Diaconis, P., Janson, S., 2008. Graph limits and exchangeable random graphs. Rendiconti Di Matematica 28 (1), 33–61.

Eagleson, G.K., Weber, N.C., 1978. Limit theorems for weakly exchangeable arrays. Mathematical Proceedings of the Cambridge Philosophical Society 84 (1), 123–130.

Fafchamps, M., Gubert, F., 2007. The formation of risk sharing networks. Journal of Development Economics 83 (2), 326–350.

Ferguson, T.S., 2005. U-Statistics. University of California, Los Angeles.

Gourieroux, C., Monfort, A., Trognon, A., 1984. Pseudo maximum likelihood methods: applications to Poisson models. Econometrica 52 (3), 701–720.

Graham, B.S., 2017. An econometric model of network formation with degree heterogeneity. Econometrica 85 (4), 1033–1063.

Graham, B.S., 2020. The econometric analysis of networks. In: Handbook of Econometrics, vol. 7. North-Holland, Amsterdam.

Graham, B.S., Imbens, G.W., Ridder, G., 2014. Complementarity and aggregate implications of assortative matching: a nonparametric analysis. Quantitative Economics 5 (1), 29–66.

Graham, B.S., Niu, F., Powell, J.L., 2019. Kernel Density Estimation for Undirected Dyadic Data. Technical report. University of California, Berkeley.

Head, K., Mayer, T., 2014. Gravity equations: workhorse, toolkit, and cookbook. In: Handbook of International Economics, vol. 4. North-Holland, Amsterdam, pp. 131–191.

Hoeffding, W., 1948. A class of statistics with asymptotically normal distribution. The Annals of Mathematical Statistics 19 (3), 293–325.

Holland, P.W., Leinhardt, S., 1976. Local structure in social networks. Sociological Methodology 7, 1–45.

Hoover, D.N., 1979. Relations on Probability Spaces and Arrays of Random Variables. Technical report. Institute for Advanced Study, Princeton, NJ.

Huber, P.J., 1967. The behavior of maximum likelihood estimates under nonstandard conditions. In: Proceedings of the Fifth Berkeley Symposium on Mathematical Statistics and Probability, vol. 1, pp. 221–233.

Kolaczyk, E.D., 2009. Statistical Analysis of Network Data. Springer, New York.

Lindsey, B.G., 1988. Composite likelihood. Contemporary Mathematics 80, 221–239.

Menzel, K., 2017. Bootstrap with clustering in two or more dimensions. Technical Report. arXiv: 1703.03043v2.

Oneal, J.R., Russett, B., 1999. The kantian peace: the pacific benefits of democracy, interdependence, and international organizations. World Politics 52 (1), 1–37.

Picard, F., Daudin, J.J., Koskas, M., Schbath, S., Robin, S., 2008. Assessing the exceptionality of network motifs. Journal of Computational Biology 15 (1), 1–20.

Portes, R., Rey, H., 2005. The determinants of cross-border equity flows. Journal of International Economics 65 (2), 269–296.

Rose, A.K., 2004. Do we really know that the wto increases trade? The American Economic Review 94 (1), 98–114.

Santos Silva, J., Tenreyro, S., 2006. The log of gravity. Review of Economics and Statistics 88 (4), 641–658.

Santos Silva, J., Tenreyro, S., 2010. Currency unions in prospect and retrospect. Annual Review of Economics 2, 51–74.

Shalizi, C.R., 2016. Lecture 1: Conditionally-Independent Dyad Models. Lecture Note. Carnegie Mellon University.

Snijders, T.A.B., Borgatti, S.P., 1999. Non-parametric standard errors and tests for network statistics. Connections 22 (2), 61–70.

Tabord-Meehan, M., 2018. Inference with dyadic data: asymptotic behavior of the dyadic-robust t-statistic. Journal of Business & Economic Statistics.

Tinbergen, J., 1962. Shaping the World Economy: Suggestions for an International Economic Policy. Twentieth Century Fund, New York.

van der Vaart, A.W., 2000. Asymptotic Statistics. Cambridge University Press, Cambridge.

# Chapter 3

# Strategic network formation[☆]

Áureo de Paula

*University College London, CeMMAP, IFS and CEPR, London, United Kingdom*

## Contents

Luck plays an important role in the establishment of links between individuals, households or firms. At the same time, agency and choice also feature prominently in the formation of business, personal or social connections. The game theoretic study of network formation seeks to model the emergence of such networks when the actors involved have clear incentives to form or dissolve relationships.[1] When both factors, luck and agency, come together to determine a social or economic network, one is left with a probabilistic model of network formation where parameters can be interpreted as payoff-relevant features guiding individual incentives to form links or extraneous shocks that might interfere with those connections. This in turn offers a statistical framework which can then be used to characterize the data.

The adaptation of game theoretical models into estimable counterparts rests on several requirements. First, one needs a well-defined environment where players, payoffs and the rules of engagement are explicitly acknowledged. In other words, one needs to specify the game and its constituents (e.g., players, payoffs and information structure). Having done that, an equilibrium concept should be adopted, explicitly prescribing how connections come about. Finally, a clear delimitation between observables and unobservables (to the researcher)

---

[☆] The author gratefully acknowledges financial support from the Economic and Social Research Council through the ESRC Centre for Microdata Methods and Practice grant RES-589-28-0001.

[1] For a very good overview of such models, see Jackson (2008). As he points out, strategic behavior does not necessarily require adversarial nor dispassionate engagement: "Individuals need not be Machiavellian and calculate their potential benefits and costs from each potential relationship. What is critical is that they have a tendency to form relationships that are (mutually) beneficial and to drop relationships that are not" (p.153).

will allow for a probability model over potential outcome realizations that can in principle be taken to data, provided the relevant parameters are identifiable by the model and sampling allows for estimation (see, e.g., Heckman, 2000 and the references therein). The first goal of this chapter is to demonstrate how such ingredients are pieced together, though an encompassing discussion on theoretical models of network formation is admittedly not within the main purposes of this chapter and better found elsewhere (see Jackson, 2008).

The protocol above will generate a mathematical structure that represents the connection between two individuals as a function of individual characteristics, unobservable features in the model and, crucially, other links in the community which themselves are dependent on observable and unobservable features and other edges and so on. Taken together these can be seen as a potentially nonlinear system of equations whose solution (or solutions) correspond to the equilibrium (or equilibria) predicted by the game theoretical framework. Whereas the study of linear systems of equations has a long history in Economics, the discrete nature of the outcomes at hand (if links or their absence are encoded in a binary variable) leads to nonlinearities that introduce a new set of issues. One important such issue is the possibility of multiple solutions to this system which might complicate not only estimation but also the mapping between the population distribution of observable variables and the parameters of interest (i.e., identification). To illustrate such issues, we will explore simpler, perhaps more conventional games where such problems arise and a few potential strategies to deal with these challenges found in the empirical games literature (see de Paula, 2013). We will then relate these to available strategies in the analysis of network models.

In what follows, this chapter initially provides basic definitions necessary for the strategic analysis of games. It then discusses issues related to multiplicity of equilibria and their consequences for identification and computation using simpler game theoretic settings. We then discuss a set of econometric models for the analysis network formation games, broadly divided across two categories: the first one deals with models where an iterative "meeting protocol" is explicitly present in the model and the second one where this is not the case.

## 3.1 Basic ingredients of the environment

When framing the network formation as a game, the basic ingredients stipulate the set of players, their actions and payoffs. Here, the set of players is given by a group of individuals which we shall call $\mathcal{N}$. These are the nodes to be connected in the (equilibrium) graph and will be individuals, households, firms or some other entity. Their actions will be related to the formation of links among them. If directional, one can simply imagine that the actions are binary indicators for whether one establishes a connection to any other individual in the game. Otherwise, the links can be thought of as mutually agreed by the parties involved. In either case, the actions will relate to the edges in the graph, which we denote by $\mathcal{E}$.

For a given graph $\mathcal{D} \equiv (\mathcal{N}, \mathcal{E})$ designating how players are connected, node $i$ is assigned a payoff $U_i(\mathcal{D})$. Whereas payoff specification may depend on context, a common parameterization (on an undirected graph, see e.g. de Paula et al., 2018) is given by

$$U_i(\mathcal{D}) \equiv \sum_{j \neq i} D_{ij} \times \left(u + \epsilon_{ij}\right) + \left|\cup_{j:D_{ij}=1} N_j(\mathcal{D}) - N_i(\mathcal{D}) - \{i\}\right| v$$

$$+ \sum_j \sum_{k>j} D_{ij} D_{ik} D_{jk} \omega, \tag{3.1}$$

where $D_{ij} = 1$ if $i$ and $j$ are connected (remember: this corresponds to an undirected network, so connections are reciprocated), $N_i(\mathcal{D})$ denotes the set of nodes directly connected to node $i$ in the graph and $|\cdot|$ is the cardinality of a given set. The first term records the utility obtained from direct connections. The second term registers utility from indirect connections: $\left|\cup_{j:D_{ij}=1} N_j(\mathcal{D}) - N_i(\mathcal{D}) - \{i\}\right|$ is the number of individuals connected to direct counterparties of $i$, but not directly connected to $i$. Finally, the last term summarizes any benefits from having two direct connections also liked to each other and induces incentives for "clustering," a commonly observed phenomenon.

We omit (observable) covariates above (individual features, pairwise proximity in characteristics), but the parameters $(u, v, \omega)$ can also be made to depend on those. For example, $u \equiv u(X_i, X_j; \theta)$, where $\theta$ is now parameter vector, and similarly for the other parameters. On the other hand, we explicitly include the variable $\epsilon_{ij}$, which is unobservable to the researcher. Once a solution concept is imposed to negotiate how networks come about, properties of such terms would deliver a distribution over (equilibrium) networks. Once payoffs are specified, it is also important to clearly establish the information structure. An often used assumption is that information is complete so agents are informed about others' (observed and unobserved) payoffs and incentives perfectly.[2]

Another feature of the environment that requires attention relates to transferability. As Chiappori writes, this relates to

*(...) whether a technology exists that would allow one to transfer utility between agents participating to a matching process. (...) [W]hen available, they allow agents to bid for their preferred mate by accepting the reduction of own gain from the match in order to increase the partner's. The exact nature of these bids depends on the context and may not take the form of monetary transfers; in family economics, for instance, they typically affect the allocation of time between paid work, domestic work, and leisure; the choice between current and future consumption; or the structure of expenditures for private or public goods. (Chiappori, 2019, pp.5–6)*

---

[2] Incomplete information, albeit possibly more plausible and epistemically more realistic especially in large groups, has less often been analyzed in the literature.

At two opposite ends of the spectrum are non-transferable utility (NTU) models, when there is no technology enabling agents to decrease their utility to benefit a potential partner, and transferable utility (TU) models, which allows transfers of utility at a constant "exchange rate" and the total gain from the matching (surplus) is what matters for stability of the relationship.[3]

Given the elements above, a strategic network formation will then rely on a solution concept prescribing how individual behaviors are aggregated to generate an equilibrium network. Whereas traditional concepts in game theory (e.g., Nash equilibrium) can be envisioned, the literature has offered additional notions to better capture the peculiarities of certain network formation contexts. Consider, for example, a simple setting where two individuals, $A$ and $B$, contemplate forming a relationship the value of this connection is positive. If the relationship is not established, both individuals collect a value normalized to zero. Information is complete and utility, non-transferable. One possible protocol is the *link announcement* game discussed by Myerson (1977). The players announce a link and a connection arises if the offers are reciprocated. In this case, a connected network on this two-node game ($A \leftrightarrow B$) corresponds to a Nash equilibrium of the link announcement game[4] and the network is typically said to be Nash stable. If $A$ offers to connect with $B$, it is a best-response for $B$ to reciprocate, and vice versa. An empty network, where $A$ and $B$ remain isolated, is nonetheless also Nash stable. If $A$ does not offer to link with $B$, she is equally well-off offering to connect with $A$ as she is by withholding the offer. In either case, the payoff obtained equals zero since the relationship is not formed. Similarly, if $B$ does not propose to $A$, $A$ is equally well not proposing as she is proposing and an equilibrium also arises where neither extends an offer to the other.

Given that it is mutually beneficial for them to establish a link, why would they not if they can deliberate about it? It seems unlikely in many situations where two individuals are contemplating the formation of a relationship that this would be the case. To amend this situation, Jackson and Wolinsky (1996) suggest an alternative solution concept: pairwise stability. A network $\mathcal{D}$ is pairwise stable according to Jackson and Wolinsky (1996) if

$$\forall ij \in \mathcal{D}, \ U_i(\mathcal{D}) \geq U_i(\mathcal{D}_{-ij}) \text{ and } U_j(\mathcal{D}) \geq U_j(\mathcal{D}_{-ij})$$

and

$$\forall ij \notin \mathcal{D}, \ U_i(\mathcal{D}) > U_i(\mathcal{D}_{+ij}) \text{ or } U_j(\mathcal{D}) > U_j(\mathcal{D}_{+ij}),$$

---

[3] Another possibility is the intermediate scenario with imperfect transferable utility (ITU) where transfers are allowed, but at an "exchange rate" between individual utilities that is not constant and possibly endogenous to the economic environment. While this would also be categorized as transferable utility, the conventional terminology focuses on the constant "exchange rate" case (see Chiappori, 2019).

[4] A Nash equilibrium is a strategy profile where each player best-responds to other players' strategies.

where $ij \in (\notin)\mathcal{D}$ signifies that the link between $i$ and $j$ pertains (not) to the set of edges in $\mathcal{D}$.[5] Here, $\mathcal{D}_{-ij}$ is the network $\mathcal{D}$ without the link between $i$ and $j$ and $\mathcal{D}_{+ij}$ is the network $\mathcal{D}$ with the link between $i$ and $j$. In English, this solution concept specifies that $\mathcal{D}$ is pairwise stable if any link present in $\mathcal{D}$ is mutually beneficial and any absent link is detrimental to at least one of the parties involved. Note that the outcome where a relationship is not formed between $A$ and $B$ above is no longer a pairwise stable network (while it still corresponds to a Nash equilibrium of the proposal game). The theoretical literature has contemplated several variations to this stability concept (e.g., pairwise Nash stability, strong stability; see the discussion in Jackson, 2008).

The concept of pairwise stability can also be extended to a transferable utility setting. Following Bloch and Jackson (2006), this corresponds to requiring a positive surplus for existing links and a negative surplus for nonexistent ones:

$$\forall ij \in \mathcal{D}, \ [U_i(\mathcal{D}) - U_i(\mathcal{D}_{-ij})] + [U_j(\mathcal{D}) - U_j(\mathcal{D}_{-ij})] \geq 0$$

and

$$\forall ij \notin \mathcal{D}, \ [U_i(\mathcal{D}_{+ij}) - U_i(\mathcal{D})] + [U_j(\mathcal{D}_{+ij}) - U_j(\mathcal{D})] < 0.$$

Since payoffs are specified in terms of parameters, covariates observable to the researcher and unobservable error terms, for a given parameter and observable covariates, the model produces a probability distribution over the equilibrium sets for the game described above. Since this probability distribution is indexed by the parameter vector defining the environment, this renders a statistical model on which one can in principle perform estimation and inference. One difficulty in doing this is that there might be more than one stable network for a given parameter value and realization of observable and unobservable random variables. This is potentially problematic for identification (i.e., the reverse mapping between observed distributions and parameters) and computation.

As will be seen later on, another possibility in generating a distribution over possible networks is to rely on an iterative procedure whereby links are formed or severed as individuals or pairs take turns in a random meeting protocol. These stochastic revision processes are not unrelated to equilibria defined above. For example, in a non-transferable utility setting, Jackson and Watts (2002) demonstrate that a process where pairs meet sequentially and are offered to (myopically) form or maintain links that are mutually beneficial and dissolve links that are not beneficial to at least one of the parties involved converges to a pairwise stable network or a cycle. Jackson and Watts (2001) provide conditions to rule out such cycles, in which case the dynamics above will "rest" on a pairwise stable network.[6]

---

[5] This is related, but different from the stability concept typically used in "marriage market" models.

[6] Such conditions relate to the existence of an ordinal potential function. This is a function mapping networks to the real line and encode whether the addition of a link is mutually beneficial to the pair

## 3.2 Relation to empirical games

Before proceeding, it pays to examine the issues brought about by equilibrium multiplicity. In doing so, we will focus on simple games well studied in the econometric literature.[7] Consider the entry game depicted in Bresnahan and Reiss (1991) (see also Bjorn and Vuong, 1985 and Tamer, 2003). The researcher observes different markets and in each market there are two potential entrant firms.

Let $D_i \in \{0, 1\}$ denote whether firm $i$ enters ($D_i = 1$) or not ($D_i = 0$). (In analogy to the link formation narrative above, we use $D$ to denote the action.) There is complete information and the payoff structure is summarized by the following two-by-two matrix:

|   | **0** | **1** |
|---|---|---|
| 0 | $(0,0)$ | $(0, \mathbf{X}_2^\top \beta_2 + \epsilon_2)$ |
| 1 | $(\mathbf{X}_1^\top \beta_1 + \epsilon_1, 0)$ | $(\mathbf{X}_1^\top \beta_1 + \Delta_1 + \epsilon_1, \mathbf{X}_2^\top \beta_2 + \Delta_2 + \epsilon_2)$ |

where firm 1's actions ($D_1 = 0$ or 1) are rows and firm 2's actions are columns ($D_2 = 0$ or 1). The first coordinate of the payoff vector in each cell corresponds to firm 1's payoff and the second one, to firm 2's payoff. The variables $\mathbf{X}_i$ and $\epsilon_i, i = 1, 2$ are observable and unobservable (to the researcher) components of profits. The joint distribution of $(\epsilon_1, \epsilon_2)$, call it $F_{\epsilon_1, \epsilon_2}$, is known (at least up to a parameter). (Firms know the payoff matrix since information is complete.) The parameters $\beta_i$ and $\Delta_i$ are ingredients one would like to estimate given a sample of markets (i.e., games). Hence, if firm $i$ decides not to enter the market, it obtains a (normalized) payoff of zero. If it enters, its payoff is given by $\mathbf{X}_i^\top \beta_i + \Delta_i D_j + \epsilon_i, i, j = 1, 2, i \neq j$.

Given that this an entry game, it is natural to suppose that $\Delta_i \leq 0, i = 1, 2$: it is less profitable to be in a duopoly than it is to be a monopolist in the market. A (pure strategy) Nash equilibrium for the game above delivers the following econometric model:

$$
\begin{aligned}
D_i^* &= \mathbf{X}_i^\top \beta_i + D_j \Delta_i + \epsilon_i, \\
D_i &= \mathbf{1}_{D_i^* \geq 0},
\end{aligned}
$$

for $i, j = 1, 2, i \neq j$. We can then represent the Nash equilibria for particular realizations of the random variables above in the space of unobservables (to the researcher):

---

involved or the deletion, detrimental to at least one of the parties involved. A potential function like this also plays an important role in the econometric model studied by Mele (2017).

[7] For a more extensive discussion, see de Paula (2013).

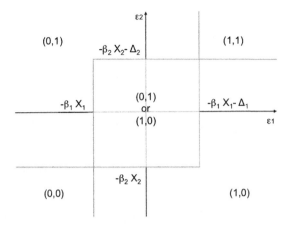

When profits are sufficiently high ($\epsilon_i \to \infty$, $i = 1, 2$), it is a dominant strategy for firm $i$ to enter the market. If they are sufficiently low ($\epsilon_i \to -\infty$, $i = 1, 2$), it is a dominant strategy for firm $i$ to stay out. This defines the four (unique) equilibria in the NE, NW, SE and SW regions of the picture above. In intermediary cases, the market is only profitable enough for a single firm and the are two possible Nash equilibria: one in which firm 1 enters and firm 2, does not; and another one where the opposite takes place.

Given parameter values and realizations for $\mathbf{X}_i, \epsilon_i, i = 1, 2$, the model predicts possibly more than one outcome ($D_1, D_2$) in the central region of the figure. The data generating process thus far defined would not deliver a clear likelihood function or reduced form on which to base the statistical analysis of a sample of markets. The model is thus "incomplete" (see, e.g., Tamer, 2003): one needs to take a stand on how equilibria are selected if the games lands on the central region of the picture.

Alternative strategies for identification and estimation may nonetheless be devised without specifying an equilibrium selection protocol. One potential avenue in this simple setting is to note that the number of entrants is invariant across equilibria in the central region and one can thus form a likelihood function based on the (equilibrium) number of entrant firms per market (i.e., zero, one or two firms) which can be used for identification and estimation. This is the solution pursued by Bresnahan and Reiss (1990) and Berry (1992), for example.[8] Theoretically, if the observable covariates have a large enough support, very large or small values for $\beta_i^\top \mathbf{X}_i$ can be seen to render entry (or not) a dom-

---

[8] The key here is to group a given equilibrium outcome with any other outcome that may appear as an alternative equilibrium for a given value of the parameters and realization of observable and unobservable variables. In the example above, this consists of considering the events $\{(0, 0)\}$, $\{(1, 1)\}$ and $\{(0, 1), (1, 0)\}$. In other situations, the grouping might differ. If $\Delta_i > 0$, for example, the multiplicity region would involve $(1, 1)$ and $(0, 0)$ instead of $(1, 0)$ and $(0, 1)$. In this case, the events to consider would be $\{(1, 0)\}$, $\{(0, 1)\}$ and $\{(0, 0), (1, 1)\}$ instead.

inant strategy for firm $i, i = 1, 2$ and the decision problem for firm $j, j \neq i$, becomes a more conventional individual decision problem potentially allowing for identification of the parameters of interest. Tamer (2003) suggests such "identification at infinity" as one additional source of identification.

Since these (or other strategies) may not always be available (especially when the number of players is larger), one common strategy abandons point identification and estimation and instead focuses on retrieving a non-singleton set of parameters that rationalizes the data (see Tamer, 2003). Since in the simple example $(1, 0)$ occurs as a unique (pure) strategy equilibrium in the SE corner of the graph, the probability of this region provides a lower bound for the probability of observing this outcome in equilibrium. This lower bound would be attained if $(0, 1)$ is never selected when there are other possible equilibria (i.e., $(1, 0)$). An upper bound would then be given by the probability that $(0, 1)$ occurs as a unique equilibrium plus the probability that it is one of possibly multiple equilibria and it is always selected as an equilibrium. In sum, we have

$$
\begin{aligned}
\mathbb{P}((D_1, D_2) = (0, 1)|\mathbf{X}_1, \mathbf{X}_2) \quad \leq \quad & F_{\epsilon_1}(-\mathbf{X}_1^\top \beta_1 - \Delta_1) \\
& -F_{\epsilon_1, \epsilon_2}(-\mathbf{X}_1^\top \beta_1 - \Delta_1, -\mathbf{X}_2^\top \beta_2)
\end{aligned}
$$

and

$$
\begin{aligned}
\mathbb{P}((D_1, D_2) = (0, 1)|\mathbf{X}_1, \mathbf{X}_2) \quad \geq \quad & F_{\epsilon_1}(-\mathbf{X}_1^\top \beta_1 - \Delta_1) \\
& -F_{\epsilon_1, \epsilon_2}(-\mathbf{X}_1^\top \beta_1 - \Delta_1, -\mathbf{X}_2^\top \beta_2) \\
& -\mathbb{P}\big((\epsilon_1, \epsilon_2) \in \\
& \quad \times_{i=1,2}[-\mathbf{X}_i^\top \beta_i, -\mathbf{X}_i^\top \beta_i - \Delta_i]\big).
\end{aligned}
$$

Similar bounds can be obtained for the probability of observing $(1, 0)$. Since $(0, 0)$ and $(1, 1)$ always arise as unique equilibria, we can define the likelihood of observing either one in terms of model primitives as an equality. Provided the left-hand sides of the inequalities above can be estimated from the data, one can produce empirical restrictions on the parameter values to be consistent with the data. Intuitively, these thus suggest estimating the identified set using the inequalities above.

As in the game above, strategic network formation models will often exhibit multiple solutions for given parameters and covariate realizations. One possibility is to emulate the ideas above and seek to characterize and estimate the set of parameters that is consistent with the data. As can be inferred from the above discussion, this suggests that, for each putative parameter vector and realizations for the unobserved variables, one needs to compute all the possible equilibria and calculate the various probabilities above.

## 3.3 Network formation

### 3.3.1 Iterative network formation

One class of strategic network formation models relies on a meeting protocol whereby individuals or pairs sequentially are offered the possibility of forming or severing links. While the protocols are not meant to be directly fit to the data, the random meeting sequences and unobservable errors guiding the decisions to establish or interrupt connections lead to a distribution over networks that can thus be taken to data. Mele (2017), Christakis et al. (2010) and Badev (2018) are notable examples for this approach. Mele (2017) focuses on a directed network, where links do not require reciprocation, and Badev (2018) expands the analysis there to the joint determination of links and behaviors.[9] Christakis et al. (2010), on the other hand, examine an undirected network. The last two present empirical applications to links among adolescents (Badev studies in addition their smoking behavior) and Mele (forthcoming) applies the methodology also to examine segregation in high schools. In this chapter we provide an overview for Mele (2017). Christakis et al. (2010) is part of this volume.

Mele (2017) models a directed network where $D_{ij} = 1$ if individual $i$ offers a link to individual $j$, and $= 0$, otherwise. Connections need not be reciprocated. (This matches the data structure in Mele (forthcoming): the survey, AddHealth, elicits friend nominations among teenagers that are not always reciprocated.) The utility function for individual $i$ is given by

$$U_i(\mathcal{D}) \equiv \sum_{j\neq i} D_{ij} u_{ij}^{\theta} + \sum_{j\neq i} D_{ij} D_{ji} m_{ij}^{\theta} + \sum_{j\neq i} D_{ij} \sum_{k\neq i,j} D_{jk} v_{ik}^{\theta}$$
$$+ \sum_{j\neq i} D_{ij} \sum_{k\neq i,j} D_{ki} p_{kj}^{\theta},$$

where $u_{ij}^{\theta} \equiv u(X_i, X_j; \theta)$ represents the direct utility from directly linking to other individuals and $v_{ij}^{\theta} \equiv v(X_i, X_j; \theta)$ encodes the utility from indirectly linking to a friend's friend. These then play the same role as $u$ and $v$ in the utility function previously introduced. This being a directed network, $m_{ij}^{\theta} \equiv m(X_i, X_j; \theta)$ denotes the utility from a mutual, reciprocated link. (In undirected networks, links are reciprocated by definition and this term does not show up in the utility function presented earlier in this chapter.) Finally, $p_{ij}^{\theta} \equiv p(X_i, X_j; \theta)$ is a term that internalizes some of the impact a link to individual $j$ generates for individuals that had offered links to $i$. The author refers to this as popularity: "When an agent forms a link, he/she automatically creates an indirect link for other agents that are connected to him/her, thus generating externalities and

---

[9] Mele (2017) was previously circulated as "A Structural Model of Segregation in Social Networks" (2015). Previous versions for Badev (2018) appeared as "Discrete Games with Endogenous Networks: Theory and Policy" (2013) and "Discrete Games in Endogenous Networks: Equilibria and Policy" (2017).

impacting his/her 'popularity.'" Utility is non-transferable and information is complete.

The model further assumes the following.

**Assumption 3.1.** Preferences are such that $m_{ij}^{\theta} = m_{ji}^{\theta}$ and $v_{ij}^{\theta} = p_{ij}^{\theta}$.

In words, the benefits from mutual links are reciprocal and $i$ internalizes the externality created on other individuals linking to her. Under these restrictions, it can be shown that the Nash equilibria of the game with payoffs thus defined correspond to the maxima of the following (potential) function:

$$Q(\mathcal{D}, X; \theta) = \sum_{(i,j)} D_{ij} u_{ij}^{\theta} + \sum_{(i,j)} D_{ij} D_{ji} m_{ij}^{\theta} + \sum_{(i,j,k)} D_{ij} D_{jk} v_{ik}^{\theta}.$$

This function is later shown to play an important role in the distribution of networks arising in equilibrium. To wrap up the model, there is a meeting sequence $m = \{m^t\}_{t=1}^{\infty}$ where $m^t = (i, j)$ means that $i$ can offer or dissolve a link to $j$ in iteration $t$. Let $\mathbb{P}(m^t = ij | \mathcal{D}^{t-1}, X) = \rho(\mathcal{D}^{t-1}, X_i, X_j)$, where $\mathcal{D}^{t-1}$ is the network in iteration $t - 1$. In addition, we have the following.

**Assumption 3.2.** $\rho(\mathcal{D}^{t-1}, X_i, X_j) = \rho(\mathcal{D}_{-ij}^{t-1}, X_i, X_j) > 0, \forall ij,$

where $\mathcal{D}_{-ij}^{t-1}$ is the network $\mathcal{D}^{t-1}$ without the link from $i$ to $j$. This means that the meeting probability between $i$ and $j$ does not depend on there being a link between them and each meeting has positive probability of occurring. This assumption ensures that the likelihood function does not depend on the meeting protocol.

Whenever a meeting opportunity is offered and $i$ can revise her linking status to $j$, it is supposed that $i$ receives idiosyncratic shocks $(\epsilon_1, \epsilon_0)$ to the utility forming a link $(D_{ij} = 1)$ or not $(D_{ij} = 0)$. A link to $j$ is established if and only if

$$U_i(D_{ij}^t = 1, \mathcal{D}_{-ij}^t, X; \theta) + \epsilon_{1t} \geq U_i(D_{ij}^t = 0, \mathcal{D}_{-ij}^t, X; \theta) + \epsilon_{0t}$$

Note that up to this point there were no unobservable errors. Once given the choice, the decision by $i$ operates much like a standard random utility model over the remaining $|\mathcal{N}| - 1$ nodes where $|\mathcal{N}|$ is the number of nodes involved in the network. (Note thus that the model produces a dense network: as $|\mathcal{N}|$ grows, the probability of forming a link does not vanish.) Once the meeting protocol is set in march and the revision process leads to subsequent additions and deletions of edges, the resulting process forms a Markov chain on networks $\{\mathcal{D}^t\}$. Were there no unobservable shocks (i.e., $\epsilon_0$ and $\epsilon_1$ are zero with probability one), the chain converges to one of the Nash equilibria of the game without $\epsilon$s. Under the assumption that the $\epsilon$s are distributed independently (across time and links) and follow an extreme value Type I distribution, the Markov chain above converges to a unique stationary distribution:

$$\pi(\mathcal{D}, X; \theta) = \frac{\exp[Q(\mathcal{D}, X; \theta)]}{\sum_{\mathcal{D}'} \exp[Q(\mathcal{D}', X; \theta)]}$$

where $Q$ is the potential function previously defined and the summation is over all possible directed networks between the individuals in the group.

This construction offers a unique distribution that can then be taken to data (either one or more networks). In fact, since the utility functions are linear in parameters, the stationary distribution above describes an exponential random graph model (ERGM), which takes this names as it is pertains to the exponential family of distributions. The model is estimated by Bayesian methods which produce a posterior distribution over parameters of interest. Schematically, given a prior distribution over those parameters, say $p(\theta)$ and a likelihood model, in this case $\pi(\mathcal{D}, X; \theta)$, a posterior distribution is given by

$$p(\theta|\mathcal{D}, X) = \frac{\pi(\mathcal{D}, X; \theta)p(\theta)}{\int_{\Theta} \pi(\mathcal{D}, X; \theta)p(\theta)d\theta}.$$

One important difficulty with such models is nonetheless the computation of the denominator $\sum_{\mathcal{D}'} \exp[Q(\mathcal{D}', X; \theta)]$ in $\pi(\mathcal{D}, X; \theta)$. With 10 individuals, there are $2^{90} \approx 10^{27}$ such network configurations. As pointed by Mele (2017), "a supercomputer that can compute $10^{12}$ potential functions in one second would take almost 40 million years to compute the constant." The issue becomes evident above as it appears necessary to compute such denominator to solve for the posterior distribution either analytically or numerically (e.g., via simulations of the posterior distribution).

Alternative strategies to circumvent this issue or to approximate the denominator in other settings include pseudo-likelihood methods (Besag, 1975; Strauss and Ikeda, 1990) and variational principles (see Jordan and Wainwright, 2008). Mele (2017) offers instead to handle it using simulation (Markov chain Monte Carlo, MCMC) methods (see also Kolaczyk, 2009 and the references therein). For a given parameter value $\theta$, a Metropolis–Hastings algorithm to simulate the distribution of networks would proceed as follows[10]:

**0.** Fix a parameter $\theta$. At iteration $r$, with current network $\mathcal{D}_r$:
**1.** propose a network $\mathcal{D}'$ from a proposal distribution $\mathcal{D}' \sim q_{\mathcal{D}}(\mathcal{D}'|\mathcal{D}_r)$;
**2.** accept network $\mathcal{D}'$ with probability

$$\alpha_{mh}(\mathcal{D}_r, \mathcal{D}') = \min\left\{1, \frac{\exp[Q(\mathcal{D}', X; \theta)]}{\exp[Q(\mathcal{D}_r, X; \theta)]} \frac{q_{\mathcal{D}}(\mathcal{D}_r|\mathcal{D}')}{q_{\mathcal{D}}(\mathcal{D}'|\mathcal{D}_r)}\right\}.$$

Following the narrative above, the proposal distribution $q_{\mathcal{D}}(\mathcal{D}'|\mathcal{D}_r)$ selects a player $i$ with probability $1/|\mathcal{N}|$ and a counterpart $j$ with probability $1/(|\mathcal{N}|-1)$ and revises their linking status according to the utility comparison for individual $i$. The network transitions from $\mathcal{D}_r$ to $\mathcal{D}'$ with probability $T(\mathcal{D}_r, \mathcal{D}') = q_{\mathcal{D}}(\mathcal{D}'|\mathcal{D}_r)\alpha_{mh}(\mathcal{D}_r, \mathcal{D}')$. The acceptance probability $\alpha_{mh}$ guarantees that the

---

[10] In the Bayesian estimation, one also needs to perform related MCMC steps to approximate the posterior distribution for the parameters of interest. The "inner" simulation of the networks above is a component of the "outer" simulation protocol presented in Mele (2017).

procedure is well behaved (i.e., it ensures what is known as "detailed balance": $\pi(\mathcal{D}_r)T(\mathcal{D}_r, \mathcal{D}') = \pi(\mathcal{D}')T(\mathcal{D}', \mathcal{D}_r)$). The important point to observe is that the quantities above do not depend on the normalizing constant.

Unfortunately, the simulation protocol above is itself not immune to problems. It is well known, for example, that parameter changes in ERGMs may lead to abrupt changes in probable graphs (see Snijders, 2002). In addition, in parameter regions where the distribution over networks is multimodal, the mixing time is slow for MCMC protocols where networks change only locally from iteration to iteration (see Bhamidi et al., 2011). In Mele (2017), he notes that, in such regions, "once the sampler reaches a local maximum, there is probability $\exp(-Cn^2)$ to escape such state of the network. As a consequence, the sampling is practically infeasible with a local sampler." Here the modes of the distribution will correspond to the maxima of the potential function $Q$ which are in turn related to the Nash equilibria for the game discussed previously. Hence, while the stationary distribution for the Markov process defined by the meeting protocol is unique, equilibrium multiplicity is also a complicating computational feature here. To accelerate convergence, the article suggests a simulation algorithm that updates networks at larger steps (see Appendix B.1 to the article).

For parameter regions where the distribution is unimodal on the other hand, Bhamidi et al. (2011) and Chatterjee and Diaconis (2013) show that graph draws are indistinguishable from a random network model with independent link formation (i.e., an Erdös–Rényi model) or mixture of such models. Mele (2017) also shows that a similar phenomenon occurs in a simplified version of his model, where only utility from direct ($u$) and reciprocated links ($m$) are maintained and mutual links bring positive utility ($m > 0$). This points to an identification issue when estimation is based on a single network in this particular example.[11] The model is observationally distinct from such a random network (i.e., an Erdös–Rényi model) if mutual links bring negative utility (i.e., $m < 0$), suggesting again that similar forces yielding multiplicity (i.e., positive externalities) may lead to complications in identification as well as in computation. The results does not allow for covariates, but the author conjectures that the sign of such externalities (on reciprocated links) will remain relevant.

The network simulation above (for a given parameter vector) is but one piece of the overall procedure in approximating the posterior distribution $p(\theta|\mathcal{D}, X)$. Here too, the article follows a Markov chain Monte Carlo procedure based on the exchange algorithm proposed by Murray et al. (2006) to avoid the computation of the normalizing constant. The model is taken to data in Mele (forthcoming), where the author studies ethnic segregation in high schools using data from AddHealth.

---

[11] When multiple networks are used, identification is attained with variation in sufficient statistics across networks: "If the sufficient statistics are not linearly dependent, then the exponential family is minimal and the likelihood is strictly concave, therefore the mode is unique" (Mele, 2017).

### 3.3.2 Non-iterative network formation

A different approach takes a non-iterative perspective and directly focuses on a simultaneous move game where players are nodes/vertices and the action space are links. This aligns these with the static game theoretical models introduced earlier. For example, Leung (2015b) studies a directed network formation model under incomplete information and Bayes–Nash as the solution concept adapting (two-step) estimation strategies commonly used in such games (see de Paula, 2013). He employs the model to analyze trust networks in India. Also modeling a directed network, Gualdani (2019) examines a complete information model with Nash equilibrium as the solution concept and uses her model to study board interlocks among firms.[12] Here we will focus on works using pairwise stability (with and without transferability) in undirected networks.

An initial impulse is to emulate the bounding strategy presented previously. Consider, for instance, a game among three individuals ($|\mathcal{N}| = 3$) with non-transferable utility and complete information. Let payoffs be given by

$$U_i(\mathcal{D}) \equiv \sum_{j \in 1,\ldots,n, j \neq i} \delta^{d(i,j;\mathcal{D})-1} \left(1 + \epsilon_{ij}\right) - |N_i(\mathcal{D})|,$$

where $d(i, j; \mathcal{D})$ is the minimum distance between $i$ and $j$ in the graph $\mathcal{D}$, $0 < \delta < 1$, $\epsilon_{ij}$ are unobservable (to the researcher) preference shocks and $|N_i(\mathcal{D})|$ is the number of direct connections of individual $i$ in graph $\mathcal{D}$. Assume that observed networks are pairwise stable. For $\epsilon_{ij} = \epsilon_{ji}$, $0 < \epsilon_{23} < \delta/(1 - \delta)$, we can represent the possible pairwise stable equilibria in the space of unobservables as

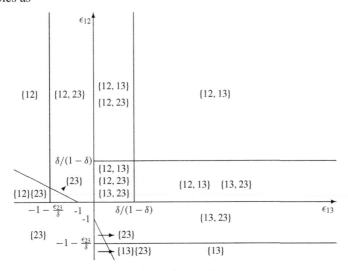

---

[12] As described in this chapter, one pressing challenge in this context relates to the dimensionality of potential networks. Gualdani (2019) offers suggestions to reduce the computational burden.

The approach introduced earlier would focus on bounds on $\delta$ corresponding to the probability that a particular network is pairwise stable (upper bound) and the probability that it is the unique pairwise stable network (lower bound). In the figure above (which does not comprise the whole space for $\epsilon$s), those would be

$$\mathbb{P}(\epsilon_{12}, \epsilon_{13} \geq 0) \geq \mathbb{P}(\{12, 13\}) \geq \mathbb{P}(\epsilon_{12}, \epsilon_{13} \geq \delta/(1 - \delta)),$$

and one could form similar bounds for all ($= 8$) possible networks (exploring the whole space of unobservables). Unfortunately, while this might be conceivable when only three individuals are involved, for even a moderate number of nodes, the number of networks one would need to consider as potential equilibria is computationally intractable. With 24 individuals, for instance, there are more potential networks than atoms in the observable universe.

Given this dimensionality issue, one possible avenue to reduce the computational burden is to focus on smaller subnetworks involving subgroups of individuals. Sheng (2016) takes this route in a model for undirected networks. She focuses on pairwise stable networks (either with transferable and non-transferable utility; see previous definitions) under complete information and a payoff structure given by

$$U_i(\mathcal{D}) \equiv \sum_{j \neq i} D_{ij}(u_{ij}^\theta + \epsilon_{ij}) + \frac{1}{|\mathcal{N}| - 2} \sum_{j \neq i} D_{ij} \sum_{k \neq i, j} D_{jk} v$$

$$+ \frac{1}{|\mathcal{N}| - 2} \sum_{j, k \neq i} D_{ij} D_{ki} D_{jk} \omega.$$

As before, $u_{ij}^\theta \equiv u(X_i, X_j; \theta)$ encodes the direct utility obtained from linking to other individuals in the group, $v$ provides benefits to indirect friendships and $\omega$ indicates additional payoff to having common connections also be linked to each other.[13] The unobservable random variables $\epsilon$ are independent and follow a known distribution (up to a finite dimensional parameter vector). (Since there are preference shocks for each potential link, isolated individuals are unlikely when $|\mathcal{N}|$.) The data is presumed to obtain from a sample of i.i.d. networks.

Under transferable utility, the game admits a potential function (as in Mele, 2017) and a pairwise stable network is shown to exist. When utility is not transferable, the author shows that a pairwise stable network exists when $v$ and $\omega$ are positive. (The game has then a supermodular structure that allows for the demonstration of a non-empty solution set; see Hellmann, 2013.) Pairwise stability (with either transferable utility or not) is determined by the marginal

---

[13] In contrast to the utility specification in the beginning of this chapter, the specification above normalizes the number of connections by $|\mathcal{N}| - 2$ and allows for some double counting: if $i, j$ and $k$ are all connected, each accrues benefits from direct connection with two individuals, indirect connections from each of the other two and the fact that the other two are also linked to each other.

utility of a link $\Delta U_{ij}(\mathcal{D}) = U_i(\mathcal{D}) - U_i(\mathcal{D}_{-ij})$ when $ij \in \mathcal{D}$ and $\Delta U_{ij}(\mathcal{D}) = U_i(\mathcal{D}_{+ij}) - U_i(\mathcal{D})$ when $ij \notin \mathcal{D}$, let PS($\Delta U(X, \epsilon)$) denote the set of pairwise stable networks for realizations of $X$ and $\epsilon$. (Depending on the context, pairwise stability is understood to be either with transferable utility or not.) Under these conditions, the probability that one observes $\mathcal{D}$ is given by

$$\mathbb{P}(\mathcal{D}|X) = \int_{\mathcal{D} \in \text{PS}(\Delta U(X,\epsilon)) \wedge |\text{PS}(\Delta U(X,\epsilon))|=1} dF(\epsilon) +$$
$$\int_{\mathcal{D} \in \text{PS}(\Delta U(X,\epsilon)) \wedge |\text{PS}(\Delta U(X,\epsilon))|>1} \lambda(\mathcal{D}|\text{PS}(\Delta U(X,\epsilon))) dF(\epsilon),$$

where $\lambda$ is the probability that $\mathcal{D}$ is selected for realizations of $\epsilon$ that allow for multiple pairwise stable networks. These deliver the following bounds emulating our previous discussion on empirical games:

$$\int_{w \in \text{PS}(\Delta U(X,\epsilon)) \wedge |\text{PS}(\Delta U(X,\epsilon))|=1} dF(\epsilon) \leq \mathbb{P}(\mathcal{D}|X) \leq \int_{w \in \text{PS}(\Delta U(X,\epsilon))} dF(\epsilon).$$

As previously discussed, these bounds are unfortunately computationally intractable for even moderately sized networks. Instead, Sheng (2016) suggests looking at subgraphs on $A \subset \mathcal{N}$ nodes: the network $\mathcal{D}_A$ comprising $A$ and all edges in $\mathcal{D}$ linking those nodes. The probability of observing such a subnetwork is then given by

$$\mathbb{P}(\mathcal{D}_A|X) = \int_{\mathcal{D}_A \in \text{PS}_A(\Delta U(X,\epsilon)) \wedge |\text{PS}_A(\Delta U(X,\epsilon))|=1} dF(\epsilon) +$$
$$\int_{\mathcal{D}_A \in \text{PS}_A(\Delta U(X,\epsilon)) \wedge |\text{PS}_A(\Delta U(X,\epsilon))|>1} \sum_{\mathcal{D}_{-A}} \lambda(\mathcal{D}_A|\text{PS}(\Delta U(X,\epsilon))) dF(\epsilon),$$

where the addition over $\mathcal{D}_{-A}$ sums over the collection of complementary nodes ($\mathcal{N}\backslash A$) and edges in $\mathcal{D}$ connecting them to each other and to nodes in $A$. $\text{PS}_A(\Delta U(X, \epsilon))$ is the subset of networks in $A$ that are part of a network in $\text{PS}(\Delta U(X, \epsilon))$. These yield

$$\int_{\mathcal{D}_A \in \text{PS}_A(\Delta U(X,\epsilon)) \wedge |\text{PS}_A(\Delta U(X,\epsilon))|=1} dF(\epsilon) \leq \mathbb{P}(\mathcal{D}_A|X_A)$$
$$\leq \int_{\mathcal{D}_A \in \text{PS}_A(\Delta U(X,\epsilon))} dF(\epsilon),$$

where the upper bound is the probability that the subnetwork $\mathcal{D}_A$ on nodes $A$ pertains to a pairwise stable network and the lower bound is the probability that the *only* subnetwork on nodes $A$ pertaining to a pairwise stable network is $\mathcal{D}_A$.

Consider for example the network formation game on three individuals presented earlier in this subsection. For the subnetwork {12} on nodes 1 and 2, the upper bound is given by the probability that $\epsilon_{12}$ is greater than zero minus the probability for the triangular region where only $\{23\}$ is pairwise stable. In this region, $\{12\}$ always pertains to a pairwise stable network. The lower bound is given by the probability that $\epsilon_{12}$ is greater than $\delta/(1+\delta)$ and $\epsilon_{13}$ is greater than zero plus the probability that $\epsilon_{13}$ is less than zero minus the subregions where $\{23\}$ is also a pairwise stable network. In this region, $\{12\}$ is the only network on nodes 1 and 2 that is part of a pairwise stable network is $\{12\}$ (even though there are multiple pairwise stable networks in the region where $\epsilon_{12}$ is greater than $\delta/(1-\delta)$ and $\epsilon_{13}$ is between zero and $\delta/(1-\delta)$).

In the article, Sheng imposes (exchangeability) restrictions (on equilibrium selection and payoff primitives) that guarantee that these bounds are non-trivial even as the number of individuals in the groups gets larger. Among of other things, such (exchangeability) restrictions also imply a dense network (as in Mele, 2017): the total number of links is $O_p(|\mathcal{N}|^2)$ (see, e.g., Orbanz and Roy, 2015). While the sets above are not sharp, i.e., more informative bounds on the parameters can intuitively be obtained by considering subnetworks on a larger number of nodes, they are potentially computable.[14] The article offers a computational algorithm to perform such computation and indicates a few additional potential simplifications. For example, when $\nu$ and $\omega$ are nonnegative (which guarantees existence of pairwise stable networks when utility is non-transferable), the game is supermodular as noted above and the solution set possesses a maximal and a minimal element. This can be explored to reduce the computational complexities here as done by Miyauchi (2016) (also in the context of pairwise stable network formation) and other authors in the empirical games literature. A Monte Carlo study in the paper demonstrates the performance of the algorithm in a transferable utility context with 50 and 100 networks varying in size from 25 individuals to 100.

Another use of subnetworks to circumvent the challenges presented in this setting appears in de Paula et al. (2018). The article works on a complete information, non-transferable utility model using pairwise stability as the solution concept. The treatment is tailored to handle large networks and the $\mathcal{N}$ is an uncountable set with continuum cardinality, taken to be an approximation to a large group of individuals.[15] To capture sparsity, they restrict payoffs, allowing only for a finite number of links $L$ such that in equilibrium one obtains a bounded degree graph on the continuum (sometimes referred to as a *graphing*). Utilities are

---

[14] Previous versions of the article (see Sheng, 2014, reviewed in de Paula, 2017) also considered simpler bounds: $\mathbb{P}(W_A = w_A | X_A) \leq \int_{\exists W_{-A} : w_A \in PS(\Delta U_A(W_{-A}, X_A, \epsilon_A))} dF(\epsilon_A)$ and $\mathbb{P}(\mathcal{D}_A | X_A) \geq \int_{\forall \mathcal{D}_{-A} : \mathcal{D}_A \in PS(\Delta U_A(\mathcal{D}_{-A}, X_A, \epsilon_A)) \wedge |PS_A(\Delta U_A(\mathcal{D}_{-A}, X_A, \epsilon_A))| = 1} dF(\epsilon_A)$. In words, the upper bound for $\mathbb{P}(\mathcal{D}_A | X_A)$ is the probability that subnetwork $\mathcal{D}_A$ is pairwise stable for some $\mathcal{D}_{-A}$ and the lower bound is the probability that, for any $\mathcal{D}_{-A}$, only subnetwork $\mathcal{D}_A$ is pairwise stable. These bounds do not require pairwise stability on the rest of the network and are thus easier to compute, but they are less informative than the ones above and might yield trivial bounds for larger groups.

[15] The approach described here starts with a "large" network. Related approaches, also focused on large networks, but taken as limits for finite sequences of networks is given in Leung (2015a), Menzel (2016) and Boucher and Mourifié (2017).

also assumed to depend only on individual characteristics (and not identities) and on indirect connections only up to a finite distance (depth $D$). This allows one to focus on "network types" defined by one's local neighborhood, whose cardinality is potentially more manageable than that of networks on individual nodes.

To illustrate the strategy, consider a very simple network formation game where individuals can only form one link and their utility depends only on this link. Here, both $L$ and $D$ are one. Nodes are characterized by $X$ which takes two values, $B$ or $W$ and there is a continuum of individuals of each type $\mu_B$ and $\mu_W$. Outcomes are thus given by ordered pairs $(x, y)$, where $x$ is the individual's characteristic and $y$, her connection's characteristic. Utilities are given by

$$U_i(\mathcal{D}) \equiv u_{xy} + \epsilon_i(y),$$

where again $x$ marks the individual's characteristic and $y$, her counterpart. If no link is formed, the payoff is normalized to zero. Hence, there are four parameters $(f_{x,y}, x, y \in \{B, W\}$ and two preference shocks for each individual: $\epsilon_i(B)$ and $\epsilon_i(W)$.[16]

The paper defines *network types* as the local network surrounding an individual in an observed network. Given the payoff structure, the network type should record payoff-relevant connections. In this simple individual, the relevant network type is given by the pair $(x, y)$. In a more general setting a network type is characterized by the individual herself, her direct connections, their direct connections and so on together with each of these nodes characteristics up to the payoff depth $D$. This thus corresponds to a network on up to $1 + L + L(L - 1) + \cdots + L(L - 1)^{D-1} = 1 + L \sum_{d=1}^{D} (L - 1)^{d-1}$ nodes and is equal to 2 when $L = 1$. The proportion of individuals of each network type is an equilibrium outcome and one would like to verify which parameter values rationalize the type shares in the data as outcomes of a pairwise stable network.

To do this, the article classifies individuals based on which network types they would not reject. Depending on the preference shocks, a $B$ individual may be content to have a $W$ connection ($f_{BW} + \epsilon_i(W) > 0$), but not a $B$ connection ($f_{BB} + \epsilon_i(B) < 0$). In this case, this individual would not have network type $BB$ in equilibrium as this would contradict pairwise stability, but would be content to be $BW$ or, should there be no $W$ individuals to link to, to remain isolated as $B0$. The authors thus form *preference classes* collecting all types that would be acceptable to an individual with given realizations of the preference shocks. In this simple example, the preference class for the individual above would be $\{BB, B0\}$. (Since there are no connections to be dropped from an isolated network type, the isolated type is an element for every preference class.)

As in the empirical games discussion and the example earlier in this subsection, this corresponds to a partition of the space of unobservable shocks,

---

[16] Additional restrictions are imposed on the preference shocks so that in equilibrium, even in large networks, there are isolated individuals.

but only for the individual. Given a distribution for the preference shocks $\epsilon$, one can compute (either analytically or numerically) the probability of each preference class for a given individual at a particular parameter value. One can then stipulate how individuals in each preference class are allocated to network types. In the paper, this is done using *allocation parameters* designating the proportion of individuals in a particular preference class that are allocated to a network type. In the example above, there are four preference classes for a $B$ individual: $H_1 = \{B0\}$, $H_2 = \{B0, BB\}$, $H_3 = \{B0, BW\}$ and $H_4 = \{B0, BB, BW\}$. Letting $\alpha_H(t)$ denote the allocation proportion of individuals in preference class $H$ to type $t$, the predicted share of $BW$ individuals is given by $\mathbb{P}(H_1|B)\alpha_{H_1}(BW) + \mathbb{P}(H_2|B)\alpha_{H_2}(BW) + \mathbb{P}(H_3|B)\alpha_{H_3}(BW) + \mathbb{P}(H_4|B)\alpha_{H_4}(BW)$ multiplied by the proportion of $B$ individuals in the group.

The key here is to offer restriction on the allocation parameters $\alpha_H(t)$ to be satisfied for a given profile of network type shares to be consistent with pairwise stability. These restrictions are necessary conditions for pairwise stability in the article. For example, nodes can only be allocated to network types that pertain to their preference class: if $t \notin H$, $\alpha_H(t) = 0$. This corresponds to the condition that links have to be beneficial to both individuals and would have $\alpha_{H_1}(BW) = \alpha_{H_2}(BW) = 0$. Second, given any pair of network types that could feasibly add a link to each other (i.e., an isolated individual of either characteristic, $B$ or $W$, in the example), the measure of individuals who would prefer to do so must be zero for at least one of the types. This corresponds to the condition that non-existing links have to be detrimental to at least one of the individuals. Another way to express this condition is to require that the product of the measure of individuals of one type that would benefit from adding links to individuals of the other type must be zero. This translates into a quadratic objective function which in equilibrium has to be zero once allocation parameters are adequately chosen. Finally, the predicted proportions of network types ought to match the observed proportions of types in the network, which in turn defines a set of linear constraints.

Once these are put together, one can express the task of verifying whether a given parameter vector can rationalize the data (observed network type shares) as that of a pairwise stable network) as a quadratic programme on the allocation parameters with constraints requiring allocation parameters to be positive, add up to one and for predicted shares to be matched in the data. Should the data be rationalized as a pairwise stable network for a given parameter vector, the optimized objective function is zero. The cardinality of the problem, while still non-trivial, is related to the cardinality of the preference classes and network types rather than the potential networks on $|\mathcal{N}|$ individuals. If this is done at each putative parameter, one can then collect those parameters that rationalize the data and form the identified set. Whereas the quadratic programme above is regrettably not a convex one (since the matrix in the quadratic form is not necessarily positive definite), the article offers simulation evidence for networks as large as $|\mathcal{N}| = 500$. Anderson and Richards-Shubik (2019) applies this framework to the analysis of co-authorships in Economics.

One interesting point to note refers to the source of statistical uncertainty here. Since there are infinitely many nodes, were the network to be completely observed, network type shares would be perfectly measured. On the other hand, if there is sampling uncertainty in the measurement of network type shares because only a sample of individuals (and their network types) is collected, sampling uncertainty in type shares would transfer to the estimation of structural parameters. This relates to what is sometimes referred to as a "design-based" paradigm in statistics (see Kolaczyk, 2009). The randomness here obtains from the probability ascribed by the survey scheme to the sampling of the various individuals in the network. The partial observability of the network is nonetheless not uncommon and rather the norm in many settings.[17]

## 3.4 Concluding remarks

This chapter provides an overview of alternative routes for the econometric analysis of strategic network formation. This review is nonetheless not exhaustive and the analysis is in its infancy. Whereas the presentation here indicates the connections with well-known statistical models (e.g., ERGMs), statistical models presented elsewhere may themselves be amenable to an interpretation as a structural model of network formation (see, e.g., Graham, 2017). On the other hand, statistical models conditionally defined may themselves not be immune to some of the pathologies identified here, like the multiplicity of potential distributions consistent with the models (see, again, the final discussion in Graham, 2017).

The connection between network formation and outcomes mediated by networks is also important. This connection has not been explored in many contexts, but one can mention articles such as Gilleskie and Zhang (2009), Goldsmith-Pinkham and Imbens (2013), Hsieh et al. (2019) and Badev (2018). Other recent article exploring networks and outcomes simultaneously are Ghili (2018), Liebman (2018) and Ho and Lee (2019).[18]

## References

Anderson, K.A., Richards-Shubik, S., 2019. Collaborative Production in Science: An Empirical Analysis of Coauthorships in Economics. CMU and Lehigh University Working Paper.

Badev, A., 2018. Nash Equilibria on (Un)Stable Networks. Federal Reserve Board Working Paper.

Berry, S.T., 1992. Estimation of a model of entry in the airline industry. Econometrica 60 (4), 889–917.

Besag, J., 1975. Statistical analysis of non-lattice data. The Statistician 24 (3), 179–195.

---

[17] Since also focused on subnetworks, the approach in Sheng (2016) may also be adapted to such contexts.

[18] The latter two articles use alternative network formation solution concepts than the ones presented here.

Bhamidi, S., Bresler, G., Sly, A., 2011. Mixing time of exponential random graphs. The Annals of Applied Probability 21 (6), 2146–2170.

Bjorn, P.A., Vuong, Q.H., 1985. Econometric Modeling of a Stackelberg Game with an Application to Labor Force Participation. Working Paper.

Bloch, F., Jackson, M.O., 2006. Definitions of equilibrium in network formation games. International Journal of Game Theory 34 (3), 305–318.

Boucher, V., Mourifié, I., 2017. My friend far far away: asymptotic properties of pairwise stable networks. Econometrics Journal 20 (3), S14–S46. Université Laval and University of Toronto Working Paper.

Bresnahan, T., Reiss, P., 1990. Entry in monopoly markets. The Review of Economic Studies 57 (4), 531–553.

Bresnahan, T., Reiss, P., 1991. Empirical models of discrete games. Journal of Econometrics 48, 57–81.

Chatterjee, S., Diaconis, P., 2013. Estimating and understanding exponential random graph models. The Annals of Statistics 41 (5), 2428–2461.

Chiappori, P.-A., 2019. Matching with Transfers: The Economics of Love and Marriage. Princeton University Press.

Christakis, N.A., Fowler, J.H., Imbens, G.W., Kalyanaraman, K., 2010. An Empirical Model for Strategic Network Formation. NBER Working Paper 16039. National Bureau of Economic Research.

de Paula, A., 2013. Econometric analysis of games with multiple equilibria. Annual Review of Economics 5, 107–131.

de Paula, A., 2017. Econometrics of network models. In: Honore, B., Pakes, A., Piazzesi, M., Samuelson, L. (Eds.), Advances in Economics and Econometrics: Theory and Applications: Eleventh World Congress. Cambridge University Press, Cambridge, pp. 268–323.

de Paula, Á., Richards-Shubik, S., Tamer, E., 2018. Identifying preferences in networks with bounded degrees. Econometrica 86 (1), 263–288.

Ghili, S., 2018. Network Formation and Bargaining in Vertical Markets: The Case of Narrow Networks in Health Insurance. Yale University Working Paper.

Gilleskie, D., Zhang, Y.S., 2009. Friendship Formation and Smoking Initiation Among Teens. University of North Carolina Working Paper.

Goldsmith-Pinkham, P., Imbens, G.W., 2013. Social networks and the identification of peer effects. Journal of Business and Economic Statistics 31 (3), 253–264.

Graham, B.S., 2017. An econometric model of link formation with degree heterogeneity. Econometrica 85 (4), 1033–1063.

Gualdani, C., 2019. An Econometric Model of Network Formation with an Application to Board Interlocks Between Firms. Toulouse School of Economics Working Paper.

Heckman, J., 2000. Causal parameters and policy analysis in economics: a twentieth century retrospective. The Quarterly Journal of Economics, 45–97.

Hellmann, T., 2013. On the existence and uniqueness of pairwise stable networks. International Journal of Game Theory 42 (1).

Ho, K., Lee, R., 2019. Equilibrium provider networks: bargaining and exclusion in health care markets. The American Economic Review 109 (2), 473–522.

Hsieh, C.-S., Lee, L.-F., Boucher, V., 2019. Specification and Estimation of Network Formation and Network Interaction Models with the Exponential Probability Distribution. CRREP Working Paper.

Jackson, M., Watts, A., 2001. The existence of pairwise stable networks. Seoul Journal of Economics 14, 299–321.

Jackson, M.O., 2008. Social and Economic Networks. Princeton University Press.

Jackson, M.O., Watts, A., 2002. The evolution of social and economic networks. Journal of Economic Theory 106 (2), 265–295.

Jackson, M.O., Wolinsky, A., 1996. A strategic model of social and economic networks. Journal of Economic Theory 71 (1), 44–74.

Jordan, M.I., Wainwright, M.J., 2008. Graphical models, exponential families, and variational inference. Foundations and Trends in Machine Learning 1 (1–2), 1–305.

Kolaczyk, E.D., 2009. Statistical Analysis of Network Data. Springer, New York.

Leung, M., 2015a. A random-field approach to inference in large models of network formation. Stanford University. Mimeo.

Leung, M., 2015b. Two-step estimation of network-formation models with incomplete information. Journal of Econometrics 188 (1), 182–195.

Liebman, E., 2018. Bargaining in Markets with Exclusion: An Analysis on Health Insurance Networks. University of Georgia Working Paper.

Mele, A., 2017. A structural model of dense network formation. Econometrica 85 (3), 825–850.

Mele, A., forthcoming. Does school desegregation promote diverse interactions? An equilibrium model of segregation within schools. American Economic Journal: Economic Policy.

Menzel, K., 2016. Strategic network formation with many agents. New York University.

Miyauchi, Y., 2016. Structural estimation of a pairwise stable network with nonnegative externality. Journal of Econometrics 195 (2), 224–235.

Murray, I., Ghahramani, Z., MacKay, D., 2006. MCMC for doubly-intractable distributions. Uncertainty in Artificial Intelligence.

Myerson, R., 1977. Graphs and cooperation in games. Mathematics of Operations Research 2, 225–229.

Orbanz, P., Roy, D.M., 2015. Bayesian models of graphs, arrays and other exchangeable randoms structures. IEEE Transactions on Pattern Analysis and Machine Intelligence 37 (2), 437–461.

Sheng, S., 2014. A Structural Econometric Analysis of Network Formation Games. Working Paper. University of California, Los Angeles.

Sheng, S., 2016. A structural econometric analysis of network formation games through subnetworks. Working Paper. University of California, Los Angeles.

Snijders, T., 2002. Markov chain Monte Carlo estimation of exponential random graph models. Journal of Social Structure 3 (2), 1–40.

Strauss, D., Ikeda, M., 1990. Pseudolikelihood estimation for social networks. Journal of the American Statistical Association 85 (409), 204–212.

Tamer, E., 2003. Incomplete simultaneous discrete response model with multiple equilibria. The Review of Economic Studies 70 (1), 147–165.

# Chapter 4

# Testing for externalities in network formation using simulation<sup>☆</sup>

## Bryan S. Graham[a,b] and Andrin Pelican[c]

[a]*Department of Economics, University of California - Berkeley, Berkeley, CA, United States,* [b]*National Bureau of Economic Research, Cambridge, MA, United States ,* [c]*Department of Economics, School of Economics and Political Science, University of St. Gallen, St. Gallen, Switzerland*

## Contents

De Weerdt (2004) studies the formation of risk-sharing links among $N = 119$ households located in the Tanzanian village of Nyakatoke. Let $\hat{P}(\triangle)$ and $\hat{P}(\wedge)$, respectively, equal the fraction of all $\binom{N}{3}$ triads which take the triangle and two-star configuration. De Weerdt (2004) finds that the transitivity of the Nyakatoke risk-sharing network

$$\hat{\mathrm{TI}} = \frac{3\hat{P}(\triangle)}{3\hat{P}(\triangle) + \hat{P}(\wedge)} = 0.1884 \tag{4.1}$$

is almost three times its density ($\hat{P}(\frown) = 0.0698$). There are several, not necessarily mutually exclusive, explanations for the clustering present in Nyakatoke. First, it may reflect the increased value of a risk-sharing relationship between two households when "supported" by a third household (Jackson et al., 2012).

---

☆ We thank Aureo de Paula and participants in the Mannheim/Bonn summer school on social networks for useful feedback. All the usual disclaimers apply. Financial support from NSF grant SES #1851647 is gratefully acknowledged.

Households $i$ and $j$ may value a risk sharing link with each other more if they are both additionally linked to household $k$. Household $k$ may then serve as a monitor, arbiter and referee for households $i$ and $j$'s relationship (increasing its value). Second, clustering may simply be an artifact of degree heterogeneity, whereby high degree households link more frequently with one-another and hence form triangles ($\triangle$) incidentally. Third, clustering may also stem from homophilous sorting on kinship, ethnicity, religion and so on (McPherson et al., 2001).

In this chapter we outline a method of randomization inference, in the spirit of Fisher (1935), that can be used to "test" for externalities, or interdependencies, in link formation.[1] Externalities arise when the utility two agents generate when forming a link varies with the presence or absence of edges elsewhere in the network. Attaching greater utility to "supported" links is one such interdependency. Externalities typically imply that an efficient network will not form when link formation is negotiated bilaterally (e.g., Bloch and Jackson, 2007). Consider household $i$, who is linked to $k$, an incidental consequence of $i$ additionally linking to $j$, is that she will then be able to "support" any link between $j$ and $k$. When evaluating whether to form a link with $j$, $i$ may not internalize this additional, non-bilateral, benefit; consequently, there may be too few risk-sharing links in Nyakatoke.

The scientific and policy implications of externalities are considerable (cf. Graham, 2016). In the presence of interdependencies small re-wirings of a network may induce a cascade of link revisions, alternating network structure, and agents' utility, substantially. In the absence of interdependencies links form bilaterally and re-wirings will not induce additional changes in network structure (see Fig. 4.1).

Testing for externalities in network formation is not straightforward; particularly if the null model allows for rich forms of agent-level heterogeneity. Allowing for heterogeneity under the null is essential, after all, such heterogeneity provides an alternative explanation for the type of link clustering which arises in the presence of externalities.

The approach outlined here draws upon Pelican and Graham (2019). Our goal here, however, is primarily pedagogical; to introduce some key ideas and methods likely to be of interest to empirical researchers interested in networks. Relative to what is presented here, Pelican and Graham (2019) additionally consider (i) directed and undirected networks, (ii) null models which allow for both degree heterogeneity *and* homophily, (iii) models with *and* without transfers, (iv) constructing test statistics to maximize power in certain directions and (v) novel Markov chain Monte Carlo (MCMC) methods of simulating the null distribution of the test statistic.

---

[1] We place "test" in quotes to emphasize that, while, as in other examples of randomization inference, the null hypothesis is explicitly formulated, rejection may arise for a variety of reasons. See Cox (2006, Chapter 3) for additional examples and discussion.

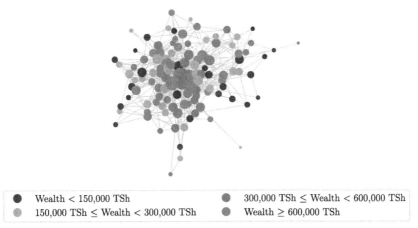

| ● | Wealth < 150,000 TSh | ● | 300,000 TSh ≤ Wealth < 600,000 TSh |
|---|---|---|---|
| ● | 150,000 TSh ≤ Wealth < 300,000 TSh | ● | Wealth ≥ 600,000 TSh |

**FIGURE 4.1** Nyakatoke risk-sharing network. *Notes:* Nodes/Households are colored according to total land and livestock wealth in Tanzanian Shillings (calculated as described by Comola and Fafchamps, 2014). Node sizes are proportional to degree. *Source:* De Weerdt (2004) and authors' calculations. Raw data available at https://www.uantwerpen.be/en/staff/joachim-deweerdt/ (Accessed January 2017).

While the presentation in this chapter is more basic, the upshot is that the method outlined here can be implemented by combining familiar heuristics (e.g., Milo et al., 2002) with a little game theory and the adjacency matrix simulation algorithm of Blitzstein and Diaconis (2011).

We begin by outlining a simple network formation game with transfers in the spirit of Bloch and Jackson (2007). We then formally describe our test. Next we discuss how to simulate the null distribution of our test statistic using an algorithm due to Blitzstein and Diaconis (2011); we also briefly discuss other applications of this algorithm and alternatives to it. We close with an illustration based upon the Nyakatoke network.

In what follows we let **D** be the adjacency matrix associated with a simple graph $G(\mathcal{V}, \mathcal{E})$ defined on $N = |\mathcal{V}|$ vertices or agents. The set $\mathcal{V} = \{1, \ldots, N\}$ includes all agents in the network and $\mathcal{E} \subseteq \mathcal{V} \times \mathcal{V}$ equals the set of undirected edges or links among them. The set of all $N \times N$ undirected adjacency matrices is denoted by $\mathbb{D}_N$.

## A strategic network formation game with transfers

In this section we outline a simple model of strategic network formation where agents may make (bilateral) transfers to one another. Let $v_i : \mathbb{D}_N \to \mathbb{R}$ be a utility function for agent $i$, which maps adjacency matrices—equivalently networks—into utils. The marginal utility for agent $i$ associated with (possible) edge $(i, j)$ is

$$MU_{ij}(\mathbf{D}) = \begin{cases} v_i(\mathbf{D}) - v_i(\mathbf{D} - ij) & \text{if } D_{ij} = 1, \\ v_i(\mathbf{D} + ij) - v_i(\mathbf{D}) & \text{if } D_{ij} = 0, \end{cases} \qquad (4.2)$$

where $\mathbf{D} - ij$ is the adjacency matrix associated with the network obtained after deleting edge $(i, j)$ and $\mathbf{D} + ij$ the one obtained via link addition.

From Bloch and Jackson (2006), a network is *pairwise stable with transfers* if the following condition holds.

**Definition 4.1** (Pairwise stability with transfers). The network $G(\mathcal{V}, \mathcal{E})$ is pairwise stable with transfers if
(i) $\forall (i, j) \in \mathcal{E}(G), MU_{ij}(\mathbf{D}) + MU_{ji}(\mathbf{D}) \geq 0$,
(ii) $\forall (i, j) \notin \mathcal{E}(G), MU_{ij}(\mathbf{D}) + MU_{ji}(\mathbf{D}) < 0$.

Definition 4.1 states that the marginal utility of all links actually present in a pairwise stable network is (weakly) positive, while that associated with links not present is negative. The definition presumes utility is transferable, since it only requires that the *sum* of utility to *i and j* associated with edge $(i, j)$ is positive. When the sum of the two marginal utilities is positive, there exists a within-dyad transfer such that both agents benefit. Note also that the definition is pairwise: the benefit of a link is evaluated conditional on the remaining network structure. It is possible, for example, that a coalition of players could increase their utility by jointly forming a set of links and making transfers to one another. Imposing more sophisticated play of this type would result in a refinement relative to the set of network configurations which satisfy Definition 4.1 (cf. Jackson, 2008).

In this chapter we will specialize to utility functions of the form

$$v_i(\mathbf{d}, \mathbf{U}; \gamma_0, \delta_0) = \sum_j d_{ij} \left[ A_i + B_j + \gamma_0 s_{ij}(\mathbf{d}) - U_{ij} \right] \qquad (4.3)$$

with $\mathbf{U} = \left[ U_{ij} \right]$. Here $A_i$ and $B_j$ capture agent-level degree heterogeneity (cf. Graham, 2017). If $A_i$ is high, then the baseline utility associated with any link is high for agent $i$ ($i$ is an "extrovert"). If $B_j$ is high, then $j$ is a particularly attractive partner for all other agents ($j$ is "popular"). We leave the joint distribution of $\mathbf{A} = [A_i]$ and $\mathbf{B} = [B_i]$ unrestricted in what follows.

The $s_{ij}(\mathbf{d})$ term is associated with externalities in link formation. We require that $s_{ij}(\mathbf{d}) = s_{ij}(\mathbf{d} - ij) = s_{ij}(\mathbf{d} + ij)$; additional restrictions might be needed to ensure the existence of a network that is pairwise stable with transfers and/or a test statistic with a non-degenerate null distribution.

Instead of formulating additional high-level conditions on $s_{ij}(\mathbf{d})$, in what follows we emphasize, and develop results for, two specific examples. In the first $s_{ij}(\mathbf{d})$ equals

$$s_{ij}(\mathbf{d}) = \sum_k d_{jk}, \qquad (4.4)$$

which implies that agents receive more utility from links with popular (or high degree) agents.

The second example specifies $s_{ij}$ (**d**) as

$$s_{ij}(\mathbf{d}) = \sum_k d_{ik}d_{jk}, \tag{4.5}$$

which implies that dyads receive more utility from linking when they share other links in common. This is a transitivity effect.

When the utility function is of the form given in (4.3) the marginal utility agent $i$ gets from a link with $j$ is

$$MU_{ij}(\mathbf{d}, \mathbf{U}; \gamma_0, \delta_0) = A_i + B_j + \gamma_0 s_{ij}(\mathbf{d}) - U_{ij}.$$

Pairwise stability then implies that, conditional on the realizations of **A**, **B**, **U** and the value of the externality parameter $\gamma_0$, the observed network must satisfy, for $i = 1, \ldots, N - 1$ and $j = i + 1, \ldots, N$

$$D_{ij} = \mathbf{1}\left(\tilde{A}_i + \tilde{A}_j + \gamma_0 \tilde{s}_{ij}(\mathbf{D}) \geq \tilde{U}_{ij}\right) \tag{4.6}$$

with $\tilde{A}_i = A_i + B_i$, $\tilde{s}_{ij}(\mathbf{d}) = s_{ij}(\mathbf{d}) + s_{ji}(\mathbf{d})$ and $\tilde{U}_{ij} = U_{ij} + U_{ji}$.

Eq. (4.6) defines a system of $\binom{N}{2} = \frac{1}{2}N(N-1)$ nonlinear simultaneous equations. Any solution to this system – and there will typically be multiple ones—constitutes a pairwise stable (with transfers) network. To make this observation a bit more explicit, similar to Miyauchi (2016), consider the mapping $\varphi(\mathbf{D}) : \mathbb{D}_N \to \mathbb{I}_{\binom{N}{2}}$:

$$\varphi(\mathbf{d}) \equiv \begin{bmatrix} \mathbf{1}\left(\tilde{A}_1 + \tilde{A}_2 + \gamma_0 \tilde{s}_{12}(\mathbf{d}) \geq U_{12}\right) \\ \mathbf{1}\left(\tilde{A}_1 + \tilde{A}_3 + \gamma_0 \tilde{s}_{13}(\mathbf{d}) \geq U_{13}\right) \\ \vdots \\ \mathbf{1}\left(\tilde{A}_{N-1} + \tilde{A}_N + \gamma_0 \tilde{s}_{N-1N}(\mathbf{d}) \geq U_{N-1N}\right) \end{bmatrix}. \tag{4.7}$$

Under the maintained assumption that the observed network satisfies Definition 4.1, the observed adjacency matrix corresponds to the fixed point

$$\mathbf{D} = \text{vech}^{-1}\left[\varphi(\mathbf{D})\right].$$

Here vech$(\cdot)$ vectorizes the $\binom{N}{2}$ elements in the lower triangle of an $N \times N$ matrix and we define its inverse operator as creating a symmetric matrix with a zero diagonal. In addition to the observed network there may be other $\mathbf{d} \in \mathbb{D}_N$ such that $\mathbf{d} = \text{vech}^{-1}\left[\varphi(\mathbf{d})\right]$. The fixed point representation is useful for showing equilibrium existence and for characterization (e.g., using Tarski's (1955) fixed point theorem).

For the two types of network formation externalities we consider, specified in Eqs. (4.4) and (4.5) above, the $\varphi\,(\mathbf{d})$ mapping is weakly increasing in $\mathbf{d}$ for $\gamma_0 \geq 0$. This allows for the application of Tarski's (1955) theorem; ensuring existence of at least one pairwise stable equilibrium.

## Test formulation

Our goal is to assess the null hypothesis that $\gamma_0 = 0$ relative to the alternative that $\gamma_0 > 0$. The extension of what follows to two-sided tests is straightforward. A feature our testing problem is the presence of a high-dimensional nuisance parameter in the form of the $N$ degree heterogeneity terms, $\tilde{\mathbf{A}} = \left[\tilde{A}_i\right]$. Since the value of these terms may range freely over the null, our null hypothesis is a *composite* one.

The composite nature of the null hypothesis raises concerns about size control. Ideally our test will have good size properties regardless of the particular value of $\tilde{\mathbf{A}}$. Assume, for example, that the distribution of the $\left\{\tilde{A}_i\right\}_{i=1}^{N}$ is right-skewed. In this case we will likely observe high levels of clustering among high $\tilde{A}_i$ agents. Measured transitivity in the network might be substantial even in the absence of any structural preference for transitive relationships. We want to avoid excessive rejection of our null hypothesis in such settings; we do so by varying the critical value used for rejection with the magnitude of a sufficient statistics for the $\left\{\tilde{A}_i\right\}_{i=1}^{N}$.

A simple example helps to fix ideas. Under the null we have, for $i = 1, \ldots, N-1$ and $j = i+1, \ldots, N$,

$$\Pr\left(D_{ij} = 1\right) = \frac{\exp\left(\tilde{A}_i + \tilde{A}_j\right)}{1 + \exp\left(\tilde{A}_i + \tilde{A}_j\right)}, \tag{4.8}$$

which corresponds to the $\beta$-model of network formation (e.g., Chatterjee et al., 2011). Assume that $\tilde{A}_i \in \left\{-\infty, \frac{1}{2}\ln\left(\frac{\rho}{1-\rho}\right)\right\}$ with $\tilde{A}_i = -\infty$ with probability $1 - \pi$. In this simple model two "high" $\tilde{A}_i$ agents link with probability $\rho$, while low-to-low and low-to-high links never form. Some simple calculations give an overall density for this network of $\pi^2 \rho$, and a (population) transitivity index of $\rho$. For $\pi$ small and or $\rho$ large, transitivity in this network may exceed density substantially even though there is no structural taste for transitive links among agents. Here the transitivity is entirely generated by high degree agents linking with one another with greater frequency and, only incidentally, forming triangles in the process. A simple comparison of density and transitivity in this case is uninformative.

Motivated in part by this inferential challenge, and to exploit classic results on testing in exponential families (e.g., Lehmann and Romano, 2005, Chapter 4) it will be convenient in what follows to assume that $\tilde{U}_{ij} \sim \text{Logistic}(0, 1)$. Next let $\mathbb{A}$ denoting a subset of the $N$ dimensional Euclidean space in which $\tilde{\mathbf{A}}$ is, a priori, known to lie, and

$$\Theta_0 = \left\{ \left( \gamma, \tilde{\mathbf{A}}' \right) : \gamma = 0, \tilde{\mathbf{A}} \in \mathbb{A} \right\}.$$

Our null hypothesis is

$$H_0 : \theta \in \Theta_0 \tag{4.9}$$

since $\tilde{\mathbf{A}}$ may range freely over $\mathbb{A} \subset \mathbb{R}^N$ under the null of no externalities in link formation ($\gamma_0 = 0$).[2] With a little manipulation we can show that, under (4.9), the probability of the event $\mathbf{D} = \mathbf{d}$ takes the exponential family form

$$P_0 \left( \mathbf{d}; \tilde{\mathbf{A}} \right) = c \left( \tilde{\mathbf{A}} \right) \exp \left( \mathbf{d}'_+ \tilde{\mathbf{A}} \right)$$

with $\mathbf{d}_+ = (d_{1+}, \ldots, d_{N+})$ equal to the degree sequence of the network.

Let $\mathbb{D}_{N, \mathbf{d}_+}$ denote the set of all undirected $N \times N$ adjacency matrices with degree counts also equal to $\mathbf{d}_+$ and $\left| \mathbb{D}_{N, \mathbf{d}_+} \right|$ denote the size, or cardinality, of this set. Under $H_0$ the conditional likelihood of $\mathbf{D} = \mathbf{d}$ given $\mathbf{D}_+ = \mathbf{d}_+$ is

$$P_0 \left( \mathbf{d} | \mathbf{D}_+ = \mathbf{d}_+ \right) = \frac{1}{\left| \mathbb{D}_{N, \mathbf{d}_+} \right|}.$$

Under the null of no externalities *all networks with identical degree sequences are equally probable*. This insight will form the basis of our test.

Let $T(\mathbf{d})$ be some statistic of the adjacency matrix $\mathbf{D} = \mathbf{d}$, say its transitivity index. We work with a (test) critical function of the form

$$\phi(\mathbf{d}) = \begin{cases} 1 & T(\mathbf{d}) > c_\alpha(\mathbf{d}_+), \\ g_\alpha(\mathbf{d}_+) & T(\mathbf{d}) = c_\alpha(\mathbf{d}_+), \\ 0 & T(\mathbf{d}) < c_\alpha(\mathbf{d}_+). \end{cases}$$

We will reject the null if our statistic exceeds some critical value, $c_\alpha(\mathbf{d}_+)$ and accept it—or fail to reject it—if our statistic falls below this critical value. If our statistic exactly equals the critical value, then we reject with probability $g_\alpha(\mathbf{d}_+)$. The critical value $c_\alpha(\mathbf{d}_+)$ and the probability $g_\alpha(\mathbf{d}_+)$ are chosen to set the rejection probability of our test under the null equal to $\alpha$ (i.e., to control size). In order to find the appropriate values of $c_\alpha(\mathbf{d}_+)$ and $g_\alpha(\mathbf{d}_+)$ we need to know the distribution of $T(\mathbf{D})$ under the null.

---

[2] There is an additional (implicit) nuisance parameter associated with equilibrium selection since, under the alternative, there may be many pairwise stable network configurations. We can ignore this complication for our present purposes, but see Pelican and Graham (2019) for additional discussion and details.

Conceptually this distribution is straightforward to characterize; particularly if we proceed conditional on the degree sequence observed in the network in hand. Under the null all possible adjacency matrices with degree sequence $\mathbf{d}_+$ are equally probable. The null distribution of $T(\mathbf{D})$ therefore equals its distribution across all these matrices. By enumerating all the elements of $\mathbb{D}_{N,\mathbf{d}_+}$ and calculating $T(\mathbf{d})$ for each one, we could directly—and exactly—compute this distribution. In practice this is not (generally) computationally feasible. Even for networks that include as few as 10 agents, the set $\mathbb{D}_{N,\mathbf{d}_+}$ may have millions of elements (see, for example, Table 1 of Blitzstein and Diaconis, 2011). Below we show how to approximate the null distribution of $T(\mathbf{D})$ by simulation, leading to a practical method of finding critical values for testing.

If we could efficiently enumerate the elements of $\mathbb{D}_{N,\mathbf{d}_+}$ we would find $c_\alpha(\mathbf{d}_+)$ by solving

$$\Pr\left(T(\mathbf{D}) \geq c_\alpha(\mathbf{d}_+) \mid \mathbf{D} \in \mathbb{D}_{N,\mathbf{d}_+}\right) = \frac{\sum_{\mathbf{D} \in \mathbb{D}_{N,\mathbf{d}_+}} \mathbf{1}\left(T(\mathbf{D}) \geq c_\alpha(\mathbf{d}_+)\right)}{\left|\mathbb{D}_{N,\mathbf{d}_+}\right|} = \alpha.$$
(4.10)

If there is no $c_\alpha(\mathbf{d}_+)$ for which (4.10) exactly holds, then we would instead find the smallest $c_\alpha(\mathbf{d}_+)$ such that $\Pr\left(T(\mathbf{D}) > c_\alpha(\mathbf{d}_+) \mid \mathbf{D} \in \mathbb{D}_{N,\mathbf{d}_+}\right) \geq \alpha$ and choose $g_\alpha(\mathbf{d}_+)$ to ensure correct size.

Alternatively we might instead calculate the p-value:

$$\Pr\left(T(\mathbf{D}) \geq T(\mathbf{d}_+) \mid \mathbf{D} \in \mathbb{D}_{N,\mathbf{d}_+}\right) = \frac{\sum_{\mathbf{D} \in \mathbb{D}_{N,\mathbf{d}_+}} \mathbf{1}\left(T(\mathbf{D}) \geq T(\mathbf{d}_+)\right)}{\left|\mathbb{D}_{N,\mathbf{d}_+}\right|}.$$
(4.11)

If this probability is very low, say less than 5 percent of all networks in $\mathbb{D}_{N,\mathbf{d}_+}$ have a transitivity index larger than the one observed in the network in hand, then we might conclude that our network is "unusual" and, more precisely, that it is *not* a uniform random draw from $\mathbb{D}_{N,\mathbf{d}_+}$ (our null hypothesis).

Below we show how to approximate the probabilities to the left of the equalities in (4.10) and (4.11) by simulation.

### Similarity of the test

In our setting, a test $\phi(\mathbf{D})$, will have size $\alpha$ if its null rejection probability (NRP) is less than or equal to $\alpha$ for *all* values of the nuisance parameter:

$$\sup_{\theta \in \Theta_0} \mathbb{E}_\theta\left[\phi(\mathbf{D})\right] = \sup_{\tilde{A} \in \mathbb{A}} \mathbb{E}_\theta\left[\phi(\mathbf{D})\right] = \alpha.$$

Since $\tilde{\mathbf{A}}$ is high dimensional, size control is non-trivial. This motivates, as we have done, proceeding conditionally on the degree sequence.

Let $\mathbb{D}_+$ be the set of all graphical degree sequences (see below for a discussion of "graphic" integer sequences). For each $\mathbf{d}_+ \in \mathbb{D}_+$ our approach is equivalent to forming a test with the property that, for all $\theta \in \Theta_0$,

$$\mathbb{E}_\theta \left[ \phi \left( \mathbf{D} \right) | \, \mathbf{D}_+ = \mathbf{d}_+ \right] = \alpha. \tag{4.12}$$

Such an approach ensures *similarity* of our test since, by iterated expectations,

$$\mathbb{E}_\theta \left[ \phi \left( \mathbf{D} \right) \right] = \mathbb{E}_\theta \left[ \mathbb{E}_\theta \left[ \phi \left( \mathbf{D} \right) | \, \mathbf{D}_+ \right] \right] = \alpha$$

for any $\theta \in \Theta_0$ (cf. Ferguson, 1967). By proceeding conditionally we ensure the NRP is unaffected by the value of the degree heterogeneity distribution $\left\{ \tilde{A}_i \right\}_{i=1}^N$. Similar tests have proved to be attractive in other settings with composite null hypotheses (cf. Moreira, 2009).

## Choosing the test statistic

Ideally the critical function is chosen to maximize the probability of correctly rejecting the null under particular alternatives of interest. It turns out that, because our network formation model is incomplete under the alternative (as we have been silent about equilibrium selection), constructing tests with good power is non-trivial. In Pelican and Graham (2019) we show how to choose the critical function, or equivalently the statistic $T(\mathbf{d})$, to maximize power against particular (local) alternatives. The argument is involved, so here we confine ourselves to a more informal development.

A common approach to choosing a test statistic, familiar from other applications of randomization testing (e.g., Cox, 2006, Chapter 3), is to proceed heuristically. This suggests, for example, choosing $T(\mathbf{D})$ to be the transitivity index, or the support measure of Jackson et al. (2012), if the researcher is interested in "testing" for whether agents prefer transitive relationships.

A variation on this approach, inspired by the more formal development in Pelican and Graham (2019), is to set $T(\mathbf{D})$ equal to

$$T(\mathbf{D}) = \sum_{i<j} \left( D_{ij} - \hat{p}_{ij} \right) \tilde{s}_{ij}(\mathbf{d}) \tag{4.13}$$

with $\hat{p}_{ij} = \dfrac{\exp\left( \hat{\tilde{A}}_i + \hat{\tilde{A}}_j \right)}{1 + \exp\left( \hat{\tilde{A}}_i + \hat{\tilde{A}}_j \right)}$ and $\hat{\tilde{\mathbf{A}}} = \left[ \hat{\tilde{A}}_i \right]$ the maximum likelihood estimate (MLE) of $\tilde{\mathbf{A}}$.[3] The intuition behind (4.13) is as follows: if it is positive, this implies that high values of the externality term, $\tilde{s}_{ij}(\mathbf{d})$, are associated with links that have low estimated probability under the null (such that $D_{ij} - \hat{p}_{ij}$ is large). The conjunction of "surprising" links with large values of $\tilde{s}_{ij}(\mathbf{d})$ is taken as evidence that $\gamma_0 > 0$.

---

[3] Chatterjee et al. (2011) present a simple fixed point algorithm for computing this MLE (see also Graham, 2017).

Consider the transitivity example with $\tilde{s}_{ij}(\mathbf{d}) = 2\sum_k d_{ik}d_{jk}$; statistic (4.13), with some manipulation, can be shown to equal

$$
T(\mathbf{D}) = 6\left[\sum_{i<j<k} D_{ij}D_{ik}D_{jk}\right.
$$

$$
\left. - \sum_{i<j<k} \frac{1}{3}\left(\hat{p}_{ij}D_{ik}D_{jk} + D_{ij}\hat{p}_{ik}D_{jk} + D_{ij}D_{ik}\hat{p}_{jk}\right)\right]. \tag{4.14}
$$

Statistic (4.14) is a measure of the difference between the actual number of triangles in the network and (a particular) expected triangle count computed under the null. To see this assume, as would be approximately true if the graph were an Erdös–Rényi one, that $\hat{p}_{ij} = \hat{P}(\!-\!)$ for all $i < j$. Recalling that $\hat{P}(\triangle)$ and $\hat{P}(\wedge)$ respectively equal the fraction of all $\binom{N}{3}$ triads which are triangles and two-stars, we would have

$$
T(\mathbf{D}) = 2\binom{N}{3}\left[3\hat{P}(\triangle) - \left(3\hat{P}(\triangle) + \hat{P}(\wedge)\right)\hat{P}(\!-\!)\right].
$$

The term in [] equals the difference between the numerator of the transitivity index and its denominator *times* density. For an Erdös–Rényi graph this difference should be approximately zero. In the presence of degree heterogeneity, the second term to the right of the equality in (4.14) is a null-model-assisted count of the expected number of triangles in $G$. A rejection therefore occurs when many "surprising" triangles are present.

Before describing how to simulate the null distribution of $T(\mathbf{D})$ we briefly recap. We start by specifying a sharp null hypothesis. Consider the network in hand with adjacency matrix $\mathbf{D} = \mathbf{d}$ and corresponding degree sequence $\mathbf{D}_+ = \mathbf{d}_+$. Our null hypothesis is that the observed network coincides with a uniform random draw from $\mathbb{D}_{N,\mathbf{d}_+}$ (i.e., the set of all networks with identical degree sequences). This null is a consequence of the form on the transferable utility network formation game outlined earlier. The testing procedure is to compare a particular statistic of $\mathbf{D} = \mathbf{d}$, say $T(\mathbf{d})$, with its distribution across $\mathbb{D}_{N,\mathbf{d}_+}$. If the observed value of $T(\mathbf{d})$ is unusually large we take this as evidence against our null.

Although we have motivated our test as one for strategic interactions or externalities, in actuality we are really assessing the adequacy of a particular null model of network formation—namely the $\beta$-model. Our test may detect many types of violations of this model, albeit with varying degrees of power. Consequently we need to be careful about how we interpret a rejection in practice. At the same time, by choosing the test statistic $T(\mathbf{D})$ with some care, we hope to generate good power to detect the violation of interest – that $\gamma_0 > 0$—and hence conclude that externalities in link formation are likely present when we reject.

## Simulating undirected networks with fixed degree

This section describes an algorithm, introduced by Blitzstein and Diaconis (2011), for sampling uniformly from the set $\mathbb{D}_{N,\mathbf{d}_+}$. Our notation and exposition tracks that of Blitzstein and Diaconis (2011), albeit with less details. As noted previously, direct enumeration of all the elements of $\mathbb{D}_{N,\mathbf{d}_+}$ is generally not feasible. We therefore require a method of sampling from $\mathbb{D}_{N,\mathbf{d}_+}$ *uniformly* and also, at least implicitly, estimating its size. The goal is to replace, for example, the exact p-value (4.11) with the simulation estimate

$$\hat{\Pr}\left(T\left(\mathbf{D}\right) \geq T\left(\mathbf{d}\right) | \mathbf{D} \in \mathbb{D}_{\mathbf{N},\mathbf{d}_+}\right) = \frac{1}{B}\sum_{b=1}^{B}\mathbf{1}\left(T\left(\mathbf{D}_b\right) \geq T\left(\mathbf{d}\right)\right), \qquad (4.15)$$

where $\mathbf{D}_b$ is a uniform random draw from $\mathbb{D}_{N,\mathbf{d}_+}$ and $B$ denotes the number of independent simulation draws selected by the researcher.

Two complications arise. First, it is not straightforward to construct a random draw from $\mathbb{D}_{N,\mathbf{d}_+}$. Second, we must draw *uniformly* from this set. Fortunately the first challenge is solvable using ideas from the discrete math literature. Researchers in graph theory and discrete math have studied the construction of graphs with fixed degrees and, in particular, provided conditions for checking whether a particular degree sequence is graphical (e.g., Sierksma and Hoogeveen, 1991). We say that $\mathbf{d}_+$ is *graphical* if there is feasible undirected network with degree sequence $\mathbf{d}_+$. Not all integer sequences are graphical. The reader can verify, for example, that there is no feasible undirected network of three agents with degree sequence $\mathbf{d}_+ = (3, 2, 1)$.

As for the second complication, although we cannot easily/directly construct a uniform random draw from $\mathbb{D}_{N,\mathbf{d}_+}$, we can use importance sampling (e.g., Owen, 2013) to estimate expectations with respect to this distribution.

The basic idea and implementation is due to Blitzstein and Diaconis (2011). A similar, and evidently independently derived, algorithm is presented in Del Genio et al. (2010). While computationally faster approaches are now available, we nevertheless present the method introduced by Blitzstein and Diaconis (2011) for its pedagogical value and easy implementation. Their approach is adequate for small to medium sized problems. Readers interested in applying the methods outlined below to large sparse graphs might consult Rao et al. (1996), McDonald et al. (2007) or Zhang and Chen (2013). Pelican and Graham (2019) introduce a more complicated MCMC simulation algorithm that holds additional graph statistics constant (besides the degree sequence). They also provide references to the fairly extensive literature on adjacency matrix simulation.

While our presentation of the Blitzstein and Diaconis (2011) algorithm is motivated by a particular formal testing problem, our view is that it is also useful for more informally finding "unusual" or "interesting" features of a given network. Are links more transitive than one would expect in networks with similar degree sequences? Is average path length exceptionally short? For this reason, the material presented below may also enter a researcher's workflow during the data summarization or exploratory analysis stage.

## The algorithm

A sequential network construction algorithm begins with a matrix of zeros and sequentially adds links to it until its rows and columns sum to the desired degree sequence. Unfortunately, unless the links are added appropriately, it is easy to get "stuck" (in the sense that at a certain point in the process it becomes impossible to reach a graph with the desired degree and the researcher must restart the process). The paper by Snijders (1991) provides examples and discussion of this phenomena.

As an example consider the graphical degree sequence $\mathbf{d}_+ = (2, 2, 1, 1)$. If we begin with an empty graph and add an edge between agents 3 and 4, we will go from the degree sequence $(2, 2, 1, 1)$ to a residual one of $(2, 2, 0, 0)$. Unfortunately $(2, 2, 0, 0)$ is not graphical. Adding more edges requires introducing self-loops or a double-edge, neither of which is allowed.

Intuitively we can avoid this phenomenon by first connecting high degree agents. Havel (1955) and Hakimi (1962) showed that this idea works for any degree sequence

**Theorem 4.1** (Havel–Hakimi). *Let $d_{i+} > 0$, if $\mathbf{d}_+$ does not have at least $d_{i+}$ positive entries other than $i$ it is not graphical. Assume this condition holds. Let $\tilde{\mathbf{d}}_+$ be a degree sequence of length $N - 1$ obtained by*
*[i] deleting the $i$th entry of $\mathbf{d}_+$ and*
*[ii] subtracting 1 from each of the $d_{i+}$ highest elements in $\mathbf{d}_+$ (aside from the $i$th one).*
*$\mathbf{d}_+$ is graphical if and only if $\tilde{\mathbf{d}}_+$ is graphical. If $\mathbf{d}_+$ is graphical, then it has a realization where agent $i$ is connected to any of the $d_{i+}$ highest degree agents (other than $i$).*

Theorem 4.1 gives a verifiable condition for whether a degree sequence is graphical. Blitzstein and Diaconis (2011) extended this condition so that we can check whether a degree sequence is graphical if one node is already connected to some other nodes. This modified condition serves as a tool in their importance sampling algorithm.

Theorem 4.1 is suggestive of a sequential approach to building an undirected network with degree sequence $\mathbf{d}_+$. The procedure begins with a target degree sequence $\mathbf{d}_+$. It starts by choosing a link partner for the lowest degree agent (with at least one link). It chooses a partner for this agent from among those with higher degree. A one is then subtracted from the lowest degree agent and her chosen partner's degrees. This procedure continues until the *residual degree sequence* (the sequence of links that remain to be chosen for each agent) is a vector of zeros.

**FIGURE 4.2** Cubic graph with six agents. *Notes:* Prism graph (a 3-regular graph) on six vertices. *Source:* Authors' calculations.

To formally describe such an approach we require some additional notation. Let $\left(\oplus_{i_1,\ldots,i_k} \mathbf{d}_+\right)$ be the vector obtained by adding a one to the $i_1, \ldots, i_k$ elements of $\mathbf{d}_+$:

$$\left(\oplus_{i_1,\ldots,i_k} \mathbf{d}_+\right)_j = \begin{cases} d_{j+} + 1 & \text{for } j \in \{i_1, \ldots, i_k\}, \\ d_{j+} & \text{otherwise.} \end{cases}$$

Let $\left(\ominus_{i_1,\ldots,i_k} \mathbf{d}_+\right)$ be the vector obtained by subtracting one from the $i_1, \ldots, i_k$ elements of $\mathbf{d}_+$:

$$\left(\ominus_{i_1,\ldots,i_k} \mathbf{d}_+\right)_j = \begin{cases} d_{j+} - 1 & \text{for } j \in \{i_1, \ldots, i_k\}, \\ d_{j+} & \text{otherwise.} \end{cases}$$

**Algorithm 4.1** (Blitzstein and Diaconis). *A sequential algorithm for constructing a random graph with degree sequence* $\mathbf{d}_+ = (d_{1+}, \ldots, d_{N+})'$ *is*

1. Let $\mathbf{D}$ be an empty adjacency matrix.
2. If $\mathbf{d}_+ = \mathbf{0}$ terminate with output $\mathbf{D}$.
3. Choose the agent $i$ with minimal positive degree $d_{i+}$.
4. Construct a list of candidate partners $\mathcal{J} = \left\{ j \neq i : D_{ij} = D_{ji} = 0 \text{ and } \ominus_{i,j} \mathbf{d}_+ \text{ graphical} \right\}$.
5. Pick a partner $j \in \mathcal{J}$ with probability proportional to its degree in $\mathbf{d}_+$.
6. Set $D_{ij} = D_{ji} = 1$ and update $\mathbf{d}_+$ to $\ominus_{i,j} \mathbf{d}_+$.
7. Repeat steps 4 to 6 until the degree of agent $i$ is zero.
8. Return to step 2.

The input for Algorithm 4.1 is the target degree sequence $\mathbf{d}_+$ and the output is an undirected adjacency matrix $\mathbf{D} \in \mathbb{D}_{\mathbf{N},\mathbf{d}_+}$ (i.e., with $\mathbf{D}'\iota = \mathbf{d}_+$).[4] Consider the 3-regular (i.e., cubic graph) depicted in Fig. 4.2. Each agent in this graph has exactly three links such that its degree sequence equals $(3, 3, 3, 3, 3, 3)$. In turns out that there are two non-isomorphic cubic graphs on six vertices: the prism graph, shown in the figure, and the utility graph (or complete bipartite graph on two sets of three vertices). We can use Algorithm 4.1 to generate a random draw from the set of all graphs with a degree sequence of $\mathbf{d}_+ = (3, 3, 3, 3, 3, 3)$.

---

[4] Here $\iota$ denotes a conformable column vector of ones.

As an example of a series of residual degree sequences (updated in Step 6 of the algorithm) associated with a random draw from $\mathbb{D}_{N,d_+}$, for $N = 6$ and $d_+ = (3, 3, 3, 3, 3, 3)$, consider:

$$(3, 3, 3, 3, 3, 3) \rightarrow (2, 2, 3, 3, 3, 3) \rightarrow (1, 2, 3, 3, 2, 3) \rightarrow (0, 2, 2, 3, 2, 3)$$
$$\rightarrow (0, 1, 2, 3, 2, 2) \rightarrow (0, 0, 2, 2, 2, 2) \rightarrow (0, 0, 1, 2, 1, 2)$$
$$\rightarrow (0, 0, 0, 2, 1, 1) \rightarrow (0, 0, 0, 1, 0, 1) \rightarrow (0, 0, 0, 0, 0, 0).$$

Labeling agents $i = 0, 1, \ldots, 5$ from left-to-right we can see that the first link is added between agents 0 and 1 (the "active" node's residual degree is bold-faced above). This is illustrated in Fig. 4.3, which begins with the labeled empty graph in the upper-left-hand corner and then sequentially adds links as we move from left-to-right and top-to-bottom. Next a link is added between agents 0 and 4, and then between agents 0 and 2. Observe that the algorithm selected agent 0 as the lowest degree agent in the initial step and continues to connect this vertex with higher degree ones until all needed edges incident to it are present.[5]

In the eighth iteration of the algorithm an edge is added between agents 3 and 4. If, instead, an edge was added between agents 4 and 5 at this point, the residual sequence degree sequence would have been updated to $(0, 0, 0, 2, 0, 0)$, which is not graphic. Step 4 of the algorithm prevents the addition of edges which, if added, lead to non-graphic degree sequences. It is in this way that the algorithm avoids getting "stuck". Getting stuck was a problem with earlier approaches to binary matrix simulation, such as the method of Snijders (1991).

### Importance sampling

Algorithm 4.1 produces a random draw from $\mathbb{D}_{N,d_+}$, however, it does not draw from this set uniformly. A key insight of Blitzstein and Diaconis (2011) is that one can construct importance sampling weights to correct for non-uniformity of the draws from $\mathbb{D}_{N,d_+}$.

Let $\mathbb{Y}_{N,d_+}$ denote the set of all possible sequences of links outputted by Algorithm 4.1 given input $d_+$. Let $\mathcal{D}(Y)$ be the adjacency matrix induced by link sequence $Y$. Let $Y$ and $Y'$ be two different sequences produced by the algorithm. These sequences are equivalent if their "end point" adjacency matrices coincide (i.e., if $\mathcal{D}(Y) = \mathcal{D}(Y')$). We can partition $\mathbb{Y}_{N,d_+}$ into a set of equivalence classes, the number of such classes coincides with the number of feasible networks with degree distribution $d_+$ (i.e., with the cardinality of $\mathbb{D}_{N,d_+}$).

Let $c(Y)$ denote the number of possible link sequences produced by Algorithm 4.1 that produce $Y$'s end point adjacency matrix (i.e., the number of different ways in which Algorithm 4.1 can generate a given adjacency matrix).

---

[5] In the event of ties for the lowest degree agent, the algorithm chooses the one with the lowest index.

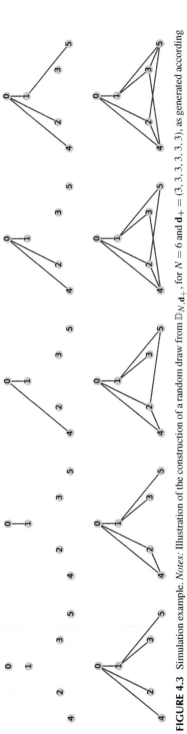

**FIGURE 4.3** Simulation example. *Notes:* Illustration of the construction of a random draw from $\mathbb{D}_{N,\mathbf{d}_+}$, for $N = 6$ and $\mathbf{d}_+ = (3, 3, 3, 3, 3, 3)$, as generated according to Algorithm 4.1. *Source:* Authors' calculations.

Let $i_1, i_2, \ldots, i_M$ be the sequence of agents chosen in step 3 of Algorithm 4.1 in which $Y$ is the output. Let $a_1, \ldots, a_m$ be the degree sequences of $i_1, \ldots, i_M$ at the time when each agent was first selected in step 3, then

$$c\,(Y) = \prod_{k=1}^{M} a_k!. \tag{4.16}$$

To see why (4.16) holds consider two equivalent link sequences $Y$ and $Y'$. Because links are added to vertices by minimal degree (see Step 3 of Algorithm 4.1), the agent sequences $i_1, i_2, \ldots, i_M$ coincide for $Y$ and $Y'$. This, in turn, means that *the exact same links*, perhaps in a different order, are added at each "stage" of the algorithm (i.e., when the algorithm iterates through steps 4 to 7 repeatedly for a given agent). The number of different ways to add agent $i_k$'s links during such a "stage" is simply $a_k!$ and hence (4.16) follows.

The second component needed to construct importance weights is $\sigma\,(Y)$, the probability that Algorithm 4.1 produces link sequence $Y$. This probability is easy to compute. Each time the algorithm chooses a link in step 5 we simply record the probability with which it was chosen (i.e., the residual degree of the chosen agent divided by the sum of the residual degrees of all agents in the choice set). The product of all these probabilities equals $\sigma\,(Y)$.

With $c\,(Y)$ and $\sigma\,(Y)$ defined we can now show how to estimate expectations with respect to uniform draws from $\mathbb{D}_{N,\mathbf{d}_+}$. Let $T\,(\mathbf{D})$ be some statistic of the adjacency matrix. Here for $\mathbf{D}$ is a draw from $\mathbb{D}_{N,\mathbf{d}_+}$ constructed using Algorithm 4.1. Consider the p-value estimation problem discussed earlier:

$$\mathbb{E}\left[\frac{\pi\,(\mathcal{D}\,(Y))}{c\,(Y)\,\sigma\,(Y)}\mathbf{1}\,(T\,(\mathcal{D}\,(Y)) > T\,(\mathbf{d}))\right]$$

$$= \sum_{y \in \mathbb{Y}_{N,\mathbf{d}}} \frac{\pi\,(\mathcal{D}\,(y))}{c\,(y)\,\sigma\,(y)}\mathbf{1}\,(T\,(\mathcal{D}\,(y)) > T\,(\mathbf{d}))\,\sigma\,(y)$$

$$= \sum_{y \in \mathbb{Y}_{N,\mathbf{d}}} \frac{\pi\,(\mathcal{D}\,(y))}{c\,(y)}\mathbf{1}\,(T\,(\mathcal{D}\,(y)) > T\,(\mathbf{d}))$$

$$= \sum_{\mathbf{D} \in \mathbb{D}_{N,\mathbf{d}_+}} \sum_{\{y\,:\,\mathcal{D}(y)=\mathbf{D}\}} \frac{\pi\,(\mathbf{D})}{c\,(y)}\mathbf{1}\,(T\,(\mathbf{D}) > T\,(\mathbf{d}))$$

$$= \sum_{\mathbf{D} \in \mathbb{D}_{N,\mathbf{d}_+}} \pi\,(\mathbf{D})\,\mathbf{1}\,(T\,(\mathbf{D}) > T\,(\mathbf{d}))$$

$$= \mathbb{E}_{\pi}\,[\mathbf{1}\,(T\,(\mathbf{D}) > T\,(\mathbf{d}))].$$

Here $\pi\,(\mathbf{D})$ is the probability attached to the adjacency matrix $\mathbf{D} \in \mathbb{D}_{N,\mathbf{d}_+}$ in the target distribution over $\mathbb{D}_{N,\mathbf{d}_+}$. The ratio $\pi\,(\mathcal{D}\,(Y))\,/c\,(Y)\,\sigma\,(Y)$ is called the likelihood ratio or the *importance weight*. We would like $\pi(\mathbf{D}) = 1 / |\mathbb{D}_{N,\mathbf{d}_+}|$ for all $\mathbf{D} \in \mathbb{D}_{N,\mathbf{d}_+}$.

Observe that $\mathbb{E}_\pi [T(\mathcal{D}(Y))] = \mathbb{E}\left[\frac{\pi(\mathcal{D}(Y))}{c(Y)\sigma(Y)} T(\mathcal{D}(Y))\right]$; setting $\pi(\mathcal{D}(Y)) = |\mathbb{D}_{N,\mathbf{d}_+}|^{-1}$ and $T(\mathcal{D}(Y)) = 1$ to the constant statistic, then suggests an estimate of $|\mathbb{D}_{N,\mathbf{d}_+}|$ equal to

$$|\mathbb{D}_{N,\mathbf{d}_+}^{\hat{}}| = \left[\frac{1}{B} \sum_{b=1}^{B} \frac{1}{c(Y_b)\sigma(Y_b)}\right], \quad (4.17)$$

and hence a p-value estimate of

$$\hat{\rho}_{T(\mathbf{G})} = \left[\frac{1}{B} \sum_{b=1}^{B} \frac{1}{c(Y_b)\sigma(Y_b)}\right]^{-1}$$

$$\times \left[\frac{1}{B} \sum_{b=1}^{B} \frac{1}{c(Y_b)\sigma(Y_b)} \mathbf{1}(T(\mathbf{D}_b) > T(\mathbf{d}))\right]. \quad (4.18)$$

An attractive feature of (4.18) is that the importance weights need only be estimated up to a constant. This feature is useful when dealing with numerical overflow issues that can arise when $|\mathbb{D}_{N,\mathbf{d}_+}|$ is too large to estimate.

Algorithm (4.1) is appropriate for simulating undirected networks. Recently Kim et al. (2012) propose a method for simulating from directed networks with both fixed indegree and outdegree sequences. Their methods is based on an extension of Havel–Hakimi type results to digraphs due to Erdös et al. (2010). Pelican and Graham (2019) introduce an MCMC algorithm for simulating digraphs satisfying various side constraints.

## Illustration using the Nyakatoke network

Fig. 4.1 plots the Nyakatoke risk-sharing network introduced earlier. The transitivity index for the Nyakatoke network, at 0.1884, is almost three times its associated network density of 0.0698. Is this excess transitivity simply a product of degree heterogeneity alone? To assess this we used Algorithm 4.1 to take 5,000 draws from the set of adjacency matrices with $N = 119$ and degree sequences coinciding with the one observed in Nyakatoke (for reference the Nyakatoke degree distribution is plotted in Fig. 4.4).

Fig. 4.5 displays estimates of the distribution of two star and triangle counts, as well as the transitivity index (and "optimal" transitivity statistic), with respect to the distribution of uniform draws from $\mathbb{D}_{N,\mathbf{d}_+}$ ($N = 119$ and $\mathbf{d}_+$ coinciding with the one observed in Nyakatoke). Measured transitivity is Nyakatoke is extreme relative to this reference distribution. This suggests that clustering of links is, in fact, a special feature of the Nyakatoke network. It is also interesting to note that the distribution of transitivity in this reference distribution is

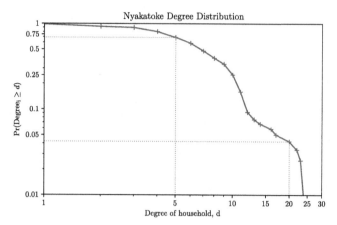

**FIGURE 4.4** Nyakatoke degree distribution. *Notes:* This figure plots the probability (vertical axis) that a random household in Nyakatoke has strictly more risk sharing links than listed on the horizontal axis. *Source:* De Weerdt (2004) and authors' calculations. Raw data available at https://www.uantwerpen.be/en/staff/joachim-deweerdt/ (Accessed January 2017).

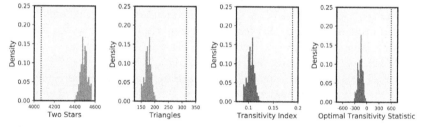

**FIGURE 4.5** Reference distribution of transitivity index for Nyakatoke network. *Notes:* Histogram of two star counts, triangle counts and transitivity index values across 5,000 draws from $\mathbb{D}_{N,\mathbf{d}_+}$ ($N = 119$ and $\mathbf{d}_+$ coinciding with the one observed in Nyakatoke). The final figure plots the distribution of the "optimal" transitivity statistic given in Eq. (4.13). *Source:* De Weerdt (2004) and authors' calculations. Raw data available at https://www.uantwerpen.be/en/staff/joachim-deweerdt/ (Accessed January 2017).

well to the right of 0.0698 (the density of all graphs in the reference distribution). The skewed degree distribution in Nyakatoke forces a certain amount of transitivity, since high degree nodes are more likely to link with one another. This highlights the value of a test which proceeds conditionally on the degree sequence.

Fig. 4.6 displays estimates of the distribution of network diameter and average distance. Nyakatoke's diameter is not atypical across networks with the same degree sequence. However, average distance is significantly longer in Nyakatoke. One interpretation of this fact is that the Nyakatoke includes a distinct periphery of poorly connected/insured households.

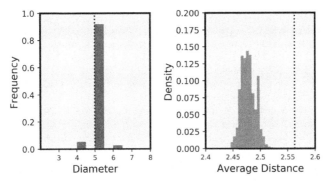

**FIGURE 4.6** Reference distribution of network diameter and average distance for Nyakatoke network. *Notes:* Histogram of values network diameter and average distance across 5,000 draws from $\mathbb{D}_{N,\mathbf{d}_+}$ ($N = 119$ and $\mathbf{d}_+$ coinciding with the one observed in Nyakatoke). *Source:* De Weerdt (2004) and authors' calculations. Raw data available at https://www.uantwerpen.be/en/staff/joachim-deweerdt/ (Accessed January 2017).

# References

Blitzstein, J., Diaconis, P., 2011. A sequential importance sampling algorithm for generating random graphs with prescribed degrees. Internet Mathematics 6 (4), 489–522.

Bloch, F., Jackson, M.O., 2006. Definitions of equilibrium in network formation games. International Journal of Game Theory 34 (3), 305–318.

Bloch, F., Jackson, M.O., 2007. The formation of networks with transfers among players. Journal of Economic Theory 113 (1), 83–110.

Chatterjee, S., Diaconis, P., Sly, A., 2011. Random graphs with a given degree sequence. The Annals of Applied Probability 21 (4), 1400–1435.

Comola, M., Fafchamps, M., 2014. Testing unilateral and bilateral link formation. The Economic Journal 124 (579), 954–976.

Cox, D.R., 2006. Principles of Statistical Inference. Cambridge University Press, Cambridge.

De Weerdt, J., 2004. Risk-sharing and endogenous network formation. In: Insurance Against Poverty. Oxford University Press, Oxford, pp. 197–216.

Del Genio, C.I., Kim, H., Toroczkai, Z., Bassler, K., 2010. Efficient and exact sampling of simple graphs with given arbitrary degree sequence. PLoS ONE 5 (4), e100012.

Erdös, P.L., Mikos, I., Toroczkai, Z., 2010. A simple Havel–Hakimi type algorithm to realize graphical degree sequences of directed graphs. The Electronic Journal of Combinatorics 17 (1), R66.

Ferguson, T.S., 1967. Mathematical Statistics: A Decision Theoretic Approach. Academic Press, New York.

Fisher, R.A., 1935. The Design of Experiments. Oliver and Boyd, Edinburgh.

Graham, B.S., 2016. Homophily and Transitivity in Dynamic Network Formation. NBER Working Paper 22186. National Bureau of Economic Research.

Graham, B.S., 2017. An econometric model of network formation with degree heterogeneity. Econometrica 85 (4), 1033–1063.

Hakimi, S.L., 1962. On realizability of a set of integers as degrees of the vertices of a linear graph. I. Journal of the Society for Industrial and Applied Mathematics 10 (3), 496–506.

Havel, V.J., 1955. A remark on the existence of finite graph. Časopis Pro Pěstování Matematiky 80, 477–480.

Jackson, M.O., 2008. Social and Economic Networks. Princeton University Press, Princeton.

Jackson, M.O., Rodriguez-Barraquer, T., Tan, X., 2012. Social capital and social quilts: network patterns of favor exchange. The American Economic Review 102 (5), 1857–1897.

Kim, H., Del Genio, C.I., Bassler, K.E., Toroczkai, Z., 2012. Constructing and sampling directed graphs with given degree sequences. New Journal of Physics 14, 023012.

Lehmann, E.L., Romano, J.P., 2005. Testing Statistical Hypotheses, 3rd edition. Springer, New York.

McDonald, J.W., Smith, P.W.F., Forster, J.J., 2007. Markov chain Monte Carlo exact inference for social networks. Social Networks 29 (1), 127–136.

McPherson, M., Smith-Lovin, L., Cook, J.M., 2001. Birds of a feather: homophily in social networks. Annual Review of Sociology 27 (1), 415–444.

Milo, R., Shen-Orr, S., Itzkovitz, S., Kashtan, N., Chklovskii, D., Alon, U., 2002. Network motifs: simple building blocks of complex networks. Science 298 (5594), 824–827.

Miyauchi, Y., 2016. Structural estimation of a pairwise stable network with nonnegative externality. Journal of Econometrics 195 (2), 224–235.

Moreira, M.J., 2009. Tests with correct size when instruments can be arbitrarily weak. Journal of Econometrics 152 (2), 131–140.

Owen, A.B., 2013. Monte Carlo Theory, Methods and Examples. Book manuscript.

Pelican, A., Graham, B.S., 2019. Testing for Strategic Interaction in Social and Economic Network Formation. Technical report. University of California, Berkeley.

Rao, A.R., Jana, R., Bandyopadhyay, S., 1996. A Markov chain Monte Carlo method for generating random (0, 1)-matrices with given marginals. Sankhya 58 (2), 225–242.

Sierksma, G., Hoogeveen, H., 1991. Seven criteria for integer sequences being graphic. Journal of Graph Theory 15 (2), 223–231.

Snijders, T.A.B., 1991. Enumeration and simulation methods for 0-1 matrices with given marginals. Psychometrika 56 (3), 397–417.

Tarski, A., 1955. A lattice-theoretical fixpoint theorem and its applications. Pacific Journal of Mathematics 5 (2), 285–309.

Zhang, J., Chen, Y., 2013. Sampling for conditional inference on network data. Journal of the American Statistical Association 108 (504), 1295–1307.

Chapter 5

# Econometric analysis of bipartite networks<sup>☆</sup>

## Stéphane Bonhomme
*University of Chicago, Chicago, IL, United States*

## Contents

## 5.1 Introduction

In bipartite networks, two types of agents interact with each other. Bipartite structures arise in many economic settings, including (but not limited to) interactions between buyers and sellers, firms and banks, workers and their employers, or exporters and importers.

A key feature of network data is the presence of unobserved heterogeneity. In bipartite networks, heterogeneity is two-sided. As a result, econometric models are more complex than single-agent models. At the same time, methods from single-agent analysis, particularly panel data analysis, are closely related to

☆ To appear in *The Econometric Analysis of Network Data*, edited by Bryan Graham and Aureo de Paula. I thank the editors, Jeremy Fox, Thibaut Lamadon and Elena Manresa for insightful comments.

those used in bipartite networks. We will make use of this connection throughout the paper.[1]

We start our review with a linear model of outcome variables which is conditional on the realized network. The underlying assumption is one of *network exogeneity*. This requires links between agents to be independent of potential outcomes, conditional on observed covariates and unobserved agent-specific heterogeneity. This assumption may or may not be plausible in applications. A recurring theme of this paper is the importance of the underlying assumptions on the network structure.

In a simple, "canonical" linear model for bipartite networks we review two general approaches. The first approach is by *two-way fixed effects*. This approach was pioneered by Abowd et al. (1999) in the context of wage regressions on matched employer-employee data. In linear models, a fixed-effect approach provides a tractable, regression-based approach to allow for two-sided unobserved heterogeneity. The "AKM" method has been extensively applied to networks of workers and firms, and also to other bipartite settings.[2]

The performance of fixed-effect estimators depends on the number of existing connections between agents in the network. This point was first made in Abowd et al. (2004) and Andrews et al. (2008), and it was recently formalized in Jochmans and Weidner (2016). In sparsely connected networks, fixed-effect estimators suffer from an incidental parameter bias due to the fixed effects being estimated based on few observations. This bias is similar to the one arising in single-agent panel data estimators in short panels (Nickell, 1981).

An alternative approach to allow for unobserved heterogeneity is to model the conditional distribution of agent-specific effects given the network and exogenous covariates, in a two-sided *correlated random-effect* fashion (Chamberlain, 1980). In bipartite settings, specifying the conditional distribution of unobserved heterogeneity given the network can be challenging, however. One approach is to assume independence of the network, as in the "mixed models" literature in statistics. Woodcock (2008, 2011) developed such an approach in the context of matched employer-employee data. Consistency of the estimator in this approach relies on the number of connections per agent being large, similarly to the AKM method. A different approach to allow for dependence between agent heterogeneity and the network structure is to explicitly model network formation. The advantage of such an approach where links and outcomes are jointly modeled is that it still delivers consistent estimates in sparsely connected networks under correct specification.

---

[1] While we focus on bipartite networks, many of the methods reviewed in this paper can be extended to deal with general multi-partite networks where more than two types of agents interact.

[2] See for example Card et al. (2013), Song et al. (2015), Card et al. (2016), and Helpman et al. (2016), among many others, for applications to employer-employee data. In other settings, Kramarz et al. (2015a) apply the method to study of students' sorting across schools, Finkelstein et al. (2014) study sorting of patients across hospitals, and Kramarz et al. (2015b) apply the AKM method to a network of exporters and importers.

An intermediate approach between fixed effects and two-sided random effects is by *one-sided random effects*. This method consists in conditioning on the side of the network where agents have a relatively large number of links (e.g., firms) using agent-specific fixed effects, while modeling the distribution of unobservables on the other, less well-connected side of the network (e.g., workers) through a correlated random-effect specification. Such an approach was recently developed for matched employer-employee panel data by Bonhomme et al. (2019). In such settings, the one-sided random-effect approach allows for consistent estimation in short panels, while preserving the tractability of single-agent models.

*Nonlinear* models of bipartite networks are often of great interest in economics. Nonlinearity may be directly motivated by economic theory. Allowing for interactions between agent-specific heterogeneity (e.g., between firm and worker heterogeneity) is key in order to capture complementaries and other features of production functions. As an example, the large theoretical and structural literature on sorting models dating back to Becker (1973) emphasizes that the structure of production has important implications on the effects of reallocations. In the many-to-many settings we consider in this paper one may assess the effects of re-allocating inputs which are *not* observed to the econometrician (such as unobserved types). This extends the scope of re-allocation effects previously studied in one-to-one settings (Graham et al., 2014).

In nonlinear models which satisfy a network exogeneity condition, identification may be established under conditional independence assumptions. Allowing for two-sided unobserved heterogeneity requires restricting the amount of dependence across links. We review nonparametric identification results for two-sided random-effect specifications (Allman et al., 2009, 2011) and one-sided random-effect specifications (Bonhomme et al., 2019).[3]

In nonlinear settings the large number of parameters involved makes estimation challenging. Although both fixed-effect and random-effect methods are conceptually easy to extend to nonlinear models, they may not be tractable in data sets of sizes typically encountered in applications. In such settings, estimation approaches based on *discrete unobserved heterogeneity* may offer tractable alternatives through a reduction of dimensionality. We review several approaches based on discrete heterogeneity: finite mixture methods, and one-sided and two-sided classification methods which generalize the *k-means* clustering algorithm to bipartite network data.

In the last part of the paper we review approaches aimed at allowing for *network endogeneity*. Work on this important topic is still scarce, so our discussion is necessarily brief. Endogenizing the network structure requires modeling the process of link formation, and thus requires taking an explicit stand on economic decisions. We illustrate how existing methods for bipartite networks can

---

[3] The identification conditions and arguments are closely related to those used in the literature on nonlinear measurement error models; see Hu (2015) for a recent survey.

be extended to allow for network endogeneity in a simple static model of network formation without network externalities. We also review several dynamic models of mobility decisions which have recently been proposed in employer-employee settings. A common feature of these approaches is the need for exclusion restrictions for identification, such as the availability of cost shifters or dynamic panel data restrictions.

### Scope of the paper and outline

There is a large literature on one-to-one matching problems in bipartite graphs, both under transferable and under non-transferable utility. Important theoretical contributions are Gale and Shapley (1962), Shapley and Shubik (1954), and Becker (1973). Recent empirical work has built on these models, see Choo and Siow (2006), Galichon and Salanié (2015), and Chiappori et al. (2015), among others. See also the reviews by Graham (2011) and Chiappori and Salanié (2015).

This paper focuses on many-to-many matching settings where agents on both sides of the network have multiple links to agents on the other side. While many-to-one and many-to-many matching models have been studied theoretically (see, e.g., Roth and Sotomayor, 1992), empirical work on these problems is less developed. Fox (2010) develops the idea of rank order inequalities, and studies a maximum score estimator for matching with applications beyond one-to-one settings. Fox (2016) considers a general setup with transferable utility, which contains as special cases the one-to-one marriage model but also many-to-many matching games with transfers.

Our focus is on settings where an output (or transfer) of the match is observed to the researcher. As in Graham et al. (2014, 2016), an advantage of this configuration is that the researcher need not take a stand on the specifics of network formation, provided a conditional independence assumption ensuring network exogeneity holds (although we also consider relaxing this assumption in the final section of the paper). However, in contrast to Graham et al. we focus on many-to-many matching settings. Unlike in one-to-one matching settings, the availability of multiple links per agent provides an opportunity to separately identify agent-specific heterogeneity and match-specific heterogeneity. The difference is analogous to the one between cross-sectional response models (e.g., Matzkin, 2013) and panel data response models (e.g., Arellano and Bonhomme, 2011).

The outline of the paper is as follows. In Section 5.2 we introduce a baseline linear model for an exogenous bipartite network, and we review fixed-effect and random-effect methods in this setting. In Section 5.3 we extend the analysis to nonlinear models. In Section 5.4 we review estimation methods. In Section 5.5 we review approaches to allow for endogenous network formation. Lastly, we conclude in Section 5.6 with some directions for future work.

## 5.2 Bipartite network models: the linear case

We start by describing a linear model of outcomes which is conditional on an exogenous network. In this setting we review two complementary approaches to estimation: fixed-effect and random-effect approaches.

### 5.2.1 Bipartite networks

Following standard terminology (e.g., Lovász and Plummer, 2009), a *graph* denotes a set of *points* (or "vertices") $V$, and *lines* (or "edges") $E$ which connect two points in $V$. We will refer to lines in $E$ alternatively as "links" or "matches". Note that two points may be connected by several lines. In this paper we focus on undirected graphs, which are common in economic applications.

A *bipartite graph* is a graph where the set of points $V$ is partitioned into two sets, $V_1$ and $V_2$, such that all lines in $E$ connect a point in $V_1$ to a point in $V_2$. In other words, there are no lines connecting two points in $V_1$, nor are there lines connecting two points in $V_2$. In economic applications, $V_1$ and $V_2$ typically correspond to different types of agents (e.g., firms and workers). Let $i = 1, ..., N$ denote agents in $V_1$ and $j = 1, ..., J$ denote agents in $V_2$. Fig. 5.1 provides an example. There are 5 agents in $V_1$, 4 in $V_2$, for a total of 9 links. Depending of the application, pairs of agents (e.g., $(i, j) = (1, 1)$) could be connected through multiple links, as in Example 1 below.

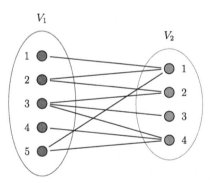

**FIGURE 5.1** A bipartite graph.

A *bipartite network* is a bipartite graph $\{V_1, V_2, E\}$, where points and lines in the graph are associated with random variables. We denote the presence of one or several links between $i$ and $j$ as $D_{ijt} = 1$, where $t = 1, ..., T$. Here $t$ accounts for the possibility of repeated or multiple links between the same pair of agents. This may happen over time or across markets, for example. $T$ is the maximum number of links connecting a pair of agents. Several configurations are possible: $T$ may be equal to one (cross-sectional bipartite graph), greater than one but small (short bipartite panel), or large (long bipartite panel).

It is assumed that match-specific outcomes $Y_{ijt}$ are observed whenever $D_{ijt} = 1$. $Y_{ijt}$ may correspond to an output of the match or to a transfer between agents. Outcome variables depend on observed characteristics $X_{ijt}$, which may include agents' characteristics or characteristics of the match $(i, j, t)$, and on unobserved characteristics $\alpha_i$, $\psi_j$, and $\varepsilon_{ijt}$, the latter denoting unobserved characteristics of the match.[4] A key feature of the setup is the presence of two-sided agent-specific unobserved heterogeneity $(\alpha, \psi)$. In the following we will refer to $i$ as workers and $j$ as firms, respectively, although bipartite network structures arise in a number of other settings and the methods we review apply generally.

We will first analyze bipartite network models under the assumption that the network is *exogenous*, where the existence of a link $(i, j, t)$ (that is, the realization of $D_{ijt}$) is independent of all match-specific shocks $\varepsilon$ conditional on observed heterogeneity (the $X$) and unobserved heterogeneity (the $\alpha$ and $\psi$).[5] Under this assumption it is natural to directly model the joint distribution of realized outcomes *conditional* on heterogeneity and the structure of the network $(\alpha, \psi, X, D)$. In contrast, endogenizing link formation requires modeling the joint distribution of potential outcomes *and* links; see Section 5.5.

Another important feature of network models is the dependence structure of the data, and in particular the $\varepsilon$. A possible starting point, which we will adopt, is to assume that outcomes are mutually independent across $(i, j)$ pairs given the conditioning variables $X$, $\alpha$, $\psi$, and $D$. Serial dependence across repeated links or multiple markets may be allowed for. However, it is generally not possible to leave the dependence structure of the $\varepsilon$ fully unrestricted.

### Linear model

As a leading example, let us consider the following additive model with two-sided heterogeneity:

$$Y_{ijt}^* = X_{ijt}'\beta + \alpha_i + \psi_j + \varepsilon_{ijt}. \tag{5.1}$$

Here $Y_{ijt}^*$ are *potential outcomes* that are realized if a link $(i, j, t)$ exists. Let $Y_{ijt} = D_{ijt}Y_{ijt}^*$ be the observed outcomes, so $Y_{ijt}$ and $Y_{ijt}^*$ coincide when $D_{ijt} = 1$.[6] Note that the potential outcome in match $(i, j, t)$ only depends on the $\alpha$ and $\psi$ through $\alpha_i$ and $\psi_j$, an assumption of *lack of spillovers* which we will maintain in most of this paper.

In this model, a common assumption is the following:

$$\mathbb{E}\left[\varepsilon_{ijt} \mid D, X, \alpha, \psi\right] = 0, \tag{5.2}$$

---

[4] Note that the "1" subscripts in $\alpha_1$ and $\psi_1$ refer to different agents. In order to remove this ambiguity an alternative notation could be $(\alpha_i, \psi^j)$ instead of $(\alpha_i, \psi_j)$.

[5] Mean independence suffices in linear models, as we shall see.

[6] Note that $X_{ijt}$ might also be *potential* covariates, depending of link formation. For example, in a network of workers and firms, $X_{ijt}$ could be the seniority of worker $i$ in firm $j$ in period $t$. Here we focus on strictly exogenous covariates and assume that $X_{ijt}$ are always observed, irrespective of the existence of a link $(i, j, t)$.

where $D$, $X$, $\alpha$, and $\psi$ denote the sequences of all $D_{ijt}$, $X_{ijt}$, $\alpha_i$, and $\psi_j$, respectively. Assumption (5.2) states that covariates $X$ are strictly exogenous, and importantly that the existence of links $D$ is strictly exogenous as well. This allows one to analyze the model *conditional on D* using simple regression techniques, as we shall see in the next subsection. In contrast, allowing for dependence between link indicators $D$ and match-specific shocks $\varepsilon$ would be more challenging as this would require specifying a joint model for $Y^*$ and $D$.

### Example 1: matched employer-employee data

Longitudinal data sets with both worker and firm identifiers have a bipartite network structure. Abowd et al. (1999) pioneered the analysis of matched employer-employee data sets. In this setting, $D_{ijt}$ denotes the fact that worker $i$ is employed by firm $j$ in period $t$. As an example, Fig. 5.1 may represent a balanced employer-employee panel with $T = 3$, worker $i = 1$ being employed by firm 1 in all three periods, worker 2 moving between firm 1 to firm 2, and so on. In this case the graph is weighted by the number of links between pairs of agents and their time occurrence.

### Example 2: buyer/seller network

More generally, data sets involving buyers and sellers on different sides of a market have a bipartite network structure. Buyer/seller networks have often been studied in one-to-one matching settings (e.g., Kranton and Minehart, 2001, Donna et al., 2015). However, empirical buyer/seller networks often feature multiple or repeated *realized* links between agents. For example this is the case of the importer/exporter network data analyzed in Kramarz et al. (2015b).

### 5.2.2   Fixed effects: the AKM estimator

Let us consider the additive model (5.1). Assuming that (5.2) holds, we have

$$\mathbb{E}\left(Y_{ijt}^* \mid D, X, \alpha, \psi\right) = X_{ijt}'\beta + \alpha_i + \psi_j. \tag{5.3}$$

It is useful to write (5.3) in matrix form. Let $\widetilde{X}$ denote the matrix with $NJT$ rows stacking the $X_{ijt}'$, and $\widetilde{A}$ and $\widetilde{B}$ be the $NJT \times N$ and $NJT \times J$ matrices stacking $i$ and $j$ indicators, respectively. Denoting as $Y^*$ a stacked $NJT \times 1$ vector, (5.3) may be written as

$$\mathbb{E}\left(Y^* \mid D, X, \alpha, \psi\right) = \widetilde{X}\beta + \widetilde{A}\alpha + \widetilde{B}\psi.$$

In order to see the observational implications of (5.3), let $L = \sum_{i,j,t} D_{ijt}$ denote the total number of links, and let $S$ be the $L \times NJT$ selection matrix which selects the elements of $Y^*$ corresponding to existing links. Hence $Y =$

$SY^*$ is the $L \times 1$ vector of observed outcomes for the links corresponding to $D_{ijt} = 1$. Moreover, denoting $X = S\widetilde{X}$, $A = S\widetilde{A}$, and $B = S\widetilde{B}$, we have

$$\mathbb{E}\,(Y \mid D, X, \alpha, \psi) = X\beta + A\alpha + B\psi, \qquad (5.4)$$

where $A$ and $B$ are functions of the $D_{ijt}$.

In (5.4) $\beta$ may be consistently estimated using a differencing strategy. To see this, consider a projection matrix $C$, function of $A$ and $B$, such that $CA = 0$ and $CB = 0$. Specifically, letting $G = [A\ B]$, take the "within" projection matrix $C = I - GG^\dagger$, with $G^\dagger$ the Moore–Penrose generalized inverse of $G$, and $I$ a conformable identity matrix. As $C$ is a projection matrix, it is symmetric and idempotent, i.e. $C' = C$ and $CC = C$. Pre-multiplying (5.4) by $C$ and taking expectations then yields

$$\mathbb{E}\,(C\,(Y - X\beta) \mid D, X) = 0. \qquad (5.5)$$

Under standard conditions (in particular $CX$ being full column rank) $\beta$ may be consistently estimated by regressing $CY$ on the columns of $CX$, that is, $\widehat{\beta} = \left(X'CX\right)^{-1} X'CY$.

Assuming that $\beta$, or a consistent estimate of it, is available, let us now focus on the simpler model

$$\mathbb{E}\,(Y \mid D, \alpha, \psi) = A\alpha + B\psi, \qquad (5.6)$$

where $Y$ is to be understood in deviation from $X\beta$. Since (5.6) is linear in the $\alpha$ and $\psi$, worker- and firm-specific effects are identified provided the design matrix $G = [A\ B]$ be full column rank. As discussed in detail in Abowd et al. (1999) and Abowd, Creecy and Kramarz (2002), ensuring complete rank requires focusing on a *connected component* of the bipartite graph, containing all workers who ever work in a firm of that component, and all firms ever employing a worker of that component. Based on this definition, it is easy to see that the graph in Fig. 5.1 is connected, for example. Intuitively, the $\alpha$ and $\psi$ in two different connected components cannot be related to each other since agents in those components do not share any (direct or indirect) links.

A simple algorithm to obtain all connected components in a bipartite graph is as follows (Abowd et al., 2002):

*For c = 1, ..., repeat until no firm remains:*
*The first firm not assigned to a component is in component c.*
*Repeat until no more firms or persons are added to component c:*
*Add all persons employed by a firm in c to component c.*
*Add all firms that have employed a person in c to component c.*
*End repeat.*
*End for.*

When focusing on a connected component of the graph, identification of the $\alpha$ and $\psi$ is then guaranteed under a single normalization. For example, one may impose that $\psi_J = 0$ and remove the corresponding column from $B$. In that case, $G = [A \ B]$ is full column rank, and the OLS estimators of the worker and firm effects are

$$\begin{pmatrix} \widehat{\alpha} \\ \widehat{\psi} \end{pmatrix} = (G'G)^{-1} G'Y, \tag{5.7}$$

or more generally $(G'G)^{-1} G'(Y - X\widehat{\beta})$ in the presence of covariates. This is the *AKM* estimator of $\beta$, the $\alpha$ and the $\psi$, after Abowd et al. (1999).

In practice, solving least-squares problems in the presence of two-sided fixed effects can be computationally challenging in large samples. Computational issues are studied in Abowd et al. (1999, 2002) and Guimaraes and Portugal (2010), among others, in the context of matched employer-employee data.

### Statistical properties

The statistical precision of least-squares estimators of agent-specific effects depends on the structure of the network. As an extreme case, when the graph is disconnected the agent-specific effects are not point-identified. More generally, models in sparsely connected networks may be weakly identified even when connectedness holds.

In a recent study, Jochmans and Weidner (2016) derive upper and lower bounds on the variances of agent-specific effects in linear network models. They compute finite-sample bounds under a Gaussianity assumption. They first derive an upper bound on the variance of $\widehat{\alpha}_i$ (respectively, $\widehat{\psi}_j$) which is inversely proportional to the product of two quantities: the *degree* of $i$ (resp. $j$), that is, the number of agents directly connected to it, and a measure of *connectivity* of the graph. They also provide refined bounds that exploit the connectivity of the neighbors of $i$ (resp. $j$). The bounds continue to hold under non-Gaussianity, and the authors also provide asymptotic results that allow for heteroskedasticity and dependence. The results in Jochmans and Weidner (2016) help to formalize the intuition that individual effects are hard to estimate in sparsely connected graphs. In the context of matched employer-employee panel data, such a situation often arises due to limited mobility of workers between firms, particularly in small samples (Abowd et al., 2004; Andrews et al., 2008).

In empirical applications interest may center on estimating $\beta$, or alternatively on estimating features of the distributions of agent-specific effects. For example, in the wage decomposition literature based on matched employer-employee data the variances of firm and worker effects and the covariance between the two sets of effects are often of interest (Abowd et al., 1999;

Card et al., 2013). Inference on such quantities may be based on conventional asymptotics where the number of agents and the number of links per agent tend to infinity jointly. Cluster-robust standard errors are often computed, a possible approach being a two-sided clustering that takes into account unrestricted dependence within $i$ and within $j$. In employer-employee data, clustering standard errors at the firm level seems to be common practice.

Conventional asymptotics may be misleading, however, particularly when the graph is not sufficiently well-connected. Due to features such as limited mobility in employer-employee panels, sampling distributions of AKM estimators may be biased. Although bias reduction techniques have been successfully developed in single-agent panel data models for both common parameters and averages of individual effects (e.g., Hahn and Newey, 2004; Arellano and Hahn, 2007), these techniques are not yet widespread in bipartite network models. See Cattaneo et al. (2015) for work on inference in linear models with a large number of incidental parameters, and the recent contribution by Kline et al. (2018). Regularization techniques may be attractive in such contexts. In Section 5.4 we will review discrete heterogeneity methods that aim at reducing the dimensionality of the model and alleviating incidental parameter biases.

### 5.2.3 Random-effect approaches

Fixed-effect methods have the attractive feature of being agnostic about unobserved heterogeneity, as they leave the $\alpha$ and $\psi$ fully unrestricted. However, while fixed-effect estimators such as the AKM estimator tend to work well in well-connected networks, their performance tends to deteriorate in sparsely connected graphs. Random-effect estimators provide a complementary approach based on an explicit modeling of the distribution of unobserved heterogeneity.

Random-effect and correlated random-effect methods are widespread in single-agent panel data models (e.g., Wooldridge, 2010). However, applying these methods to bipartite networks raises subtle issues. In this subsection we review three different approaches that have been proposed.

#### 5.2.3.1 Conditionally independent random effects

Consider model (5.1), now viewing $\alpha_1, ..., \alpha_N$ and $\psi_1, ..., \psi_J$ as draws from a joint distribution conditional on $D$ and $X$. A simple specification is to model $\alpha_i$ and $\psi_j$ as *conditionally* i.i.d. and independent of each other. For example, a possibility is to specify

$$
\begin{pmatrix} \alpha_1 \\ \cdots \\ \alpha_N \\ \psi_1 \\ \cdots \\ \psi_J \end{pmatrix} \Bigg| (D, X) \sim \mathcal{N} \left( \begin{pmatrix} 0 \\ \cdots \\ 0 \\ 0 \\ \cdots \\ 0 \end{pmatrix}, \begin{pmatrix} \sigma_\alpha^2 & \cdots & 0 & 0 & \cdots & 0 \\ \cdots & \cdots & \cdots & \cdots & \cdots & \cdots \\ 0 & \cdots & \sigma_\alpha^2 & 0 & \cdots & 0 \\ 0 & \cdots & 0 & \sigma_\psi^2 & \cdots & 0 \\ \cdots & \cdots & \cdots & \cdots & \cdots & \cdots \\ 0 & \cdots & 0 & 0 & \cdots & \sigma_\psi^2 \end{pmatrix} \right).
$$

$$(5.8)$$

Independent Gaussian specifications such as (5.8) are commonly assumed in the literature on variance components and *mixed models* in statistics (e.g., Searle et al., 2009; Robinson, 1991). Combining the random-effect specification (5.8) with a Gaussian likelihood for $Y$ given $(D, X, \alpha, \psi)$ yields "REML" estimates (for "restricted maximum likelihood") of $\beta$, $\sigma_\alpha^2$, and $\sigma_\psi^2$. Woodcock (2008, 2011) shows how to allow for correlation between $\alpha_i$ and $X$ based on a correlated random-effect approach (Chamberlain, 1980). Abowd et al. (Abowd et al., 2008) review approaches based on mixed models in the context of matched employer-employee data.

REML estimators have an interesting Bayesian interpretation. Indeed, viewing (5.8) as a prior specification, and endowing $\beta$, $\sigma_\alpha^2$, and $\sigma_\psi^2$ with independent diffuse priors, REML estimates correspond to posterior means of these parameters. In addition, in applications it is common to report posterior mean estimates of the $\alpha_i$ and $\psi_j$, which are sometimes referred to as "BLUP" (Robinson, 1991) for "best linear unbiased predictors". Frequentist properties of REML estimators (consistency and asymptotic normality) have been derived under conditions that do not rely on Gaussianity (Jiang, 1996).

However, conditions for REML consistency rest on $\alpha_1, ..., \alpha_N, \psi_1, ..., \psi_J$ being independent of each other and independent of $D$ in the population (possibly conditional on $X$ as in Woodcock, 2008, 2011). Absent those conditions, the model for $(\alpha, \psi)$ in (5.8) is misspecified and random-effect estimators are not consistent in general. This situation is analogous to the fixed-$T$ inconsistency of independent random-effect estimators in linear single-agent panel data models when individual effects and covariates are correlated with each other in the population.

As in standard panel data settings (Arellano and Bonhomme, 2009), one may expect consistency to hold as the number of observations used to estimate each $\alpha_i$ and $\psi_j$ becomes large, irrespective of the true relationship between individual effects and the network structure. In this case it is natural to expect that the effect of the "prior" information in (5.8) will become asymptotically negligible as the data accumulates. In fact, as shown in Woodcock (2011), the AKM fixed-effect estimator is a limiting case of REML when prior variances tend to infinity. Hence, imposing (5.8) in estimation may be interpreted as "shrinking" the AKM estimator in an empirical Bayes fashion.[7]

Similarly to fixed-effect estimators, conditionally independent random-effect estimators are thus expected to work well in sufficiently well-connected networks. For these methods to remain consistent in sparsely connected graphs, however, the joint distribution of agent-specific effects conditional on the network needs to be correctly specified, in the sense that conditional independence (as in (5.8), for example) needs to hold in the population. However, we will see next that this situation is unlikely to arise in most network models.

### 5.2.3.2 Random effects and network formation

In order to assess the plausibility of distributional assumptions such as (5.8), one needs to specify a network formation process. To fix ideas, consider a very simple model where there are no covariates, $T = 1$ (no repeated links between agents), and the link indicators $D_{ij}$ are i.i.d. between $(i, j)$ conditional on $\alpha_i$ and $\psi_j$. Assume in addition that $\alpha_1, ..., \alpha_N$ and $\psi_1, ..., \psi_J$ are *unconditionally* i.i.d. and independent of each other. Lastly, for concreteness focus on $N = 2$ and $J = 1$. In this case, $\alpha_1$ and $\alpha_2$ are dependent of each other *conditional* on $D$, since, by Bayes' rule,

$$f(\alpha_1, \alpha_2 \mid D_{11} = d_1, D_{21} = d_2)$$
$$= \frac{f(\alpha_1) f(\alpha_2) \mathbb{E}\left[\Pr(D_{11} = d_1 \mid \alpha_1, \psi_1) \Pr(D_{21} = d_2 \mid \alpha_2, \psi_1)\right]}{\Pr(D_{11} = d_1, D_{21} = d_2)},$$

where the expectation is taken with respect to $\psi_1$. This density is not separable in $\alpha_1$ and $\alpha_2$ when $\psi_1$ affects the probability of link formation. In addition, it depends on $(d_1, d_2)$ in general.

More generally, $\alpha_1, ..., \alpha_N$ are typically *not* independent conditionally on $D$, and likewise for $\psi_1, ..., \psi_J$. The conditional distribution of $(\alpha, \psi)$ given $D$ generally exhibits a complex dependence structure.[8] Given the difficulty to specify conditional random-effect distributions in a way that is consistent with models of link formation, it may be appealing to specific a *joint* model for $Y$, $D$, and $(\alpha, \psi)$, possibly conditional on exogenous covariates $X$. Such a joint approach is obviously needed when attempting to account for endogenous network formation, as we will see in Section 5.5. In addition, perhaps less obviously, the present discussion shows that a joint modeling of links and outcomes may prove useful in exogenous network models too. We will see an example of such a joint approach in Section 5.3.

---

[7] Note that the "shrinkage" here is toward a *random allocation* benchmark; that is, toward a distribution where all agent-specific effects are independent of the network and independent of each other.

[8] At the same time, note that $\alpha_1, ..., \alpha_N$ are independent conditional on $D$ *and* $\psi$ (and symmetrically on the other side of the network). This observation is instrumental to the one-sided random-effect approach reviewed below.

## Illustration on simulated data

To illustrate that unconditionally i.i.d. agent-specific types can be dependent conditional on the network, we next simulate data from the following two-equations model of links and outcomes:

$$D_{ij} = \mathbf{1}\left\{c + dX_{ij} + \rho(\alpha_i + \psi_j) + V_{ij} \geq 0\right\}, \tag{5.9}$$

$$Y_{ij} = a + bX_{ij} + \alpha_i + \psi_j + \varepsilon_{ij}. \tag{5.10}$$

The parameterization is as follows: all $\alpha_i$ and $\psi_j$ are drawn from independent standard normal distributions; $\varepsilon_{ij}$ and $V_{ij}$ are i.i.d. standard normal and independent of each other; $X_{ij} = \frac{1}{2}(\alpha_i + \psi_j) + U_{ij}$, where $U_{ij}$ are independent normal with zero mean and variance $1/2$; $a = 0$, $b = 1$, $c = -1$, $d = 1$; lastly, for this illustration we take $\rho = 3$.

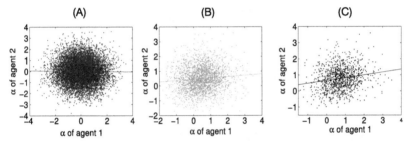

**FIGURE 5.2**  Draws of $(\alpha_1, \alpha_2)$ conditional on the network. (A) Unconditional $Corr = -.01$; (B) $D_{11} = D_{21} = 1$, $Corr = .09$; (C) $D_{11} = D_{21} = D_{12} = D_{22} = 1$, $Corr = .18$. *Notes:* 10,000 simulations from model (5.9)–(5.10). Graph (A) shows all 10,000 draws. Graph (B) shows the 2,602 draws for which $D_{11} = D_{21} = 1$ holds. Graph (C) shows the 1,071 draws for which $D_{11} = D_{21} = D_{12} = D_{22} = 1$ holds. The x-axis shows $\alpha_1$, the y-axis shows $\alpha_2$. Straight lines show the regression fit.

In Fig. 5.2 we plot the $\alpha$ draws of the first two workers (that is, $\alpha_1$ and $\alpha_2$) in three cases: all draws (graph (A)); draws corresponding to networks where workers 1 and 2 are both linked to firm 1 (graph (B)); and draws corresponding to networks where workers 1 and 2 are both linked to firm 1 and to firm 2 (graph (C)). The results are based on 10,000 simulations. Graph (A) confirms that $\alpha_1$ and $\alpha_2$ are unconditionally independent. In turn, graphs (B) and (C) show that they are *not* independent conditional on particular configurations of the network. As argued above this situation is the rule rather than the exception: conditional dependence is a general feature of two-sided models of bipartite networks.

### 5.2.3.3   One-sided random effects

In fixed-effect methods the researcher conditions the analysis on both worker and firm effects and estimates their realized values, while in two-sided random-effect methods she specifies the joint distribution of worker and firm effects. An intermediate approach is to condition on one type of effects only, while specifying the distribution of the other effect using a correlated random-effect specification. To fix ideas, and since this corresponds to the structure of many (short) matched employer-employee panel data sets, here we describe an approach which conditions on firm effects and treats worker heterogeneity as random effects. Bonhomme et al. (2019) recently used such a one-sided random-effect approach to estimate models of wage determination in short employer-employee panel data.

Let $D_i$ denote the set $\{D_{ijt}, j = 1, .., J, t = 1, ..., T\}$ of link indicators for worker $i$, and let $X_i$ similarly denote the set $\{X_{ijt}, j = 1, .., J, t = 1, ..., T\}$. Let us specify $(\alpha_i, D_i, X_i)$ as i.i.d. across $i$ conditional on $\psi$. A general correlated random-effect specification for $\alpha$ is then

$$f(\alpha \mid D, X, \psi) = \prod_{i=1}^{N} f(\alpha_i \mid D_i, X_i, \psi). \tag{5.11}$$

It is worth pointing out that, as it is conditional on the entire sequence of realizations $\psi_j$, this specification is consistent with models of exogenous network formation where links are independently formed across workers given $\psi$. This is in contrast with the conditionally independent random-effect approach previously described in 5.2.3.2.

Eq. (5.11) has a similar structure to correlated random-effect specifications in single-agent panel data models. Taking advantage of this fact, one may use results from the panel data random coefficients literature (e.g., Chamberlain, 1992; Graham and Powell, 2012; Arellano and Bonhomme, 2012) to provide conditions for identification in model (5.1) under a one-sided random-effect specification, as we now show. Importantly, here the analysis does not require the availability of a large number of links for each workers. For example, consistency will hold in a panel data set of workers and firms of fixed length $T$, as $N$ and $J$ tend to infinity such that connectedness patterns are sufficiently strong.

### Identification

Let us consider model (5.1), now treating the $\psi_j$ as fixed effects and the $\alpha_i$ as i.i.d. draws from the correlated random-effect distribution in (5.11). The slope parameter $\beta$ and the firm effects $\psi_j$ can be identified as described in the analysis of fixed-effect estimators. In particular, to identify the $\psi_j$ up to normalization graph connectedness is needed.

In this setting the individual $\alpha_i$ are not identifiable in general, due to the small number of observations per worker $i$. The goal is to identify their distribution conditional on $(D, X, \psi)$. Let us start with the mean. Re-writing the conditional mean restrictions implied by the model net of the effects of $X$ and $\psi$, we have

$$\mathbb{E}\left(Y \mid D, X, \alpha, \psi\right) = A\alpha, \tag{5.12}$$

where $Y$ is now to be understood in deviation from $X\beta + B\psi$. Hence, taking expectations we have

$$\mathbb{E}(Y \mid D, X, \psi) = A\mathbb{E}(\alpha \mid D, X, \psi). \tag{5.13}$$

From (5.13) and (5.11) we thus have

$$\mathbb{E}(\alpha_i \mid D_i, X_i, \psi) = \mathbb{E}(\widehat{\alpha}_i \mid D_i, X_i, \psi),$$

where $\widehat{\alpha}_i$, the $i$th element of $A^\dagger Y$, is the AKM fixed-effect estimator of $\alpha_i$. For example, the mean of $\alpha_i$ in the realized network is identified as $\frac{1}{N}\sum_{i=1}^{N}\mathbb{E}(\alpha_i \mid D) = \frac{1}{N}\sum_{i=1}^{N}\mathbb{E}(\widehat{\alpha}_i \mid D)$, which may be estimated as the sample mean of the $\widehat{\alpha}_i$, weighted by the number of firms connected to $i$. This approach mimics the one in Chamberlain (1992) to recover average individual effects in single-agent random coefficients panel data models.

Likewise, given the one-sided random-effect model in (5.11), and under suitable restrictions on the dependence structure of $\varepsilon$, it is possible to identify the variance, higher-order moments, and entire distribution of $\alpha_i$ in model (5.1). This can be done by following similar arguments as in Arellano and Bonhomme (2012), who generalize the Kotlarski (1967) identification result to linear panel data models subject to independence restrictions. Identification requires restricting the amount of dependence between $\varepsilon_{ijt}$ across $(j, t)$. Here identification is semi-parametric as it leaves the conditional distribution of worker effects unrestricted beyond (5.11).[9]

## 5.3   Identification in nonlinear models

In this section we outline a nonlinear generalization of model (5.1), while maintaining the focus on exogenous networks.

### 5.3.1   Motivation for nonlinearity

Linear models such as (5.1) are useful for exposition, and two-way regression methods have proven useful in many empirical applications. At the same time, economic structure typically leads to nonlinearity. A case in point is the study of sorting patterns between workers and firms. Since the seminal work of Becker (1973), a large theoretical and structural literature has emphasized the link between the sign and strength of sorting and the presence of complementarities in production and wages.[10]

---

[9] Note that in this one-sided random-effect setting the identification analysis is conducted conditionally on the network. Such an approach, which mimics the identification arguments used in single-agent models, cannot be used in two-sided random-effect settings. See Subsection 5.3.3 for an analysis of identification for two-sided random-effect approach.

[10] See, among others, Shimer and Smith (2000), Eeckhout and Kircher (2011), De Melo (2009), and Hagedorn, Law and Manovskii (Hagedorn et al., 2014).

A second motivation for studying nonlinear models in bipartite networks is related to policy analysis. Policy parameters of interest often involve assessing the effect of a marginal increase in an input on average individual outcomes; see Wooldridge (2010), for example. It is well-known that estimates of such policy parameters may be sensitive to linearity assumptions, so a nonlinear framework may be needed for robust estimation. Moreover, in models with two-sided heterogeneity other policy parameters involve *re-allocating* inputs across agents, as introduced and analyzed in Graham, Imbens and Ridder (2014, GIR hereafter). In linear models, such re-allocations have no effect on average outcomes. Hence, accounting for nonlinearities is key in this setting.

A nonlinear model for an exogenous bipartite network is as follows:

$$Y_{ijt}^* = g\left(X_{ijt}, \alpha_i, \psi_j, \varepsilon_{ijt}\right), \qquad (5.14)$$

where it is assumed that $\varepsilon_{ijt}$ are fully independent of $D$, $X$, $\alpha$, and $\psi$. Full independence strengthens the exogeneity assumption made in the linear models studied in Section 5.2.

Let us assume for now that the response function $g$ and the distribution of $(\alpha, \psi)$ are known. Later we will discuss conditions for their identification. A number of policy-relevant effects may be considered in this setup. As an example, consider the following average marginal response to a change in co-variates $X_{ijt}$:

$$\int \int \int \frac{\sum_{i,j,t} D_{ijt} \overline{g}_x\left(X_{ijt}, \alpha_i, \psi_j\right)}{\sum_{i,j,t} D_{ijt}} f_{X,\alpha,\psi \mid D}(X, \alpha, \psi)\, dX d\alpha d\psi,$$

where

$$
\begin{aligned}
\overline{g}(x, \alpha, \psi) &= \mathbb{E}\left[g\left(x, \alpha, \psi, \varepsilon_{ijt}\right)\right] \\
&= \mathbb{E}\left[Y_{ijt} \mid D_{ijt} = 1, X_{ijt} = x, \alpha_i = \alpha, \psi_j = \psi\right],
\end{aligned}
$$

and $\overline{g}_x$ denotes the derivative of $\overline{g}$ with respect to its first argument. To simplify the notation we have assumed that $\overline{g}$ and $\overline{g}_x$ are constant across $(i, j, t)$. This type of estimand keeps the allocation of the $X$, $\alpha$ and $\psi$ unchanged.

A different type of estimand is introduced in GIR in one-to-one bipartite networks. To proceed it is useful to focus on the case where $X_{ijt} = (X_{it}^w, X_{jt}^f)$ contains characteristics specific to worker $i$ and firm $j$, respectively. In GIR's approach, re-allocation effects will result from altering the joint distribution of $(X_{it}^w, \alpha_i, X_{jt}^f, \psi_j)$ while keeping the marginal distributions of $(X_{it}^w, \alpha_i)$ and $(X_{jt}^f, \psi_j)$ constant. Doing so will affect the sorting patterns between the $i$ and $j$, but leave the distributions of inputs unchanged. Here inputs are both observed $(X^w, X^f)$ and unobserved $(\alpha, \psi)$ to the econometrician.

Although GIR focus on a one-to-one matching setting, the many-to-many settings we study here thus allow us to consider reallocation effects in terms of *unobservables*, as well as in terms of observed covariates. This is an important point, as allocating worker $i$ to another firm $j$ will affect the $(i, j)$ outcome through both observed $X_i^w$ and unobserved $\alpha_i$. In other words, GIR's exogeneity assumption is generally not satisfied in the presence of correlated unobserved heterogeneity.

Let $C$ denote a copula with conformable dimensions, and let $c$ denote the associated copula density.[11] A generic average re-allocation effect (ARE) indexed by $C$ is as follows:

$$
\int \int \int \int \frac{\sum_{i,j,t} D_{ijt} \overline{g}\left(X_{it}^w, X_{jt}^f, \alpha_i, \psi_j\right)}{\sum_{i,j,t} D_{ijt}} f_{X^w, \alpha \mid D}(X^w, \alpha) \, f_{X^f, \psi \mid D}(X^f, \psi)
$$
$$
\times c\left[F_{X^w, \alpha \mid D}(X^w, \alpha), F_{X^f, \psi \mid D}(X^f, \psi)\right] dX^w dX^f d\alpha d\psi,
$$
$$
\tag{5.15}
$$

where $F_Z$ denotes the cdf of $Z$. Random matching is obtained by taking $C$ to be the independent copula, hence $c = 1$. This case provides a "no-sorting" average counterfactual outcome, which may be of interest in applications. Positive and negative assortative matching are obtained as limiting cases, as $C$ approaches the upper and lower Fréchet bounds for copulas (Fréchet, 1951).[12]

Note that the densities in (5.15) are weighted by the number of links. For example, in matched employer-employee panel data $f_{\psi \mid D}$ is weighted by the overall firm size pooled over all periods. This suggests the possibility to document other counterfactual quantities in addition to those in GIR. In a many-to-many matching setting counterfactual changes could also involve changing the number of connections (that is, the degree) of different agents. For example, in the analysis of workers and firms one could modify (5.15) to account for changes in firm size. Another difference with GIR concerns estimation, since estimating quantities such as (5.15) requires estimating $f_{\alpha \mid D, X^w}$ and $f_{\psi \mid D, X^f}$. The presence of unobservables also creates challenges for identification, as we discuss next.

### 5.3.2 Identification in one-sided random effects

Here we follow Bonhomme et al. (2019, BLM), who studied identification in short employer-employee panel data models under one-sided random-effect specifications. In the next subsection we will turn to identification in two-sided random-effect settings.

---

[11] Comprehensive references on copulas are Joe (1997) and Nelsen (1999).

[12] If output is additive in inputs, then estimands such as (5.15) are not interesting as they all coincide with the average observed outcome. However, in that case one may consider averages of nonlinear transformations of outcomes such as second- or higher-order moments. This amounts to redefining $\widetilde{g} = h \circ g$, where $h$ is a nonlinear function.

As an illustration let us focus on the following nonlinear generalization of model (5.1) with one-dimensional worker effect $\alpha_i$ and two-dimensional firm effect $\psi_j = (a_j, b_j)$:

$$Y^*_{ijt} = X'_{ijt}\beta + a_j + b_j\alpha_i + \varepsilon_{ijt}, \qquad (5.16)$$

where $\mathbb{E}\left[\varepsilon_{ijt} \mid X, D, \alpha, \psi\right] = 0$. Model (5.16) allows for interactions between the two heterogeneous effects $\alpha$ and $\psi$, hence for complementarities.

Let us assume that $b_j \neq 0$ for all $j$. We are interested in studying identification in a one-sided random-effect model based on the following mean restrictions which hold whenever $D_{ijt} = 1$:

$$\tau_j\mathbb{E}\left[Y_{ijt} \mid X, D, \psi\right] = X'_{ijt}\mu_j + c_j + \mathbb{E}\left[\alpha_i \mid X, D, \psi\right], \qquad (5.17)$$

where $\tau_j = b_j^{-1}$, $\mu_j = \tau_j\beta$, and $c_j = \tau_j a_j$.

Define $X$ and $C$ as in Section 5.2, so $CA = 0$ and $CB = 0$. Let $\tau = (\tau_1, ..., \tau_J)'$ and $\mu = (\mu'_1, ..., \mu'_J)'$. Finally, let $M_Y$ denote the $L \times J$ matrix with $\{(i, j, t), j'\}$-element $Y_{ijt}\mathbf{1}\{j = j'\}$. From (5.17) we have

$$\mathbb{E}\left(C\left(M_Y\tau - X\mu\right) \mid D, X, \psi\right) = 0. \qquad (5.18)$$

The system of conditional moment restrictions (5.18) can be used to test for the presence of complementarities, by testing the null hypothesis that the $\tau_j$ are equal to each other. Following BLM we now outline how it can be used to identify and estimate the model's parameters.

Note that $\tau$ is not identified unless one of its elements is normalized. Let us set $\tau_J = 1$, and denote as $[CM_Y]_{J-1}$ the matrix formed by the first $J - 1$ columns of $CM_Y$. A sufficient condition for identification of the complementarities $b_j = \tau_j^{-1}$ and the parameter vector $\beta$ is that the matrix $\left[\mathbb{E}\left([CM_Y]_{J-1} \mid D, X, \psi\right), -CX\right]$ be full-column rank.[13] Given the $\tau_j$ and $\beta$, the $a_j$ and $\mathbb{E}(\alpha_i \mid D, X, \psi)$ are then identified, provided the network be connected.

As BLM point out, identification of the complementarity parameters $b_j = \tau_j^{-1}$ relies on additional conditions beyond connectedness of the graph component. In particular, in a simple two-period model without covariates identification of the $b_j$ based on mean restrictions fails whenever links are randomly distributed across workers. In other words, non-random sorting is needed if one wishes to identify complementarity patterns.

The $\tau_j$ and $\mu_j$ in (5.18) satisfy a system of linear restrictions. BLM proposed to use the limited information maximum likelihood (LIML) estimator to estimate these parameters. Given those, the $a_j$ and means and variances of $\alpha_i$

---

[13] The reason why this condition is not necessary in general is that there are additional nonlinear restrictions on the parameters $\mu_j = \tau_j\beta$.

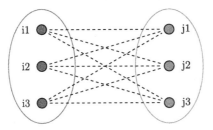

**FIGURE 5.3** Subnetwork.

given $D$ can be estimated using a minimum-distance approach which exploits mean and covariance restrictions.

Lastly, although it is in principle possible to estimate a different complementarity parameter $b_j = \tau_j^{-1}$ for each firm $j$, in practice, due to the presence of firms of moderate size with limited worker mobility it may be advantageous to discretize firm-level heterogeneity and estimate complementarities at the firm-type level. In addition, a discrete heterogeneity approach allows one to identify and estimate more complex nonlinear models, with richer complementarity patterns, than the interactive regression (5.16). We refer the reader to BLM for details on identification of more general nonlinear static and dynamic models. We will review estimation methods based on a discretization of heterogeneity in Section 5.4.

### 5.3.3   Identification in two-sided random effects

In order to study identification in two-sided environments it is convenient to focus on a setup where the unobserved heterogeneity terms $\alpha_i$ and $\psi_j$ have finite support. Identification in finite mixture models has been studied in Hall and Zhou (2003), Hall et al. (2005), Hu (2008), Kasahara and Shimotsu (2009), and Allman et al. (2009), among others, and recently by Allman et al. (2011) in the context of exponential graph models. Below we will briefly discuss how to generalize the analysis to allow for continuous heterogeneity.

Consider a finite mixture model with $\alpha_i \in \{1, ..., M\}$ and $\psi_j \in \{1, ..., K\}$. Here the values of $\alpha_i$ and $\psi_j$ are simple labels, so identification is defined up to permutation of these labels. $\alpha_i$ and $\psi_j$ are i.i.d., independent of each other, conditional on $X$. Link indicators $D_{ijt}$ are assumed to be conditionally independent across $(i, j)$ given $\alpha, \psi$ and $X$, and to only depend on the $\alpha$ and the $\psi$ through $\alpha_i$ and $\psi_j$. In turn, potential outcomes $Y_{ijt}^*$ are assumed conditionally independent across $(i, j)$ given $\alpha, \psi, X$ and $D$, with unrestricted conditional cdf given $\alpha_i$ and $\psi_j$. Models (5.1) and (5.16) are special cases of this setup, provided $\varepsilon_{ijt}$ are independent across $(i, j)$, and link indicators $D_{ijt}$ are conditionally independent of each other across $(i, j)$ and only depend on the $\alpha$ and $\psi$ through $\alpha_i$ and $\psi_j$.

Here we outline an identification strategy which relies on subnetworks based on triplets of firms and workers, as shown in Fig. 5.3. The analysis is closely related to Allman et al. (2009, 2011), who similarly focus on subgraphs to study identification. To simplify the notation let us focus on the case without repeated interactions (that is, $T = 1$), since this is sufficient for the identification analysis. Let $\widetilde{Y}_{ij} = (D_{ij}, Y_{ij})$. Let $\mathcal{I} = (i_1, i_2, i_3)$ and $\mathcal{J} = (j_1, j_2, j_3)$ denote triplets of workers and firms, respectively. It is worth noting that the analysis in this subsection is *not* conditional on the network, but exploits joint restrictions on outcomes *and* network indicators $\widetilde{Y}_{ij}$.

The identification argument proceeds in two steps. In the first step we write, for all $\mathcal{I}$, $\mathcal{J}$, and all $y_{ij}$ in the support of $\widetilde{Y}_{ij}$ for $(i, j) \in \mathcal{I} \times \mathcal{J}$,

$$
\Pr\left[\widetilde{Y}_{ij_1} \leq y_{ij_1}, \widetilde{Y}_{ij_2} \leq y_{ij_2}, \widetilde{Y}_{ij_3} \leq y_{ij_3} \text{ for all } i \in \mathcal{I}\right]
$$
$$
= \sum_{k=1}^{K} \sum_{k'=1}^{K} \sum_{k''=1}^{K} \Pr\left(\psi_{j_1} = k, \psi_{j_2} = k', \psi_{j_3} = k''\right)
$$
$$
\times \prod_{i \in \mathcal{I}} \Pr\left[\widetilde{Y}_{ij_1} \leq y_{ij_1}, \widetilde{Y}_{ij_2} \leq y_{ij_2}, \widetilde{Y}_{ij_3} \leq y_{ij_3} \mid \psi_{j_1} = k, \psi_{j_2} = k', \psi_{j_3} = k''\right],
$$

$$(5.19)$$

where all probabilities are conditional on covariates $X$, although the conditioning is omitted for conciseness. Eq. (5.19) holds because outcomes, link indicators and the $\alpha_i$ are independent across $i$ conditional on the relevant set of $\psi_j$. Note that, in this setup, outcomes are generally *not* conditionally independent across $i$ conditionally on link indicators, for the reasons we explained in 5.2.3.2.

Hall and Zhou (2003) and subsequent authors provides conditions under which both the type probabilities of $\psi_{j_1}, \psi_{j_2}, \psi_{j_3}$, and the distributions of $(\widetilde{Y}_{ij_1}, \widetilde{Y}_{ij_2}, \widetilde{Y}_{ij_3})$ conditional on $\psi_{j_1}, \psi_{j_2}, \psi_{j_3}$ for $i \in \mathcal{I}$, are identified. Identification is up to permutation of the $\psi_j$. For the result to hold, two conditions are needed: a *support* condition, that all $\Pr\left(\psi_j = k\right)$ be positive, and a *rank* condition, that the cdfs inside the product sign in (5.19) be linearly independent; see for example Allman et al. (2009) and Bonhomme et al. (2016). Together, these two assumptions impose a connectedness condition at the firm type level.

In the second step of the argument, we write

$$
\Pr\left[\widetilde{Y}_{ij_1} \leq y_{ij_1}, \widetilde{Y}_{ij_2} \leq y_{ij_2}, \widetilde{Y}_{ij_3} \leq y_{ij_3} \mid \psi_{j_1} = k, \psi_{j_2} = k', \psi_{j_3} = k''\right]
$$
$$
= \sum_{m=1}^{M} \Pr(\alpha_i = m \mid \psi_{j_1} = k, \psi_{j_2} = k', \psi_{j_3} = k'')
$$
$$
\times \Pr\left[\widetilde{Y}_{ij_1} \leq y_{ij_1} \mid \psi_{j_1} = k, \alpha_i = m\right]
$$
$$
\times \Pr\left[\widetilde{Y}_{ij_2} \leq y_{ij_2} \mid \psi_{j_2} = k', \alpha_i = m\right]
$$
$$
\times \Pr\left[\widetilde{Y}_{ij_3} \leq y_{ij_3} \mid \psi_{j_3} = k'', \alpha_i = m\right].
$$

$$(5.20)$$

Since the first step above has shown that the left-hand side in (5.20) is identified up to permutation of firm types, Hall and Zhou (2003)'s identification result then applies once again to show that the probabilities of $\alpha_i$ given $(\psi_{j_1}, \psi_{j_2}, \psi_{j_3})$, and the cdfs of $\widetilde{Y}_{ij}$ conditional of $\psi_j$ and $\alpha_i$, are identified. Those quantities are unique, up to permutation of the $\alpha_i$ and permutation of the $\psi_j$, subject to a support condition that $\Pr(\alpha_i = m \mid \psi_{j_1} = k, \psi_{j_2} = k', \psi_{j_3} = k'') > 0$ for all $k, k', k''$, and a rank condition that the cdfs on the right-hand side of (5.20) be linearly independent. This requires that connectedness should hold for all worker types, a stronger connectedness condition than in linear models such as (5.1). This condition is needed due to the absence of linearity or other functional forms on the relationship between outcomes and unobservables.[14]

The identification argument outlined above could be adapted to allow for continuous unobserved heterogeneity, in the case where outcomes are continuously distributed and $\alpha_i$ and $\psi_j$ are scalar unobservables. Following Hu and Schennach (2008), dealing with the continuous case would require strengthening linear independence and imposing *completeness* conditions (Newey and Powell, 2003). This would also require imposing monotonicity conditions, such as mean outcomes $\mathbb{E}(Y_{ij} \mid \psi_j, D, X)$ and $\mathbb{E}(Y_{ij} \mid \alpha_i, \psi_j, D, X)$ being increasing in $\psi_j$ and $\alpha_i$, respectively.

A particular case of the setup with continuous heterogeneity is a two-sided generalization of Kotlarski (1967) in the following additive model:

$$Y_{ijt}^* = \alpha_i + \psi_j + \varepsilon_{ijt}, \quad Y_{ijt} = D_{ijt} Y_{ijt}^*,$$

under the assumptions that $(D_{ijt}, \varepsilon_{ijt})$ are independent across $(i, j)$ conditional on $(\alpha_i, \psi_j)$. Identification could be analyzed by exploiting *joint* independence restrictions on links and outcomes, similarly as above. However, providing formal identification arguments in such models with continuous unobserved heterogeneity exceeds the scope of this review.

Lastly, note that the identification analysis presented here does not require imposing a network exogeneity condition. Indeed, the main assumption concerns the joint distributions of link indicators and potential outcomes, $(D_{ijt}, Y_{ijt}^*)$. When link indicators and potential outcomes are dependent on each other conditional on heterogeneity, and excluded covariates such as cost shifters are available, a similar approach may be used in order to identify models allowing for network endogeneity. We will consider such models in Section 5.5.

---

[14] This result is complementary to the analysis in Bonhomme et al. (2019, BLM). In two-sided random-effect approach the number of links can be small on both sides of the network. Such a setting may be well-suited in buyer/seller networks or import/export relationships, for example. In contrast, the analysis in BLM is tailored to matched employer-employee data settings, where one side of the network (firms) has fewer agents and more links than the other one (workers). At the same time, BLM only require the availability of two links per worker, corresponding to a job move, to be independent given types. Assuming three independent links as in the argument above would require exploiting repeated job moves, which may be empirically restrictive.

## 5.4 Estimation in nonlinear models

In this section we start by reviewing general fixed-effect and random-effect estimation in nonlinear models for bipartite networks. We then review two approaches based on discrete unobserved heterogeneity: finite mixture methods and classification-based methods.

### 5.4.1 Fixed-effect and random-effect approaches

The fixed-effect and random-effect estimation methods reviewed in Section 5.2 may be extended to nonlinear models. In two-way fixed-effect estimation of nonlinear models the presence of a large number of parameters creates challenges for computation and statistical analysis. In particular, while incidental parameter biases have been characterized in large classes of single-agent panel data models and various bias reduction methods have been proposed (Hahn and Newey, 2004; Arellano and Hahn, 2007), biases in nonlinear bipartite network models have not been extensively studied so far. Jochmans (2016) is a recent exception, in the context of a dyadic network formation model.

To describe random-effect approaches in nonlinear models it is useful to study the general form of random-effect likelihood functions. Conditional on observed and unobserved heterogeneity and conditional on the links, the likelihood of all *potential* outcomes indexed by a finite or infinite dimensional parameter $\theta$ is

$$f(Y^* \mid X, \alpha, \psi; \theta) = f(Y^* \mid D, X, \alpha, \psi; \theta),$$

provided that potential outcomes be conditionally independent of link formation. Note that this network exogeneity condition is stronger than (5.2). Selecting the observations corresponding to $D_{ijt} = 1$ then yields the conditional likelihood for *observed* outcomes given existing links[15]

$$f(Y \mid D, X, \alpha, \psi; \theta).$$

As an illustration, consider two assumptions which are commonly made in models with exogenous networks and lead to simplifications in the expression of the likelihood. First, assume that potential outcomes $Y_{ijt}^*$ are mutually independent of each other given observed and unobserved heterogeneity and given the exogenous network structure. Second, suppose that $f(Y_{ijt}^* \mid X, \alpha, \psi) = f(Y_{ijt}^* \mid X_{ijt}, \alpha_i, \psi_j)$; that is, outcomes only depend on pair- and period-specific characteristics (absence of spillovers). In that case the conditional likelihood of potential outcomes is

---

[15] We use the notation $f(Y \mid D, X, \alpha, \psi; \theta)$ although a more precise notation would indicate that it is obtained from $f(Y^* \mid X, \alpha, \psi; \theta)$ by selecting certain arguments of the likelihood function of $Y^*$ depending on the values of $D$. For example, an alternative notation could be $f_S(Y \mid X, \alpha, \psi; \theta)$, where $S$ is the selection matrix introduced in Subsection 5.2.2.

$$\prod_{i,j,t} f(Y^*_{ijt} \mid X_{ijt}, \alpha_i, \psi_j; \theta),$$

so the conditional likelihood of *observed* outcomes takes the following form:

$$f(Y \mid D, X, \alpha, \psi; \theta) = \prod_{i,j,t} f(Y_{ijt} \mid X_{ijt}, \alpha_i, \psi_j; \theta)^{D_{ijt}}. \qquad (5.21)$$

It can be noted that, in model (5.1) with $\varepsilon_{ijt}$ i.i.d. $\mathcal{N}(0, \sigma^2)$, maximizing the conditional likelihood with respect to $\beta$, $\alpha$ and $\psi$ yields the fixed-effect estimator of Abowd et al. (1999).

In a correlated random-effect approach, the likelihood in (5.21) is integrated with respect to the joint distribution of $\alpha$ and $\psi$, which is conditional on the network $D$ and may also be conditioned on exogenous covariates $X$. Let $\xi$ be a parameter vector indexing that distribution. Then the integrated likelihood is

$$L(\theta, \xi) = \int \cdots \int f(Y \mid D, X, \alpha, \psi; \theta)$$
$$\times f(\alpha_1, ..., \alpha_N, \psi_1, ..., \psi_J \mid D, X; \xi) \, d\alpha_1 ... d\alpha_N \, d\psi_1 ... d\psi_J. \quad (5.22)$$

Likelihood functions associated with conditionally independent random-effect specifications take this form (see 5.2.3.1). Similarly, the integrated likelihood function takes a similar form as in (5.22) in joint random-effect approaches where the likelihood of $(Y^*, D)$ is jointly modeled conditional on heterogeneity.

In bipartite network models with two-sided unobserved heterogeneity the integrated likelihood does not factor into a product of low-dimensional terms in general. As a result, evaluating the integrated likelihood in (5.22) requires computing high-dimensional integrals with respect to *all* $\alpha_i$ and $\psi_j$. This situation contrasts with single-agent panel data models, where random-effect likelihoods with scalar heterogeneity can be evaluated by computing $N$ single-dimensional integrals. The two-sided structure in (5.22) also contrasts with the one-sided random-effect approaches reviewed in 5.2.3.3.

The presence of multiple integrals in the likelihood is a pervasive feature of network data, which prevents one from applying standard numerical approximation methods. Bayesian methods are popular for estimation of latent variables models; see Rossi et al. (1995) and Lancaster (2004) for examples of economic applications. However, in the context of network models with two-sided heterogeneity it may be challenging to efficiently draw from the joint posterior distribution due to the high dimension of heterogeneity and to possible multimodality of the objective function. In the next subsection we provide more details in the context of models with discrete heterogeneity.

### 5.4.2 Discrete heterogeneity I: finite mixture methods

In this subsection and the next we describe discrete heterogeneity approaches. In discrete settings $\alpha_i$ and $\psi_j$ are modeled as taking a finite number of values $M$

and $K$, respectively. Random-effect and fixed-effect approaches are both popular in such settings, the former corresponding to finite mixture approaches while the latter comprise discrete fixed-effect (or "grouped fixed-effect") classification approaches, which we will review in the next subsection.

A simple finite mixture model with binary, conditionally independent outcomes and no covariates has been extensively studied in the literature. A *stochastic blockmodel* (Holland et al., 1983; Snijders and Nowicki, 1997) relates binary indicators $D_{ijt}$ to unobserved types $\alpha_i$ and $\psi_j$ through the probabilities $\Pr(D_{ijt} = 1 \mid \alpha_i = m, \psi_j = k)$. This model may be generalized in a number of ways, in particular to account for conditioning covariates and non-binary data (e.g., Nowicki and Snijders, 2001).[16]

When adopting a random-effect approach, a specification for the joint distribution of heterogeneity $(\alpha, \psi)$ is needed. In a simple stochastic blockmodel without covariates a natural possibility is to assume that $(\alpha, \psi)$ are i.i.d. draws from a discrete distribution with unrestricted type probabilities. Applying these methods to bipartite networks requires modeling the relationship between link indicators $D_{ijt}$ and unobserved types $(\alpha, \psi)$ (and possibly observed covariates $X$). As we pointed out in 5.2.3.2, conditional random-effect approaches given the realized network $D$ may be challenging to specify. An alternative is to model unconditional type probabilities of $(\alpha, \psi)$, possibly given $X$, together with the joint distribution of $(Y^*, D)$ given $(\alpha, \psi)$ and $X$. Conditions for the identification of such two-sided finite mixture models were discussed in Subsection 5.3.3.

A number of estimation techniques have been proposed in the literature. Snijders and Nowicki (1997, 2001) described direct maximum likelihood estimation, strategies based on the expectation maximization (EM) algorithm, and Markov chain Monte Carlo (MCMC) methods based on Gibbs sampling. Likelihood maximization is often intractable even for moderate sample size, given the presence of high-dimensional sums of terms (which are discrete counterparts to the multiple integrals in (5.22)). EM and MCMC also face challenges for computation, due to the high-dimensionality of the model, and, in the case of MCMC, the invariance of the model to the labeling of the types.

Variational inference represents an alternative approach to estimation, and its popularity is growing within statistics and machine learning. Daudin et al. (2008) develop a variational method for stochastic blockmodels for network data, based on mean-field approximations. The hope is that substituting the objective function associated with the mixture model by a simpler, easier to evaluate function, the computational burden will be reduced while biases will remain moderate. It would be interesting to apply variational inference methods to matched employer-employee data or other bipartite network data in economics.

---

[16] For example, a blockmodel with continuous outcomes could be used to model the following cdf $\Pr(Y_{ijt}^* \leq y \mid \alpha_i = m, \psi_j = k, X_{ijt} = x)$, which is an $(x, \alpha, \psi)$-specific distribution of potential outcomes. In a wage regression, such a specification substantially relaxes additive specifications such as (5.1) as it allows for general interaction effects between worker and firm heterogeneity by allowing for general forms of complementarity between worker and firm attributes $\alpha_i$ and $\psi_j$.

Statistical properties of maximum likelihood and variational inference for stochastic blockmodels have been studied in Celisse et al. (2012) and in Bickel et al. (2013). The setup considered by these authors is one where $M$ and $K$ are fixed and the sample size as well as the average number of connections per agent (that is, the average degree in the graph) tend to infinity simultaneously. Bickel et al. (2013) allow for the average degree in the network to increase at log-rate with sample size. They focus on a simple, non-bipartite stochastic blockmodel for binary data without covariates. Their results establish that, as the sample size tends to infinity, perfect classification of the types is achieved. In populations with discrete heterogeneity, this "oracle" property is shared by the classification-based methods which we now review.

### 5.4.3 Discrete heterogeneity II: classification-based methods

Classification-based (or "clustering"-based) techniques are widely used in machine learning, computer science and statistics as a way of performing community detection and reducing dimensionality. Clustering consists in classifying observations (e.g., workers and firms) into a finite number of types. Hence, unlike in random-effect mixtures, in those approaches the researcher estimates the individual type memberships. Classification-based methods are becoming increasingly popular in the statistical analysis of network data. As we emphasize below, their justification does not rely on discreteness holding in the population, so the discrete modeling is viewed as a dimension reduction device, as opposed to a substantive assumption about population heterogeneity. We first describe a one-sided random-effect method, and then turn to two-sided methods.

#### Two-step grouped fixed effects

Consider a likelihood model with two-sided heterogeneity, $f(Y_{ij} \mid D_{ij}, X_{ij}, \alpha_i, \psi_j; \theta)$, independent across $(i, j)$, where $Y_{ij}$, $D_{ij}$ and $X_{ij}$ contain all period-specific $Y_{ijt}$, $D_{ijt}$ and $X_{ijt}$. We will treat the $\psi_j$ as fixed-effect parameters to be estimated, and the $\alpha_i$ as draws from a correlated random-effect distribution, hence following a one-sided random-effect approach as in 5.2.3.3. Specifically, we consider a parametric specification of the form $f(\alpha_i \mid D_i, X_i, \psi; \xi)$, where $\xi$ is a parameter vector.

In a full likelihood setting, the two-step *grouped fixed-effect* approach proposed by Bonhomme et al. (2017, 2019) is as follows. Let

$$h_j = \frac{\sum_{i=1}^{N} \sum_{t=1}^{T} D_{ijt} h(Y_{ijt}, X_{ijt})}{\sum_{i=1}^{N} \sum_{t=1}^{T} D_{ijt}}, \quad j = 1, ..., J$$

denote firm-specific moment vectors.[17]

---

[17] In order for the method to be consistent those moment vectors need to be informative about $\psi_j$; formally, a condition of asymptotic injectivity is needed, see Bonhomme et al. (2017).

1. Estimate a partition of firms, $\{\widehat{k}_j\}$, by discretizing the $h_j$; that is:

$$\left(\widetilde{h}, \widehat{k}_1, ..., \widehat{k}_J\right) = \underset{(\widetilde{h}, k_1, ..., k_J)}{\text{argmin}} \sum_{j=1}^{J} \left\| h_j - \widetilde{h}(k_j) \right\|^2, \qquad (5.23)$$

where $(k_1, ..., k_J) \in \{1, ..., K\}^J$ are partitions of $\{1, ..., J\}$ into $K$ groups, and $\widetilde{h} = (\widetilde{h}(1)', ..., \widetilde{h}(K)')'$ are vectors.

2. Maximize the log-likelihood function with respect to common parameters and group-specific firm effects, where the groups are given by the $\widehat{k}_j$ estimated in the first step; that is:

$$\left(\widehat{\theta}, \widehat{\xi}, \widehat{\psi}\right) = \underset{(\theta, \xi, \psi)}{\text{argmax}} \sum_{i=1}^{N} \sum_{j=1}^{J} \ln \left[ \int f(Y_{ij} \mid D_{ij}, X_{ij}, \alpha_i, \psi(\widehat{k}_j); \theta) \right.$$

$$\left. f(\alpha_i \mid D_i, X_i, \psi(\widehat{k}_j); \xi) d\alpha_i \right]. \qquad (5.24)$$

The first step in two-step grouped fixed effects is to solve a *k-means* classification problem, based on a suitable set of firm-specific moments. The second step is a single-agent random-effect likelihood problem, at the worker level. When $K$ is chosen to be much smaller than $J$, this approach may result in substantial computational gains due to a reduction in dimensionality, compared to traditional fixed-effect and random-effect methods. The discrete regularization can also result in a reduction in incidental parameter biases.

A simple algorithm to solve (5.23), Lloyd's algorithm, is to iterate back and forth between estimating the $\widetilde{h}(k)$ and classifying the $j$ by updating the $\widehat{k}_j$. In practice the algorithm is repeated with multiple starting values. It typically provides fast and reliable solutions. A number of heuristic and exact algorithms to solve (5.23) are available, see Steinley (2006) and Bonhomme and Manresa (2015) for references.

Alternative classification methods which do not require optimizing (5.23) have been recently proposed in the literature. Convex clustering methods (Pelckmans et al., 2005; Hocking et al., 2011; Lindsten et al., 2011) rely on fully convex objectives. These methods are closely related to the Lasso (Tibshirani, 1996). Similarly to the Lasso, the level of sparsity (that is, the number of types $K$) is not specified *ex-ante*, but discreteness arises due to the presence of an $\ell^1$ penalty term. While these alternative clustering methods seem promising, the optimization problem is distinct from (5.23), and it has been much less studied; see Tan and Witten (2015) for recent work on the statistical properties of convex clustering methods. A related method based on a non-convex multiplicative penalty has been recently introduced in Su et al. (2015).

Theoretical properties of grouped fixed-effect estimators have been derived under two distinct population frameworks. A first approach is to assume that firm-specific unobserved heterogeneity is discrete in the population, and the true number of groups is known or consistently estimated. Hahn and Moon (2010) and Bonhomme and Manresa (2015) provide conditions under which the classification is consistent; that is, asymptotically as $J$ and $N$ tend to infinity at suitable rates the estimated group membership $\widehat{k}_j$ converges in probability to the population group membership $k_j$ (up to arbitrary labeling of the groups). As a result two-step grouped fixed-effect estimators are asymptotically equivalent to the infeasible estimators based on the true population group membership. Related perfect classification results have been recently established in Lin and Ng (2012), Saggio (2012), Bai and Ando (2015), Su et al. (2015), and Vogt and Linton (2015). These results are also related to the analysis of finite mixture estimators under correct specification in Celisse et al. (2013) and Bickel et al. (2013) reviewed above.

A second approach is to study the properties of two-step grouped fixed-effect estimators as the number of groups $K$ tends to infinity together with the sample size, in an environment where heterogeneity is *not* assumed to be discrete in the population. Focusing on single-agent panel data settings, Bonhomme et al. (2017) show that grouped fixed-effect estimators suffer from two types of bias. The first one is an *approximation* bias, which decreases as $K$ increases and reflects that a small-$K$ approximation might be too coarse. However, due to the number of groups growing perfect classification is no longer possible and the estimators generally suffer from an *incidental parameter* bias. Bonhomme et al. (2017) show that the latter is closely related to the small-$T$ bias of fixed-effect estimation, and exploit this connection to develop bias reduction methods. They show that, in practice, bias correction may substantially improve the performance of grouped fixed-effect estimators.[18]

Lastly, related classification approaches have been recently proposed in some models of economic networks. In a many-to-one matching setting, Krasnokutskaya et al. (2014a) develop a method to estimate type membership based on pairwise comparisons, and they study its properties under discrete heterogeneity in the population in Krasnokutskaya et al. (2014b). Hagedorn et al. (2014) propose a rank-based clustering algorithm to estimate worker types in matched employer-employee data, relying on long panels.

---

[18] In addition, Bonhomme et al. (2017) propose a model-based iteration which may provide further finite-sample improvements. A continuously updated version of it is the following "one-step" estimator:

$$\left(\widehat{\theta}, \widehat{\xi}, \widehat{\psi}, \{\widehat{k}_j\}\right)$$

$$= \operatorname*{argmax}_{(\theta, \xi, \psi, \{k_j\})} \sum_{i=1}^{N} \sum_{j=1}^{J} \ln \left[ \int f(Y_{ij} \mid D_{ij}, X_{ij}, \alpha_i, \psi(k_j); \theta) f(\alpha_i \mid D_i, X_i, \psi(k_j); \xi) d\alpha_i \right],$$

$$(5.25)$$

where here the optimization is with respect to $\theta, \xi, \psi$, and all partitions $\{k_j\}$ of $\{1, ..., J\}$ into at most $K$ groups.

## Co-clustering

"Co-clustering" techniques (also referred to as "bi-clustering") are popular in statistics and machine learning. These are two-way classification methods, which extend *k-means* clustering to network structures. A typical application is to stochastic blockmodels. As an example, Dhillon (2001) consider the joint classification of documents and words. Other applications include co-clustering of genes and experimental conditions. Co-clustering is a convenient approach to handle unobserved heterogeneity in general bipartite networks, as we now describe.

Consider as an example the linear model (5.1) on an exogenous network. In this case a co-clustering estimator solves the following problem:

$$\min_{(\beta,\alpha,\psi,\{m_i\},\{k_j\})} \sum_{i,j,t} D_{ijt} \left(Y_{ijt} - X'_{ijt}\beta - \alpha(m_i) - \psi(k_j)\right)^2, \qquad (5.26)$$

where the minimum is taken with respect to all partitions $\{m_i\} \in \{1, ..., M\}^N$ of $\{1, ..., N\}$ into at most $M$ groups, and $\{k_j\} \in \{1, ..., K\}^J$ of $\{1, ..., J\}$ into at most $K$ groups.[19]

More generally, in a likelihood model with an exogenous network a co-clustering maximum likelihood estimator solves (assuming conditionally independent observations for simplicity)

$$\max_{(\theta,\alpha,\psi,\{m_i\},\{k_j\})} \sum_{i,j,t} D_{ijt} \ln f \left(Y_{ijt} \mid X_{ijt}, \alpha(m_i), \psi(k_j); \theta\right). \qquad (5.27)$$

Given a parametric specification, co-clustering may thus also be used to estimate a model of network formation where links $D_{ijt}$ are treated as outcome variables, such as

$$\max_{(\gamma,\alpha,\psi,\{m_i\},\{k_j\})} \sum_{i,j,t} D_{ijt} \ln \Pr \left(D_{ijt} = 1 \mid X_{ijt}, \alpha(m_i), \psi(k_j); \gamma\right)$$
$$+ (1 - D_{ijt}) \ln \Pr \left(D_{ijt} = 0 \mid X_{ijt}, \alpha(m_i), \psi(k_j); \gamma\right). \qquad (5.28)$$

The optimization problems in (5.26), (5.27) and (5.28) are combinatorial, NP hard problems. While simple and efficient heuristic algorithms exist for the standard one-way k-means problem, such as Lloyd's algorithm, no comparable algorithm has yet been developed for co-clustering. Methods to optimize such criteria are reviewed in Madeira and Oliveira (2004). The fact that combinatorial optimization may be prohibitive has motivated the recent development of alternative approaches to computation, such as the variational inference methods

---

[19] An interesting modification of (5.26) is to allow for general interactions between worker and firm types, through a function $\mu(m_i, k_j)$.

we reviewed above and spectral clustering methods. Spectral clustering algorithms are increasingly popular in the statistical analysis of network data; see Von Luxburg (2007) for a survey. Lastly, recently a convex approach to co-clustering was proposed in Chi et al. (2017).

Deriving statistical properties of co-clustering estimators is an active research area. Similarly to the analysis of grouped fixed-effect methods, two different approaches have been pursued. Most of the work focuses on block-models with binary outcomes, as in (5.28), without covariates. In this setting, consistency properties have been studied under the assumption that unobserved heterogeneity is discrete in the population and that the model is correctly specified; see Bickel and Chen (2009), Rohe et al. (2011), and Choi et al. (2012), among others. These authors have characterized conditions under which estimated types $\widehat{m}_i$ and $\widehat{k}_j$ converge in probability to the population types $m_i$ and $k_j$. These conditions typically rely on exchangeable graphs, where the average number of links per agent tends to infinity together with the number of agents. Choi et al. (2012) and Rohe et al. (2011) establish asymptotically perfect classification while allowing the number of population types to grow with the sample size. Rohe et al. (2011) and Lei and Rinaldo (2015) study the consistency of spectral clustering methods.

Recently, co-clustering methods have also been studied in settings that allow for the discrete model to be misspecified, in the spirit of White (1982). Choi and Wolfe (2014) characterize statistical properties of pseudo-true values in a "separately exchangeable" setup where the underlying types are continuous and uniformly distributed, and co-clustering is used to estimate type membership. In this setting, although asymptotically perfect classification of worker and firm types is no longer achievable Choi and Wolfe (2014) derive rates of convergence. Recently, limiting network structures (or "graphons") in non-bipartite settings have been studied in Gao et al. (2015), who characterize optimal rates of convergence, and Wolfe and Ohlede (2014). To this date these methods do not yet allow for statistical testing or the construction of asymptotically valid confidence intervals.

### Illustration on simulated data (cont.)

To illustrate the performance of classification-based methods, we next perform a Monte-Carlo simulation exercise based on model (5.9)–(5.10). This model generates relatively dense networks, for which co-clustering methods can be well-suited. Specifically, we use a two-sided version of the two-step grouped fixed-effect method to estimate the coefficients of covariates $b$ and $d$.

The two-step method is as follows. In a first step we classify *both* workers *and* firms based on the moments $\sum_{j=1}^{N} D_{ij}$ and $\sum_{j=1}^{N} D_{ij} Y_{ij}$ (resp. $\sum_{i=1}^{N} D_{ij}$ and $\sum_{i=1}^{N} D_{ij} Y_{ij}$), weighted by the inverse of their standard deviations. In the second step we estimate the parameters in (5.9)–(5.10) by performing a probit regression and a linear regression which control for additive group indicators;

**TABLE 5.1** Results of the simulation exercise.

| | $\widehat{b}$ (mean) | $\widehat{b}$ (std) | $\widehat{d}$ (mean) | $\widehat{d}$ (std) | Corr($\alpha_i, \widehat{\alpha}(\widehat{m}_i)$) (mean) | Corr($\psi_j, \widehat{\psi}(\widehat{k}_j)$) (mean) |
|---|---|---|---|---|---|---|
| $N = J = 20$ | 1.03 | .16 | 1.11 | .21 | .92 | .91 |
| $N = J = 50$ | 1.01 | .05 | 1.02 | .07 | .96 | .96 |
| $N = J = 100$ | 1.01 | .03 | 1.01 | .04 | .97 | .98 |

Notes: True values are $b = d = 1$. The numbers of groups in the three rows are 4, 7, 10. 500 simulations.

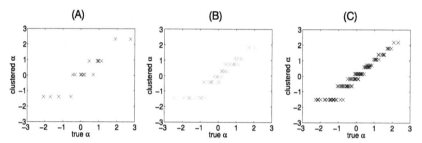

**FIGURE 5.4** True $\alpha_i$ against clustered estimate $\widehat{\alpha}(\widehat{m}_i)$. (A) $N = J = 20$; (B) $N = J = 50$; (C) $N = J = 100$. *Notes:* One simulation of model (5.9)–(5.10), for different sample sizes. The x-axis shows the true $\alpha_i$, the y-axis shows the estimated $\widehat{\alpha}(\widehat{m}_i)$.

that is, for indicators of groups of workers and groups of firms. This method combines features from two-step grouped fixed effects and co-clustering.[20]

In Table 5.1 we report the means and standard deviations of the estimates of $b$ and $d$ across 500 simulations. The number of groups is set to the square root of the number of workers (resp. firms); that is: 4, 7 or 10, depending on the sample size. We use the same parameterization as in 5.2.3.2 except that we set $\rho = 1$. In particular, $\alpha_i$ and $\psi_j$ are continuously distributed in the population. We see that while the estimators are biased when $N = J = 20$ the biases decrease rapidly with the sample size, although we have not attempted to use a bias reduction method. In addition we see that the standard deviations decrease approximately at the rate $\sqrt{NJ}$.

The last two columns in Table 5.1 show the average value of the correlation between the true worker effect $\alpha_i$ and the (discrete) grouped fixed-effect estimate $\widehat{\alpha}(\widehat{m}_i)$, and similarly for firm effects. We see that correlations are high, and increase with the sample size. This suggests that the discrete model provides an accurate approximation to the underlying continuous heterogeneity in this setting. In Fig. 5.4 we confirm this by plotting the values of $\alpha_i$ and $\widehat{\alpha}(\widehat{m}_i)$ corresponding to one simulation for every sample size. This small-scale simulation

---

[20] The performance of the estimator depends on the dimensionality of heterogeneity, which is low in this case since individual and firm heterogeneity are only driven by the scalar terms $\alpha_i$ and $\psi_j$. See Bonhomme et al. (2017) for a discussion of the role of the underlying dimension of heterogeneity.

suggests that classification-based methods can be useful in bipartite networks, including in environments where population heterogeneity is not discrete.

## 5.5 Endogenous link formation and network dynamics

In this last section we focus on a key issue in bipartite network analysis: network endogeneity. In such settings it is necessary to jointly model potential outcomes and link formation. Our discussion is very brief despite the importance of the subject. We expect more work in this area in the near future.

We will focus on endogenous networks where the joint likelihood takes the form

$$f(D, Y^* \mid X, \alpha, \psi; \theta),$$

that is, on situations where the likelihood is conditioned on $\alpha$, $\psi$, and $X$, and the only source of endogeneity arises from the formation of links. Interesting extensions of this setup would include relaxing the exogeneity of covariates $X$, and allowing for non-exogenous time-varying unobserved types.

When the network is exogenous, the above likelihood simplifies to

$$f(D \mid X, \alpha, \psi; \theta) f(Y^* \mid X, \alpha, \psi; \theta).$$

This simplification only occurs when $Y^*$ and $D$ are independent of each other given $(\alpha, \psi)$ and $X$. Hence, network endogeneity arises whenever the link indicators $D_{ijt}$ depend on the match-specific shocks $\varepsilon_{ijt}$.

While the economic literature on endogenous network formation is progressing rapidly (see for example the recent reviews in Graham, 2015; Chandrasekhar, 2015, and De Paula, 2016) there remain a number of fundamental challenges. We will first illustrate some features of the problem in a simple static model. Then we will review existing approaches and challenges when attempting to allow for dynamics and network externalities.

### 5.5.1 A static model of network formation

Recent work aims at modeling both the formation of a network and how it affects individual outcomes. See for example Goldsmith-Pinkham and Imbens (2013), Johnsson and Moon (2015), Arduini et al. (2015), Hsieh and Lee (2016), and Auerbach (2016). Here we outline an identification argument in a nonlinear static model which is an extension of the model analyzed in Subsection 5.3.2 allowing for endogeneity of the network.

Consider a nonlinear model with conditionally independent outcomes and link indicators. As already mentioned, the identification argument in Subsection 5.3.2 does not rely on network exogeneity. For example, consider the following model:

$$Y_{ijt}^* = g(X_{ijt}, \alpha_i, \psi_j, \varepsilon_{ijt}), \tag{5.29}$$

$$D_{ijt} = \mathbf{1}\{\eta_{ijt} \leq h(Z_{ijt}, \alpha_i, \psi_j)\}, \qquad (5.30)$$

where $(\varepsilon_{ijt}, \eta_{ijt})$ are independent of $(\alpha, \psi, X, Z)$ and independent across $(i, j, t)$, but $\varepsilon_{ijt}$ and $\eta_{ijt}$ are allowed to depend on each other. For example, $\eta_{ijt}$ could be a signal about the match quality $\varepsilon_{ijt}$, revealed to agents before they decide whether or not to form a link.

In Subsection 5.3.2 we outlined an identification argument for the type probabilities and the type-conditional distributions $\Pr(D_{ijt} = d, Y_{ijt} \leq y \mid X_{ijt}, Z_{ijt}, \alpha_i, \psi_j)$. In order to identify the function $g$, one then needs to solve the *sample selection* problem which arises due to endogenous network formation, as only outcomes of realized matches (that is, corresponding to $D_{ijt} = 1$) are observed to the econometrician.

In additively separable models, a number of methods are available to deal with sample selection. As an example, in the following model:

$$Y_{ijt}^* = g(X_{ijt}, \alpha_i, \psi_j) + \varepsilon_{ijt},$$

we have

$$\mathbb{E}\left(Y_{ijt} \mid D_{ijt} = 1, X_{ijt}, Z_{ijt}, \alpha_i, \psi_j\right)$$
$$= g(X_{ijt}, \alpha_i, \psi_j) + \mathbb{E}\left(\varepsilon_{ijt} \mid \eta_{ijt} \leq h(Z_{ijt}, \alpha_i, \psi_j), X_{ijt}, Z_{ijt}, \alpha_i, \psi_j\right),$$
$$(5.31)$$

where the second term on the right-hand side is a selection-correction factor. Identification requires the presence of excluded covariates in $Z_{ijt}$ that are not part of $X_{ijt}$, such as determinants of costs of forming a link. Since Heckman (1974, 1979), various semi-parametric and nonparametric estimation methods have been developed in this setting; see Vella (1998) and Das et al. (2003), for example.

In nonseparable models, sample selection methods are not as well developed. Point-identification may be established under "identification at infinity" (that is, under large support on the propensity score) or extrapolation based on analytic restrictions on the dependence structure; see Arellano and Bonhomme (2017). Bounds on $g$ may be constructed absent such assumptions (Manski, 1994).[21]

### 5.5.2 Network dynamics and externalities

Model (5.29)–(5.30) relies on two strong assumptions. The first one is that link formation and outcomes are independent across $(i, j)$ pairs. This rules out the presence of network externalities, through which the probability of forming a link depends on the other links that the agent may form. The second, related assumption is that the model is static, in that links formed at $t$ do not depend on

---

[21] A survey of sample selection methods in nonseparable, quantile-based models may be found in Arellano and Bonhomme (2016).

links at $t - 1, t - 2, ...,$ and neither are agents forward-looking when deciding whether to form a link at $t$. Relaxing these assumptions is a challenging task, however. In this last subsection we review recent innovations in the literature on matched employer-employee networks which make some progress in this direction.

In networks of workers and firms, modeling network endogeneity requires modeling mobility decisions of workers and hiring decisions of firms. The labor literature has proposed several approaches, mostly based on setups with search frictions. As a recent example, Sorkin (2015) augments the linear wage model (5.1) with an employment equation for $D_{ijt}$. In the model worker mobility depends on firm attributes in a dynamic manner, following a job posting model, while worker unobserved heterogeneity has no effect on mobility due to the additive structure of wages. Mobility decisions imply the presence of a selection-correction factor, as in (5.31).

Bonhomme et al. (2019) consider a setting allowing for worker and firm attributes to affect mobility in the presence of endogenous mobility. In their model exclusion restrictions are obtained under Markovian restrictions on mobility and wages. As an example, they let both the firm type $\psi$ at $t - 1$ and the wage $Y$ at $t - 1$ affect workers' decisions to move between firms. However, conditional on those, worker type $\alpha$, and covariates $X$, firm types and wages before period $t - 2$ are assumed not to affect the mobility decisions. In turn, the wage at $t$ may depend on the firm types at $t$ and $t - 1$ and on the wage at $t - 1$, in addition to $\alpha$ and $X$, but not on firm types or wages before $t - 2$. Bonhomme et al. (2019) show that those restrictions are implied by a number of economic models of worker/firm sorting, including job posting models and models with wage bargaining, in the presence of general wage functions allowing for complementarities. They show how to estimate these models using a one-sided random-effect approach based on discretizing firm types.

Other models of endogenous network formation for workers and firms have been proposed in the literature. As an example, Beffy et al. (2003) augment the setup of Buchinsky et al. (2010) to allow for firm heterogeneity. In their model, potential wages are additive functions of unobserved types, and mobility decisions may be driven by match effects, thus leading to network endogeneity. Abowd et al. (2015) propose a model of endogenous mobility where match effects play a key role in mobility decisions. The estimation problems in both papers are high-dimensional, and the authors rely on Markov chain Monte Carlo methods.

All the models reviewed in this section abstract from the joint matching problem between workers and firms. They either focus on partial equilibrium models of the labor market, or are based on equilibrium analyses where matches are one-to-one or firm production has constant returns to scale, as in Shimer and Smith (2000) and subsequent structural work. Modifying these approaches to modeling many-to-many matches in the presence of capacity or organizational constraints on the firm side is an interesting research avenue; see Eeckhout and

Kircher (2016) for recent work in this direction. At the same time, specifying and estimating dynamic models of link formation allowing for general network externalities raises a number of technical challenges, due to the large dimensions involved and multiplicity of equilibria. A recent example of such an approach is the model of bilateral contracting among upstream and downstream firms in Lee and Fong (2013).[22]

## 5.6 Conclusion

Econometric methods for bipartite networks are now well-understood in exogenous networks. Recent advances allow for identification of general relationships between outcomes and heterogeneous types, in the presence of flexible complementarity patterns. Such methods can be put to work to estimate rich effects of actual or counterfactual policies, including effects of re-allocating observed or unobserved inputs across agents. There are many potential applications of these techniques, for example in labor economics (workers and firms), in the economics of education (students, teachers, schools), or in health economics (patients and hospitals).

Network externalities and dynamics are important topics for future research. Building dynamic matching models with forward-looking agents which remain tractable and can be taken to the data seems a natural next step for research in this area, with numerous applications in industrial organizations or finance where endogenizing the evolution of market structure is key. We conjecture that, particularly in dynamic "many-to-many" matching settings, progress will come from better integrating econometric frameworks with theoretical economic models.

In models with exogenous or endogenous networks alike, estimation approaches relying on a discretization of heterogeneity and classification algorithms seem promising in order to alleviate the curse of dimensionality which arises in these models. More generally, substantial progress is currently being made in machine learning and statistics. Computational techniques and approximation methods developed in those fields could prove very useful in economics.

Lastly, two issues which we have not touched in this survey are models with aggregate effects and models with time-varying unobserved heterogeneity. The first question is an important one in the perspective of building network models able to capture macroeconomic effects such as business cycle fluctuations. Regarding the second question, allowing for time-varying unobservables may improve empirical realism, although this raises issues for both identification and estimation.

## References

Abowd, J.M., Creecy, R.H., Kramarz, F., 2002. Computing person and firm effects using linked longitudinal employer-employee data. Cornell University. Mimeo.

---

[22] See also the recent study of hospital-insurer bargaining in Ho and Lee (2017).

Abowd, J., Kramarz, F., Lengermann, P., Pérez-Duarte, S., 2004. Are good workers employed by good firms? A test of a simple assortative matching model for France and the United States. Unpublished manuscript.

Abowd, J., Kramarz, F., Margolis, D., 1999. High wage workers and high wage firms. Econometrica 67 (2), 251–333.

Abowd, J., Kramarz, F., Woodcock, S., 2008. Econometric analyses of linked employer-employee data. In: The Econometrics of Panel Data. Springer, Berlin, Heidelberg, pp. 727–760.

Abowd, J.M., McKinney, K.L., Schmutte, I.M., 2015. Modeling Endogenous Mobility in Wage Determination. Paper No. CES-WP-15-18. US Census Bureau Center for Economic Studies.

Allman, E.S., Matias, C., Rhodes, J.A., 2009. Identifiability of parameters in latent structure models with many observed variables. The Annals of Statistics, 3099–3132.

Allman, E.S., Matias, C., Rhodes, J.A., 2011. Parameter identifiability in a class of random graph mixture models. Journal of Statistical Planning and Inference 141 (5), 1719–1736.

Andrews, M.J., Gill, L., Schank, T., Upward, R., 2008. High wage workers and low wage firms: negative assortative matching or limited mobility bias? Journal of the Royal Statistical Society. Series A 171 (3), 673–697.

Arduini, T., Patacchini, E., Rainone, E., 2015. Parametric and Semiparametric IV Estimation of Network Models with Selectivity. Working paper No. 1509. Einaudi Institute for Economics and Finance (EIEF).

Arellano, M., Bonhomme, S., 2009. Robust priors in nonlinear panel data models. Econometrica 77, 489–536.

Arellano, M., Bonhomme, S., 2011. Nonlinear panel data analysis. Annual Review of Economics 3 (1), 395–424.

Arellano, M., Bonhomme, S., 2012. Identifying distributional characteristics in random coefficients panel data models. The Review of Economic Studies 79, 987–1020.

Arellano, M., Bonhomme, S., 2016. Sample selection in quantile regression: a survey. In: Handbook of Quantile Regression. In press.

Arellano, M., Bonhomme, S., 2017. Quantile selection models with an application to understanding changes in wage inequality. Econometrica 85 (1), 1–28.

Arellano, M., Hahn, J., 2007. Understanding bias in nonlinear panel models: some recent developments. In: Blundell, R., Newey, W., Persson, T. (Eds.), Advances in Economics and Econometrics, Ninth World Congress. Cambridge University Press.

Auerbach, E., 2016. Identification and estimation of models with endogenous network formation. Unpublished manuscript.

Bai, J., Ando, T., 2015. Panel data models with grouped factor structure under unknown group membership. Journal of Applied Econometrics.

Becker, G.S., 1973. A theory of marriage: part I. Journal of Political Economy, 813–846.

Beffy, M., Kamionka, T., Kramarz, F., Robert, C., 2003. Job Mobility and Wages with Worker and Firm Heterogeneity. Crest working paper.

Bickel, P.J., Chen, A., 2009. A nonparametric view of network models and Newman-Girvan and other modularities. Proceedings of the National Academy of Sciences of the United States of America 106, 21068–21073.

Bickel, P., Choi, D., Chang, X., Zhang, H., 2013. Asymptotic normality of maximum likelihood and its variational approximation for stochastic blockmodels. The Annals of Statistics 41 (4), 1922–1943.

Bonhomme, S., Jochmans, K., Robin, J.M., 2016. Nonparametric estimation of finite mixtures from repeated measurements. Journal of the Royal Statistical Society, Series B, Statistical Methodology 78 (1), 211–229.

Bonhomme, S., Manresa, E., 2015. Grouped patterns of heterogeneity in panel data. Econometrica 83 (3), 1147–1184.

Bonhomme, S., Lamadon, T., Manresa, E., 2017. Discretizing unobserved heterogeneity. Unpublished manuscript.

Bonhomme, S., Lamadon, T., Manresa, E., 2019. A distributional framework for matched employer-employee data. Econometrica 87 (3), 699–739.

Buchinsky, M., Fougere, D., Kramarz, F., Tchernis, R., 2010. Interfirm mobility, wages and the returns to seniority and experience in the United States. The Review of Economic Studies 77 (3), 972–1001.

Card, D., Cardoso, A.R., Kline, P., 2016. Bargaining, sorting, and the gender wage gap: quantifying the impact of firms on the relative pay of women. The Quarterly Journal of Economics 131 (2), 633–686.

Card, D., Heining, J., Kline, P., 2013. Workplace heterogeneity and the rise of West German wage inequality. The Quarterly Journal of Economics 128 (3), 967–1015.

Cattaneo, M.D., Jansson, M., Newey, W.K., 2015. Alternative asymptotics and the partially linear model with many regressors. arXiv preprint arXiv:1505.08120.

Celisse, A., Daudin, J.J., Pierre, L., 2012. Consistency of maximum-likelihood and variational estimators in the stochastic block model. Electronic Journal of Statistics 6, 1847–1899.

Chamberlain, G., 1980. Analysis of covariance with qualitative data. The Review of Economic Studies 47, 225–238.

Chamberlain, G., 1992. Efficiency bounds for semiparametric regression. Econometrica 60, 567–596.

Chandrasekhar, A., 2015. Econometrics of network formation. In: Bramoullé, Yann, Galeotti, Andrea, Rogers, Brian (Eds.), Oxford Handbook on the Economics of Networks. In press.

Chi, E.C., Allen, G.T., Baraniuk, R.G., 2017. Convex biclustering. Biometrics 73 (1), 10–19.

Chiappori, P.-A., Salanié, B., 2015. The econometrics of matching models. Journal of Economic Literature. In press.

Chiappori, P.-A., Salanié, B., Weiss, Y., 2015. Partner choice and the marital college premium: analyzing marital patterns over several decades. Unpublished manuscript.

Choi, D., Wolfe, P.J., 2014. Co-clustering separately exchangeable network data. The Annals of Statistics 42 (1), 29–63.

Choi, D.S., Wolfe, P.J., Airoldi, E.M., 2012. Stochastic blockmodels with a growing number of classes. Biometrika 99, 273–284.

Choo, E., Siow, A., 2006. Who marries whom and why. Journal of Political Economy 114 (1), 175–201.

Das, M., Newey, W.K., Vella, F., 2003. Nonparametric estimation of sample selection models. The Review of Economic Studies 70, 33–58.

Daudin, J.J., Picard, F., Robin, S., 2008. A mixture model for random graphs. Statistics and Computing 18 (2), 173–183.

De Melo, R.L., 2009. Sorting in the labor market: theory and measurement. Unpublished manuscript.

De Paula, A., 2016. Econometrics of Network Models. Cemmap working paper No. CWP06/16.

Dhillon, I.S., 2001. Co-clustering documents and words using bipartite spectral graph partitioning. In: Proceedings of the Seventh ACM SIGKDD International Conference on Knowledge Discovery and Data Mining.

Donna, J., Schenone, P., Veramendi, G., 2015. Networks, frictions, and price dispersion. Unpublished manuscript.

Eeckhout, J., Kircher, P., 2011. Identifying sorting? In theory. The Review of Economic Studies.

Eeckhout, J., Kircher, P., 2016. Assortative matching with large firms. Unpublished manuscript.

Finkelstein, A., Gentzkow, M., Williams, H., 2014. Sources of Geographic Variation in Health Care: Evidence from Patient Migration. NBER working paper No. w20789.

Fox, J.T., 2010. Identification in matching games. Quantitative Economics 1 (2), 203–254.

Fox, J.T., 2016. Estimating matching games with transfers. Unpublished manuscript.

Fréchet, M., 1951. Sur les Tableaux de Corrélation dont les Marges sont Données. Annales de L'Université de Lyon, Sér. 3 14, 53–77.

Gale, D., Shapley, L.S., 1962. College admissions and the stability of marriage. The American Mathematical Monthly 69 (1), 9–15.

Galichon, A., Salanié, B., 2015. Cupid's invisible hand: social surplus and identification in matching models. Unpublished manuscript.

Gao, C., Lu, Y., Zhou, H.H., 2015. Rate-optimal graphon estimation. The Annals of Statistics 43 (6), 2624–2652.

Goldsmith-Pinkham, P., Imbens, G.W., 2013. Social networks and the identification of peer effects. Journal of Business and Economic Statistics 31 (3), 253–264.

Graham, B., 2011. Econometric methods for the analysis of assignment problems in the presence of complementarity and social spillovers. In: Handbook of Social Economics, vol. 1, pp. 965–1052.

Graham, B.S., 2015. Methods of identification in social networks. Annual Review of Economics 7 (1), 465–485.

Graham, B.S., Imbens, G.W., Ridder, G., 2014. Complementarity and aggregate implications of assortative matching: a nonparametric analysis. Quantitative Economics 5 (1), 29–66.

Graham, B.S., Imbens, G.W., Ridder, G., 2016. Identification and Efficiency Bounds for the Average Match Function Under Conditionally Exogenous Matching. No. w22098 National Bureau of Economic Research.

Graham, B.S., Powell, J.L., 2012. Identification and estimation of irregular correlated random coefficient models. Econometrica 80 (5), 2105–2152.

Guimaraes, P., Portugal, P., 2010. A simple feasible procedure to fit models with high-dimensional fixed effects. Stata Journal 10 (4), 628–649.

Hagedorn, M., Law, T.H., Manovskii, I., 2014. Identifying equilibrium models of labor market sorting. Econometrica. In press.

Hahn, J., Moon, H., 2010. Panel data models with finite number of multiple equilibria. Econometric Theory 26 (3), 863–881.

Hahn, J., Newey, W.K., 2004. Jackknife and analytical bias reduction for nonlinear panel models. Econometrica 72, 1295–1319.

Hall, P., Neeman, A., Pakyari, R., Elmore, R., 2005. Nonparametric inference in multivariate mixtures. Biometrika 92 (3), 667–678.

Hall, P., Zhou, X.H., 2003. Nonparametric estimation of component distributions in a multivariate mixture. The Annals of Statistics, 201–224.

Heckman, J.J., 1974. Shadow prices, market wages and labour supply. Econometrica 42, 679–694.

Heckman, J.J., 1979. Sample selection bias as a specification error. Econometrica 47, 153–161.

Helpman, E., Muendler, M., Itskhoki, O., Redding, S., 2016. Trade and inequality: from theory to estimation. The Review of Economic Studies. In press.

Ho, K., Lee, R., 2017. Insurer competition in health care markets. Econometrica 85 (2), 379–417.

Hocking, T.D., Joulin, A., Bach, F., Vert, J.P., 2011. Clusterpath: an algorithm for clustering using convex fusion penalties. In: 28th International Conference on Machine Learning, p. 1.

Holland, P.W., Laskey, K.B., Leinhardt, S., 1983. Stochastic blockmodels: first steps. Social Networks 5 (2), 109–137.

Hsieh, C.S., Lee, L.F., 2016. A social interactions model with endogenous friendship formation and selectivity. Journal of Applied Econometrics 31 (2), 301–319.

Hu, Y., 2008. Identification and estimation of nonlinear models with misclassification error using instrumental variables: a general solution. Journal of Econometrics 144 (1), 27–61.

Hu, Y., 2015. Microeconomic Models with Latent Variables: Applications of Measurement Error Models in Empirical Industrial Organization and Labor Economics. Technical report, Cemmap Working Papers, CWP03/15.

Hu, Y., Schennach, S.M., 2008. Instrumental variable treatment of nonclassical measurement error models. Econometrica 76 (1), 195–216.

Jiang, J., 1996. REML estimation: asymptotic behavior and related topics. The Annals of Statistics 24 (1), 255–286.

Jochmans, K., 2016. Modified-likelihood estimation of fixed-effect models for dyadic data. Unpublished working paper. Sciences-Po.

Jochmans, K., Weidner, M., 2016. Fixed-effect regressions on network data. Unpublished manuscript.

Joe, H., 1997. Multivariate Models and Dependence Concepts. Chapman & Hall, London.

Johnsson, I., Moon, H.R., 2015. Estimation of peer effects in endogenous social networks: control function approach. Unpublished manuscript.

Kasahara, H., Shimotsu, K., 2009. Nonparametric identification of finite mixture models of dynamic discrete choices. Econometrica 77 (1), 135–175.

Kline, P., Saggio, R., Solvsten, M., 2018. Leave-out estimation of variance components. Unpublished manuscript.

Kotlarski, I., 1967. On characterizing the gamma and normal distribution. Pacific Journal of Mathematics 20, 69–76.

Kramarz, F., Machin, S., Ouazad, A., 2015a. Using compulsory mobility to identify school quality and peer effects. Oxford Bulletin of Economics and Statistics 77 (4), 566–587.

Kramarz, F., Martin, J., Mejean, I., 2015b. Volatility in the small and in the large: the lack of diversification in international trade. Unpublished manuscript.

Kranton, R.E., Minehart, D.F., 2001. A theory of Buyer-Seller networks. The American Economic Review 91 (3), 485–508.

Krasnokutskaya, E., Song, K., Tang, X., 2014a. The role of quality in Internet service markets. Johns Hopkins University. Mimeo.

Krasnokutskaya, E., Song, K., Tang, X., 2014b. Estimating unobserved individual heterogeneity through pairwise comparisons. Johns Hopkins University. Mimeo.

Lancaster, T., 2004. An Introduction to Modern Bayesian Econometrics. Blackwell.

Lee, R.S., Fong, K., 2013. Markov Perfect network formation: an applied framework for bilateral oligopoly and bargaining in buyer-seller networks. Unpublished manuscript.

Lei, J., Rinaldo, A., 2015. Consistency of spectral clustering in stochastic block models. The Annals of Statistics 43 (1), 215–237.

Lin, C.C., Ng, S., 2012. Estimation of panel data models with parameter heterogeneity when group membership is unknown. Journal of Econometric Methods 1 (1), 42–55.

Lindsten, F., Ohlsson, H., Ljung, L., 2011. Clustering using sum-of-norms regularization: with application to particle filter output computation. In: 2011 IEEE Statistical Signal Processing Workshop (SSP), pp. 201–204.

Lovász, L., Plummer, M.D., 2009. Matching Theory, vol. 367. American Mathematical Society.

Madeira, S.C., Oliveira, A.L., 2004. Biclustering algorithms for biological data analysis: a survey. IEEE/ACM Transactions on Computational Biology and Bioinformatics 1 (1), 24–45.

Manski, C.F., 1994. The selection problem. In: Sims, C. (Ed.), Advances in Econometrics, Sixth World Congress, vol. 1. Cambridge University Press, Cambridge, U.K., pp. 143–170.

Matzkin, R.L., 2013. Nonparametric identification in structural economic models. Annual Review of Economics 5 (1), 457–486.

Nelsen, R.B., 1999. An Introduction to Copulas. Springer Verlag, New-York.

Newey, W., Powell, J., 2003. Instrumental variable estimation of nonparametric models. Econometrica 71 (5), 1565–1578.

Nickell, S., 1981. Biases in dynamic models with fixed effects. Econometrica, 1417–1426.

Nowicki, K., Snijders, T.A.B., 2001. Estimation and prediction for stochastic blockstructures. Journal of the American Statistical Association 96 (455), 1077–1087.

Pelckmans, K., De Brabanter, J., Suykens, J.A.K., De Moor, B., 2005. Convex clustering shrinkage. In: PASCAL Workshop on Statistics and Optimization of Clustering Workshop.

Robinson, G.K., 1991. That BLUP is a good thing: the estimation of random effects. Statistical Science, 15–32.

Rohe, K., Chatterjee, S., Yu, B., 2011. Spectral clustering and the high-dimensional stochastic blockmodel. The Annals of Statistics, 1878–1915.

Rossi, P., McCulloch, R.E., Allenby, G.M., 1995. Hierarchical modelling of consumer heterogeneity: an application to target marketing. In: Kass, Singpurwalla (Eds.), Case Studies in Bayesian Statistics. Springer Verlag, New York, pp. 323–350.

Roth, A.E., Sotomayor, M., 1992. Two-sided matching. In: Handbook of Game Theory with Economic Applications, vol 1, pp. 485–541.

Saggio, R., 2012. Discrete Unobserved Heterogeneity in Discrete Choice Panel Data Models. CEMFI Master Thesis.

Searle, S.R., Casella, G., McCulloch, C.E., 2009. Variance Components. John Wiley and Sons.

Shapley, L.S., Shubik, M., 1954. A method for evaluating the distribution of power in a committee system. American Political Science Review 48 (03), 787–792.

Shimer, R., Smith, L., 2000. Assortative matching and search. Econometrica 68 (2), 343–369.

Snijders, T.A., Nowicki, K., 1997. Estimation and prediction for stochastic blockmodels for graphs with latent block structure. Journal of Classification 14 (1), 75–100.

Song, J., Price, D.J., Guvenen, F., Bloom, N., Von Wachter, T., 2015. Firming Up Inequality. NBER working paper No. w21199.

Sorkin, I., 2015. Ranking firms using revealed preference. Unpublished manuscript.

Steinley, D., 2006. K-means clustering: a half-century synthesis. British Journal of Mathematical & Statistical Psychology 59, 1–34.

Su, L., Shi, Z., Phillips, P.C.B., 2015. Identifying latent structures in panel data. Econometrica. In press.

Tan, K.M., Witten, D., 2015. Statistical properties of convex clustering. Electronic Journal of Statistics 9 (2), 2324–2347.

Tibshirani, R., 1996. Regression shrinkage and selection via the lasso. Journal of the Royal Statistical Society, Series B 58, 267–288.

Vella, F., 1998. Estimating models with sample selection bias: a survey. The Journal of Human Resources 33 (1), 127–169.

Vogt, Linton, O., 2015. Classification of nonparametric regression functions in heterogeneous panels. Unpublished manuscript.

Von Luxburg, U., 2007. A tutorial on spectral clustering. Statistics and Computing 17 (4), 395–416.

White, H., 1982. Maximum likelihood estimation of misspecified models. Econometrica, 1–25.

Wolfe, P.J., Ohlede, S.C., 2014. Nonparametric graphon estimation. ArXiv.

Woodcock, S.D., 2008. Wage differentials in the presence of unobserved worker, firm, and match heterogeneity. Labour Economics 15 (4), 771–793.

Woodcock, S.D., 2011. Match effects. Unpublished manuscript.

Wooldridge, J.M., 2010. Econometric Analysis of Cross Section and Panel Data. MIT Press.

Chapter 6

# An empirical model for strategic network formation[☆]

Nicholas Christakis[a], James Fowler[b], Guido W. Imbens[c,d], and
Karthik Kalyanaraman[e]

[a]*Department of Sociology, Internal Medicine and Biomedical Engineering, Yale University, New
Haven, CT, United States,* [b]*Department of Political Science, University of California at San Diego,
San Diego, CA, United States,* [c]*Department of Economics and Graduate School of Business,
Stanford University, Stanford, CA, United States,* [d]*NBER, Cambridge, MA, United States,* [e]*64/1,
Bengaluru, India*

## Contents

## 6.1 Introduction

In this paper we develop and analyze an empirical model for strategic network formation. The example we have in mind is the formation of a network of friendship links between individuals in a community. Following Jackson (2010) we

[☆] We are grateful for discussions with Paul Goldsmith-Pinkham, Matt Jackson and Markus Möbius, and for comments from participants at seminars at Harvard/MIT and the University of Chicago Booth School of Business. The first version of this paper was prepared in 2010. Financial support for this research was generously provided through NSF grants 0631252 and 0820361.

refer to these models as strategic network formation models. Such models are also referred to as network evolution models (Toivonen et al., 2009), or actor-based models (Snijders, 2005; Snijders et al., 2010). Starting with an empty network, with a finite set of individuals, each with a fixed set of characteristics,[1] we model the network as the result of a sequential process, driven by a combination of what Currarini et al. (2010) call chance (through randomly arising opportunities for the formation of links) and choice (in the form of optimal decisions by the individuals whether to establish the potential links), culminating in a complete network. See Moody (2001), Snijders et al. (2010), and Zeng and Xie (2008) for related models.

The goal of the current paper is to develop an empirical model that, using observations from a single network, at a single point in time, in combination with information on the characteristics of the participants, can be used for predicting features of the network that would arise in a population of agents with different characteristics or different constraints. To make this specific, in the application we consider the effects that alternative assignments of students to classes (e.g., based on ability tracking, or single sex classrooms) might have on the topology of the network of friendships in a high school.

The motivation for focusing on determinants of network formation comes from the large literature that has found that links in networks are associated with correlations in outcomes. For example, Christakis and Fowler (2007) find that changes in weight of individuals is a predictor of weight changes in their friends. Calvo-Armengol and Jackson (2004) find that social networks are correlated with employment prospects. Uzzi (1996) and Uzzi and Spiro (2005) find that certain network configurations are correlated with improved group performance. In educational settings Goldsmith-Pinkham and Imbens (2013) find that outcomes are correlated with network structure. In experimental settings Leider et al. (2009), and Fowler and Christakis (2010), find the networks matter for altruism. See Christakis and Fowler (2009) and Jackson (2010) for surveys of this literature. In the related literature on peer effects, researchers have found that outcomes and measures of behavior of an individual's classmates predicts outcomes for that individual (Angrist and Lang, 2004; Carrell et al., 2009). In the peer effect literature the peer group is often defined broadly in terms of easily measurable characteristics, e.g., being in the same class. It is plausible that these correlations are stronger for individuals who identify themselves as connected through friendship or other social networks.

If policy makers have preferences over these outcomes, and if the correlations between networks or peer groups and outcomes found in the aforementioned studies are causal, policy makers may be interested in policies that affect the formation of networks. The current study is potentially useful in understanding how the various manipulations policymakers may be able to carry out affect the networks, and thus indirectly affect the outcomes of interest. It will also shed light on the plausibility of the causal interpretation of the claims by adding

---

[1] The model could be extended to allow for time-varying characteristics.

to the understanding of the determinants of network formation. The models for network formation developed in the game-theoretic literature (e.g., Myerson, 1977; Aumann and Myerson, 1988; Jackson and Wolinsky, 1996) often imply that networks are at least partly the result of random shocks (through randomly arising opportunities for forming links) that imply that established links are partially exogenous, even if individuals optimally decide to form links when such opportunities arise.

We focus on models for network formation based on individual choices motivated by utility maximization. This follows in the econometric tradition on discrete choice established by McFadden (1980, 1984), and the theoretical work on strategic network formation by Jackson (2003, 2010). One approach would be to consider the utilities each individual associates with all possible networks, and formulate rules for the game that determines the realized network given the preferences of all individuals simultaneously. This set up often leads to multiple equilibria. Such models also tend to be computationally extremely demanding, both for the agents and for the econometrician, even in moderately sized networks, given that the number of links is quadratic in the number of nodes, and the number of possible networks is exponential in the number of possible links. In the context of our application with 669 individuals, these considerations severely constrain the ability to analyze such models.

Here, we side-step these complications by modeling the network formation as a sequential process, where at each step a single pair of individuals is offered the chance to establish a link. Alternative sequential network formation models have been considered in Myerson (1977), Currarini et al. (2010), and Snijders et al. (2010). In our model both members of the pair that is given the opportunity to form a link, weigh the options open to them, taking into account the current state of the network and their own, as well as their potential partner's, characteristics. If both individuals view the link as beneficial (that is, if their utility from establishing the link is higher than the utility of not establishing the link), the link materializes. After a number of opportunities for links have arisen, the network is complete. A key restriction we impose is that at each step (that is, at each opportunity to form a link), the potential partners take into account the current state of the network, but do not anticipate future changes in the network: they compare the net utility from forming (or breaking) a link as if the current state of the network will remain unchanged in the future. Such myopic behavior eases the computational burden for both the agents and the econometrician substantially, as well as removes the complications arising from multiple equilibria. Jackson (2010) discusses some arguments in support of such behavior, and the relation to pairwise stability. Despite this assumption, the computational burden for this model remains large. With $N$ nodes the number of different sequences of meetings (opportunities to form links) is equal to $(N \times (N - 1)/2)!$. Nevertheless, we illustrate in the application that for these data with $N = 669$ this model is still tractable.

We specify the function that describes the utility an individual derives from a link in terms of characteristics of the individual and the potential partner, and the current state of the network, as a function of the unknown preference parameters. A key feature is that we explicitly allow the decision of the individuals to form a link to depend on features of the current state of the network. Earlier work, (e.g., in a similar context, Moody (2001), and in a different context, Fox (2010, 2008)), allows the utility to depend only on individual characteristics, which greatly improves the computational tractability. Specifically, in our application, we allow the utility of a link to depend on *ex ante* degrees of separation between the potential friends and the number of friends they already have. We shall demonstrate in the context of our application that this dependence on network features substantially improves the ability of the model to generate commonly observed features of networks, such as clustering.

We focus on Bayesian methods for inference and computation (see also Goldsmith-Pinkham and Imbens, 2013). One reason is that no large sample asymptotic theory has been developed for the maximum likelihood estimator in such models (see Kolaczyk, 2009, for some discussion). A second argument is that obtaining draws from the posterior distribution is much easier than calculating the maximum likelihood estimates. We illustrate these methods using data from a network of high school friends with 669 individuals and 1,541 mutual friendships (hence an average of 4.5 friendships per person).

## 6.2 Set up

Consider a population of $N$ individuals, the nodes, indexed by $i = 1, \ldots, N$. Individual $i$ has observed attributes $X_i$, where $X_i$ is a $K$-vector. In our application to a network of friendships among high school students, these attributes include sex, age, current grade, and participation in organized sports. Let $\mathbf{X}$ be the $N \times K$ matrix with $i$th row equal to $X_i'$. Pairs of individuals $i$ and $j$, with $i, j \in \{1, \ldots, N\}$, may be linked. The symmetric matrix $\mathbf{D}$, of dimension $N \times N$, with

$$D_{ij} = \begin{cases} 1 & \text{if } i \text{ and } j \text{ are friends,} \\ 0 & \text{otherwise,} \end{cases}$$

is called the adjacency matrix. This is the dependent variable in our analysis. The diagonal elements $D_{ii}$ are normalized to zero. We focus in the current paper on undirected links (so $\mathbf{D}$ is symmetric). In some settings it may be more appropriate to allow the links to have a direction, and the methods here can be extended to cover such cases. We will also allow for link-specific covariates. For ease of exposition we only allow for one link-specific covariate, although generalizing this is straightforward in principle. For pair $(i, j)$, let $C_{ij}$ be the link-specific covariate, with $\mathbf{C}$ the symmetric $N \times N$ matrix with typical element $C_{ij}$. In our application $C_{ij}$ is the number of classes individuals $i$ and $j$

have in common. One can think of $C_{ij}$ as a function of individual characteristics, that is, a function of the list of all classes taken by each individual, but we analyze it here as a link-specific covariate.

There are $N \cdot (N - 1)/2$ different pairs $(i, j)$ with $i \neq j$. For each such pair there either is, or is no, friendship link, so there are $2^{N \cdot (N-1)/2}$ different values possible for the adjacency matrix $\mathbf{D}$. We are interested in modeling the probability associated with adjacency matrix $\mathbf{D}$, given the matrix of individual characteristics $\mathbf{X}$, and given the matrix of link-specific characteristics $\mathbf{C}$. Let $p(\mathbf{D}|\mathbf{X}, \mathbf{C}; \theta)$ denote this probability, as a function of an unknown vector of parameters denoted by $\theta$.

Using the observed data, including the adjacency matrix $\mathbf{D}_{\text{obs}}$, the individual characteristics $\mathbf{X}_{\text{obs}}$, and the link characteristics $\mathbf{C}_{\text{obs}}$, and postulating a prior distribution for $\theta$, we can use the model $p(\mathbf{D}|\mathbf{X}, \mathbf{C}; \theta)$ to derive the posterior distribution of $\theta$ given $(\mathbf{D}_{\text{obs}}, \mathbf{X}_{\text{obs}}, \mathbf{C}_{\text{obs}})$:

$$p(\theta|\mathbf{D}_{\text{obs}}, \mathbf{X}_{\text{obs}}, \mathbf{C}_{\text{obs}}) \propto p(\mathbf{D}_{\text{obs}}|\mathbf{X}_{\text{obs}}, \mathbf{C}_{\text{obs}}; \theta) \cdot p(\theta). \tag{6.1}$$

We then use this model to calculate the probabilities of (features of) particular networks given alternative populations of individuals, associated with alternative values for $\mathbf{X}$ and $\mathbf{C}$, say $\mathbf{X}'$ and $\mathbf{C}'$. The predictive distribution of the network for this new configuration of characteristics, conditional on the parameters $\theta$, is $p(\mathbf{D}|\mathbf{X}', \mathbf{C}'; \theta)$. Unconditionally, the predictive distribution that is ultimately the main object of interest in our analysis, is

$$p(\mathbf{D}|\mathbf{X}', \mathbf{C}') = \int_{\theta} p(\mathbf{D}|\mathbf{X}', \mathbf{C}'; \theta) p(\theta|\mathbf{D}_{\text{obs}}, \mathbf{X}_{\text{obs}}, \mathbf{C}_{\text{obs}}) d\theta. \tag{6.2}$$

Specifically, in our example of a network of high school students, one may be interested in features of the network that would emerge if classes were configured in different ways. Leading examples include ability tracking, where students would be allocated to classes based on prior grades, or single sex classes. Given a fixed set of individuals (or a fixed distribution from which future cohorts are drawn), such changes in allocation rules would change the value of some components of the matrices $\mathbf{X}$ and $\mathbf{C}$, and thus generate different probabilities on future networks. A school administration may care about the network, for example wishing to avoid networks where many students have no friends, networks with many separate cliques, or networks that are associated with undesirable behavior, and generally preferring networks with a high degree of cohesion and a well-connected student body. We do not directly address the question of the optimal configuration of classes, that is, the optimal assignment of $\mathbf{X}$ and $\mathbf{C}$ given restrictions (see for some related discussion Graham et al., 2008), but note that the derivation of a predictive distribution for the network would be an important component of some such analyses.

There are two main challenges confronting these analyses. First, we need to specify a model for the adjacency matrix given characteristics, $p(\mathbf{D}|\mathbf{X}, \mathbf{C}; \theta)$.

We do not do so directly, instead specifying a technology for sequential network formation that implies a distribution for $\mathbf{D}$ given $(\mathbf{X}, \mathbf{C})$, indexed by a parameter $\theta$. This model need not merely fit the data well. In order for the prediction exercise to be accurate, it also needs to be a structural model in the Goldberger (1991) sense that its parameters $\theta$ do not change if we change the distribution of the covariates $\mathbf{X}$ and $\mathbf{C}$. Second, we need computational methods for drawing from the predictive distribution of $\mathbf{D}$ given the observed data. The main specific challenge in this is obtaining draws from the posterior distribution of $\theta$ given the observed data, in the context of a single, fairly large network and a rich model for network formation. In our application there are 669 individuals, with 1,541 friendships among the set of 223,446 potential links.

It is useful to have some additional notation. Let $\mathbf{F}$ to be the $N \times N$ matrix equal to $\mathbf{D}'\mathbf{D}$. The diagonal element $F_{ii}$ of $\mathbf{F}$ is equal to the number of friends individual $i$ has, and $F_{ij}$, for $i \neq j$, is equal to the number of friends individuals $i$ and $j$ have in common. Define $\mathbf{G}$ to be the $N \times N$ matrix that gives the degree of separation between individuals, or the geodesic:

$$
G_{ij} = \begin{cases}
0 & \text{if } i = j, \\
1 & \text{if } D_{ij} = 1, \\
2 & \text{if } D_{ij} = 0, \text{ and } F_{ij} \geq 1, \\
3 & \text{if } D_{ij} = 0, \ F_{ij} = 0, \exists (k \neq m), D_{ik} = 1, D_{km} = 1, D_{mj} = 1, \\
\vdots & \\
\infty & \text{if there is no path between } i \text{ and } j.
\end{cases}
$$

## 6.3 Exponential random graph and strategic network formation models

In this section we discuss two approaches to modeling network formation. Models in the first approach are referred to exponential random graph (ERG) models. These models directly focus on distributions for the adjacency matrix itself. Models in the second approach are referred to as strategic network formation (SNF) models. They start by modeling the probability of two nodes forming a link. See for a discussion of some of these models from a statistics perspective Kolaczyk (2009).

### 6.3.1 Exponential random graph models

Exponential random graph models, for example those developed by Holland and Leinhardt (1981) and Frank and Strauss (1986), Anderson et al. (1999) and Snijders (2005), can capture commonly observed structures in the network such as transitivity and clustering. ERG models tend to be parsimonious models effective at generating commonly observed structure in networks, and these models often do well at matching the predicted and actual degree distribution.

The basic approach is to specify the probability of a network $\mathbf{D}$ in terms of some functions of $\mathbf{D}$. The simplest model is the Erdös–Reny model, where the probability of any link is the same:

$$p(\mathbf{D} = \mathbf{d}) = \prod_{i<j} \alpha^{D_{ij}} (1 - \alpha)^{1-D_{ij}}.$$

An important early extension is the $p_1$ model by Holland and Leinhardt (1981), who allow the probability of a link to vary by node. Holland and Leinhardt model the probability of a network $\mathbf{D}$ (in the absence of attribute information), simplified to the undirected link case, as

$$p(\mathbf{D} = \mathbf{d}) = \exp\left(\sum_{i=1}^{N} \alpha_i f_{ii}(\mathbf{D}) - k(\alpha_1, \ldots, \alpha_N)\right).$$

Here $f_{ii}(\mathbf{d})$ is the number of friends individual $i$ has in network $\mathbf{d}$, $f_{ii}(\mathbf{d}) = \sum_{j=1}^{N} d_{ij}$. The unknown parameters are $\alpha_1, \ldots, \alpha_N$, and $k(\alpha_1, \ldots, \alpha_N)$ is a constant that ensures that the probability distribution sums up to one, with the summing over all $2^{N \times (N+1)/2 - N}$ possible values of the adjacency matrix $\mathbf{D}$.

Alternative versions of these models, for example the $p^*$ models in Anderson et al. (1999) use additional functions $h(\mathbf{d})$ in the exponential specification,

$$p(\mathbf{D} = \mathbf{d}) = \exp\left(\theta' h(\mathbf{d}) - k(\theta)\right).$$

These functions may include the number of triangles (the number of triples $(i, j, k)$ such that $d_{ij} = d_{jk} = d_{ik} = 1$), and other features of the network topology.

There are two features of these models that make them unattractive for our purposes. The main problem is that, once estimated, it is difficult to simulate networks from these models in new settings with a different number of nodes, or a different distribution of characteristics. There is no clear reason why the parameters of the ERG models remain the same under such changes. As a result, they do not naturally lead to the prediction of network features in new settings, e.g., the prediction of networks given alternative rules for assigning students to classes. A second problem is that these models are difficult to estimate. The function $k(\theta)$ is difficult to evaluate, and as a result the likelihood function cannot easily be evaluated at multiple values for $\theta$. Various approximations have been suggested but the accuracy of these methods is not clear. For a recent survey, see Kolaczyk (2009).

### 6.3.2 Strategic network formation models

The second approach to modeling networks consists of what Jackson (2010) refers to as strategic network formation (SNF) models. Such models are also referred to as network evolution models (Toivonen et al., 2009), or actor-based models (Snijders, 2005). These models share features with the structural matching models studied in the econometric literature by Fox (2010, 2008), Choo and Siow (2006), and Galichon and Salanié (2010), and the models studied in the sociology and physics literature by Moody (2001), Barabási and Albert (1999), and Fowler et al. (2009). The game-theoretic background to these models is discussed in Myerson (1977), Roth and Sotomayor (1992), and Jackson (2003). Empirical examples of such models include Fox (2010, 2008), Currarini et al. (2009, 2010), and Snijders et al. (2010).

The key feature of these models is the recognition that links are at least partially the result of individual choices. These models assume that links between individuals are established, conditional on an opportunity for such a link arising, if both individual view these links as beneficial. The specific models differ in the amount of structure they place on the objective functions of the individuals. Most of the matching models (e.g., Fox, 2010, 2008; Choo and Siow, 2006; and Galichon and Salanié, 2010) where each individual matches with at most one other individual, and some of the general network models (Moody, 2001) assume that the utility function depends only on the characteristics of the potential partner. Here, in a context where individuals can form links with multiple others, we explicitly allow the utility of a link between $i$ and $j$ to depend on the existence of common friends of $i$ and $j$. As in our application, Snijders et al. (2010) allow for network effects in the utility function. Their model is very rich in allowing the probability of opportunities to form links to arise as a function of individual's characteristics, but in order to do so they can only deal with a small number of nodes (their application has 32 individuals), and need multiple observations on the network over time.

## 6.4 The model

There are three components to our model. The first component concerns the arrival of opportunities for the formation of links. Starting with a fixed population of $N$ individuals or nodes, and an empty network, a sequence of opportunities or meetings (the "chances" in the terminology of Currarini et al. (2009, 2010)) arises. In each period a single pair of individuals is given the opportunity to form a link. The second component of the model determines whether a link gets formed or discontinued. Whether it does depends on the utility the two potential partners derive from such a link (the "choice" in the terminology of Currarini et al. (2010)). The rule for forming a link may require that both potential partners derive positive net utility from the link, or there may be transfers so that a combination of the utilities determines whether the link is formed. The third part of the model consists of the preferences, in the form of a utility function relating the attributes of the potential partners and the current state of the network to the utility derived from a potential link. In the next three subsections we discuss these three aspects of the model.

## 6.4.1 Opportunities for establishing links

In our model there are $T$ periods in the network formation, starting with an empty network. The total number of periods may be tied to the number of individuals in the network, $N$. In fact, when we implement the model the number of periods is exactly equal to the number of distinct pairs, $T = N \times (N - 1)/2$. More generally, we may allow each pair of individuals to meet more than once, and there may be many periods, possibly an infinite number of them. When a pair of individuals is presented with an opportunity to evaluate a link, there are two possible states they may find themselves in. If they currently have no link, they must decide to form a link or not. If they currently have a link, they must decide whether or not to continue the link. This process leads to a slowly evolving network.

This decision to form or discontinue a link is assumed to be based on their characteristics, and on features of the current state of the network. Let $\mathbf{D}_t$ denote the value of the adjacency matrix, that is, the state of the network, at the end of period $t$, with $\mathbf{D}_0$ the empty network, with $\mathbf{D}_{0,ij} = 0$ for all $(i, j)$, and $\mathbf{D} = \mathbf{D}_T$ the final network. In period $t$, two individuals, say individuals $i$ and $j$ have the opportunity to form or discontinue a link. The only possible change in the network in that period is in the values of the $(i, j)$ (and, by symmetry, the $(j, i)$) th element of $\mathbf{D}_{t-1}$. Thus, for $(k, l) \neq (i, j)$ and $(k, l) \neq (j, i)$, it follows that $D_{t,kl} = D_{t-1,kl}$, whereas $D_{t,ij}$ may differ from $D_{t-1,ij}$. In the next period a new pair of individuals gets the opportunity to consider a link. After $T$ periods the network is complete.

In the current version of the model we assume $T = N \cdot (N - 1)/2$, with a unique pair of individuals presented with an opportunity to evaluate the benefits of a link, so that each pair of individuals has exactly one opportunity to meet. The order in which the pairs meet is completely random. Because each pair meets only once, links, once established, will never get dissolved. Conceptually it is straightforward to extend the technology to allow for multiple meetings of pairs of individuals. If a pair of individuals has already formed a link, such subsequent opportunities can lead to the re-evaluation of the link, and through that channel to a severance of the existing link. If a new meeting takes place between individuals whose previous meeting did not result in a link, the change in the network status may lead the individual to reconsider and establish a link. The main restriction in extending the model to allow for multiple meetings between pairs is computational. A second extension involves allowing the probability of a meeting to depend on the current state of the network, or on characteristics of the individuals. Although in the absence of direct information on the sequence of meetings it may be difficult to separate the parameters from the technology of meetings from those of the preferences for links, such extensions may lead to additional flexibility of the models. These extensions may also make the assumption that individuals do not take into account possible future changes to the network more palatable.

## 6.4.2 Link formation

The decision to form a link between a pair, at the point when they meet, is based on their stochastic utility. The utility, for individual $i$, of forming a link with $j$, depends on the characteristic of $i$, the characteristics of $j$, and the current state of the network, and the time period $t$ in which they meet. Thus, if $i$ and $j$ meet in period $t$, with the state of the network at the beginning of period $t$ equal to $\mathbf{D}_{t-1}$, the net utility for $i$ of forming a link can be written, without loss of generality, as

$$U_i(j|\mathbf{X}, \mathbf{C}, \mathbf{D}_{t-1}, t).$$

Similarly, the net utility for individual $j$ of forming a link is

$$U_j(i|\mathbf{X}, \mathbf{C}, \mathbf{D}_{t-1}, t).$$

Whether or not a link gets formed, or whether a link gets discontinued if already formed, depends on these two utilities. We consider three different link formation rules.

One possibility, and the one we focus on in the application, is the non-cooperative version. If $i$ and $j$ meet at in period $t$, they will form a link if both potential partners $i$ and $j$ see the link as increasing their utility:

$$D_{t,ij} = 1 \text{ if } U_i(j|\mathbf{X}, \mathbf{C}, \mathbf{D}_{t-1}, t) \geq 0, \text{ and } U_i(j|\mathbf{X}, \mathbf{C}, \mathbf{D}_{t-1}, t) \geq 0. \quad (6.3)$$

This is the link formation rule we will use in the application in Section 6.6.

A second link formation rule allows for cooperative behavior through the possibility of transfers:

$$D_{t,ij} = 1 \text{ if } \left( U_i(j|\mathbf{X}, \mathbf{C}, \mathbf{D}_{t-1}, t) + U_i(j|\mathbf{X}, \mathbf{D}_{t-1}, t) \right) \geq 0. \quad (6.4)$$

Fox (2010, 2008) considers such matching models for marriage markets.

More generally, one can allow for the possibility of partial transfers of utility, making the link formation an increasing function of both utilities, with some limited degree of substitutability:

$$D_{t,ij} = 1 \text{ if } g\left( U_i(j|\mathbf{X}, \mathbf{C}, \mathbf{D}_{t-1}, t), U_i(j|\mathbf{X}, \mathbf{C}, \mathbf{D}_{t-1}, t) \right) \geq 0. \quad (6.5)$$

Both the non-cooperative version (6.3) and the cooperative version (6.4) are special cases of the general rule (6.5). Although we focus in the current paper on settings with mutual friendships, often data are available on directed friendships where $i$ may consider $j$ a friend, but $j$ need not consider $i$ a friend. In such cases the value of $D_{ij}$ may reflect the net benefits for $i$ of being friends with $j$, not depending on the utility $j$ attaches to a friendship with $i$.

### 6.4.3 Preferences

The first, and most important restriction we impose on the utility function is that it does not depend on $t$:

$$U_i(j, \mathbf{X}, \mathbf{C}, \mathbf{D}, t) = U_i(j, \mathbf{X}, \mathbf{C}, \mathbf{D}). \tag{6.6}$$

This is a crucial restriction. In the early periods of the game the adjacency matrix is still relatively sparse: few friendships have been established at that point. In deciding to evaluate the benefits of potential links, however, we assume that individuals do not anticipate future changes to the network. Given the current network, the probability of a link does not depend on whether the opportunity arose early (and therefore the network is likely to subsequently change) or late (when it the network is close to its final value). This restriction to myopic behavior is more plausible if the technology allows for multiple meetings between each pair of individuals, and it allows for opportunities to sever existing links. See Jackson (2010) for more discussion on this and the link to the concept of pairwise stability of the resulting network. Relaxing this assumption is difficult. It would require individuals to take into account the likelihood of further links, and the impact such links would have on the utility of their own links. Problems concerning the presence of multiple equilibria would arise, as well as severe computational difficulties.

Next, we specify a parametric form for the stochastic utility function $U_i(j, \mathbf{X}, \mathbf{D})$ in terms of some unknown preference parameters $\theta$. This follows in the econometric tradition established by McFadden (1980, 1984). Call this function $U_i(j, \mathbf{X}, \mathbf{C}, \mathbf{D}, \varepsilon_{ij}; \theta)$. In this expression $\varepsilon_{ij}$ represents a component of the utility that is not observed by the econometrician. Combined with a parametric model for the joint distribution of the unobserved components $\varepsilon_{ij}$ for all $i$ and $j$, this leads to a parametric form for the probability of a link with individual $j$ having positive net utility for individual $i$:

$$P_i(j, \mathbf{X}, \mathbf{C}, \mathbf{D}; \theta) = \Pr\left(U_i(j, \mathbf{X}, \mathbf{D}, \mathbf{C}, \varepsilon_{ij}; \theta) > 0\right).$$

The methods we suggest for inference work generally for any specification of the probability, although in practice we need to limit the dependence of the utility (and thus indirectly the dependence of the probability of a profitable link) on the state of the network. Here we discuss some of the restrictions we may impose on the utility function.

First, we restrict the dependence of the utility function $U_i(j, \mathbf{X}, \mathbf{C}, \mathbf{D}, \varepsilon_{ij}; \theta)$ on the current state of the network to be a function of the number of friends $j$ already has, $F_{jj}$; the degree of separation (distance, or geodesic), $G_{ij}$; the match-specific covariate $C_{ij}$; and a scalar stochastic term indexed by the match $(i, j)$. Moreover the dependence on the characteristics is only through the characteristics of $i$ and $j$ themselves:

$$U_i(j, \mathbf{X}, \mathbf{D}, \mathbf{C}; \varepsilon_{ij}; \theta) = U\left(X_i, X_j, F_{jj}, G_{ij}, C_{ij}, \varepsilon_{ij}; \theta\right).$$

The particular parametric form we use in the application in Section 6.6 is

$$U(x_1, x_2, f_{22}, g_{12}, \epsilon; \theta) = \beta_0 + \beta_1' x_2 \qquad (6.7)$$
$$- (x_1 - x_2)' \Omega (x_1 - x_2)$$
$$+ \alpha_1 f_{22} + \alpha_2 f_{22}^2 + \alpha_3 \mathbf{1}_{g_{12}=2} + \alpha_4 \mathbf{1}_{g_{12}=3}$$
$$+ \delta C_{ij} + \epsilon,$$

where full parameter vector is $\theta = (\beta_0, \beta_1, \Omega, \alpha)$. There are four components to the utility function. First, individuals may have direct preferences over the attributes of the potential partners. This is captured by the $\beta_1' x_2$ term. More generally, the preferences of individual $i$ for attributes of potential partners, captured by $\beta - 1$, may vary by characteristics of $i$, and we could model $\beta_1$ as $\beta_{i1} = B' x_i$, leading the first term of the utility function to have the form $x_i' B x_j$. This component of the utility is similar to the way utility functions are specified in the analysis of the demand for differentiated products in the Industrial Organization literature (e.g., Ackerberg et al., 2007), where $x_j$ would capture characteristics of choice $j$ and $x_i$ would correspond to characteristics of the agent that affect the marginal utility of choice characteristics. A component of the utility function that is less familiar from the traditional econometric discrete choice literature is the second term, $(x_1 - x_2)' \Omega (x_1 - x_2)$. This term captures the disutility associated with differences in the characteristics between the two potential partners. The tendency of individuals to form links with individuals who are similar to them, referred to as homophily in the network literature (Jackson, 2010; Christakis and Fowler, 2009), has been found to be pervasive in social networks (e.g., Christakis and Fowler, 2009). In our specification $\Omega$ is a diagonal matrix. The third component, including four terms, captures network effects. The utility is allowed to depend quadratically on the number of friends the alter already has, $f_{22}$, and whether the degree of separation is two or three. The first two terms simply capture that the utility of having $j$ as a friend may depend on how many friends $j$ has already. On the one hand, one may not want to have friends who have too many friends already, but on the other hand there may be benefits associated with having very popular friends. Including a quadratic function in the number of friends in the specification of the utility function allows us to potentially capture both effects. A common finding in the social network literature is that if $i$ and $j$ are friends, and $j$ and $k$ are friends, $i$ and $k$ are more likely to be friends than one would expect if links were formed randomly. The dependence of the utility function on attributes of the potential partners, and in particular the homophily, may already generate such patterns in the network, but $\alpha_3$ and $\alpha_4$ allow for more flexibility in generating patterns commonly observed in networks. Finally, the fourth component allows the utility of the link to depend directly on the link-specific characteristic $C_{ij}$.

As second, more restrictive, specification we use

$$U(x_1, x_2, f_{11}, f_{22}, f_{12}, g_{12}, \epsilon; \theta)$$
$$= \beta_0 + \beta_1' x_2 - (x_1 - x_2)' \Omega (x_1 - x_2) + \delta C_{ij} + \epsilon. \tag{6.8}$$

Here we rule out network effects ($\alpha_1 = \alpha_2 = \alpha_3 = \alpha_4 = 0$), so that the utility of a link between $i$ and $j$ depends only on characteristics of $i$ and $j$, and not on the degree of separation between $i$ and $j$, or on how many friends they already have. This model is more in the spirit of the models used by Moody (2001) and Fox (2010, 2008), and so we will pay particular attention to the empirical evidence that the additional parameters that explicitly capture the network dependence, contribute substantially to the explanatory power of the model.

In the implementation below, we assume that the $\epsilon_{ij}$ are independent across all pairs $(i, j)$, including independent of $\varepsilon_{ji}$, and that the $\varepsilon_{ij}$ have a logistic distribution. We also assume that the $\varepsilon_{ij}$ do not vary across meetings between the same pair. Thus, if individuals $i$ and $j$ meet more than once, their decision whether to form or dissolve a link may change over time. The reason for the difference in the decision comes from the changes in the network between meetings. This property implies that if the number of meetings $T$ is infinitely large, so that all pairs meet at least once after the final network has been established, and if the sequence of networks converge, the final network will be pairwise stable (Jackson, 2010).

The assumption of a type I extreme value distribution for $\epsilon_{ij}$ implies that the log odds of individual $i$ being in favor of establishing the link is

$$\ln \left( \frac{P_i(j, \mathbf{X}, \mathbf{C}, \mathbf{D}; \theta)}{1 - P_i(j, \mathbf{X}, \mathbf{C}, \mathbf{D}; \theta)} \right) = \beta_0 + \beta_1' X_j - (X_i - X_j) \Omega (X_i - X_j)$$
$$+ \alpha_1 F_{jj} + \alpha_2 F_{jj}^2 + \alpha_3 \mathbf{1}_{G_{ij}=2} + \alpha_4 \mathbf{1}_{G_{ij}=3} + \delta C_{ij},$$

where again

$$P_i(j, \mathbf{X}, \mathbf{C}, \mathbf{D}; \theta) = \Pr \left( U_i(j, \mathbf{X}, \mathbf{D}, \mathbf{C}; \varepsilon_{ij}; \theta) > 0 \right).$$

As a result of the independence of the $\varepsilon_{ij}$, the probability of the establishment of a link between individuals $i$ and $j$ in period $t$, given their characteristics and given the current state of the network, and given that the opportunity for establishing a link between $i$ and $j$ arises in period $t$, is the product of the probabilities that both individuals perceive a net benefit from such a link:

$$\Pr(D_{t,ij} = 1 | X_i, X_j, \mathbf{D}_{t-1}, \mathbf{C}, (m_{1t}, m_{2t}) = (i, j))$$
$$= P_i(j, \mathbf{X}, \mathbf{C}, \mathbf{D}_{t-1}; \theta) \cdot P_j(i, \mathbf{X}, \mathbf{C}, \mathbf{D}_{t-1}; \theta).$$

### 6.4.4 The likelihood function

The model outlined above describes a stochastic mechanism for generating a network, given a population of $N$ individuals, with characteristics $X_1, \ldots, X_N$, and given link characteristics $C_{ij}$. Associated with a matrix of characteristics $\mathbf{X}$ and a matrix of match characteristics $\mathbf{C}$, and conditional on a vector of parameters $\theta$, there is therefore a probability for the adjacency matrix $\mathbf{D}$,

$$\Pr(\mathbf{D}|\mathbf{X}, \mathbf{C}; \theta),$$

leading to a likelihood function associated with the sample $(\mathbf{D}, \mathbf{X}, \mathbf{C})$,

$$\mathcal{L}(\theta|\mathbf{D}, \mathbf{X}, \mathbf{C}) = \Pr(\mathbf{D}|\mathbf{X}, \mathbf{C}; \theta).$$

How can we analyze and estimate such models? The difficulty is that even in settings with only a moderate number of nodes and links, the likelihood function can be hard to evaluate directly.

To see this, let us rewrite the likelihood function in terms of the ordered meetings. Let $\mathbf{M}$ be the matrix of ordered meetings. The matrix $\mathbf{M}$ is an $(N \cdot (N-1)/2) \times 2$ dimensional matrix, with $t$th row $m_t$ a pair of indices, $m_t = (m_{t1}, m_{t2})$, such that $m_{t1}, m_{t2} \in \{1, \ldots, N\}$. The set of possible values for $\mathbf{M}$, denoted by $\mathbb{M}$, has $(N \times (N-1)/2)!$ distinct elements.

First we construct the augmented data likelihood function $\Pr(\mathbf{D}, \mathbf{M}|\mathbf{X}, \mathbf{C}; \theta)$. In order to get the observed data likelihood function we then sum over the distribution of opportunities $\mathbf{M}$:

$$\mathcal{L}(\theta|\mathbf{D}, \mathbf{X}, \mathbf{C}) = \Pr(\mathbf{D}|\mathbf{X}, \mathbf{C}; \theta) = \sum_{\mathbf{M} \in \mathbb{M}} \Pr(\mathbf{M}|\mathbf{X}, \mathbf{C}; \theta) \cdot \Pr(\mathbf{D}|\mathbf{M}, \mathbf{X}, \mathbf{C}; \theta).$$

A key observation is the fact that, given $\mathbf{M}$ and $\mathbf{D}$, we can recover the entire sequence of networks, $\mathbf{D}_0, \mathbf{D}_1, \ldots, \mathbf{D}_{N \cdot (N+1)/2-N}$, and thus recover the full set of decisions faced and made by each agent. First let us look at the augmented data likelihood of a sequence of networks and opportunities. Let $\mathbf{M}_t$ be the $t \times 2$-dimensional matrix containing the first $t$ rows of $\mathbf{M}$, so that $\mathbf{M}_{N \cdot (N+1)/2-N} = \mathbf{M}$, and let $\mathbf{M}_0 = 0$. Then the complete data likelihood function is

$$\Pr(\mathbf{D}, \mathbf{M}|\mathbf{X}, \mathbf{C}; \theta)$$
$$= \Pr(\mathbf{D}_0, \mathbf{D}_1, \ldots, \mathbf{D}_{N \cdot (N-1)/2}, \mathbf{M}_1, \ldots, \mathbf{M}_{N \cdot (N-1)/2}|\mathbf{X}, \mathbf{C}; \theta)$$
$$= \prod_{t=1}^{N \cdot (N-1)/2} \Pr(\mathbf{M}_t|\mathbf{D}_{t-1}, \mathbf{M}_{t-1}, \mathbf{X}; \theta) \cdot \Pr(\mathbf{D}_t|\mathbf{D}_{t-1}, \mathbf{M}_t, \mathbf{X}, \mathbf{C}; \theta)$$
$$= \Pr(\mathbf{M}) \cdot \prod_{t=1}^{N \cdot (N-1)/2} \Pr(\mathbf{D}_t|\mathbf{D}_{t-1}, \mathbf{M}_t, \mathbf{X}, \mathbf{C}; \theta)$$
$$= \Pr(\mathbf{M})$$
$$\cdot \prod_{t=1}^{N \cdot (N-1)/2} \left\{ \left( P_{m_{t1}}(m_{t2}, \mathbf{X}, \mathbf{C}, \mathbf{D}_t; \theta) \cdot P_{m_{t2}}(m_{t1}, \mathbf{X}, \mathbf{C}, \mathbf{D}_t; \theta) \right)^{D_{m_{t1}, m_{t2}}} \right.$$

$$\times \left( 1 - P_{m_{t1}}(m_{t2}, \mathbf{X}, \mathbf{C}, \mathbf{D}_t; \theta) \cdot P_{m_{t2}}(m_{t1}, \mathbf{X}, \mathbf{C}, \mathbf{D}_t; \theta) \right)^{1 - D_{m_{t1}, m_{t2}}} \Bigg\}$$

The marginal (or conditional) probability of the sequence of meetings is simply

$$\Pr(\mathbf{M}) = \Pr(\mathbf{M}|\mathbf{X}, \mathbf{C}) = \frac{1}{(N \cdot (N-1)/2)!}.$$

Hence the (observed data) likelihood function is

$$\mathcal{L}(\theta|\mathbf{D}, \mathbf{X}, \mathbf{C}) = \Pr(\mathbf{D}|\mathbf{X}, \mathbf{C}; \theta) = \sum_{\mathbf{M} \in \mathbb{M}} \Pr(\mathbf{M}|\mathbf{X}, \mathbf{C}; \theta) \cdot \Pr(\mathbf{D}|\mathbf{M}, \mathbf{X}, \mathbf{C}; \theta)$$

$$= \frac{1}{(N \cdot (N-1)/2)!}$$

$$\cdot \sum_{\mathbf{M} \in \mathbb{M}} \Bigg[ \prod_{t=1}^{N \cdot (N-1)/2} \Bigg\{ \left( P_{m_{t1}}(m_{t2}\mathbf{X}, \mathbf{C}, \mathbf{D}_t; \theta) \cdot P_{m_{t2}}(m_{t1}, \mathbf{X}, \mathbf{C}, \mathbf{D}_t; \theta) \right)^{D_{m_{t1}, m_{t2}}}$$

$$\times \left( 1 - P_{m_{t1}}(m_{t2}, \mathbf{X}, \mathbf{C}, \mathbf{D}_t; \theta) \cdot P_{m_{t2}}(m_{t1}\mathbf{X}, \mathbf{C}, \mathbf{D}_t; \theta) \right)^{1 - D_{m_{t1}, m_{t2}}} \Bigg\} \Bigg].$$

$$(6.9)$$

The likelihood function is a sum over $(N \cdot (N-1)/2)!$ terms, each of which is a product over $(N \cdot (N-1)/2)$ factors. In our application the number of nodes is $N = 669$, so that directly evaluating the likelihood function is not feasible. We therefore use simulation methods.

Note that these difficulties in evaluating the likelihood function with network effects would not arise if the network effects were not present (all the parameters $\alpha_k$ equal to zero). If the probability of a link between $i$ and $j$ depends only on the characteristics of the individuals $i$ and $j$, and not on the current state of the network, the order of meetings does not matter, and calculating the log likelihood function for a given value of the parameters is straightforward. In that case

$$P(i \langle j | \mathbf{X}, \mathbf{C}, \mathbf{D}; \theta) = P(X_i, X_j, C_{ij}; \theta),$$

and we can write the likelihood function as

$$\mathcal{L}(\theta|\mathbf{D}, \mathbf{X}, \mathbf{C}) =$$

$$\prod_{i=1}^{N-1} \prod_{j=i+1}^{N} \left( P(X_i, X_j, C_{ij}; \theta) P(X_j, X_i, C_{ij}; \theta) \right)^{D_{ij}}$$

$$\times \left( 1 - P(X_i, X_j, C_{ij}; \theta) P(X_j, X_i, C_{ij}; \theta) \right)^{1 - D_{ij}}.$$

Although the number of factors in the likelihood function is larger than the sample size $(N \cdot (N-1)/2)$, this likelihood function is straightforward to work with, and standard properties apply.

## 6.5 Markov-chain-Monte-Carlo methods

A key insight is that the likelihood function for the model with network effects would be easier to evaluate if we knew the history of opportunities, and, by implication, the history of the network formation. Snijders et al. (2010) exploit this in a setting with repeated observations on a network.

We exploit this by imputing the unobserved sequence of meetings in a Bayesian approach. The Markov-chain-Monte-Carlo algorithm consists of two parts. Given the parameters $\theta$ and the observed data, and given an initial value for the sequence of meetings $\mathbf{M}$, we use a Metropolis-Hastings step to update the sequence of meetings. In the second step, given the sequence of meetings, parameters and data we update the vector of parameters, again in a Metropolis-Hastings step. Let $(\theta_k, \mathbf{M}_k)$ denote the sequence of values in the chain. We describe these two steps in more detail in the next two subsections.

### 6.5.1 Drawing from the posterior distribution of the parameters given the augmented data

Let the prior distribution for $\theta$ be $p(\theta)$. (We will use independent Gaussian prior distributions for all elements of $\theta$, centered at zero, and with unit variance, but the algorithms apply more generally.) Then, given the augmented data $(\mathbf{X}, \mathbf{C}, \mathbf{D}, \mathbf{M}_k)$, including the imputed sequence of meetings $\mathbf{M}_k$, and given a current value for the parameters $\theta_k$, we draw $\theta$ from a candidate distribution $q_\theta(\theta | \theta_k, \mathbf{X}, \mathbf{C}, \mathbf{D}, \mathbf{M}_k)$. We then calculate the ratio

$$\rho_\theta(\theta, \theta_k, \mathbf{X}, \mathbf{C}, \mathbf{D}, \mathbf{M}_k)$$
$$= \min \left\{ 1, \frac{\Pr(\mathbf{D}|\mathbf{M}_k, \mathbf{X}, \mathbf{C}; \theta) \cdot p(\theta) \cdot q_\theta(\theta_k | \theta, \mathbf{X}, \mathbf{C}, \mathbf{D}, \mathbf{M}_k)}{\Pr(\mathbf{D}|\mathbf{M}, \mathbf{X}, \mathbf{C}; \theta_k) \cdot p(\theta_k) \cdot q_\theta(\theta | \theta_k, \mathbf{X}, \mathbf{C}, \mathbf{D}, \mathbf{M}_k)} \right\}.$$

As the candidate distribution $q_\theta(\theta | \theta_k, \mathbf{X}, \mathbf{C}, \mathbf{D}, \mathbf{M}_k)$ we take a gaussian distribution:

$$q_\theta(\theta | \theta_k, \mathbf{X}, \mathbf{C}, \mathbf{D}, \mathbf{M}_k) \sim \mathcal{N}(\theta_k, \Sigma),$$

where $\Sigma$ is a positive definite matrix. (In the application we run an initial chain with a diagonal matrix $\Sigma$ and then choose $\Sigma$ proportional to the covariance matrix of $\theta$ based on the results from that initial chain.) As a result of the choice of $q_\theta(\cdot)$ it follows that

$$q_\theta(\theta_k | \theta, \mathbf{X}, \mathbf{C}, \mathbf{D}, \mathbf{M}_k) = q_\theta(\theta | \theta_k, \mathbf{X}, \mathbf{C}, \mathbf{D}, \mathbf{M}_k),$$

which implies that the candidate distribution $q_\theta(\cdot | \cdot)$ drops out of the expression for the transition probability $\rho_\theta(\cdot)$, leaving us with

$$\rho_\theta(\theta, \theta_k, \mathbf{X}, \mathbf{C}, \mathbf{D}, \mathbf{M}_k) = \min \left\{ 1, \frac{\Pr(\mathbf{D}|\mathbf{M}_k, \mathbf{X}; \theta) \cdot p(\theta)}{\Pr(\mathbf{D}|\mathbf{M}_k, \mathbf{X}; \theta_k) \cdot p(\theta_k)} \right\}.$$

The MCMC chain jumps to the new value with probability $\rho_\theta(\theta, \theta_k, \mathbf{X}, \mathbf{C}, \mathbf{D}, \mathbf{M}_k)$, so that the new value is

$$\theta_{k+1} = \begin{cases} \theta & \text{with probability } \rho_\theta(\theta, \theta_k, \mathbf{X}, \mathbf{C}, \mathbf{D}, \mathbf{M}_k), \\ \theta_k & \text{with probability } 1 - \rho_\theta(\theta, \theta_k, \mathbf{X}, \mathbf{C}, \mathbf{D}, \mathbf{M}_k). \end{cases}$$

### 6.5.2 Updating the sequence of opportunities

Now consider imputing $\mathbf{M}_{k+1}$ given current $\theta_k$ and given the data $\mathbf{D}$, $\mathbf{X}$, and $\mathbf{C}$, and the currently imputed $\mathbf{M}_k$. The conditional probability for a value $\mathbf{M}$ given the data $(\mathbf{X}, \mathbf{C}, \mathbf{D})$ and the current value of the parameter $\theta_k$ is

$$\Pr(\mathbf{M}|\mathbf{D}, \mathbf{X}, \mathbf{C}; \theta_k) = \frac{\Pr(\mathbf{M}) \cdot \Pr(\mathbf{D}|\mathbf{M}, \mathbf{X}, \mathbf{C}; \theta_k)}{\Pr(\mathbf{D}|\mathbf{X}, \mathbf{C}; \theta_k)}.$$

We draw a potential new value $\mathbf{M}$ from a distribution $q_\mathbf{M}(\mathbf{M}|\mathbf{M}_k, \mathbf{X}, \mathbf{C}, \mathbf{D}; \theta_k)$. Then define the transition probability

$$\rho_\mathbf{M}(\mathbf{M}, \mathbf{M}_k, \mathbf{X}, \mathbf{C}, \mathbf{D}, \theta_k)$$
$$= \min\left\{ 1, \frac{\Pr(\mathbf{D}|\mathbf{M}, \mathbf{X}, \mathbf{C}; \theta_k) \cdot \Pr(\mathbf{M}) \cdot q_\mathbf{M}(\mathbf{M}_k|\mathbf{M}, \mathbf{X}, \mathbf{C}, \mathbf{D}, \theta_k)}{\Pr(\mathbf{D}|\mathbf{M}_k, \mathbf{X}, \mathbf{C}; \theta_k) \cdot \Pr(\mathbf{M}_k) \cdot q_\mathbf{M}(\mathbf{M}|\mathbf{M}_k, \mathbf{X}, \mathbf{C}, \mathbf{D}, \theta_k)} \right\}.$$

With the marginal distribution of $\mathbf{M}$ uniform on $\mathbb{M}$, so that $\Pr(\mathbf{M}) = \Pr(\mathbf{M}_k)$, this transition probability simplifies to

$$\rho_\mathbf{M}(\mathbf{M}, \mathbf{M}_k, \mathbf{X}, \mathbf{C}, \mathbf{D}, \theta_k)$$
$$= \min\left\{ 1, \frac{\Pr(\mathbf{D}|\mathbf{M}, \mathbf{X}, \mathbf{C}; \theta_k) \cdot q_\mathbf{M}(\mathbf{M}_k|\mathbf{M}, \mathbf{X}, \mathbf{C}, \mathbf{D}, \theta_k)}{\Pr(\mathbf{D}|\mathbf{M}_k, \mathbf{X}, \mathbf{C}; \theta_k) \cdot q_\mathbf{M}(\mathbf{M}|\mathbf{M}_k, \mathbf{X}, \mathbf{C}, \mathbf{D}, \theta_k)} \right\}.$$

For the candidate distribution $q_\mathbf{M}(\mathbf{M}|\mathbf{M}_k, \mathbf{X}, \mathbf{C}, \mathbf{D}; \theta_k)$ we random re-order a fraction $p_\mathbf{M}$ of the elements of $\mathbf{M}_k$. (In the application we fix $p_\mathbf{M} = 0.01$, so that 2,234 out of the 223,446 meetings are randomly reordered. The fraction $p_\mathbf{M} = 0.01$ is set by trial and error so that the jump probabilities are not too high or too low on average, aiming for a jump probability of 0.4.) This choice of $q_\mathbf{M}(\cdot)$ implies that the candidate distribution is symmetric in $\mathbf{M}$ and $\mathbf{M}_k$, implying $q_\mathbf{M}(\mathbf{M}|\mathbf{M}_k, \mathbf{X}, \mathbf{C}, \mathbf{D}; \theta_k) = q_\mathbf{M}(\mathbf{M}_k|\mathbf{M}, \mathbf{X}, \mathbf{C}, \mathbf{D}; \theta_k)$, so that the expression for the transition probability is free of dependence on the candidate distribution $q_\mathbf{M}(\cdot|\cdot)$:

$$\rho_\mathbf{M}(\mathbf{M}, \mathbf{M}_k, \mathbf{X}, \mathbf{C}, \mathbf{D}, \theta_k) = \min\left\{ 1, \frac{\Pr(\mathbf{D}|\mathbf{M}, \mathbf{X}, \mathbf{C}; \theta_k)}{\Pr(\mathbf{D}|\mathbf{M}_k, \mathbf{X}, \mathbf{C}; \theta_k)} \right\}.$$

The MCMC chain jumps to the new value with probability $\rho_\mathbf{M}(\mathbf{M}, \mathbf{M}_k, \mathbf{X}, \mathbf{C}, \mathbf{D}, \theta_k)$, so that the new value is

$$\mathbf{M}_{k+1} = \begin{cases} \mathbf{M} & \text{with probability } \rho_\mathbf{M}(\mathbf{M}, \mathbf{M}_k, \mathbf{X}, \mathbf{C}, \mathbf{D}, \theta_k), \\ \mathbf{M}_k & \text{with probability } 1 - \rho_\mathbf{M}(\mathbf{M}, \mathbf{M}_k, \mathbf{X}, \mathbf{C}, \mathbf{D}, \theta_k). \end{cases}$$

## 6.6 An application to high school friendships

In this section, we estimate the model for network formation on a network of friendships among high school students. We estimate the specific parametric model with utility function

$$U(x_1, x_2, f_{22}, g_{12}, \epsilon; \theta) = \beta_0 + \beta_1' x_2 - (x_1 - x_2)' \Omega (x_1 - x_2)$$
$$+ \alpha_1 f_{22} + \alpha_2 f_{22}^2 + \alpha_3 \mathbf{1}_{g_{12}=2} + \alpha_4 \mathbf{1}_{g_{12}=3}$$
$$+ \delta C_{ij} + \epsilon,$$

with a type I extreme value distribution for the $\epsilon$, independent across all pairs of students. We assume there are $T = N \cdot (N + 1)/2 - N$ periods in the network formation phase, with each pair of individuals having a single opportunity to establish a link. Links are formed if both potential partners derive net positive utility from the link. There are no utility transfers in the model. We also estimate a restricted version of this model with no network effects, where $\alpha_1 = \alpha_2 = \alpha_3 = \alpha_4 = 0$. We refer to this as the covariates-only model or the no-network-effects model.

We will first estimate these two models using MCMC methods. Next we investigate the fit of the model, focusing on network features such as clustering, the degree or distance distribution, and the distribution of the number of friendships or links. We assess the fit by comparing the actual feature, e.g., the clustering coefficient, to the predictive distribution of the clustering coefficient given the data. Third, we predict the effect, on the network characteristics, of an alternative distribution of characteristics, corresponding to making all classrooms single sex, so that the number of classes in common for pairs of students of different sex is zero.

### 6.6.1 Data

The data are from a single school in the AddHealth data set. The data set contains information on 669 students (nodes) in this school, and a total of 1,541 friendships (links), out of a set of 223,446 pairs of distinct students. We use four student characteristics, an indicator for sex (0 for male, 1 for female), grade (ranging from 8 to 13), age (ranging from 13.3 to 21.3), and an indicator for participation in sports. We also use a match-specific characteristic, $C_{ij}$, the number of classes individuals $i$ and $j$ have in common. When estimating the model we subtract 10 from the grade and 17 from the age variables.

Table 6.1 presents some summary statistics for the 669 students. Table 6.2 presents some summary statistics for the 223,446 pairs. Table 6.3 gives the triangle census of the network and the overall clustering coefficient. (The overall clustering coefficient is calculated as the ratio of the number of distinct triples with three friendships to the number of distinct triples with at least two friendships.) Given that the number of individuals in our sample is 669 and given that there are 1,541 links, if the links were formed completely randomly, the

**TABLE 6.1** Summary statistics of student characteristics (N=669).

| Characteristic | Mean | Standard Deviation | median | Min | Max |
|---|---|---|---|---|---|
| Sex (0 Male, 1 Female) | 0.48 | (0.50) | 0 | 0 | 1 |
| Grade | 10.7 | (1.1) | 11.0 | 8.0 | 13.0 |
| Age | 17.3 | (1.3) | 17.3 | 13.3 | 21.3 |
| Sports Participation | 0.49 | (0.50) | 0 | 0 | 1 |
| Number of Friendships | 4.6 | (3.3) | 4 | 0 | 18 |

**TABLE 6.2** Summary statistics of student pair characteristics (223,446 pairs).

| Characteristic | All (223,446) | | Friends (1,541) | | Not Friends (221,905) | |
|---|---|---|---|---|---|---|
| | *Mean* | *SD* | *Mean* | *SD* | *Mean* | *SD* |
| # Classes in Common | 0.65 | 1.45 | 2.13 | 2.48 | 0.64 | 1.44 |
| Abs Diff in Gender | 0.50 | 0.50 | 0.41 | 0.49 | 0.50 | 0.50 |
| Abs Dif in Grade | 1.21 | 1.01 | 0.43 | 0.67 | 1.22 | 1.01 |
| Abs Diff in Age | 1.43 | 1.07 | 0.70 | 0.64 | 1.43 | 1.07 |
| Abs Dif in Sports Participation | 0.50 | 0.50 | 0.40 | 0.49 | 0.50 | 0.50 |

**TABLE 6.3** Triangle census (total number of triples 49,679,494).

| Triangle Type | Actual Count | Predicted Count | |
|---|---|---|---|
| | | *Model I* Covariates Only | *Model II* Network Effects |
| No Edges | 48,660,171 | 48,660,484.8 | 48,697,654.4 |
| Single Edge | 1,011,455 | 1,010,674.3 | 974,304.9 |
| Two Edges | 7,212 | 8,294.5 | 7,075.2 |
| Three Edges | 656 | 40.3 | 459.6 |
| Overall Clustering Coefficient | 0.083 | 0.005 | 0.061 |

expected number of triangles with three edges would be 16.3, and the clustering coefficient would be 0.0023. In the actual network there are 656 triangles with three edges, and the clustering coefficient is 0.083, much higher than can be explained by completely random formation of links. The finding that there are many more triangles in the actual network than in a corresponding random network is common in the network literature, and developing models that are consistent with such clustering is one of the challenges facing researchers.

Table 6.4 presents summary statistics on the degree distribution. On average, students have 4.6 friends. Out of the full population of 669 students, 70 students have no friends in the grades surveyed. There is one student with 17, and one with 18 friends. The two modes of the distribution of the number of friends are 4 and 5.

Table 6.5 provides statistics on the distribution of the degree of separation or geodesic. There is one large community, comprising 579 of the 669 students in

**TABLE 6.4** Number of friendships (669 individuals).

| Number of Friendships | Number of Students | | |
|---|---|---|---|
| | Actual Network | Predicted Network | |
| | | Model I Covariates Only | Model II Network Effects |
| 0 | 70 | 39.7 | 50.8 |
| 1 | 67 | 59.5 | 72.8 |
| 2 | 60 | 77.0 | 8545 |
| 3 | 77 | 87.5 | 89.1 |
| 4 | 79 | 89.6 | 82.6 |
| 5 | 79 | 81.3 | 71.8 |
| 6 | 57 | 69.7 | 58.9 |
| 7 | 52 | 55.0 | 47.6 |
| 8 | 38 | 41.0 | 35.7 |
| 9 | 35 | 27.5 | 25.4 |
| 10 | 21 | 17.6 | 17.5 |
| 11 | 14 | 6.3 | 7.6 |
| 12 | 10 | 3.5 | 4.8 |
| 13 | 4 | 1.6 | 3.1 |
| 14 | 3 | 0.7 | 1.5 |
| 15 | 1 | 0.3 | 0.9 |
| 16 | 0 | 0.2 | 0.7 |
| 17 | 1 | 0.1 | 0.3 |
| 18 | 1 | 0.0 | 021 |
| 19 | 0 | 0.0 | 0.1 |
| 20 | 0 | 0.0 | 0.1 |
| 21 | 0 | 0.0 | 0.0 |
| 22 | 0 | 0.0 | 0.0 |
| 23 | 0 | 0.0 | 0.0 |
| 24 | 0 | 0.0 | 0.0 |
| ≥ 25 | 0 | 0.0 | 0.0 |
| Average Number of Friendships | 4.60 | 4.60 | 4.44 |
| Stand Dev of Number of Friendships | 3.29 | 2.92 | 3.15 |

the sample. The remaining 120 students consist of 70 students with no friends in the sample, 8 pairs, and 1 groups of four.

## 6.6.2   Estimation and inference

We estimate two versions of the model in (6.7). First, the model with all network parameters fixed at zero (the "no-network-effects" model, or the "covariates-only" model), and then the model allowing for network effects (the "network-effects" model). For the covariates-only model we use two estimation methods.

**TABLE 6.5** Distribution of degree of separation (number of pairs 223,446).

| Degree of Separation | Number of Pairs | | |
|---|---|---|---|
| | *Actual* | *Average Prediction* | |
| | | *Model I* Covariates Only | *Model II* Network Effects |
| 1 | 1,541 | 1,540.3 | 1,484.0 |
| 2 | 5,893 | 7,998.2 | 6,159.3 |
| 3 | 18,090 | 33,775.0 | 21,320.8 |
| 4 | 38,828 | 73,457.7 | 47,553.0 |
| 5 | 49,053 | 56,698.9 | 55,079.7 |
| 6 | 33,032 | 17,662.0 | 33,607.2 |
| 7 | 14,211 | 3,269.8 | 13,205.5 |
| 8 | 4,837 | 497.7 | 4,033.9 |
| 9 | 1,447 | 7.6 | 1,090.7 |
| 10 | 350 | 9.7 | 291.4 |
| 11 | 59 | 0.8 | 78.3 |
| 12 | 4 | 0.0 | 18.5 |
| 13 | 0 | 0.0 | 3.8 |
| 14 | 0 | 0.0 | 0.7 |
| 15 | 0 | 0.0 | 0.1 |
| 16 | 0 | 0.0 | 0.0 |
| 17 | 0 | 0.0 | 0.0 |
| 18 | 0 | 0.0 | 0.0 |
| 19 | 0 | 0.0 | 0.0 |
| 20 | 0 | 0.0 | 0.0 |
| Infinity | 56,101 | 28,459.8 | 39,519.2 |

First, we calculate the maximum likelihood estimates. As discussed in Section 6.4.4, in the model without network effects we can evaluate the likelihood function relatively easily. Next we approximate the posterior distribution for the parameters in the covariates-only model. There are a couple of reasons for focusing on posterior distributions. One is computational. Obtaining draws from the posterior distribution is easier than evaluating the likelihood function. Second, ultimately our goal is to predict features of the network given chances in the distribution of the characteristics of the individuals, and for such a prediction problem Bayesian methods are particularly well suited.

We use independent normal prior distributions on all parameters, with prior mean equal to zero, and prior variance equal to one. For both versions of the model we run one initial MCMC chain with 1,000 iterations. We fit a multivariate normal distribution to the output from these chains, after taking out the first 500 iterations. We then randomly draw 10 starting values for $\theta$ from this normal distribution, after multiplying the variance by 100 to ensure that the starting values are dispersed relative to the posterior distribution. We run

**TABLE 6.6** Estimates of preference parameters.

| Parameter | Description | ML Estimates | | Moments of Posterior Distribution | | | |
|---|---|---|---|---|---|---|---|
| | | Model I | | Model I | | Model II | |
| | | No Network Effects | | No Network Effects | | Network Effects | |
| | | est. | s.e. | mean | s.d. | mean | s.d. |
| $\alpha_1$ | # of friends of alter | 0 | – | 0 | – | −0.14 | (0.03) |
| $\alpha_2$ | total # of friends of alter sq | 0 | – | 0 | – | 0.004 | (0.003) |
| $\alpha_3$ | degr of sep is two | 0 | – | 0 | – | 2.66 | (0.07) |
| $\alpha_4$ | degr of sep is three | 0 | – | 0 | – | 1.22 | (0.07) |
| $\beta_0$ | intercept | −2.12 | (0.05) | −2.11 | (0.04) | −2.11 | (0.06) |
| $\beta_1$ | female | -0.06 | (0.04) | −0.06 | (0.04) | −0.04 | (0.05) |
| $\beta_2$ | alter grade | 0.08 | (0.03) | 0.08 | (0.03) | 0.07 | (0.03) |
| $\beta_3$ | alter age | 0.05 | (0.03) | 0.05 | (0.03) | 0.05 | (0.03) |
| $\beta_4$ | participates in sport | 0.10 | (0.04) | 0.09 | (0.04) | 0.04 | (0.05) |
| $\Omega_{11}$ | diff in sex | 0.19 | (0.03) | 0.19 | (0.03) | 0.20 | (0.03) |
| $\Omega_{22}$ | diff in grades squared | 0.17 | (0.02) | 0.17 | (0.01) | 0.14 | (0.01) |
| $\Omega_{33}$ | diff in age squared | 0.10 | (0.02) | 0.10 | (0.01) | 0.09 | (0.01) |
| $\Omega_{44}$ | diff in sports participation | 0.21 | (0.03) | 0.22 | (0.03) | 0.19 | (0.03) |
| $\delta$ | # of classes in common | 0.14 | (0.01) | 0.14 | (0.01) | 0.12 | (0.01) |

the ten MCMC chains until, for all 14 (full model with network effects) or ten (covariates-only model) parameters, the ratio of the between-chain-variance of the ten chain means, and average of the ten within-chain-variances, is less than 0.1, following the suggestion in Gelman and Rubin (1992). Table 6.6 presents summary statistics for the posterior distribution. Prior to the estimation, we normalize two of the two covariates, subtracting 10 from the grade and 17 from the age.

There are a couple of interesting observations from the posterior distributions. First, the link-specific variable, the number of classes potential friends have in common, with parameter $\delta$ is very important in explaining friendship patterns. Each additional class in common increases the log odds ratio of friendship by approximately 0.12. Note that friends have on average 2.1 classes in common, and non-friends have on average 0.6 classes in common. Conditional on that grade, age, sex and sports participation are only moderately predictive of friendships.

Second, the homophily effects as captured by $\Omega$ are substantial, for all four covariates.

Third, network effects are very important. The number of friends a potential friend already has, $F_{jj}$, is somewhat important, with people preferring, everything else equal, friends who do not have many friends yet. Much more important though is the distance between individuals in the current network. If potential friends already have friends in common, the log odds go up by 2.66, and even if the degree of separation or geodesic distance is three (some friends of $i$ have friends in common with $j$), the log odds goes up by 1.22. Compared to the effect of the covariates and the number of classes in common, these effects are large.

### 6.6.3 Goodness of fit

Here we look at the two estimated models and compare features of the predicted networks with actual features of the network to assess the goodness of fit. We focus on three features of the network.

First, we focus on the triangle census and the clustering coefficient. The results are presented in Table 6.3. The model with the covariates only does a poor job in replicating the clustering present in the actual network. This model predicts that there would be very few full triangles (39.0), compared to the 656 triangles in the actual network. The model with the network effects predicts 459.6 triangles, ten times as much as the model without network effects, although still a little less than the actual number of closed triangles.

Second, we look at the degree distribution, that is, the distribution of the number of friends each individual has. The results are presented in Table 6.4. Not surprisingly, both models predict accurately the mean number of friendships. The model with network effects does slightly better than the model with only covariates in terms of matching the dispersion of the distribution.

Third, we compare the distribution of the geodesic or degree of separation. The results are presented in Table 6.5. Here the model with network effects does a considerably better job than the model with covariates only. The model with covariates under predicts the number of pairs with high degrees of separation.

### 6.6.4 The effect of single-sex classrooms on network formation

Now let us consider the effect on network formation of policies the school may consider. Here we take a fairly extreme policy. Instead of the current mixed-sex classrooms, we impose single sex classrooms, so that all boys and girls have no classes in common. Keeping the values of the individual characteristics $X_i$ the same as in the actual data set, we change the value of $C_{ij}$ to zero if $(i, j)$ are a mixed-sex pair ($X_{i1} \neq X_{j1}$). Given the new values for $\mathbf{C}$, and the current values for $\mathbf{X}$, we simulate the network multiple times, and calculate the number of boy-boy, boy-girl and girl-girl friendships. Table 6.7 presents the results. The main quantity of interest is the rate of boy-girl friendships. In the actual network this is 0.0056. The network model predicts that to be 0.0055, again a sign that the model fits well. If we change $\mathbf{C}$ so that boys and girls have no classes in common, the model predicts that this rate will decrease to 0.0037.

**TABLE 6.7** Friendship rates by sex composition.

| Friendship Type | Actual # of Friendship | | Predicted Rate Network Model | |
|---|---|---|---|---|
| | Pairs | Rate | Current Assignment (Mixed Sex Classrooms) | Counterfactual (Single Sex Classrooms) |
| Boy–Boy | 61,075 | 0.0087 | 0.0082 | 0.0079 |
| Boy–Girl | 111,650 | 0.0056 | 0.0055 | 0.0037 |
| Girl–Girl | 50,721 | 0.0076 | 0.0074 | 0.0071 |

More generally, the school may consider various policies of assigning students to classes and grades, for example tracking students by ability. Such policies would change the interactions the students would have and as a result would change the social network in desirable or undesirable ways.

## 6.7 Conclusion

In this paper we develop an empirical model for network formation. The model allows for the formation of links depending on the characteristics of the nodes as well as on the status of the network. The model proposed here may be used for several analytic objectives. Its flexibility, and the fact that it can include information about the attributes of the nodes as well as capture aspects of topological constraints on tie formation, allows us to estimate the relative importance of such factors. Moreover, nested models allow for the determination of which elements of network structure are responsible for the formation of modules or communities in the network. For example, the tendency of students of the same race to form cliques may be a function of their attributes or at least partly a result of the tendency of people to befriend their friends' friends.

Such models may also be used in the service of policy objectives. For example, a school may face decisions concerning the assignment of a cohort of students to a number of classrooms. They can create homogeneous classrooms by putting students together with similar characteristics, e.g., similar academic record, or on the basis of other interests, or create more heterogeneous classrooms by putting together students with different characteristics. As a focal policy, consider a school contemplating segregating classrooms by sex. Such a policy will likely affect the properties of the network of friendships that will emerge, including the number of friendships, and the degree distribution. The school may have preferences over the possible networks that may arise, because they expect that peers affect educational outcomes, such as test scores. Other policy makers might directly intervene in networks, pairing high and low productivity students, or introducing, or closing triads.

One alternative approach would be to focus directly on the effect of the manipulable variables (e.g., classroom composition) on the ultimate outcomes (e.g., test scores). Graham et al. (2014, 2008) follow such an approach. The attraction of explicitly modeling the network formation first is that it requires fewer data: to evaluate the effect of classroom participation on test scores would require a substantial number of classrooms, whereas the approach in the current paper allows for estimation of the network formation parameters from a single network.

Our model also offers certain other potentially desirable properties for future exploration. The explicit inclusion of situations in which utilities $U_i(j)$ and $U_j(i)$ are unequal allows the existence of a continuous measure of tie asymmetry, and not just the simple directionality of a tie. It may be possible to use such tie asymmetry as an identification strategy Christakis and Fowler (2007); Bramoullé et al. (2009).

# References

Ackerberg, Daniel, Lanier Benkard, C., Berry, Steven, Pakes, Ariel, 2007. Econometric tools for analyzing market outcomes. Handbook of Econometrics 6, 4171–4276.

Anderson, Carolyn J., Wasserman, Stanley, Crouch, Bradley, 1999. A p* primer: logit models for social networks. Social Networks 21 (1), 37–66.

Angrist, Joshua D., Lang, Kevin, 2004. Does school integration generate peer effects? Evidence from Boston's Metco program. The American Economic Review 94 (5), 1613–1634.

Aumann, Robert, Myerson, Roger, 1988. Endogenous formation of links between players and coalitions: an application of the Shapley value. In: The Shapley Value, pp. 175–191.

Barabási, Albert-László, Albert, Réka, 1999. Emergence of scaling in random networks. Science 286 (5439), 509–512.

Bramoullé, Y., Djebbaria, H., Fortin, B., 2009. Identification of peer effects through social networks. Journal of Econometrics 150 (1), 41–55.

Calvo-Armengol, Antoni, Jackson, Matthew O., 2004. The effects of social networks on employment and inequality. The American Economic Review 94 (3), 426–454.

Carrell, Scott E., Fullerton, Richard L., West, James E., 2009. Does your cohort matter? Measuring peer effects in college achievement. Journal of Labor Economics 27 (3), 439–464.

Choo, Eugene, Siow, Aloysius, 2006. Who marries whom and why. Journal of Political Economy 114 (1), 175–201.

Christakis, Nicholas, Fowler, James, 2007. The spread of obesity in a large social network over 32 years. The New England Journal of Medicine (357), 370–379.

Christakis, Nicholas A., Fowler, James H., 2009. Connected: The Surprising Power of Our Social Networks and How They Shape Our Lives. Little, Brown.

Currarini, Sergio, Jackson, Matthew O., Pin, Paolo, 2009. An economic model of friendship: homophily, minorities, and segregation. Econometrica 77 (4), 1003–1045.

Currarini, Sergio, Jackson, Matthew O., Pin, Paolo, 2010. Identifying the roles of choice and chance in network formation: racial biases in high school friendships. Proceedings of the National Academy of Sciences 107, 4857–4861.

Fowler, James H., Christakis, Nicholas A., 2010. Cooperative behavior cascades in human social networks. Proceedings of the National Academy of Sciences 107 (12), 5334–5338.

Fowler, James H., Dawes, Christopher T., Christakis, Nicholas A., 2009. Model of genetic variation in human social networks. Proceedings of the National Academy of Sciences 106 (6), 1720–1724.

Fox, Jeremy T., 2008. Estimating Matching Games with Transfers. Technical report. National Bureau of Economic Research.

Fox, Jeremy T., 2010. Identification in matching games. Quantitative Economics 1 (2), 203–254.

Frank, Ove, Strauss, David, 1986. Markov graphs. Journal of the American Statistical Association 81 (395), 832–842.

Galichon, Alfred, Salanié, Bernard, 2010. Matching with Trade-Offs: Revealed Preferences Over Competing Characteristics.

Gelman, Andrew, Rubin, Donald B., 1992. Inference from iterative simulation using multiple sequences. Statistical Science, 457–472.

Goldberger, Arthur Stanley, 1991. A Course in Econometrics. Harvard University Press.

Goldsmith-Pinkham, Paul, Imbens, Guido W., 2013. Social networks and the identification of peer effects. Journal of Business & Economic Statistics 31 (3), 253–264.

Graham, Bryan S., Imbens, Guido, Ridder, Geert, 2008. Measuring the average outcome and inequality effects of segregation in the presence of social spillovers. Univ. Calif., Berkeley. Unpublished manuscript.

Graham, Bryan S., Imbens, Guido W., Ridder, Geert, 2014. Complementarity and aggregate implications of assortative matching: a nonparametric analysis. Quantitative Economics 5 (1), 29–66.

Holland, P., Leinhardt, S., 1981. An exponential family of probability distributions for directed graphs. Journal of the American Statistical Association 76 (373), 33–50.

Jackson, M., 2003. The stability and efficiency of economies and social networks. In: Sertel, Koray (Eds.), Advances in Economic Design.

Jackson, Matthew, 2010. Social and Economic Networks. Princeton University Press.

Jackson, Matthew, Wolinsky, Asher, 1996. A strategic model of social and economic networks. Journal of Economic Theory 71 (1), 890–915.

Kolaczyk, Eric D., 2009. Statistical Analysis of Network Data: Methods and Models, 1st edition. Springer Publishing Company, Incorporated. ISBN 038788145X, 9780387881454.

Leider, Stephen, Möbius, Markus M., Rosenblat, Tanya, Do, Quoc-Anh, 2009. Directed altruism and enforced reciprocity in social networks. The Quarterly Journal of Economics 124 (4), 1815–1851.

McFadden, Daniel, 1980. Econometric models for probabilistic choice among products. Journal of Business, S13–S29.

McFadden, Daniel L., 1984. Econometric analysis of qualitative response models. Handbook of Econometrics 2, 1395–1457.

Moody, James, 2001. Race, school integration, and friendship segregation in America. American Journal of Sociology 107 (3), 679–716.

Myerson, Roger B., 1977. Graphs and cooperation in games. Mathematics of Operations Research 2 (3), 225–229.

Roth, Alvin E., Sotomayor, Marilda, 1992. Two-sided matching. In: Handbook of Game Theory with Economic Applications, vol. 1, pp. 485–541.

Snijders, Tom A.B., 2005. Models for longitudinal network data. In: Models and Methods in Social Network Analysis, vol. 1, pp. 215–247.

Snijders, Tom A.B., Koskinen, Johan, Schweinberger, Michael, 2010. Maximum likelihood estimation for social network dynamics. Annals of Applied Statistics 4 (2), 567.

Toivonen, Riitta, Kovanen, Lauri, Kivelä, Mikko, Onnela, Jukka-Pekka, Saramäki, Jari, Kaski, Kimmo, 2009. A comparative study of social network models: network evolution models and nodal attribute models. Social Networks 31 (4), 240–254.

Uzzi, Brian, 1996. The sources and consequences of embeddedness for the economic performance of organizations: the network effect. American Sociological Review, 674–698.

Uzzi, Brian, Spiro, Jarrett, 2005. Collaboration and creativity: the small world problem. American Journal of Sociology 111 (2), 447–504.

Zeng, Zhen, Xie, Yu, 2008. A preference-opportunity-choice framework with applications to intergroup friendship. American Journal of Sociology 114 (3), 615–648.

# Chapter 7

# Econometric analysis of models with social interactions[☆]

Brendan Kline[a] and Elie Tamer[b]

[a]*University of Texas at Austin, Austin, TX, United States,* [b]*Harvard University, Cambridge, MA, United States*

## Contents

## 7.1 Introduction

Models with social interactions accommodate the possibility that an individual's outcome may be related to the outcomes, choices, treatments, and/or other characteristics of other individuals. Consequently, these models can involve simultaneity in the determination of the outcomes that does not exist in classical models of treatment response. Such models have been used to study alcohol use (e.g., Kremer and Levy, 2008), education outcomes (e.g., Epple and Romano, 2011; Sacerdote, 2011), obesity (e.g., Christakis and Fowler, 2007), smoking (e.g., Powell et al., 2005), and substance use (e.g., Lundborg, 2006), among other applications.

Models of social interactions may often be written in terms of a response function $y_{ig}(\cdot)$ that relates the outcome $y_{ig}$ of individual $i$ in group $g$ to the

---

[☆] Some of this chapter had been previously distributed as "The empirical content of models with social interactions" and "Some interpretation of the linear-in-means model of social interactions" by the same authors.

*The Econometric Analysis of Network Data.* https://doi.org/10.1016/B978-0-12-811771-2.00013-4
**149**

treatment $d_{ig}$ of individual $i$ in group $g$ and the outcomes $y_{-ig}$ and treatments $d_{-ig}$ of other individuals in group $g$, according to $y_{ig} = y_{ig}(d_{ig}, d_{-ig}, y_{-ig})$. Factors other than the treatments and others' outcomes that affect the outcome are implicitly captured by the functional form of $y_{ig}(\cdot)$. In particular, if applicable, the network of interactions among the individuals in the group are implicitly captured by the functional form of $y_{ig}(\cdot)$. Moreover, as discussed further later in the chapter, the response function can be written to depend on different quantities. For example, the response function could be written in "reduced form" to depend only on the treatments but not the outcomes of the other individuals in the group. In a model of infectious diseases, $y_{ig}(\cdot)$ might be the health outcome of individual $i$ as a function of the vaccination status of individual $i$, the vaccination status of the other people in individual $i$'s reference group, and health outcomes of the other people in individual $i$'s reference group. Or for another example, in a model of classroom production, $y_{ig}(\cdot)$ might be the test score of student $i$ as a function of the test scores of the students in student $i$'s classroom. This chapter discusses a variety of specifications of these response functions, including the linear-in-means model and nonlinear models and links these response functions to models of social interactions in economics and the corresponding identification problems. In some settings, these response functions correspond to best response functions of an underlying game. In other settings, these response functions are statistical objects that are used to define a particular treatment effect. Both interpretations are considered.

Specifically, this chapter discusses two main issues relating to the econometrics of models of social interactions. First, this chapter discusses the identification of models of social interactions. Models with social interactions are typically estimated with data on many small groups. For each group, the data typically consist of the outcome and treatment of each individual and perhaps other data like the demographic characteristics. The identification question asks whether it is possible to use such data to recover information about the underlying model that generated the data. And second, this chapter discusses the interpretation and policy relevance of models of social interactions. An important consideration in the application of models of social interactions concerns the adequacy of the specification of the model. Models of social interactions inevitably involve assumptions, either explicit or implicit, about the nature of the interactions. These assumptions often times entail significant restrictions on behavior that are not necessarily implied by economic theory for all applications. These assumptions also concern the relationship between the observed data and the underlying model that generated the data. Therefore, such assumptions are important considerations in the assessment of the adequacy of models of social interactions for particular applications. Another important consideration in the application of models of social interactions concerns policy relevance, which relates to the question of how to use the model to evaluate policy interventions.

The chapter leaves out other important issues, such as the nontrivial question of statistical inference. In addition, the chapter does not address the important problems related to social welfare, characterizing winners and losers in models with social interactions.

Finally, the literature on social interactions is large, and so this chapter cannot cover all important issues in the literature. Hence, this chapter is a complement rather than a substitute for other already existing reviews, perspectives, and work like Manski (2000), Glaeser and Scheinkman (2001), Scheinkman (2008), Durlauf and Ioannides (2010), Blume et al. (2011), Graham (2015), and de Paula (2017).

## 7.2 Identification of models of social interactions

### 7.2.1 The linear-in-means model

The most commonly used model of social interactions is the linear-in-means model. There are many variants of the linear-in-means model, all of which are similar to the specification that is specifically considered in this section:

$$y_{ig} = \alpha + x_{ig}\beta + \left(\sum_{j \neq i} g_{ij}^w x_{jg}\right)\gamma + \left(\sum_{j \neq i} g_{ij}^w y_{jg}\right)\delta + \epsilon_{ig}, \qquad (7.1)$$

where $y_{ig}$ is the outcome of individual $i$ in group $g$, $x_{ig}$ are exogenous observables (i.e., "explanatory variables") relating to individual $i$ in group $g$, and $\epsilon_{ig}$ are exogenous unobservables relating to individual $i$ in group $g$. If $\gamma = 0$ and $\delta = 0$, then the linear-in-means model is a standard linear model for $y_{ig}$.

Social interactions are accommodated by including $\left(\sum_{j \neq i} g_{ij}^w x_{jg}\right)\gamma +$ $\left(\sum_{j \neq i} g_{ij}^w y_{jg}\right)\delta$ in the model for $y_{ig}$. This allows that $y_{ig}$ is affected by the explanatory variables of the other individuals in group $g$, and by the outcomes of the other individuals in group $g$. Specifically, the linear-in-means model assumes that explanatory variables of the other individuals in group $g$ affect $y_{ig}$ through the linear weighted sum $\sum_{j \neq i} g_{ij}^w x_{jg}$ and that outcomes of the other individuals in group $g$ affect $y_{ig}$ through the linear weighted sum $\sum_{j \neq i} g_{ij}^w y_{jg}$.

Therefore, $g_{ij}^w$ is a measure of the weighted social influence that individual $j$ in group $g$ has on individual $i$ in group $g$. These weighted social influences are derived from an underlying network of connections amongst individuals in group $g$, represented by an adjacency matrix $g$. By definition, $g_{ij} = 1$ means that individual $j$ in group $g$ is "connected to" individual $i$ in group $g$, and therefore has influence on individual $i$ in group $g$. Conversely, $g_{ij} = 0$ means that individual $j$ in group $g$ is "not connected to" individual $i$ in group $g$, and therefore does not have an influence on individual $i$ in group $g$. Typically, these connections are friendships or other social relations. This network is usually (but not always) assumed to be observed in the data, so that $g_{ij}$ reflects whether individual $i$ in group $g$ has nominated individual $j$ in group $g$ as a social influence. Then, in the typical specification of the linear-in-means model,

$$
g_{ij}^w = \begin{cases} 0 & \text{if } g_{ij} = 0, \\ \frac{1}{\sum_{k \neq i} g_{ik}} & \text{if } g_{ij} = 1. \end{cases} \tag{7.2}
$$

Consequently, in the typical specification of the linear-in-means model, $\sum_{j \neq i} g_{ij}^w x_{jg}$ is the average of the observable explanatory variables of the individuals that influence individual $i$ in group $g$, and $\sum_{j \neq i} g_{ij}^w y_{jg}$ is the average of the outcomes of the individuals that influence individual $i$ in group $g$. Therefore, as motivates the name of the model, the outcome $y_{ig}$ depends linearly on the mean characteristics of the individuals that influence individual $i$ in group $g$.

The analysis of the linear-in-means model proceeds by writing the model at the group level rather than the individual level, where group $g$ has $N_g$ individuals. Let $Y_g$ be the $N_g \times 1$ vector that stacks the elements $y_{ig}$. Let $X_g$ be the $N_g \times K$ matrix that stacks the vectors $x_{ig}$ for different individuals in different rows, where $K$ is the dimension of the exogenous explanatory variables. Let $\epsilon_g$ be the $N_g \times 1$ vector that stacks the elements $\epsilon_{ig}$. And let $G^w$ be the $N_g \times N_g$ matrix of weighted social influence, with $g_{ij}^w$ in row $i$ and column $j$. Then

$$
Y_g = 1_{N_g \times 1} \alpha + X_g \beta + G^w X_g \gamma + G^w Y_g \delta + \epsilon_g.
$$

The standard linear-in-means model uses the assumption that $X_g$ and $G^w$ are mean independent of the unobservables, in the sense that $E(\epsilon_g | X_g, G^w) = 0$. The mean independence of $G^w$ from $\epsilon_g$ requires that friendship or link formation is suitably independent of the unobservables.

The corresponding reduced form, which expresses the endogenous outcomes of all individuals in the group as a function of the exogenous variables of all individuals in the group, is

$$
Y_g = (I - \delta G^w)^{-1} \left( 1_{N_g \times 1} \alpha + X_g \beta + G^w X_g \gamma + \epsilon_g \right).
$$

The existence of this reduced form depends on nonsingularity of $I - \delta G^w$. As long as $|\delta| < 1$, $I - \delta G^w$ is strictly diagonally dominant, and therefore nonsingular. Therefore, using the exogeneity assumption $E(\epsilon_g | X_g, G^w) = 0$, it follows that

$$
E(Y_g | X_g, G^w) = (I - \delta G^w)^{-1} \left( 1_{N_g \times 1} \alpha + X_g \beta + G^w X_g \gamma \right), \tag{7.3}
$$

and therefore

$$
E(y_{ig} | X_g, G^w) = e_i' (I - \delta G^w)^{-1} \left( 1_{N_g \times 1} \alpha + X_g \beta + G^w X_g \gamma \right),
$$

where $e_i$ is the unit vector of length $N_g$, with 1 as the $i$th element and 0 as every other element. By tracing out the effect of the exogenous explanatory variables on the outcomes, it is possible to recover $\frac{\partial E(y_{ig}|X_g,G^w)}{\partial X_g}$ from the data. Applying matrix calculus rules,

$$\frac{\partial E(y_{ig}|X_g, G^w)}{\partial X_g} = \beta e'_i(I - \delta G^w)^{-1} + \gamma e'_i(I - \delta G^w)^{-1}G^w. \qquad (7.4)$$

Per the standard convention, the $(k, j)$ element of $\frac{\partial E(y_{ig}|X_g,G^w)}{\partial X_g}$ is $\frac{\partial E(y_{ig}|X_g,G^w)}{\partial x_{jkg}}$, the marginal effect of the $k$th explanatory variable of individual $j$ on the outcome of individual $i$. Therefore, the effect of $X_g$ on the outcome depends in a complicated way on all of the model parameters, $\beta$, $\gamma$, and $\delta$, and also the weighted social influence matrix $G^w$. This reflects the fact that manipulating $X_g$ has three interrelated effects on $y_{ig}$.

First, the exogenous explanatory variables of individual $i$ have a direct effect on the outcome of individual $i$, per the parameter $\beta$. If $\gamma = 0$ and $\delta = 0$, then $\frac{\partial E(y_{ig}|X_g,G^w)}{\partial X_g} = \beta e'_i$ so this would be the entire effect of the exogenous explanatory variables, with only the individual $i$ exogenous explanatory variables having an effect on the outcome of individual $i$. However, note that if $\gamma \neq 0$ and $\delta \neq 0$, then $\beta$ does not fully summarize the effect of the exogenous explanatory variables of individual $i$ on the outcome of individual $i$, because manipulating the exogenous explanatory variables of individual $i$ will influence the outcomes of the other individuals in the group, which will influence the outcome of individual $i$. In other words, $\beta$ describes the "effect" of the exogenous explanatory variables of individual $i$ on the outcome of individual $i$ "holding fixed" the outcomes of the other individuals, which generically would also change in response to manipulating the exogenous explanatory variables of individual $i$.

Second, the exogenous explanatory variables of the other individuals have a direct effect on the outcome of individual $i$, per the parameter $\gamma$ and social influence matrix $G^w$. If $\delta = 0$, then $\frac{\partial E(y_{ig}|X_g,G^w)}{\partial X_g} = \beta e'_i + \gamma e'_i G^w$, so the exogenous explanatory variables of all individuals affect the outcomes of other individuals as determined by $G^w$. As above, note that if $\delta \neq 0$, then $\beta$ and $\gamma$ and $G^w$ do not fully summarize the effect of the exogenous explanatory variables on the outcome of individual $i$, because manipulating the exogenous explanatory variables will influence the outcomes of the other individuals in the group, which will influence the outcome of individual $i$. In other words, $\beta$ and $\gamma$ and $G^w$ describe the "effect" of the exogenous explanatory variables on the outcome of individual $i$ "holding fixed" the outcomes of the other individuals, which generically would also change in response to manipulating the exogenous explanatory variables.

Third, the exogenous explanatory variables of all individuals have an indirect effect on the outcome of individual $i$ through their effects on the outcomes, and then the effects of outcomes on other outcomes, according to the social influence matrix $G^w$ and parameter $\delta$.

In the data, only the combination of all of these effects of the exogenous explanatory variables is observed. This suggests that the model parameters may not be point identified under all conditions. Essentially, the question is whether the parameters $\beta$, $\gamma$, and $\delta$ can be recovered from either the reduced form in Eq. (7.3) or the marginal effects in Eq. (7.4).

Specifically, suppose that the underlying network is such that all individuals in the group have influence on all other individuals in the group, in the sense that $g_{ij} = 1$ for all $i \neq j$. This could arise in empirical applications particularly if group membership but not connections within a group are observed by the econometrician. Then

$$(I - \delta G^w)^{-1} = u_1^{-1} I_{N_g \times N_g} - u_2 u_1^{-1} (u_1 + N_g u_2)^{-1} 1_{N_g \times N_g}$$

where $u_1 = 1 + \frac{\delta}{N_g - 1}$ and $u_2 = -\frac{\delta}{N_g - 1}$.

Then the effect of the $k$th explanatory variable of individual $i$ on the outcome of individual $i$ is the same as the effect of the $k$th explanatory variable of individual $j$ on the outcome of individual $j$, for all $k$ and $i, j$. And, the effect of the $k$th explanatory variable of individual $j$ on the outcome of individual $i$ is the same as the effect of the $k$th explanatory variable of individual $m$ on the outcome of individual $l$, for all $k$ and $i \neq j$ and $l \neq m$. Therefore, there are a total of only $2K$ distinct effects of the explanatory variables, but $2K + 1$ parameters that determine the effects of the explanatory variables. Consequently, the model parameters should not be expected to be point identified from these marginal effects.

In assorted variants of the specification of the linear-in-means model discussed here, both Manski (1993) and Moffitt (2001) have established details of this source of non-identification in the linear-in-means model. Manski (1993) referred to this source of non-identification as the "reflection problem," based on the idea that it is difficult to distinguish between a group average "reflecting" the average of the individual outcomes and a group average influencing individual outcomes.

An intuition for the identification analysis of the linear-in-means model comes from thinking about the linear-in-means model as a system of simultaneous equations. If all individuals influence all other individuals, then there are no exclusion restrictions in the structural form of the outcome $y_{ig}$, from Eq. (7.1), in the sense that all exogenous explanatory variables of all individuals appear directly in the structural form of the outcome $y_{ig}$. Therefore, since that specification of the model does not have any exclusion restrictions, for similar reasons to identification analysis of general simultaneous equations model, the parameters from that specification of the model should not be expected to be point identified (e.g., Wooldridge, 2010, Chapter 9).

Conversely, if not all individuals influence all other individuals, then there is an exclusion restriction in the structural form of the outcomes, and therefore the potential for valid instruments that could identify the parameters of the model.

Specifically, suppose there is an individual $l$ such that $g_{il} = 0$, so that individual $l$ has no direct influence on individual $i$. And suppose further there is an individual $j$ such that $g_{ij} = 1$ and $g_{jl} = 1$, so that individual $j$ has a direct influence on individual $i$ and individual $l$ has a direct influence on individual $j$. Then $x_{lg}$ does not appear directly in the structural form of the outcome $y_{ig}$, but $x_{lg}$ are relevant instruments for the outcome $y_{jg}$ in the structural form of the outcome $y_{ig}$, since $x_{lg}$ directly affects $y_{lg}$, which therefore directly affects $y_{jg}$ since $g_{jl} = 1$, which therefore directly affects $y_{ig}$ since $g_{ij} = 1$. This arrangement of the weighted social influences of individuals $i$, $j$, and $l$ is known as an intransitive triad, and was the source of identification studied by Bramoullé et al. (2009).

Specifically, Bramoullé et al. (2009) formalize this identification strategy and establish that an important (nearly) sufficient condition for point identification of assorted variant specifications of the linear-in-means model is that $I$, $G$, and $G^2$ (and $G^3$ in some specifications) are linearly independent. If indeed there is the intransitive triad involving individuals $i$, $j$, and $l$, then it would follow that the $(i, l)$ element of $G^2$ is strictly positive, since by applying the standard formula for matrix multiplication, that element of $G^2$ is weakly greater than $g_{ij} g_{jl}$, which is 1. Equivalently, since the $(i, l)$ element of $G^2$ counts the number of paths of length two between individual $i$ and $l$, it is at least 1, because of the path going through individual $j$. But the $(i, l)$ element of $I$ is 0 since $i \neq l$, and the $(i, l)$ element of $G$ is 0, since $g_{il} = 0$. Therefore, any linear combination of $I$ and $G$ would also have 0 as the $(i, l)$ element, so $G^2$ cannot be a linear combination of $I$ and $G$, and hence $I$, $G$, and $G^2$ are linearly independent. See also De Giorgi et al. (2010).

An important consideration in the application of these identification strategies is whether or not this linear independence condition holds. It is a stylized fact that social networks tend to exhibit triadic closure, otherwise known as transitivity of links or clustering, as in "the friend of my friend is my friend." In other words, if two "sides" of a triad are present in a network, then the third "side" is likely to also be present. Therefore, although intransitive triads generically do exist in social networks, leading to the linear independence required above, they are less frequent than if links in the network formed independently without clustering. Another important consideration in the application of this identification strategy is whether or not there is sufficient intransitive triads to result in precise estimates.

Other sources of identification are also possible in the linear-in-means model. Lee (2007) and Davezies et al. (2009) show that variation in group size can result in point identification, in particular even if all individuals within a group influence all other individuals within that group, so that there are no intransitive triads as discussed above. The intuition for why variation in group size can result in point identification is evident in the marginal effects from the linear-in-means model in Eq. (7.4). Even if $G$ involves connections between all individuals in the group, variation in group size implies that $G^w$ would be different for groups of different size. Hence, the effect of the exogenous explanatory variables on outcomes is different in groups of different sizes, providing additional sources of identification of the model parameters from the marginal effects in different group sizes. For example, in an extreme case of groups of size one, the effect of the exogenous explanatory variables would not involve any of the social interaction parameters, providing identification of the other parameters. An important consideration in the application of this identification strategy is whether or not it is reasonable to assume that the same model parameters apply to all group sizes. Another important consideration in the application of this identification strategy is whether or not there is sufficient variation in group size to result in precise estimates. In particular, if all groups are relatively large, then "variation" in group size may have a small impact on the marginal effects of the explanatory variables, potentially resulting in imprecise estimates. Specifically, approaches that rely on variation in group size can suffer from weak identification and weak instruments problems, in the sense of the inability of standard asymptotic analysis to capture finite sample behavior. Blume et al. (2015) show a connection between groups of equal size and the condition that $I$, $G$ and $G^2$ are linearly dependent (stacking groups into one network), as discussed also in de Paula (2017). Therefore, identification can be weak unless there is enough heterogeneity in the number of individuals per group. This chapter leaves out these issues of statistical inference.

Besides identification analysis, it is useful to note that the linear-in-means model can be interpreted as the equilibrium of a certain game with quadratic utility functions. Specifically, consider the utility function for individual $i$ in group $g$ given by

$$u_{ig}(y_{ig}, y_{-ig}) = \theta_{ig} y_{ig} - \frac{(1-\delta) y_{ig}^2}{2} - \frac{\delta}{2}(y_{ig} - \zeta_{ig})^2,$$

with corresponding first order condition that implies the response function

$$y_{ig} = \theta_{ig} + \delta \zeta_{ig},$$

which is the linear-in-means model from Eq. (7.1) with $\theta_{ig} = \alpha + x_{ig}\beta + \left(\sum_{j \neq i} g_{ij}^w x_{jg}\right)\gamma + \epsilon_{ig}$ and $\zeta_{ig} = \sum_{j \neq i} g_{ij}^w y_{jg}$. Hence, the linear-in-means model may be interpreted as a game with quadratic utility functions, where each unit of outcome provides the individual with "individual" utility $\theta_{ig}$, where the "cost" of the outcome is $\frac{(1-\delta) y_{ig}^2}{2}$, and where individuals want to conform their outcome to the aggregate outcome $\zeta_{ig}$ according to the parameter $\frac{\delta}{2}$ when $\delta > 0$ and "non-conform" their outcome to the aggregate outcome $\zeta_{ig}$ according to the parameter $\frac{\delta}{2}$ when $\delta < 0$. Therefore, in the leading case of $\delta > 0$, perhaps as expected given Eq. (7.1), the linear-in-means model involves a preference for conformity of outcomes, which results in a particular linear relationship between outcomes. Of course, positive affine transformations of this utility function would also result in the linear-in-means model. See also Blume et al. (2015)

for a similar analysis for incomplete information versions of the linear-in-means model.

Other details of the specification of the linear-in-means model are important considerations in empirical applications. For example, the econometrician may specify the functional form of $G^w$ as a function of $G$ in at least two leading ways. In the typical specification, as discussed above through Eq. (7.2), the structural equation for $y_{ig}$ in Eq. (7.1) depends on the average outcome of the individuals that influence individual $i$. Therefore, for example, if the outcome is the number of cigarettes smoked, then individual $i$ is affected by the average number of cigarettes smoked by the individuals that influence individual $i$. Consequently, an individual with 1 friend that smokes 10 cigarettes is influenced equally to an individual with 2 friends that each smoke 10 cigarettes. In an alternative specification, $g_{ij}^w = g_{ij}$, so that the structural equation for $y_{ig}$ in Eq. (7.1) depends on the summed outcome of the individuals that influence individual $i$. Consequently, an individual with 1 friend that smokes 10 cigarettes is less influenced than an individual with 2 friends that each smoke 10 cigarettes. Liu et al. (2014) consider a variant of the linear-in-means model that includes both modes of interactions.

Another important consideration in the specification of the linear-in-means model is whether the social interaction happens through the actual realized outcomes or the expected outcomes. As specified above in the structural equation for $y_{ig}$ in Eq. (7.1), $y_{ig}$ depends on the actual realized $y_{jg}$. Alternatively, $y_{ig}$ could be given a structural equation that depends on the expected value of the outcomes of the individuals that influence individual $i$. Viewing the linear-in-means model as a game, this corresponds respectively to a game of complete information and a game of incomplete information. Games of incomplete information may be more appropriate for social interactions among relatively large groups of relatively anonymous individuals, where the condition that individuals have private information may be more realistic. Games of complete information may be more appropriate for social interactions among relatively small groups of individuals, where the condition that individuals do not have private information may be more realistic. Further, pure strategy Nash equilibria of a game of complete information have the feature that the equilibrium outcomes are also in ex-post equilibrium, in the sense that by definition the individuals would not want to change their outcome even after observing the outcomes of the other individuals, making it a possible approximation to a long-run equilibrium of a dynamic process. By contrast, equilibria of a game of incomplete information tend to not involve realizations of equilibrium outcomes that are in ex-post equilibrium, in these sense that generally individuals would want to change their outcome after observing the realized outcomes of the other individuals.

It may be desirable also to incorporate unobserved group fixed effects, which can allow that outcomes depend on some features of the group shared by all individuals in the group and unobserved by the econometrician. Graham and Hahn (2005) show how to analyze identification of the linear-in-means model with group fixed effects using panel data methods, viewing the "cross-sectional" dimension as the groups and the "time" dimension as individuals in the groups. Bramoullé et al. (2009) require further conditions on $G$ to accommodate such group fixed effects.

Finally, it may be desirable to allow heterogeneity in the social interaction effects, which can allow that different pairs of individuals have different influences on each other. Masten (2017) shows identification results for a system of simultaneous equations model, and applies these results to the linear-in-means model.

### 7.2.2 Non-linear models

The linear-in-means model hypothesizes a particular linear relationship between the outcome of an individual and the outcomes of the other individuals in the group. Non-linear models hypothesize a non-linear relationship instead.

One motivation for using non-linear models of social interactions is to reduce the dependence on the implicit assumptions imposed by the linear-in-means model. As discussed in more detail in Section 7.3, the linear-in-means model is an example of a model of social interactions that makes a variety of behavioral assumptions that do not necessarily apply to all empirical applications. The linear model of a conditional expectation can be viewed as an approximation to a wide class of possibly non-linear conditional expectations, indeed even if the outcome is binary as in the linear probability model. However, the linear-in-means model does not share those same approximation properties, because it also involves assumptions about the nature of the social interaction. These issues are particularly salient when the outcome is discrete rather than continuous. For example, as discussed in more detail in Section 7.3, social interactions with discrete outcomes should be generally expected to involve issues like multiple equilibria, which is not a feature of the linear-in-means model, suggesting that it may not be a good approximation to settings with discrete outcomes.

Often, non-linear models applicable to social interactions are based on game theory, often when the outcome of the social interaction is discrete or even binary, and begin with a specification of the utility function. In these models, the outcome is the actions taken by individuals in the game. Consider for example a model of a social interaction when the outcome is binary, with utility functions given by

$$u_{ig}(1, y_{-ig}) = \alpha + x_{ig}\beta + \left( \sum_{j \neq i} g_{ij}^w y_{jg} \right) \delta + \epsilon_{ig} \text{ and } u_{ig}(0, y_{-ig}) = 0.$$

Thus, individual $i$ is normalized to get 0 utility from taking action 0, and gets utility from taking action 1 that is similar to the specification of the linear-in-means model. Importantly, the exogenous explanatory variables of the other individuals in the group do not affect the utility of individual $i$, because they are generally used as excluded variables in the identification strategies. However, it would be possible to allow *some* but not *all* exogenous explanatory variables of other individuals to affect the utility of individual $i$, or to allow some exogenous explanatory variables to affect the utility of all individuals, by including those factors in $x_{ig}$. If $\delta > 0$, then the utility individual $i$ gets from taking action 1 increases as a function of $\sum_{j \neq i} g_{ij}^w y_{jg}$, so that for example the utility from smoking increases as a function of the smoking decisions of the other individuals in the group. Such models have been considered by Bresnahan and Reiss (1991), Berry (1992), Tamer (2003), Krauth (2006), Soetevent and Kooreman (2007), Ciliberto and Tamer (2009), Bajari et al. (2010b), Kline (2015, 2016), and Fox and Lazzati (2017). Similar models, except with incomplete information, have been considered by Brock and Durlauf (2001, 2007), Aradillas-Lopez (2010, 2012), Bajari et al. (2010a), Tang (2010), Grieco (2014), Lee et al. (2014), Wan and Xu (2014), Lewbel and Tang (2015), and Xu (2018). See also for example Berry and Tamer (2006) or Berry and Reiss (2007). Note that many of these models do not explicitly allow for a network to affect the utility functions, in which case the assumption would be that all individuals within a group affect all other individuals within that group. Such models may still be directly applicable to social interactions, and such models are without loss of generality if the social interaction concerns pairs of individuals (e.g., Card and Giuliano, 2013, for "best friend" pairs).

Models of social interactions based on game theory also require the specification of a solution concept, a behavioral assumption that describes the predicted outcome of the model as a mapping from the utility functions. Even strong behavioral assumptions like pure strategy Nash equilibrium results in multiple equilibria outcomes, in which case the model only predicts that the outcome of the social interaction lies within some set of possible equilibria, but does not predict the outcome uniquely. Using weaker behavioral assumptions like mixed strategy Nash equilibrium or rationalizability would only exacerbate the multiplicity of outcomes. See also Section 7.3 for more discussion of the possibility of multiple equilibria in social interactions.

Consider the basic intuition for a common identification strategy for these models, when the social interaction involves the outcome of whether individuals smoke cigarettes. In general, such models could result in multiple potential equilibrium outcomes for any given specification of utility functions. For example, consider a social interaction among pairs of friends. For a particular specification of utility functions, it could be an equilibrium for neither individual to smoke cigarettes, if both individuals find it undesirable to smoke alone. For the same specification of utility functions, it could also be an equilibrium for both to smoke cigarettes, if both individuals find it desirable to smoke alongside a friend despite not finding it desirable to smoke alone.

Despite these complications, it is possible to point identify the utility parameters if there is at least one exogenous explanatory variable per individual that appears exclusively in that individual's utility function. If so, those explanatory variables can be used to exogenously drive the smoking decisions of all *other* individuals, relative to some specific individual $i$. In particular, by taking particularly extreme values of those explanatory variables, the smoking decisions of the other individuals can be taken to be essentially exogenously either to smoke or not to smoke. Equivalently, this overcomes the problems relating to multiple equilibria, because it results in dominant strategies to either smoke or not to smoke, as appropriate depending on whether the exogenous explanatory variables of the individuals other than $i$ are taken to be extremely positive or to be extremely negative. By tracing out the effect of those "exogenous" smoking decisions on the smoking decision of the individual $i$, it is possible to identify the utility parameters for that individual $i$.

Hence, an important consideration in the application of such an identification strategy is whether or not the application actually does have such a large support explanatory variable. Identification based on large support in these games are subject to similar concerns as in other areas of econometrics. Under weaker assumptions, the model parameters may only be partially identified, as in Aradillas-Lopez and Tamer (2008), Ciliberto and Tamer (2009), Beresteanu et al. (2011), Kline (2015), or Kline and Tamer (2016).

Note that these identification strategies do not rely on the same restrictions on the network as do the identification strategies for the linear-in-means model in Section 7.2.1. Instead, these identification strategies rely on exogenous explanatory variables that each affect a specific individual but are excluded from the utility functions of all other individuals. So the exclusion restriction used in the linear-in-means model comes from the structure of the network, whereas the exclusion restriction used in the models of games comes from more standard excluded regressors.

Most of the literature on social interactions has focused on models that ignore the timing of the outcomes subject to social interactions. However, some social interactions are mainly about the timing of taking an action. For example, married couples might prefer to coordinate the timing of their retirement decisions (e.g., Honoré and de Paula, 2018). de Paula (2009) and Honoré and de Paula (2010) study a duration model with social interactions. An intuition for an identification strategy for such models is that social interactions in timing should result in simultaneous timings (e.g., simultaneous retirements) that could not be explained otherwise.

### 7.2.3 Response functions

Manski (2013) and Lazzati (2015) study partial identification of the response function that expresses the outcome of an individual as a function of the treatments of all individuals in the individual's reference group. Thus, generically, the response function $y_{ig}(\cdot)$ relates the outcome of individual $i$ in group $g$ to the treatment $d_{ig}$ of individual $i$ in group $g$ and the treatments $d_{-ig}$ of other individuals in group $g$. Such models do not explicitly model the possibility that outcomes are affected by the outcomes of other individuals. However, under certain assumptions, these response functions could be interpreted as the "reduced form" that maps the treatments to the outcomes, with an un-modeled intervening stage in which outcomes affect other outcomes. For example, in the context of the linear-in-means model, this reduced form would correspond to Eq. (7.3). However, as discussed in more detail in Section 7.3, such a reduced form does not exist in all models. For example, if the social interaction induces multiple equilibria, then it is not possible to associate a unique outcome to particular profiles of treatments, since depending on the equilibrium that is selected, different outcomes are possible.

Identification of the response function faces the fundamental problem of causal inference. An individual's response function is observed at the observed profile of treatments, but it is not observed at any other counterfactual profile of treatments. Therefore, similar to identification of response functions in the absence of any social interactions (e.g., Manski, 1997; Manski and Pepper, 2000, 2009; Okumura and Usui, 2014), shape restrictions help to tighten the identified bounds on the response functions. For example, it can be assumed that the outcome of each individual is a weakly monotone function of the treatment(s) of all individuals in the group, which tightens the identified bounds. Such bounds would allow the econometrician to conclude, for example, bounds on the probability that a randomly selected individual would smoke as a function of a specified (possibly counterfactual) arrangement of policy intervention treatments affecting the individual and each of the individual's friends.

Kline and Tamer (2012) study partial identification of the best responses in complete information binary games. These games involve the decision between two possible actions per individual. The best response function describes the utility maximizing decision of a particular individual as a function of any counterfactual specification of decisions of the other individuals. Thus, generically, the response function $y_{ig}(\cdot)$ relates the utility maximizing outcome of individual $i$ in group $g$ to the outcomes $y_{-ig}$ of other individuals in group $g$. For example, the best response function could be an individual's utility maximizing decision of whether or not to smoke cigarettes, as a function of the smoking decisions of the individual's friends. Under a variety of behavioral assumptions, including Nash equilibrium assumptions and non-equilibrium assumptions like level-$k$ rationality, interval bounds on these best response functions can be derived and therefore estimated based on the literature on interval identified parameters. Such bounds would allow the econometrician to conclude, for example, bounds on the probability that a randomly selected individual would smoke as a function of a specified (possibly counterfactual) arrangement of smoking decisions of the individual's friends. The identification result depends on the specific set of assumptions maintained, but the intuition for the identification strategy is always to ask what an observed set of decisions must necessarily imply about the utility function, and therefore about utility maximizing decisions. For example, suppose the game models the decision to smoke cigarettes, and suppose the econometrician assumes that there is a positive peer effect, in the sense that a peer smoking increases the utility from smoking. Suppose, for simplicity of exposition, that the "peer group" is a pair of friends. And suppose a particular individual is observed to smoke, despite the friend in the pair not smoking. What would happen if the friend in the pair started smoking? It is possible to conclude that individual would *also* smoke if the friend in the pair smoked, under appropriate behavioral assumptions and the maintained assumption of a positive peer effect, since if it was already utility maximizing to smoke with a friend that does not smoke, it would also be utility maximizing to smoke with a friend that does smoke.

### 7.2.4 Treatment effects mediated through networks

In standard models of treatment response in which treatments are assigned and outcomes are observed at the assigned treatments, it may be of interest to learn how much of the treatment effect is mediated through a network. For example, if some treatment is assigned at random to individuals within a group, then it is possible to learn the group treatment effect. But, how much of this effect is due to the network of connections within the group? This mediated treatment effect can be examined in the context of (endogenous) networks. This section takes a counterfactual notation approach to studying networks that is more common in the study of randomized experiments and abstracts away from the economics of games, multiple equilibria, best response functions, and other similar issues discussed elsewhere in this chapter. The stylized approach presented here is built toward estimating average treatment effects and similar objects of interest. This approach is complementary to the "economic" approach taken in Section 7.3, where interest is focused on best response functions directly related to utility functions in the context of an economic model.

Let the outcome for individual $i$ be $y_i$, determined by a response function according to

$$y_i = f(d_i, G_i, \epsilon_i),$$

where $f(\cdot)$ is the response function, $d_i$ is the binary treatment of individual $i$, $G_i$ is the network (or some network summary statistic) for individual $i$, and $\epsilon_i$ is an arbitrary unobservable for individual $i$. Also, network $G_i$ is determined by a response function according to

$$G_i = m(d_i, \eta_i),$$

where $\eta_i$ is an arbitrary unobservable for individual $i$.

The functions $f(\cdot)$ and $m(\cdot)$ are not best response functions in a game theoretic sense as in Section 7.3, since they encode a selection mechanism that determines an equilibrium outcome. For example, the network formation model may have multiple equilibria, but the function $G = m(d, \eta)$ delivers a unique network $G$. The unobservable $\eta$ therefore must involve the unobserved role of a selection mechanism. For example, if the selection mechanism is modeled as a coin flip, then $\eta$ must capture the unobserved "outcome" of that coin flip. These functions are statistical relationships that can be used to define average treatment effects. Whether these average treatment effects or these functions are useful is application specific.

In counterfactual notation, the "overall" treated outcome is

$$y_i(1) = f(1, m(1, \eta_i), \epsilon_i)$$

and the "overall" untreated outcome is

$$y_i(0) = f(0, m(0, \eta_i), \epsilon_i).$$

Similarly, define the counterfactuals that separately specify the treatment and network as

$$y_i(d, G) = f(d, G, \epsilon_i).$$

The subsequent analysis can be conditioned on predetermined variables, and it is assumed that $(y, d, G)$ are observed. In this setup, in addition to the standard "overall" average treatment effect

$$ATE \equiv E(y_i(1) - y_i(0)) = E\left(f(1, m(1, \eta_i), \epsilon_i) - f(0, m(0, \eta_i), \epsilon_i)\right),$$

there is the direct treatment effect at some fixed network $G_0$,

$$DTE(G_0) \equiv E(y_i(1, G_0) - y_i(0, G_0)) = E\left(f(1, G_0, \epsilon_i) - f(0, G_0, \epsilon_i)\right)$$

and the indirect treatment effect at some fixed treatment $d_0$,

$$ITE(d_0) \equiv E(y_i(d_0, m(1, \eta_i)) - y_i(d_0, m(0, \eta_i)))$$
$$= E\left(f(d_0, m(1, \eta_i), \epsilon_i) - f(d_0, m(0, \eta_i), \epsilon_i)\right).$$

The direct treatment effect is the "effect" of the treatment on the outcome, holding fixed the network at some fixed/predetermined $G_0$. The indirect treatment effect is the "effect" on the outcome in response to a change in the network in response to a change in the treatment, holding fixed the "direct" treatment received by the individual at some fixed $d_0$.

### 7.2.4.1 Identification with random assignment of treatment

When the treatment $d$ is randomly assigned, in the sense that $(\epsilon, \eta) \perp d$, the "overall" average treatment effect can be point identified in the standard way:

$$ATE \equiv E(y(1) - y(0)) = E\left(f(1, m(1, \eta), \epsilon) - f(0, m(0, \eta), \epsilon)\right)$$
$$= E(y|d = 1) - E(y|d = 0).$$

This is the "overall" average effect of the treatment on the outcome. This allows individuals to choose other actions or choose a different network in intervening stages after treatment. Now, consider the direct treatment effect, $DTE(G_0)$. The data reveal

$$E(y|d=1, G_0) = E(f(1, G_0, \epsilon)|m(1, \eta) = G_0),$$
$$E(y|d=0, G_0) = E(f(0, G_0, \epsilon)|m(0, \eta) = G_0).$$

It is difficult to learn anything beyond this, and especially it is difficult to learn the direct treatment effect, without further assumptions even when $d$ is randomly assigned unless $\eta$ is independent of $\epsilon$. It is possible to get bounds as follows. For simplicity, suppose that $G \in \{G_0, G_1\}$. Then, using the law of iterated expectations, $E(f(1, G_0, \epsilon)) = \underline{E(f(1, G_0, \epsilon)|d=1, G = G_0)P(1, G_0)} + E(f(1, G_0, \epsilon)|d=1, G = G_1)\underline{P(1, G_1)} + E(f(1, G_0, \epsilon)|d=0, G = G_0)$ $P(0, G_0) + E(f(1, G_0, \epsilon)|d=0, \overline{G = G_1})\underline{P(0, G_1)}$, with a similar expression for $E(f(0, G_0, \epsilon))$. Only the underlined quantities can be point identified directly from the data. A similar analysis is also possible for $DTE(G_1)$.

There are other approaches to identification, motivated by the large literature on partial identification in treatment response models. See also Manski (2013) or Lazzati (2015), or Manski (2009) more generally. Simple bounds can be obtained via exclusion restrictions. Again, for simplicity, suppose that $G \in \{G_0, G_1\}$ and suppose there exists a binary instrumental variable $Z \in \{Z_0, Z_1\}$ such that

$$G_i = m(d_i, Z_i, \eta_i).$$

Let the following exclusion restriction hold:

$$f(d, G, Z, \epsilon) \equiv f(d, G, \epsilon) \quad \text{and} \quad (\epsilon, \eta) \perp (d, Z)$$

and assume the relevance condition that $m(d, Z, \eta)$ is a nontrivial function of $Z$. Then the exclusion restriction and random assignment of treatment implies for any given $s$ that

$$
\begin{aligned}
P(y(1, G_1) \le s) \ &= \ P(y(1, G_1) \le s | d=1, Z) \\
&\le \ P(y(1, G_1) \le s | d=1, G_1, Z)P(G_1 | d=1, Z) \\
&\quad + (1 - P(G_1 | d=1, Z)) \\
&= \ P(y \le s | d=1, G_1, Z)P(G_1 | d=1, Z) \\
&\quad + (1 - P(G_1 | d=1, Z)),
\end{aligned}
$$

which implies that

$$
\begin{aligned}
P(y(1, G_1) \le s) \ &\le \ \min_{Z \in \{Z_0, Z_1\}} P(y \le s | d=1, G_1, Z)P(G_1 | d=1, Z) \\
&\quad + (1 - P(G_1 | d=1, Z)).
\end{aligned}
$$

And similarly,

$$P(y(1, G_1) \leq s) \geq \max_{Z \in \{Z_0, Z_1\}} P(y \leq s | d = 1, G_1, Z) P(G_1 | d = 1, Z).$$

Similar bounds can be derived on the distribution functions of $y(1, G_0)$, $y(0, G_0)$, and $y(0, G_1)$.

If point identification is required, it is possible to "reverse engineer" a parameter that is point identified. This can be done through a choice model via the reduced forms:

$$
\begin{aligned}
E(y | d = 1, Z_1) &= E(f(1, G_1, \epsilon) 1 \left[ \eta \in A_1(1, Z_1) \right] \\
&\quad + f(1, G_0, \epsilon) 1 \left[ \eta \in A_1^c(1, Z_1) \right]), \\
E(y | d = 1, Z_0) &= E(f(1, G_1, \epsilon) 1 \left[ \eta \in A_1(1, Z_0) \right] \\
&\quad + f(1, G_0, \epsilon) 1 \left[ \eta \in A_1^c(1, Z_0) \right]),
\end{aligned}
$$

where $A_1(1, Z_1)$ and $A_1(1, Z_0)$ are the regions for $\eta$ derived from the network formation model that result in the network $G_1$, at $Z = Z_1$ and $Z = Z_0$ respectively, when the treatment is $d = 1$. Similarly, $A_1(0, Z_1)$ and $A_1(0, Z_0)$ would be regions for when the treatment is $d = 0$. This can be equivalently written as

$$
\begin{aligned}
E(y | d = 1, Z_1) &= E((f(1, G_1, \epsilon) - f(1, G_0, \epsilon)) 1 \left[ \eta \in A_1(1, Z_1) \right]) \\
&\quad + E(f(1, G_0, \epsilon)), \\
E(y | d = 1, Z_0) &= E((f(1, G_1, \epsilon) - f(1, G_0, \epsilon)) 1 \left[ \eta \in A_1(1, Z_0) \right]) \\
&\quad + E(f(1, G_0, \epsilon)),
\end{aligned}
$$

which yields

$$
\begin{aligned}
&E(y | d = 1, Z_1) - E(y | d = 1, Z_0) \\
&= E \left( (f(1, G_1, \epsilon) - f(1, G_0, \epsilon)) \left( 1 \left[ \eta \in A_1(1, Z_1) \right] - 1 \left[ \eta \in A_1(1, Z_0) \right] \right) \right).
\end{aligned}
$$

Going further involves assumptions on the network formation model. One possibility is a model like Vytlacil (2002) (see also Imbens and Angrist, 1994) with a unidimensional unobservable (i.e., with monotonicity) as the network formation model. In particular, assume that $G_i = 1[\eta_i \leq g(d_i, Z_i)]$ where $\eta_i$ is a scalar unobservable. Then $A_1(d, Z_1) = \{\eta : \eta \leq g(d, Z_1)\}$ and $A_1(d, Z_0) = \{\eta : \eta \leq g(d, Z_0)\}$ and so taking for example the case of $g(1, Z_0) \leq g(1, Z_1)$,

$$1 \left[ \eta \in A_1(1, Z_1) \right] - 1 \left[ \eta \in A_1(1, Z_0) \right] = 1[g(1, Z_0) < \eta \leq g(1, Z_1)].$$

These can be known as the complier networks when treatment is $d = 1$. Hence,

$$
\begin{aligned}
&E(f(1, G_1, \epsilon) - f(1, G_0, \epsilon) | g(1, Z_0) < \eta \leq g(1, Z_1)) \\
&= \frac{E(y | d = 1, Z_1) - E(y | d = 1, Z_0)}{P(G = G_1 | d = 1, Z_1) - P(G = G_1 | d = 1, Z_0)}.
\end{aligned}
$$

And so, this local average indirect treatment effect for network compliers, for when treatment is $d = 1$, is point identified. Similar steps can be taken for when treatment is $d = 0$.

It is not clear in general whether such a network formation model with a scalar unobservable is relevant. In particular, in networks with many decision makers, it is harder to obtain network formation models with scalar unobservables.

### 7.2.4.2 Identification without random assignment of treatment

Without random assignment of treatment, it is even more difficult to identify the direct and indirect treatment effects without further assumptions, because unobservables/confounders can influence both treatment selection and network formation. Aside from worst case bounds, one approach is to make assumptions from the econometrics of games literature. In particular, assume that there exists a binary variable $Z \in \{Z_0, Z_1\}$ such that

$$(Z = Z_1) \implies (G = G_1) \quad \text{and} \quad (Z = Z_0) \implies (G = G_0)$$

and $Z$ is independent of $(\epsilon, \eta)$. This approximates the idea of "identification at infinity," whereby a certain explanatory variable can drive the decision making. For example, in models of airline markets, $Z$ could be an indicator of whether a market is particularly profitable, and when that is the case a particular network arises (e.g., all potential entrants serve the market). These conditions render network formation exogenous conditional on these values of the variable $Z$, in which case the identification problem reverts back to a standard treatment response model. For example, without any further assumptions, it is possible to derive the standard worst case bounds on $DTE(G_0)$ and $DTE(G_1)$. These bounds can be tightened, for example by adding monotonicity assumptions on treatment response, like assuming that $y_i(1, G_0) \geq y_i(0, G_0)$ and $y_i(1, G_1) \geq y_i(0, G_1)$. It is also possible to have another instrument $W \in \{0, 1\}$, satisfying the exclusion restriction that

$$f(d, G, W, \epsilon) \equiv f(d, G, \epsilon) \quad \text{and} \quad ((\epsilon, \eta) \perp W)|Z,$$

in which case it is possible to identify the local average direct treatment effect for compliers in a model with a scalar/monotone unobservable. This use of double instruments (one for network formation and another for the usual treatment selection problem) can be used to identify the direct effect and the indirect effect.

### 7.2.5 Other approaches to identification

In some applications, detecting the existence (and direction) of a social interaction effect, but not the magnitude of the social interaction effect, may be an object of interest. It is possible to do so under weaker conditions than are used to identify the magnitude of the social interaction effect. In the context of various game theory models that could be used to model a social interaction, this identification problem has been addressed by de Paula and Tang (2012) and Kline (2016).

de Paula and Tang (2012) applies to incomplete information games. Consider the basic intuition for the de Paula and Tang (2012) identification strategy as applied to social interactions in the decision to smoke cigarettes. In equilibrium, the individuals will tend to either make similar (positively correlated)' smoking decisions if there is a positive effect of a peer smoking on the utility from smoking, or dissimilar (negatively correlated) smoking decisions if there is a negative effect of a peer smoking on the utility from smoking. Hence, the direction of the peer effect is identified by the sign of the correlation in smoking decisions across peers.

Kline (2016) applies to complete information games. Consider the basic intuition for the Kline (2016) identification strategy as applied to social interactions in the decision to smoke cigarettes. Increasing the level of an excluded instrument that affects the utility an individual gets from smoking cigarettes but not the utility function of the other individual will (despite the complications in a game, like multiple equilibria) tend to increase the probability that individual smokes cigarettes. Then, as a consequence, in equilibrium, the other individual will either increase or decrease the probability of smoking cigarettes, depending on whether there is a positive effect of a peer smoking on the utility from smoking or a negative effect of a peer smoking on the utility from smoking.

Most identification analysis of models of social interactions, particularly in the context of continuous outcomes like variants of the linear-in-means models, focuses on mean outcomes. However, higher order moments of the outcomes, particularly variances, can also be informative about social interactions. Graham (2008) shows that comparing between-group variation in outcomes, between large and small groups, to the within-group variation in outcomes, between large and small groups, is informative about social interaction effects, under suitable random assignment assumptions. The intuition for this identification strategy is that social interactions will tend to "amplify" the differences in outcomes when comparing between groups rather than comparing within groups.

It is also possible to use random or quasi-random variation to identify models of social interactions. For example, Sacerdote (2001) uses random assignment of roommates and dormmates to investigate social interactions in college GPA and other educational outcomes. Or for example, Imberman et al. (2012) uses inflows of evacuees from Hurricane Katrina into receiving schools to study impacts on incumbent students.

## 7.3 Specification of models of social interactions

### 7.3.1 Empirical individual treatment response

An important consideration in the specification of an econometric model of social interactions is whether or not the model (and empirical setting) satisfies the assumption of *empirical individual treatment response* (EITR):

**Definition 7.1** (Empirical individual treatment response). Consider a model with response functions $y_{ig}(\mathbf{y}_{-ig}, \mathbf{d}_g)$, which is the response of individual $i$ in group $g$, where $\mathbf{y}_{-ig}$ is a possibly counterfactual specification of the outcomes of the other individuals in group $g$ and $\mathbf{d}_g$ is a possibly counterfactual specification of the treatments of all individuals in group $g$. The model satisfies empirical individual treatment response, or EITR, if the data satisfy $y_{ig} = y_{ig}(Y_{-ig}, D_g)$, where $y_{ig}$ is the actual outcome of individual $i$ in group $g$, $Y_{-ig}$ are the actual outcomes of the other individuals in group $g$, and $D_g$ are the actual treatments of all individuals in group $g$.

This assumption relates the model to the data. As above, the response function is the object of interest, so the EITR assumption relates the data to the object of interest. If there were no social interaction, then this assumption is standard and uncontroversial: the response function at treatment $d$ for individual $i$ is observed if $i$ is treated with $d$. In contrast, the assumption of EITR in models with social interaction entails implicit behavioral assumptions that are not necessarily implied by economic theory. Note that by construction, the specification of the linear-in-means model discussed in Section 7.2.1 satisfies EITR. Therefore, any criticism of models that satisfy EITR apply in particular to that specification of the linear-in-means model. The terminology *individual treatment response* refers to the fact that, from the perspective of each individual, the individual is "treated" by the treatments of all individuals in the group *and* the outcomes of the other individuals in the group.

Before analyzing the EITR assumption, it is necessary and nontrivial to make the assumption that such a response function even exists as an autonomous relationship between outcomes and treatments (e.g., Wooldridge, 2010, Section 9.1). Hence, in this chapter, and in analogy to the standard interpretation of response functions without social interactions, it is supposed that the response function gives the utility maximizing "response" of individual $i$ in group $g$ to being "treated" with the treatments of all individuals in the group and the outcomes of the other individuals in the group. This sort of response function was the focus of Kline and Tamer (2012), as discussed in Section 7.2.3.

EITR can be too strong in models with social interactions because it imposes the assumption that the observed outcome of each individual $i$ is the response to the observed outcome of individuals $-i$. Viewing the model of the social interaction as a game theory model, so that the outcomes $\mathbf{y}_g$ are determined as the outcome of a game theory model, this is essentially the definition of pure strategy Nash equilibrium play with complete information.

It is well known that pure strategy Nash equilibrium with complete information often is not a reasonable characterization of actual behavior in some settings (e.g., Camerer, 2003). Even with the maintained assumption of complete information, many alternatives to pure strategy Nash equilibrium play are entertained both in the theoretical game theory literature and also the experimental literature. Among many other examples this includes mixed strategy Nash equilibrium, rationalizability (i.e., Bernheim, 1984 and Pearce, 1984), quantal response (i.e., McKelvey and Palfrey, 1995), and models of "bounded reasoning" (i.e., Camerer et al., 2004 and Costa-Gomes and Crawford, 2006). Conceivably, individuals might also randomize over the decision rule / solution concept that they use, as explored in Kline (2018). This would also lead to similar issues.

For example, if mixed strategies are used, then it is possible even in Nash equilibrium play for the condition that $y_{ig} = y_{ig}(Y_{-ig}, D_g)$ to be false, since with mixed strategies it is possible that the realizations of the mixed strategies do not (considered as pure strategies) comprise mutual best responses. In many games that could be used to model social interactions, it is not reasonable to rule out mixed strategies, because many games do not have a Nash equilibrium in pure strategies, and in others it may be "reasonable" that when there are multiple equilibria the mixed strategy equilibrium is selected.

The assumption of complete information is also a strong assumption. The assumption of EITR essentially rules out incomplete information basically for the same reason that it rules out mixed strategies: if there is incomplete information then it is possible even in a Bayesian Nash equilibrium in which each type plays a pure strategy for the condition that $y_{ig} = y_{ig}(Y_{-ig}, D_g)$ to be false, since with incomplete information each individual is effectively interacting with other individuals using mixed strategies induced by the distribution over types. Therefore, the choice of $y_{ig}$ in the data may not actually be made with knowledge of the choices of $Y_{-ig}$ of the other individuals. In contrast, in models without social interactions, the econometrician observes the response to the realized treatment, for essentially any plausible specification of how that treatment is selected.

### 7.3.2 Empirical group treatment response

Another possible specification of the response function expresses the outcomes of all individuals in the group as a function of the exogenous treatments of all individuals in the group. Thus, generically, this specification of the response function $y_{ig}(\cdot)$ relates the outcome of individual $i$ in group $g$ to the treatment $d_{ig}$ of individual $i$ in group $g$ and the treatments $d_{-ig}$ of other individuals in group $g$.

This is relatively more similar to a standard response function in models without social interactions, but with vector outcomes and treatments. The model of the social interaction presumably places additional structure on this response function.

As with the assumption that the response function even existed in the previous section, it is an assumption that the social interaction process has a unique outcome, as a function of the profile of exogenous treatments. This specification of the response function does not reveal anything about the mechanism of the social interaction, but nevertheless can be the object of interest when the question is the relationship between exogenous treatments and outcomes. This sort of response function was the focus of Manski (2013) and Lazzati (2015), as discussed in Section 7.2.3.

The assumption of *empirical group treatment response* (EGTR) is the assumption that $Y_g = y_g(D_g)$ in the data. As with EITR, in models with social interaction this assumption involves implicit behavioral assumptions that are not necessarily implied by economic theory.

**Definition 7.2** (Empirical group treatment response). Consider a model with a group response function $y_g(\mathbf{d}_g)$, which is the response of all individuals in group $g$, where $\mathbf{d}_g$ is a possibly counterfactual specification of the treatments of all individuals in group $g$. The model is said to satisfy empirical group treatment response, or EGTR, if the data satisfies $Y_g = y_g(D_g)$, where $Y_g$ are the actual outcomes of all individuals in group $g$ and $D_g$ are the actual treatments of all individuals in group $g$.

The terminology *group treatment response* refers to the fact that, from the perspective of the entire group, the group of individuals is "treated" by the treatments of all individuals in the group.

EGTR implicitly entails the assumption of a unique equilibrium of the social interaction process. Otherwise, if there are multiple equilibrium outcomes, there are multiple potential outcomes for the group for certain profiles of treatments $\mathbf{d}$. And, indeed, in many settings of social interaction there are multiple equilibria according to reasonable solution concepts, like Nash equilibrium. Similarly, EGTR entails the assumption of the use of pure strategies in the social interaction process, although not necessarily in Nash equilibrium. If there were mixed strategies, then again there could be multiple potential outcomes even for a fixed profile of treatments $\mathbf{d}$. Therefore, in general $y_g(\mathbf{d}_g)$ is a correspondence rather than a function, so $Y_g \in y_g(D_g)$ but not $Y_g = y_g(D_g)$. Note that the "reduced form" of the linear-in-means model in Eq. (7.3) shows that the linear-in-means model does satisfy EGTR.

### 7.3.3 Recap

Consequently, in models with social interactions, EITR and EGTR can imply significant assumptions on behavior that are not necessarily implied by economic theory. Many models, including the linear-in-means model, satisfy these assumptions, and therefore imply these signification assumptions on behavior.

The next section illustrates these considerations by a concrete example of a setting with social interactions. Note that neither of EITR and EGTR necessarily implies the other. EITR can hold while EGTR fails if there is an interaction with pure strategy Nash equilibrium play with complete information and multiple equilibria. EGTR can hold while EITR fails if there is a unique potential outcome according to some solution concept that describes the behavior of the group, but the outcome is not comprised of mutual best responses considered as pure strategies. For example, if there is non-equilibrium behavior, then there can still be a unique potential outcome for the group so EGTR holds. But in general non-equilibrium behavior does not comprise mutual best responses considered as pure strategies, so EITR fails. EITR and EGTR can both hold if there is a unique pure strategy Nash equilibrium with complete information. And both can fail if there are multiple potential outcomes that do not comprise mutual best responses considered as pure strategies, which may happen when the equilibrium is in mixed strategies.

However, in addition to the considerations already discussed, there are settings in which EITR and/or EGTR may be satisfied. In particular, if there is perfect information, so that some individuals observe the decisions of the other individuals before making their own decisions, then it may be reasonable to assume EITR for some individuals. Treatment response models without social interaction can be viewed as a game with perfect information in which "nature" selects the treatments, and then the individuals "respond" to that treatment. This justifies the implicit assumption of EITR in models without social interactions.

### 7.3.4 Immunization and infectious disease with social interaction

Infectious disease involves social interactions, and can be used to illustrate issues relating to the specification of models of social interactions. This section discusses two related models of infectious disease. The first is a model of the *decision to get immunized*, in which the object of interest is the response function that gives an individual's decision to immunize as a function of the immunization decisions by others in the individual's group. The second model is a model of *health outcomes under a policy intervention*, in which the object of interest is the health production function that relates an individual's health outcome to the treatments of everyone in that individual's group. Although the discussion relates to this specific application, the general issues raised would equally apply to other empirical settings.

#### 7.3.4.1 Models of the decision whether to get immunized

Suppose the decision to get immunized made by individual $i$ in group $g$, $y_{ig}$, is subject to a response function $y_{ig}(\mathbf{y}_{-ig})$, which relates the immunization decision of individual $i$ in group $g$ to the immunization decisions of the other individuals in group $g$. The econometrics problem is to learn about functionals of $y_{ig}(\cdot)$ using a data set $(Y_g : g = 1, \ldots, G)$ of group immunization decisions. The response function is written as a function only of the immunization decision of others, but, as with all such models, can be made implicitly to depend on exogenous observed and unobserved variables (i.e., $y_{ig}(\mathbf{y}_{-ig}) \equiv y(\mathbf{y}_{-ig}, X_{ig}, \epsilon_{ig})$) through the indexing by $i$ and $g$.

Consider the immunization decisions of two people in close contact who take as given the immunization decisions of the rest of their reference group. Similar ideas apply to immunization decisions of larger groups, like immunization decisions of students in a classroom or immunization decisions of residents of a local community. Since the two people are in close contact it is very likely the immunization status and health outcome of one individual affects the health outcomes of the other individual.

There is a private cost to getting immunized (e.g., the monetary cost, the time cost, or the health cost of perceived negative effects of immunization), but a group benefit. Therefore, the individuals may wish either to anti-coordinate or coordinate their immunization decisions, as described in the following two specifications. Such considerations would be important when considering an empirical analysis of immunization decisions, as they would impact the specification of the econometric model.

First, suppose that if at least one of the pair gets immunized they both "avoid" the disease and get $\beta$ utils from health. However, there is a private cost of $\theta$ utils to getting the immunization. If neither gets immunized they both "get" the disease and get 0 utils from health. Assume that $0 < \theta < \beta$, and assume that these payoffs are common knowledge.

This interaction can be modeled by the normal form game specified in game 7.1(A), where action 0 is not get immunized and action 1 is get immunized. This game has three Nash equilibria, which are reasonable candidates for predictions of the immunization decisions of the two individuals. There are two pure strategy equilibria in which one person gets immunized and the other does not, and there is a mixed strategy equilibrium in which both people play a strategy to get immunized with probability $\frac{\beta-\theta}{\beta}$. Hence, with these payoffs, there is a preference for anti-coordination. This basically results in the payoffs of the game of chicken, as described in Fudenberg and Tirole (1991, p. 18) among many places, where the "weak" action corresponds to getting immunized and the "tough" action corresponds to not getting immunized.

Second, suppose instead that both need to get immunized to avoid the illness. The payoffs are similar to the case above, but modified to account for the fact that now both individuals need to get immunized for there to be a health benefit. This is described in game 7.1(B). This is basically a coordination game where both individuals get the same payoff to coordinating, and the payoff depends on what they coordinate on, after a payoff normalization. As with the previous specification, this game has three Nash equilibria. There are two pure strategy equilibria, one in which both individuals get immunized and one in which neither individual gets immunized, and there is a mixed strategy equilibrium in which both individuals play a strategy to get immunized with probability $\frac{\theta}{\beta}$.

Similar models that suggest that immunization decisions involve strategic interaction, and in particular randomization of individual immunization decisions,

**TABLE 7.1** Two specifications of games for immunization decisions: (a) preference for anti-coordination and (b) preference for coordination.

| | $y_2 = 0$ | $y_2 = 1$ | | $y_2 = 0$ | $y_2 = 1$ |
|---|---|---|---|---|---|
| $y_1 = 0$ | $0, 0$ | $\beta, \beta - \theta$ | $y_1 = 0$ | $0, 0$ | $0, -\theta$ |
| $y_1 = 1$ | $\beta - \theta, \beta$ | $\beta - \theta, \beta - \theta$ | $y_1 = 1$ | $-\theta, 0$ | $\beta - \theta, \beta - \theta$ |
| (A) Anti-coordination | | | (B) Coordination | | |

include Bauch et al. (2003), Bauch and Earn (2004), Galvani et al. (2007), Vardavas et al. (2007), and Bauch et al. (2010). In the games described above the randomization is due to the possible use of mixed strategies, but there can also be randomization that is due to incomplete information, for example when individuals do not know the others' preferences over health and other goods. In that case, there is effectively randomization, from the perspective of each individual, induced by the distribution over types.

In addition to randomization of individual immunization decisions, it is also plausible in this sort of setting that there is not Nash equilibrium play. For example, in the case of preference for anti-coordination it is plausible that the outcome is that neither individual gets immunized, even though this is not a pure strategy Nash equilibrium. This is plausible because it could be that each individual believes the other individual will get immunized, which is a reasonable belief since getting immunized is the best response if the other individual does not get immunized, and so on. In other words, neither individual getting immunized is a rationalizable outcome. Consequently, neither individual getting immunized is a reasonable candidate for the prediction of the immunization decisions of the two individuals, even though it is not a pure strategy Nash equilibrium. This outcome could also arise from the realization of the mixed strategy Nash equilibrium.

Consider the econometrics problem of recovering information about this model of immunization decisions, based on data that consists of the immunization decisions of pairs of individuals. The assumption of EITR implies that, for example, for a pair of individuals in the data in which both are observed to get immunized, the response of each individual to the other individual getting immunized is to get immunized itself.

This rules out the possibility that the data comes from the mixed strategy equilibrium, or a rationalizable outcome. In either such case, and also for other reasons like the existence of incomplete information that also results in randomization, it need not be that immunization decisions $Y_g$ in the data satisfy $y_{ig} = y_{ig}(Y_{-ig})$. Consequently, in those cases, EITR does not hold, and so using a model based on EITR can lead to misleading conclusions. Consider for example a public health organization that observes data on immunization decisions of married couples, and finds that fraction $p$ of husbands whose wives are immunized also gets immunized himself, for some $p \in (0, 1)$. This is consistent with the mixed strategy Nash equilibrium behavior both when there is preference for anti-coordination and preference for coordination. The public health organization might conclude from this, based on an implicit or explicit assumption of EITR, that it is worthwhile to promote immunization among women, with the "understanding" from the data that the husbands would be reasonably likely to also get immunized if their wives get immunized, assuming that $p$ is reasonably large. However, the validity of this conclusion depends on whether there is preference for anti-coordination or preference for coordination. In the first case this policy intervention would have the result of reducing the rate of immunization among men to 0 (among married couples in which the wife does get immunized) while in the second case it would have the result of increasing the rate of immunization among men to 1 (among married couples in which the wife does get immunized).

Obviously, these two scenarios have very different implications for the public health organization, but these considerations are essentially ignored when assuming EITR. In the case in which the immunization rate among men goes to 0, for example, it may be the case that this intervention is not worth the cost. The same reasoning holds for other policy interventions. For example, a public health organization might consider whether to promote vaccination among some subpopulation of a school (e.g., a particular grade level, or the teachers and staff), using the observed data to help predict the behavioral response of the rest of the school. The same considerations imply that assuming EITR can lead to misleading conclusions that the health organization draws from the data about such a policy intervention. It could be, for example, that the data would suggest that the result of this policy intervention is that, again, roughly fraction $p$ of the rest of the school would get immunized, if a focal individual like an instructor is immunized, because that is observed in the data. But as before that analysis relies on behavioral assumptions that may not apply in all empirical settings.

### 7.3.4.2 Models of health outcomes

Now suppose that the object of interest is the "production function" of health outcomes as a function of the vector of treatments in a group. The treatments could be provision or subsidization of immunization, supply of bed nets, some sort of public health awareness campaign, or anything else that a social planner can manipulate that affects health outcomes. Let the health outcome of individual $i$ in group $g$, $h_{ig}$, be given by $h_{ig} = h_{ig}(\mathbf{d}_g, \mathbf{A}_g)$ where $h_{ig}(\cdot)$ is a function, and $\mathbf{A}_g$ is an unobservable that represents actions that individuals take, possibly in response to the treatments $\mathbf{d}_g$. For example, given the treatments in $\mathbf{d}_g$, $\mathbf{A}_g$ can capture the decision of individuals in the group of whether (and how much) to interact with other individuals who may have the disease. If $\mathbf{A}_g$ is a deterministic function of $\mathbf{d}_g$ then it is without loss of generality to write that $h_{ig} = v_{ig}(\mathbf{d}_g) = h_{ig}(\mathbf{d}_g, \mathbf{A}_g(\mathbf{d}_g))$. Consequently, EGTR is plausible under this condition, because then the group health outcome is a unique function of the treatment, even though there is an intermediate behavior stage that also affects health outcomes. For recent work on identification in these settings of treatment response where an outcome is a function of the treatments of others, see Manski (2013) and Lazzati (2015), as discussed in Section 7.2.3.

There are two important cases where $\mathbf{A}_g$ is not a unique function of $\mathbf{d}_g$. The first case is when the behavioral stage of the model, considered as conditional on the "parameters" $\mathbf{d}_g$, can have multiple equilibria. In this case, $\mathbf{A}_g$ can take many different values for some $\mathbf{d}_g$. As a consequence, it is not credible to assume EGTR, because for a fixed vector of treatments, the group can have multiple different potential outcomes. The second case is when the behavioral stage of the model involves mixed strategies. Then again, $\mathbf{A}_g$ can take many different values for some $\mathbf{d}_g$.

The possibility of models of behavior with mixed strategies has already been discussed above. For example, suppose that $\mathbf{d}_g$ amounts to some sort of intervention that affects $\theta$, the private util cost of immunization, in the model of Section 7.3.4.1. Then $\mathbf{A}_g$ is not a function. For example, $\mathbf{d}_g$ could be a subsidy to get vaccinated, and $\mathbf{A}_g$ could be some action that depends on $\mathbf{d}_g$ that affects payoffs, like whether to actually get immunized. In general, the health outcome differs depending on which actions are actually realized from the mixed strategies. For example, in both games, if it happens that both individuals get immunized, then neither individual gets the disease. But, if it happens that neither individual gets immunized, then both individuals get the disease. Consequently, under this model, there are multiple potential outcomes for the group given a fixed treatment $\mathbf{d}_g$. There are also multiple potential outcomes because of the existence of multiple equilibria in those games. For example, in the game with a preference for coordination, if it happens that the equilibrium in which both individuals get immunized is selected, then neither individual gets the disease. But, if it happens that the equilibrium in which neither individual gets immunized is selected, then both individuals get the disease.

Further, for another example of a social interaction with multiple equilibria, consider models of disease in which individuals can modify their behavior (denoted above as $\mathbf{A}_g$) as a function of the prevalence of the disease. For example, in the case of a sexually transmitted infection (i.e., Kremer, 1996) this can be the number of sexual partners per period. More generally, the behavior can be the decisions relating to interaction with other individuals who may have the disease. As before, $\mathbf{d}_g$ is a vector of treatments like those discussed above, like subsidization of some sort of medical care. The actions $\mathbf{A}_g$ are the decisions of individuals about interacting with others. Kremer (1996) shows that these models can have multiple equilibria that have different prevalences of the disease. Consequently, the assumption of EGTR rules out this class of model of disease and behavior. The intuition for existence of multiple equilibria in such settings is described in detail in Kremer (1996).

Even though the vector of treatments is exogenous to the model of health outcomes, the assumption of EGTR rules out models which have the potential for multiple equilibria. The assumption of EGTR also rules out mixed strategies. All of these considerations apply equally to observational data and experimental data. There are many advantages of experiments, for example because experiments can solve endogeneity problems. Experimental data and econometric modeling of social interaction provide complementary features to an analysis. The experiment helps to solve issues with endogeneity with respect to the relation between observable and unobservable characteristics of the individuals, while the econometric modeling helps resolve the issues discussed in this section, that are unrelated to the endogeneity problem, but they are related to how to link data and models in settings where social interactions are important.

## 7.4 Policy relevance of models of social interactions

Models of social interactions are often used to make policy relevant claims like that peers cause each other to have certain outcomes, as in claims like that a student who has high achieving peers has increased educational achievement itself. In some settings it is plausible that a social planner could directly manipulate the outcome of some individuals, for example by preventing some actions for some individuals as in drug and alcohol policy, or by a mandatory immunization policy. However, in general, because the outcomes in models of social interactions are simultaneously determined, it may not be possible for a social planner to directly manipulate the outcomes of individuals. This suggests that caution is warranted when interpreting the results of estimating models of social interactions, particularly when making claims about the effect of the outcomes on other outcomes. It may be more straightforward to investigate the effect of manipulating the exogenous explanatory variables, accounting for the effects of the social interaction. For example, in the context of the linear-in-means model, the effect of the exogenous explanatory variables is given by Eq. (7.4). Similar ideas were addressed in Kline and Tamer (2013). Beyond the specific context of the linear-in-means model, these considerations suggest the role of the response functions discussed in Section 7.2.3, that are the "reduced form" that map the treatments of all individuals to the outcomes of all individuals. Note that it may not be desirable to simply run a linear regression of "outcomes" on "exogenous explanatory variables" even if the reduced form is the object of interest, because the reduced form of a social interactions model is not necessarily a linear model, as demonstrated for the linear-in-means model in Eq. (7.3). In particular, even for the linear-in-means model with a linear structural form, the reduced form depends in a complicated non-linear way on the network $G$ and parameter $\delta$.

Nevertheless, the "interaction effects" can be useful to understand the "partial" effect of outcomes on other outcomes, even if outcomes cannot actually be directly manipulated. The response functions can be useful to get a sense of the social interaction mechanism when considering a policy intervention that directly affects the outcomes of individuals privately, for example some treatment (e.g., subsidized immunization), but because of the social interaction process may indirectly affect the outcomes of everyone in the group.

It is also useful to consider possible "re-equilibrization" effects of policy interventions or other manipulations of outcomes. In particular, if a particular outcome is somehow directly manipulated, then the outcomes of other individuals in the group will change in response, according to the equilibrium of the social interaction. Then, unless the originally manipulated outcome is still held fixed by the manipulation, the original outcome might change in equilibrium in response to the changes of the outcomes of the other individuals. In other words, there can be a difference between a one-time manipulation of an outcome, in which case that outcome might subsequently change due to re-equilibrization, and a permanent manipulation of an outcome to a fixed outcome, in which case that outcome is "removed" from the model of the social interaction and no longer is "re-equilibriated."

Particularly in the context of social interactions models with an underlying network structure of interactions within groups, an important consideration is the joint determination of outcomes and the network. Interventions, whether they be related to manipulating outcomes directly or the exogenous explanatory variables, can be suspected to also have effects on the network. If so, then counterfactual predictions of the outcomes after the intervention may be poor predictions if they assume that the network will be unaffected by the intervention, although such a counterfactual that "holds fixed" the network can still be useful to understand the "partial" effect of the intervention on outcomes, even if it is not predictive of the actual outcomes. This is the direct effect of the intervention. For example, it could be possible to use a model of network formation to predict the resulting network after the intervention, and then use that predicted model in the model of social interactions to predict the resulting outcomes after the intervention. Carrell et al. (2013) find evidence that such considerations can be practically relevant, in that when they attempted to manipulate peer groups, individuals formed a network of connections within each manipulated peer group that lead to individuals avoiding interacting with individuals that the manipulated peer group had been designed for them to interact with.

It is also useful to understand the mediating effect of networks in models of social interactions. Does a particular policy intervention have different effects in different groups that have different networks of connections? In many applications, the network will be sufficiently "stable" that a relatively minor intervention affecting one outcome (out of many outcomes affected by the network) may be reasonably assumed to have negligible effect on the network. Moreover, it is useful to measure how much of the change in outcomes is due to changes in the network. This is the indirect effect of the intervention. It may be possible to parametrize the link between the treatment and the network and outcomes and use a full model to learn all the causal effects of interest.

# References

Aradillas-Lopez, A., 2010. Semiparametric estimation of a simultaneous game with incomplete information. Journal of Econometrics 157 (2), 409–431.

Aradillas-Lopez, A., 2012. Pairwise-difference estimation of incomplete information games. Journal of Econometrics 168 (1), 120–140.

Aradillas-Lopez, A., Tamer, E., 2008. The identification power of equilibrium in simple games. Journal of Business & Economic Statistics 26 (3), 261–283.

Bajari, P., Hong, H., Krainer, J., Nekipelov, D., 2010a. Estimating static models of strategic interactions. Journal of Business & Economic Statistics 28 (4), 469–482.

Bajari, P., Hong, H., Ryan, S.P., 2010b. Identification and estimation of a discrete game of complete information. Econometrica 78 (5), 1529–1568.

Bauch, C., Bhattacharyya, S., Ball, R., Boni, M., 2010. Rapid emergence of free-riding behavior in new pediatric immunization programs. PLoS ONE 5 (9), 505–514.

Bauch, C., Earn, D., 2004. Vaccination and the theory of games. Proceedings of the National Academy of Sciences of the United States of America 101 (36), 13391–13394.

Bauch, C., Galvani, A., Earn, D., 2003. Group interest versus self-interest in smallpox vaccination policy. Proceedings of the National Academy of Sciences of the United States of America 100 (18), 10564–10567.

Beresteanu, A., Molchanov, I., Molinari, F., 2011. Sharp identification regions in models with convex moment predictions. Econometrica 79 (6), 1785–1821.

Bernheim, B., 1984. Rationalizable strategic behavior. Econometrica 52 (4), 1007–1028.

Berry, S., Reiss, P., 2007. Empirical models of entry and market structure. In: Armstrong, M., Porter, R. (Eds.), Handbook of Industrial Organization, vol. 3. North-Holland, Amsterdam, pp. 1845–1886.

Berry, S., Tamer, E., 2006. Identification in models of oligopoly entry. In: Blundell, R., Newey, W.K., Persson, T. (Eds.), Advances in Economics and Econometrics, Theory and Applications, Ninth World Congress, vol. 2. Cambridge University Press, Cambridge, pp. 46–85.

Berry, S.T., 1992. Estimation of a model of entry in the airline industry. Econometrica 60 (4), 889–917.

Blume, L.E., Brock, W.A., Durlauf, S.N., Ioannides, Y.M., 2011. Identification of social interactions. In: Benhabib, J., Bisin, A., Jackson, M.O. (Eds.), Handbook of Social Economics, vol. 1. North-Holland, Amsterdam, pp. 853–964.

Blume, L.E., Brock, W.A., Durlauf, S.N., Jayaraman, R., 2015. Linear social interactions models. Journal of Political Economy 123 (2), 444–496.

Bramoullé, Y., Djebbari, H., Fortin, B., 2009. Identification of peer effects through social networks. Journal of Econometrics 150 (1), 41–55.

Bresnahan, T., Reiss, P., 1991. Empirical models of discrete games. Journal of Econometrics 48 (1–2), 57–81.

Brock, W.A., Durlauf, S.N., 2001. Discrete choice with social interactions. The Review of Economic Studies 68 (2), 235–260.

Brock, W.A., Durlauf, S.N., 2007. Identification of binary choice models with social interactions. Journal of Econometrics 140 (1), 52–75.

Camerer, C., 2003. Behavioral Game Theory: Experiments in Strategic Interaction. Princeton University Press, Princeton, NJ.

Camerer, C., Ho, T., Chong, J., 2004. A cognitive hierarchy model of games. The Quarterly Journal of Economics 119 (3), 861–898.

Card, D., Giuliano, L., 2013. Peer effects and multiple equilibria in the risky behavior of friends. Review of Economics and Statistics 95 (4), 1130–1149.

Carrell, S.E., Sacerdote, B.I., West, J.E., 2013. From natural variation to optimal policy? The importance of endogenous peer group formation. Econometrica 81 (3), 855–882.

Christakis, N.A., Fowler, J.H., 2007. The spread of obesity in a large social network over 32 years. The New England Journal of Medicine 357 (4), 370–379.

Ciliberto, F., Tamer, E., 2009. Market structure and multiple equilibria in airline markets. Econometrica 77 (6), 1791–1828.

Costa-Gomes, M., Crawford, V., 2006. Cognition and behavior in two-person guessing games: an experimental study. The American Economic Review 96 (5), 1737–1768.

Davezies, L., d'Haultfoeuille, X., Fougère, D., 2009. Identification of peer effects using group size variation. Econometrics Journal 12 (3), 397–413.

De Giorgi, G., Pellizzari, M., Redaelli, S., 2010. Identification of social interactions through partially overlapping peer groups. American Economic Journal: Applied Economics 2 (2), 241–275.

Durlauf, S.N., Ioannides, Y.M., 2010. Social interactions. Annual Review of Economics 2, 451–478.

Epple, D., Romano, R., 2011. Peer effects in education: a survey of the theory and evidence. In: Benhabib, J., Bisin, A., Jackson, M.O. (Eds.), Handbook of Social Economics, vol. 1. North-Holland, Amsterdam, pp. 1053–1163.

Fox, J.T., Lazzati, N., 2017. A note on identification of discrete choice models for bundles and binary games. Quantitative Economics 8 (3), 1021–1036.

Fudenberg, D., Tirole, J., 1991. Game Theory. MIT Press, Cambridge, MA.

Galvani, A., Reluga, T., Chapman, G., 2007. Long-standing influenza vaccination policy is in accord with individual self-interest but not with the utilitarian optimum. Proceedings of the National Academy of Sciences of the United States of America 104 (13), 5692–5697.

Glaeser, E., Scheinkman, J., 2001. Measuring social interactions. In: Durlauf, S.N., Young, H.P. (Eds.), Social Dynamics. MIT Press, Cambridge, MA, pp. 83–132.

Graham, B.S., 2008. Identifying social interactions through conditional variance restrictions. Econometrica 76 (3), 643–660.

Graham, B.S., 2015. Methods of identification in social networks. Annual Review of Economics 7, 465–485.

Graham, B.S., Hahn, J., 2005. Identification and estimation of the linear-in-means model of social interactions. Economics Letters 88 (1), 1–6.

Grieco, P.L., 2014. Discrete games with flexible information structures: an application to local grocery markets. The Rand Journal of Economics 45 (2), 303–340.

Honoré, B.E., de Paula, Á., 2010. Interdependent durations. The Review of Economic Studies 77 (3), 1138–1163.

Honoré, B.E., de Paula, Á., 2018. A new model for interdependent durations. Quantitative Economics 9 (3), 1299–1333.

Imbens, G.W., Angrist, J.D., 1994. Identification and estimation of local average treatment effects. Econometrica 62 (2), 467–475.

Imberman, S.A., Kugler, A.D., Sacerdote, B.I., 2012. Katrina's children: evidence on the structure of peer effects from hurricane evacuees. The American Economic Review 102 (5), 2048–2082.

Kline, B., 2015. Identification of complete information games. Journal of Econometrics 189 (1), 117–131.

Kline, B., 2016. The empirical content of games with bounded regressors. Quantitative Economics 7 (1), 37–81.

Kline, B., 2018. An empirical model of non-equilibrium behavior in games. Quantitative Economics 9 (1), 141–181.

Kline, B., Tamer, E., 2012. Bounds for best response functions in binary games. Journal of Econometrics 166 (1), 92–105.

Kline, B., Tamer, E., 2013. Comment. Journal of Business & Economic Statistics 31 (3), 276–279.

Kline, B., Tamer, E., 2016. Bayesian inference in a class of partially identified models. Quantitative Economics 7 (2), 329–366.

Krauth, B.V., 2006. Simulation-based estimation of peer effects. Journal of Econometrics 133 (1), 243–271.

Kremer, M., 1996. Integrating behavioral choice into epidemiological models of AIDS. The Quarterly Journal of Economics 111 (2), 549–573.

Kremer, M., Levy, D., 2008. Peer effects and alcohol use among college students. The Journal of Economic Perspectives 22 (3), 189–206.

Lazzati, N., 2015. Treatment response with social interactions: partial identification via monotone comparative statics. Quantitative Economics 6 (1), 49–83.

Lee, L.-f., 2007. Identification and estimation of econometric models with group interactions, contextual factors and fixed effects. Journal of Econometrics 140 (2), 333–374.

Lee, L.-f., Li, J., Lin, X., 2014. Binary choice models with social network under heterogeneous rational expectations. Review of Economics and Statistics 96 (3), 402–417.

Lewbel, A., Tang, X., 2015. Identification and estimation of games with incomplete information using excluded regressors. Journal of Econometrics 189 (1), 229–244.

Liu, X., Patacchini, E., Zenou, Y., 2014. Endogenous peer effects: local aggregate or local average? Journal of Economic Behavior & Organization 103, 39–59.

Lundborg, P., 2006. Having the wrong friends? Peer effects in adolescent substance use. Journal of Health Economics 25 (2), 214–233.

Manski, C., 1993. Identification of endogenous social effects: the reflection problem. The Review of Economic Studies 60 (3), 531–542.

Manski, C.F., 1997. Monotone treatment response. Econometrica 65 (6), 1311–1334.

Manski, C.F., 2000. Economic analysis of social interactions. The Journal of Economic Perspectives 14 (3), 115–136.

Manski, C.F., 2009. Identification for Prediction and Decision. Harvard University Press, Cambridge, MA.

Manski, C.F., 2013. Identification of treatment response with social interactions. Econometrics Journal 16 (1), S1–S23.

Manski, C.F., Pepper, J.V., 2000. Monotone instrumental variables: with an application to the returns to schooling. Econometrica 68 (4), 997–1010.

Manski, C.F., Pepper, J.V., 2009. More on monotone instrumental variables. Econometrics Journal 12 (s1), S200–S216.

Masten, M.A., 2017. Random coefficients on endogenous variables in simultaneous equations models. The Review of Economic Studies 85 (2), 1193–1250.

McKelvey, R., Palfrey, T., 1995. Quantal response equilibria for normal form games. Games and Economic Behavior 10 (1), 6–38.

Moffitt, R.A., 2001. Policy interventions, low-level equilibria, and social interactions. In: Durlauf, S.N., Young, H.P. (Eds.), Social Dynamics, chapter 3. MIT Press, Cambridge, MA, pp. 45–82.

Okumura, T., Usui, E., 2014. Concave-monotone treatment response and monotone treatment selection: with an application to the returns to schooling. Quantitative Economics 5 (1), 175–194.

de Paula, Á., 2009. Inference in a synchronization game with social interactions. Journal of Econometrics 148 (1), 56–71.

de Paula, Á., 2017. Econometrics of network models. In: Honoré, B., Pakes, A., Piazzesi, M., Samuelson, L. (Eds.), Advances in Economics and Econometrics, Eleventh World Congress, vol. 1. Cambridge University Press, Cambridge, pp. 268–323.

de Paula, Á., Tang, X., 2012. Inference of signs of interaction effects in simultaneous games with incomplete information. Econometrica 80 (1), 143–172.

Pearce, D., 1984. Rationalizable strategic behavior and the problem of perfection. Econometrica 52 (4), 1029–1050.

Powell, L.M., Tauras, J.A., Ross, H., 2005. The importance of peer effects, cigarette prices and tobacco control policies for youth smoking behavior. Journal of Health Economics 24 (5), 950–968.

Sacerdote, B., 2001. Peer effects with random assignment: results for Dartmouth roommates. The Quarterly Journal of Economics 116 (2), 681–704.

Sacerdote, B., 2011. Peer effects in education: how might they work, how big are they and how much do we know thus far? In: Hanushek, E.A., Machin, S.J., Woessmann, L. (Eds.), Handbook of the Economics of Education, vol. 3. Elsevier, Amsterdam, pp. 249–277.

Scheinkman, J.A., 2008. Social interactions. In: Durlauf, S.N., Blume, L.E. (Eds.), The New Palgrave Dictionary of Economics, vol. 2. Palgrave Macmillan, London.

Soetevent, A.R., Kooreman, P., 2007. A discrete-choice model with social interactions: with an application to high school teen behavior. Journal of Applied Econometrics 22 (3), 599–624.

Tamer, E., 2003. Incomplete simultaneous discrete response model with multiple equilibria. The Review of Economic Studies 70 (1), 147–165.

Tang, X., 2010. Estimating simultaneous games with incomplete information under median restrictions. Economics Letters 108 (3), 273–276.

Vardavas, R., Breban, R., Blower, S., 2007. Can influenza epidemics be prevented by voluntary vaccination? PLoS Computational Biology 3 (5), e85.

Vytlacil, E., 2002. Independence, monotonicity, and latent index models: an equivalence result. Econometrica 70 (1), 331–341.

Wan, Y., Xu, H., 2014. Semiparametric identification of binary decision games of incomplete information with correlated private signals. Journal of Econometrics 182 (2), 235–246.

Wooldridge, J.M., 2010. Econometric Analysis of Cross Section and Panel Data, 2nd ed. The MIT Press, Cambridge, MA.

Xu, H., 2018. Social interactions in large networks: a game theoretic approach. International Economic Review 59 (1), 257–284.

## Chapter 8

# Many player asymptotics for large network formation problems<sup>☆</sup>

**Konrad Menzel**
*New York University, New York, NY, United States*

### Contents

## 8.1 Introduction

This chapter presents a limiting theory for models of network formation that assumes that the number of nodes (agents) grows large. We illustrate how asymptotic representations of large but finite networks are useful for identification analysis, estimation, and approximate inference on structural parameters of the economic model.

Asymptotic approximations to distributions of estimators and other sample statistics are one of the most widely used tools in contemporary econometrics.

☆ The author gratefully acknowledges support from the NSF (SES-1459686).

*The Econometric Analysis of Network Data.* https://doi.org/10.1016/B978-0-12-811771-2.00014-6
**183**

In its most common form, the limiting argument assumes a hypothetical experiment in which the researcher repeatedly evaluates the statistic of interest at successively larger samples from a fixed or drifting distribution of observable variables. "Many-player" asymptotics applies the same reasoning to the data-generating process itself, where part of the observable data is the outcome of a game-theoretic model that is re-solved for a successively larger number of players drawn from a fixed distribution of types. As with conventional "large sample" asymptotics, the overarching goal is to produce tractable approximations to distributions of statistical quantities from a finite-player version of the model. The formal properties and interpretation of these approximations differ in a few subtle aspects, which we will highlight over the course of the presentation in this chapter.

Most importantly, identification of parameters from the limiting model may differ from identification in the finite-$n$ network. Also, depending on how data from the network is sampled, the (generally stochastic) "model approximation error" from replacing the exact finite-$n$ distribution of network outcomes with the many-player limit may be of the same order of magnitude or larger than classical sampling uncertainty. This chapter assumes that the researcher is interested in asymptotic properties of estimators from data on finitely many networks whose size grows large, rather than for draws from an increasing number of finite networks.

Our description of the network regards nodes $i = 1, \ldots, n$ as exchangeable units with exogenous attributes $x_i$. We also use network statistics $s_i$ to describe relevant aspects of the absolute position of node $i$, and $t_{ij}$ to describe her relative position to another node $j$ in the network. In economic settings, link formation may follow strategic motives, e.g. if a network link provides access to a resource distributed through the network, a more centrally located node may be a more attractive target for a new connection. Mutual network neighbors may build trust to support a potentially risky transaction between $i$ and $j$, but could also erode either party's bargaining power in a negotiation. Hence allowing network variables $s_i, s_j, t_{ij}$ to affect the value of an additional link constitutes an important aspect of our framework.

The main asymptotic result concerns a joint distribution $f(x_1, x_2; s_1, s_2, t_{12})$ describing the relative frequency with which nodes with exogenous attributes $x_1, x_2$ and (endogenous) network attributes $s_1, s_2, t_{12}$ form links. We refer to this description of the network as the *link frequency distribution* which will be introduced more formally in section 8.4.[1] We derive the limit for any link frequency distribution generated by pairwise stable networks. This limiting characterization can also be used to describe the large-network limits of homomorphism densities (i.e. subgraph counts) for triads or larger groups of nodes.[2] In the ap-

---

[1] This object shares a superficial resemblance with graphons (see Lovasz, 2012), however, our framework models the network as a sparse rather than a dense graph, and for the link frequency distribution units are indexed by observable attributes rather than a scalar latent variable.

[2] See Lovasz (2012), Bickel et al. (2011) for definitions.

pendix we give an illustrative example of subgraph counts among triads with preferences for transitivity.

The results in this chapter complement other approaches that apply simulation techniques directly to the finite-player model (see e.g. Miyauchi, 2012; Mele, 2012, and Sheng, 2014) or a continuum model for network formation (de Paula et al., 2014). The asymptotic framework presented here relies on symmetric, rather than weak dependence assumptions which were used by Boucher and Mourifié (2012), Leung (2015), and Kallenberg (2016). The conceptual focus of this chapter is on problems with strategic interdependence among links, where the benefit to the player of adding a new link may depend on the structure of the remainder of the network. Techniques for models without strategic interference have been proposed by Graham (2014) and Dzemski (2014).

## 8.2 Model

We present the theory for a leading case of a network formation model in which network connections are undirected and binary, that is, we do not assign separate weights indicating the importance of frequency of use of a link. We also abstract from the possibility of various types of discrete links.

### 8.2.1 Data

We denote the adjacency matrix for the network graph with $\mathbf{D} := (d_{ij})_{i,j=1}^{n}$, where $d_{ij}$ is an indicator variable that equals one if there is a direct connection between nodes $i$ and $j$, and zero otherwise. We also use the notation $\mathbf{D} + \{ij\}$ and $\mathbf{D} - \{ij\}$ for the network $\mathbf{D}$ after setting the link $ij$ to $d_{ij} = 1$ ($d_{ij} = 0$, respectively).

The covariate information for the nodes is given by the matrix $\mathbf{X} = (x_i')_{i=1}^{n}$, where $x_i \in \mathbb{R}^k$ is a column vector characterizing the potentially payoff-relevant exogenous attributes of node $i$. The primary focus of this chapter is on the leading case in which the researcher observes the entire graph $(\mathbf{D}, \mathbf{X})$ for a single network, but most results can be readily extended to cases in which the data set constitutes an incomplete sample of the network under various sampling protocols. The extension of the main results to multiple networks is straightforward.

### 8.2.2 Link preferences

Our framework treats utility as non-transferable, where link preferences are described by a utility function $\Pi_i(\mathbf{D})$, which gives the total payoff to node $i$ from the network $\mathbf{D}$. The function $\Pi_i(\cdot)$ may also depend on $i$'s and other nodes' exogenous attributes. It is also convenient to represent preferences and stability conditions in terms of payoff increments from adding a link $ij$ to the network $\mathbf{D}$,

$$U_{ij}(\mathbf{D}) - MC_{ij}(\mathbf{D}) = \Pi_i(\mathbf{D} + \{ij\}) - \Pi_i(\mathbf{D} - \{ij\}).$$

In the following, we refer to $U_{ij}(\mathbf{D})$ as node $i$'s marginal benefit, and $MC_i(\mathbf{D})$ as the marginal cost, respectively, of adding a direct connection to $j$. With strategic interaction effects between links, marginal benefits generally depend on the absolute and relative positions of $i$ and $j$ in the network $\mathbf{D}$. For a representation of decision utility, the distinction between (gross) marginal benefits and (negative) costs is entirely arbitrary, but turns out to be convenient for specifying payoffs below.

### 8.2.3 Network statistics

The position of nodes in the network can be characterized by various network statistics, as e.g. its network degree, or its distance to a specific other node. The model described in this chapter allows link preferences to depend on network attributes of this type. We distinguish between node-specific and edge-specific network characteristics, where the former describes the absolute position of a node $i$ in the network, and the latter its position relative to another node $j$.

Specifically, we let the payoff-relevant node-level characteristics for node $i$ be given by a vector-valued function

$$s_i := S(\mathbf{D}, \mathbf{X}; i)$$

where we assume that the function $S(\cdot)$ is invariant to permutation of player indices.[3] Examples for network attributes of this type include the network degree of node $i$,

$$S_1(\mathbf{D}, \mathbf{X}; i) = \sum_{j=1}^{n} d_{ij}$$

the average value of exogenous attribute $x_{j1}$ among $i$'s direct neighbors,

$$S_2(\mathbf{D}, \mathbf{X}; i) = \frac{\sum_{j=1}^{n} d_{ij} x_{j1}}{\sum_{j=1}^{n} d_{ij}},$$

eigenvector centrality of node $i$ in the network, or other measures of her (absolute) position in the network. Degree centrality is generally part of the description of the network distribution regardless whether payoffs depend on it, so in the following we assume that the first component of $s_i$ corresponds to the network degree of node $i$, $s_{i1} = \sum_{j=1}^{n} d_{ij}$.

As another example, node-level endogenous network attributes can be used to describe discrete network games, where agent $i$ chooses a binary action $y_i \in \{0, 1\}$ with payoffs depending on the average action among the (endogenously determined) network neighbors. Models of this type may for instance describe

---

[3] Formally, we assume that, for any one-to-one map $\pi : \{1, \ldots, n\} \to \{1, \ldots, n\}$ and $i = 1, \ldots, n$, we have $S(\mathbf{D}^\pi, \mathbf{X}^\pi; \pi(i)) = S(\mathbf{D}, \mathbf{X}; i)$, where the matrices $\mathbf{X}^\pi$ and $\mathbf{D}^\pi$ are obtained from $\mathbf{X}$ and $\mathbf{D}$ by permuting the rows (rows and columns, respectively) of the matrix according to $\pi$.

friendship formation and smoking behavior among youth, where smokers might be more likely to form friendships among themselves.[4] Suppose that the optimal action is described as a cutoff rule

$$y_i = \mathbb{1}\left\{ z_i'\gamma + \delta\frac{\sum_{j=1}^n d_{ij}y_j}{\sum_{j=1}^n d_{ij}} + v_i \geq 0 \right\}$$

where $(z_i', v_i)'$ is a subvector of $x_i$, and $v_i$ is not observed by the econometrician. A complete information Nash equilibrium of the resulting network game with endogenous link decisions can then be represented using the node-specific statistic

$$S_3(\mathbf{D}, \mathbf{X}, \mathbf{y}; i) := \mathbb{1}\left\{ z_i'\gamma + \delta\frac{\sum_{j=1}^n d_{ij}y_j}{\sum_{j=1}^n d_{ij}} + v_i \geq 0 \right\}$$

provided a solution to the recursive system exists, where $\mathbf{y} = (y_1, \ldots, y_n)$. If $\delta \geq 0$, this model corresponds to a game with strategic complementarities so that a pure-strategy Nash equilibrium is guaranteed to exist.[5]

The payoff-relevant edge-level characteristics for the dyad $i, j$ are given by

$$t_{ij} := T(\mathbf{D}, \mathbf{X}; i, j)$$

where $T(\cdot)$ may again be vector-valued, and we assume that the function $T(\cdot)$ is invariant to permutations of player indices.[6] For example, the propensity of the dyad $(i, j)$'s forming a link could depend on whether $i$ and $j$ share a network neighbor, in which case we can define the indicator variable

$$T_1(\mathbf{D}, \mathbf{X}; i, j) = \max_{k \neq i,j} d_{ik}d_{jk},$$

which is equal to one if in the absence of a direct link, the shortest path between $i$ and $j$ on the network graph is of length two or shorter. Edge-specific network attributes could more generally include other measures of network distance between $i$ and $j$ in the absence of a direct connection between the two nodes, the number of common network neighbors, or indicators whether a link between $i$ and $j$ would produce a clique of size three or larger.

### 8.2.4 Payoff specification

Our model assumes payoffs that are realizations of a random utility model with marginal benefits are of the form

$$U_{ij} = U(x_i, x_j; s_i, s_j, t_{ij}) + \sigma \eta_{ij}.$$

---

[4] Models with peer effects and endogenous network formation have been analyzed by Goldsmith-Pinkham and Imbens (2012) and Badev (2016).

[5] See Milgrom and Roberts (1990).

[6] That is, we assume that, for any permutation $\pi : \{1, \ldots, n\} \to \{1, \ldots, n\}$ and $i, j = 1, \ldots, n$, we have $T(\mathbf{D}^\pi, \mathbf{X}^\pi; \pi(i), \pi(j)) = T(\mathbf{D}, \mathbf{X}; i, j)$.

We refer to $U(x_i, x_j; s_i, s_j, t_{ij})$ as the systematic part of random utility, where dependence on the structure of the network is restricted to a finite number of node- and dyad-specific network statistics. The idiosyncratic taste shocks $\eta_{ij}$ are assumed to be random draws from a common distribution with c.d.f. $G(\eta)$ that are independent of $x_i, x_j$ and across dyads $i, j$, and $\sigma > 0$ is a scale parameter. The main application of our asymptotic results concerns identification of—parametric or nonparametric models for the function $U(x_1, x_2; s_1, s_2, t_{12})$, where the distribution of taste shocks $G(\cdot)$ need not be specified by the researcher as long as its upper tail is assumed to satisfy the shape restriction in Assumption 8.2 below.

Dependence of $U(\cdot)$ on $x_i$ and $x_j$ allows for heterogeneity in the propensity of nodes to form links, as well as homophily with respect to components of $x_i$. In addition, this specification allows for anonymous interaction effects through the (endogenous) network structure by including node-specific network characteristics $s_i, s_j$, as well as non-anonymous endogenous interaction effects by including edge-specific characteristics $t_{ij}$.

Marginal costs are of the form

$$MC_{ij} \equiv MC_i = \log J + \sigma \eta_{i0}$$

where $\eta_{i0}$ is a draw from $G(\eta)$ independent from $x_i$ and idiosyncratic shocks. In the definition of the asymptotic sequence of networks, the location and scale parameters $J = J_n$ and $\sigma = \sigma_n$ will be allowed to change in $n$, depending on the shape of the distribution $G(\eta)$ in a way to be discussed in more detail below.

The specification for marginal costs implicitly assumes that, for each node $i$, marginal costs for forming a new link do not depend on existing links or attributes of the target node. Noting that the distinction between marginal costs and (negative) marginal benefits in the model is rather arbitrary, this is without loss of generality as long as dependence on any of these quantities can be included in the specification of marginal benefits. Moreover, $MC_{ij}$ includes a preference shock $\eta_{i0}$ that is common across all possible "target" nodes $j \neq i$, generating conditional heterogeneity in network degrees $s_{1i}$ given other characteristics $x_i$.

For our formal results, we make the following assumptions on the systematic parts of payoff functions.

**Assumption 8.1** (Systematic part of payoffs). (a) The systematic parts of payoffs are uniformly bounded in absolute value for some value of $t = t_0$, $|U(x, x', s, s', t_0)| \leq \bar{U} < \infty$. Furthermore, (b) at all values of $s, s'$, the function $U(x, x', s, s', t_0)$ is $p \geq 1$ times differentiable in $x$ with uniformly bounded partial derivatives. (c) The supports of the payoff-relevant network statistics, $\mathcal{S}$ and $\mathcal{T}$, and the type space $\mathcal{X}$ are compact sets.

In particular, the bound in part (a) ensures that the influence of attributes $x_i, x_j$ and network outcomes $s_i, s_j$ on link preferences never dominates that of idiosyncratic taste shifters, so that there is always a nontrivial amount of preference heterogeneity even after conditioning on these characteristics. To give an example, this assumption is satisfied for a linear index model

$$U(x_1, x_2; s_1, s_2, t_{12}) = x_1'\beta_1 + x_2'\beta_2 + |x_2 - x_1|'\beta_3 + s_1'\gamma_1 + s_2'\gamma_2 + t_{12}'\delta$$

if the values of the covariates $x_1, x_2$ and network variables $s_1, s_2, t_{12}$ are bounded.

We do not assume a specific distribution for the unobserved taste shifters $\eta_{ij}$, but impose a condition on its tails that guarantees that the distribution of the maximum over a growing number of i.i.d. draws converges to the extreme-value type-I (Gumbel) distribution associated with the (discrete choice) conditional Logit model. For the following assumption, we say that the upper tail of the distribution $G(\eta)$ is of type I if there exists an auxiliary function $a(s) \geq 0$ such that the c.d.f. satisfies

$$\lim_{s \to \infty} \frac{1 - G(s + a(s)v)}{1 - G(s)} = e^{-v}$$

for all $v \in \mathbb{R}$.

**Assumption 8.2** (Idiosyncratic part of payoffs). $\eta_{ij}$ and $\eta_{i0,k}$ are i.i.d. draws from the distribution $G(s)$, and are independent of $x_i, x_j$, where (a) the c.d.f. $G(s)$ is absolutely continuous with density $g(s)$, and (b) the upper tail of the distribution $G(s)$ is of type I with auxiliary function $a(s) := \frac{1 - G(s)}{g(s)}$.

This property is shared for most standard specifications of discrete choice models, e.g. if $\eta_{ij}$ follows the extreme-value type I, normal, or Gamma distribution; see Resnick (1987).[7] As an important caveat, note that convergence to the extreme-value distribution is in some cases very slow—e.g. for the standard normal only at the $\log n$ rate, which would dominate all other approximation errors as we take limits of the network distribution. As a practical matter, it may therefore be preferable to assume taste shifters that are extreme-value type-I, or follow another distribution for which extrema converge at a sufficiently fast rate. Nevertheless its stability property under maxima also singles out the extreme-value distribution as a plausible reference case for discrete choice models with a large number of alternatives and independent taste shifters.

### 8.2.5 Solution concept

We assume that the observed network $\mathbf{D}^*$ is pairwise stable following the definition proposed by Jackson and Wolinsky (1996), which we state below in terms of payoff increments:

---

[7] Counterexamples include short-tailed distributions, or distributions with bounded support, as well heavy-tailed distributions like Pareto or power law distributions, whose extrema converge to the Fréchet rather than the Gumbel distribution.

**Definition 8.1** (Pairwise stable network, PSN). The undirected network $\mathbf{D}^*$ is a **pairwise stable** if for any link $ij$ with $d_{ij}^* = 1$,

$$U_{ij}(\mathbf{D}^*) \geq MC_{ij}(\mathbf{D}^*), \quad \text{and } U_{ji}(\mathbf{D}^*) \geq MC_{ji}(\mathbf{D}^*)$$

and any link $ij$ with $d_{ij}^* = 0$,

$$U_{ij}(\mathbf{D}^*) < MC_{ij}(\mathbf{D}^*), \quad \text{or } U_{ji}(\mathbf{D}^*) < MC_{ji}(\mathbf{D}^*)$$

Pairwise stability is commonly regarded as a default solution concept for strategic models of network formation (see Jackson, 2008), and it only requires stability against deviations from $\mathbf{D}^*$ by a single link. Certainly, in the actual network formation process generating one or several agents may well be able to coordinate on more elaborate departures from a given network that makes all participants in such a coalition better off. Nevertheless, pairwise stability imposes a fairly tractable set of necessary conditions for other plausible, but more sophisticated notions of equilibrium choice.

Pairwise stability has some appealing features as a solution concept for decentralized network formation. While the stability conditions in Definition 8.1 can be interpreted as assuming complete information, it is only necessary that agents be aware of the link opportunities available to them in the PSN, and evaluate their payoffs from forming a link, taking the structure of the remaining network as given. Furthermore, Jackson and Watts (2002) showed that pairwise stable networks are fixed-points of myopic adjustment (tâtonnement) dynamics, which require only minimal assumptions on agents' foresight or strategic sophistication.

Note, however, that a pairwise stable network need in general not exist, rather we make the following high-level assumption.

**Assumption 8.3** (Pairwise stability). Let $\mathcal{N}_s \subset \{1, \ldots, n\}$ be the subset of nodes for which the network $\mathbf{D}^*$ satisfies the payoff conditions for pairwise stability in Definition 8.1. Then, for any $\varepsilon > 0$, $|\mathcal{N}_s|/n > 1 - \varepsilon$ with probability approaching 1 as $n$ increases.

If the network $\mathbf{D}^*$ is pairwise stable, then $|\mathcal{N}_s| = n$, so that the condition is trivially true. Sufficient conditions for existence of pairwise stable networks include cases in which links are strategic complements (see Hellmann, 2012). As another example, Pęski (2014) showed for the stable roommate problem (which can be cast as a network formation problem with at most one link for each node) that while a pairwise stable assignment need not exist, the share of "mismatched" nodes becomes arbitrarily small as $n$ increases.

A pairwise stable network also need not be unique, in which case the outcome of tâtonnement generally depends on the initial condition as well as the adjustment process. Theory typically does not give much guidance regarding equilibrium selection, or the precise form of tâtonnement. It is therefore crucial to characterize the full set of pairwise stable outcomes and establish convergence for that set in order to arrive at methods for estimation and inference that do not rely on auxiliary hypotheses regarding equilibrium selection.

For our analysis below, we recast the pairwise stability conditions as single-agent discrete choice problems given the (endogenous) alternative set

$$W_i(\mathbf{D}) := \left\{ j \in \mathcal{N} \backslash \{i\} : U_{ji}(\mathbf{D}) \geq MC_{ji}(\mathbf{D}) \right\}.$$

The following characterization of pairwise stability is given as Lemma 2.1 in Menzel (2015b):

**Lemma 8.1.** *Assuming that all preferences are strict, a network* $\mathbf{D}^* = (d_{ij}^*)_{i,j=1}^n$ *is pairwise stable if and only if*

$$d_{ij}^* = \begin{cases} 1 & \text{if } U_{ij}(\mathbf{D}^*) \geq MC_{ij}(\mathbf{D}^*), \\ 0 & \text{if } U_{ij}(\mathbf{D}^*) < MC_{ij}(\mathbf{D}^*), \end{cases} \qquad (8.1)$$

*for all* $j \in W_i(\mathbf{D}^*)$, *and* $i = 1, \ldots, n$.

We also refer to $W_i(\mathbf{D})$ as node $i$'s *link opportunity set*, and link formation corresponds to non-exclusive choice from $W_i(\mathbf{D})$.

### 8.2.6 Tâtonnement and equilibrium selection

With the possibility of multiple pairwise stable outcomes, the distribution over networks is not uniquely determined by the distribution over random payoffs. Rather, a complete description of the model has to include a rule for selecting among the equilibria, which can be formulated as a distribution over different pairwise stable networks. Specifying such a distribution explicitly would require knowledge of its support, which means that solving for all pairwise stable networks for any given realization of payoffs. The problem of identification and estimation for economic models with multiple equilibria is best understood in the case of games (see de Paula, 2013, for a recent summary of the literature). The challenges from multiplicity of pairwise stable networks are not conceptually different from those encountered in the context of discrete games, however, network formation models involve a much larger number of agents, and decisions available to each agent, than typical applications to discrete games.

To sidestep that difficulty, we treat the selected network as the outcome of a hypothetical process in which nodes readjust their connections myopically, where the pairwise stable network is determined by the initial condition of that tâtonnement process. Specifically, we assume that the adjustment process is initialized at a network $\mathbf{D}^{(0)}$—possibly dependent on the realized values of node attributes $x_i$, and taste shifters $\eta_{ij}, MC_i$. Then at the $s$th iteration, we keep $d_{ij}^{(s+1)} = d_{ij}^{(s)}$ if the pairwise stability conditions for the link $ij$ is satisfied under $\mathbf{D}^{(s)}$, and set $d_{ij}^{(s+1)} = 1 - d_{ij}^{(s)}$ otherwise. From the arguments in Jackson and

Watts (2002) it follows that, for any initial condition, tâtonnement of this form converges to a pairwise stable network or a closed cycle.[8]

Clearly, any pairwise stable network is a fixed point of tâtonnement, and therefore reachable by this myopic adjustment process from an appropriately chosen starting point. We can therefore without loss of generality represent the selection mechanism as a conditional distribution for the initial value $\mathbf{D}^{(0)}$ given node attributes and taste shifters. As an important caveat, note, however, that even if a pairwise stable network exists, tâtonnement from certain initial conditions may result in nontrivial closed cycles (i.e. cycles of more than one distinct network), and ruling out this possibility generally implies constraints on the equilibrium selection rule that are not straightforward to formulate. An important class of settings for which there exist no nontrivial closed cycles are link preferences with strategic complementarities; see Menzel (2015b) for a discussion.

The general convergence results in Menzel (2015b) do not impose any restrictions on equilibrium selection, however, for some cases the asymptotic representation of the network distribution simplifies considerably if we impose some qualitative restrictions on the selection mechanism. For expositional ease, the primary focus of this paper is on the case in which equilibrium selection is independent across dyads.

**Assumption 8.4** (Independent equilibrium selection). The initial condition $d_{ij}^{(0)}$ corresponds to independent draws from a common distribution with conditional probability mass function $p(d_{ij}^{(0)}|x_i, x_j)$.

Note that this condition does not uniquely determine an equilibrium selection rule since the distribution of the initial condition is left unspecified and may depend on node attributes in an arbitrary fashion. Rather, it imposes a certain degree of homogeneity on how the equilibrium selection rule treats different nodes of the same type across the network. This auxiliary assumption is not needed for any of the results regarding convergence of individual model components, but results in a more straightforward characterization of the set of limiting distributions. In practice, whenever plausible, imposing Assumption 8.4 may constitute a pragmatic compromise for applied work, maintaining a substantial degree of robustness while also yielding a very tractable empirical model for the network.

## 8.3 Many player asymptotics for economic models

We now give an informal outline of the limiting approximations to the different model components and to illustrate how the asymptotic argument greatly simplifies the analysis of the model. The exact model for the finite-player network

---

[8] A closed cycle corresponds to a finite sequence of networks $\mathbf{D}^{(s)}, \ldots, \mathbf{D}^{(s+r)}$, where the myopic adjustment step moves from network $\mathbf{D}^{(s+k)}$ to $\mathbf{D}^{(s+k+1)}$ for each $k = 0, \ldots, r - 1$, and from $\mathbf{D}^{(s+r)}$ to $\mathbf{D}^{(s)}$.

has a fairly complicated state space. Most importantly, that state space needs to represent (a) the (unobserved) set of available link opportunities for each of the $n$ nodes, and (b) the potential values for the network statistics for each node (edge, respectively) under all possible configurations of the network. Either of these aspects is not directly observable to the researcher and determined endogenously in the model. This state space grows in dimension with the size of the network and contains both discrete and continuous components.

Our arguments reduce the complexity of this state space exploiting the "ex-ante" anonymity of the network formation model in combination with asymptotic approximation arguments. Specifically, our model for network preferences is independent of node identities, so that we can treat any finite subset of the unlabeled nodes as random draws from a common population. Therefore, potential values for, and availability to these nodes can be fully characterized in terms of distributions over unordered elements instead of labeled lists. Furthermore, the many-player approximation yields asymptotically sufficient statistics for these distributions with respect to link formation probabilities. Finally, under the appropriate regularity conditions, these sufficient statistics converge to deterministic limits that only depend on exogenous node attributes and can be described by aggregate equilibrium conditions.

### 8.3.1 Asymptotic sequence

We now turn to a more detailed account of the approximation arguments leading to the limiting model described further below. We first need to define the asymptotic sequence along which the relevant limits are taken.

Clearly, increasing the number of nodes in the network alters the strategic structure of the model, so that we need to be careful in how the finite-player network is embedded into a (hypothetical) asymptotic sequence of models of growing size. For the purposes of this chapter, the main objective is to approximate the distributional features of the (exact) finite-player network, and we therefore need to choose that asymptotic sequence in a fashion that preserves its main qualitative features. Specifically:

(a) We take the network to be approximated to be sparse in the sense that each node is directly connected to only a small proportion of the full population of nodes. In particular, we want to allow for the possibility that nodes may remain isolated in arbitrarily large networks.

(b) Furthermore, unobserved heterogeneity in link preferences should remain relevant in arbitrarily large networks. Specifically, the limiting distribution of $d_{ij}$ and network statistics $S_i$ should be non-degenerate conditional on $x_i, x_j$.

(c) We may also want the limiting network to retain other qualitative features, like e.g. a non-degenerate clustering coefficient or other measures of "cliquishness" of the network that can be described using edge-specific network characteristics $t_{ij}$.

In order for the limiting model to match these properties of a finite network, we have to allow the distribution of link preferences to change along the asymptotic sequence. Certainly if the aim of the asymptotic analysis were to describe the changes from adding a large number of new nodes to an actual network, the appropriate limiting experiment would instead leave the payoff distribution unchanged and document the corresponding asymptotic degeneracies for the economic model.

For requirement (a), conditional link formation probabilities at the level of any dyad have to decrease to zero uniformly, which can, without loss of generality, be characterized by an increase in $MC_i$ towards infinity. However, this means that all realized links correspond to draws of marginal benefits $U_{ij}$ from the upper tail of their distribution, where for distributions for $\eta_{ij}$ with very thin tails, likelihood ratios of the form $P(U + \sigma \eta_{ij} > v)/P(U' + \sigma \eta_{ij} \geq v) = (1 - G((v - U)/\sigma))/(1 - G((v - U')/\sigma))$ diverge to infinity whenever $U > U'$ as $v \to \infty$, leading to deterministic link formation patterns given systematic parts of marginal benefits. Hence, for some distributions part (b) may only hold if we increase the scale parameter $\sigma$ at an appropriate rate as $n$ grows. Finally, with constant link formation preferences, the support of certain edge-specific statistics of the form $t_{ij}$ may degenerate as $n$ grows. For example, if links form independently and each node has only a finite network degree, the share of dyads which share a common network neighbor is mechanically driven to zero. To retain non-degeneracy in edge-level network characteristics, we have to model their effect on link preferences as growing stronger in $n$.

To formalize this, we maintain the following assumption on the asymptotic sequence of networks.

**Assumption 8.5** (Network size). The number $n$ of agents in the network grows to infinity, where (a) the location shift for marginal costs $MC_i$ is governed by the sequence $J = [n^{1/2}]$, where $[x]$ denotes the value of $x$ rounded to the closest integer. (b) The scale parameter for the taste shifters $\sigma \equiv \sigma_n = \frac{1}{a(b_n)}$, where $b_n = G^{-1}\left(1 - \frac{1}{\sqrt{n}}\right)$, and $a(s)$ is the auxiliary function specified in Assumption 8.2 (b). Furthermore, (c) for any values $t_1 \neq t_2 \in \mathcal{T}$, $|U(x, x', s, s', t_1) - U(x, x', s, s', t_2)|$ may increase with $n$, and there exists a constant $B_T < \infty$ such that $\sup_{x,x',s,s'}\left(\mathbb{E}\left[\exp\{2|U(x, x', s, s', T(\mathbf{D}_n^*, x, x', i, j)) - U(x, x', s, s', t_0)|\}\right]\right)^{1/2} \leq \exp\{B_T\}$ for any sequence of selection mechanisms and $n$ sufficiently large.

This choice of relative rates for the asymptotic sequence picks out a "knife-edge" case in which several countervailing effects are balanced against each other to achieve a limit that is non-degenerate in the sense of the three requirements specified above. Increasing marginal costs at a rate faster than specified in part (a) would result in an empty graph in the limit, whereas boosting the scale of the taste shifter distribution at a rate faster than in part (b) would lead to a limiting distribution which no longer depends on systematic parts $U_{ij}(\mathbf{D})$.

### 8.3.2 Cross-sectional dependence

We can generally distinguish between two broader approaches to constraining dependence between cross-sectional units such as the nodes of a network—for one, nodes may be located on a latent space—geographic, or defined by other exogenous attributes—where "distant" nodes are unlikely to form direct connections, or dependence of link formation decisions decreases by other means in distance. Alternatively, dependence may be symmetric in that the model for link formation does not depend on any identity or label of nodes, but only on node attributes, and the endogenous network structure. Symmetric dependence does not generally exhibit the type of ergodicity that is needed for arguments relying on weak dependence, but frequently allows for representations using (potentially random) aggregate state variables that capture any sources of (long or short range) dependence and affect all units symmetrically.

The first notion is captured by various alternative conditions for weak dependence, with asymptotic results typically relying on an "increasing domain" assumption under which the distance between a typical pair of nodes increases as the network grows. Many-agent limits of network formation games exploiting this structure have been considered by Boucher and Mourifié (2012) and Leung (2015).

In the remainder of the paper, we will focus on the second notion of symmetric dependence instead, which is closely related to the concept of exchangeability: a vector of random variables $Y_1, \ldots, Y_n$ is (finitely) exchangeable if its joint distribution is the same for any permutation $\pi(1), \ldots, \pi(n)$ of the indices $1, \ldots, n$, i.e. its p.d.f. satisfies $f_{Y_{\pi(1)}, \ldots, Y_{\pi(n)}}(y_1, \ldots, y_n) = f_{Y_1, \ldots, Y_n}(y_1, \ldots, y_n)$. Moreover, an infinite sequence $Y_1, Y_2, \ldots$ is infinitely exchangeable if each of its finite subsequences is (finitely) exchangeable in the sense of the preceding definition. An important result to clarify the dependence structure of exchangeable arrays is de Finetti's theorem: If $Y_1, Y_2, \ldots$ are infinitely exchangeable, then the joint distribution of the sequence can be represented as a mixture of i.i.d. sequences:

$$f_{Y_1, \ldots, Y_k}(y_1, \ldots, y_k) = \int \prod_{i=1}^{k} h_{Y_1}(y_i) d\mu \left( h_{Y_1} \right) \qquad \text{for any } k = 1, 2, \ldots \quad (8.2)$$

where $\mu$ is some distribution over marginal distributions $h_{Y_1}(y)$.[9] In particular, conditional on the (random) marginal distribution $h_{Y_1}(\cdot)$ the sequence $Y_1, Y_2, \ldots$ are i.i.d. draws from that marginal distribution. Hence the marginal distribution $h_{Y_1}(\cdot)$ can serve as an aggregate state variable, where conditioning on $h_{Y_1}(\cdot)$ breaks dependence across the exchangeable units.

---

[9] Note that de Finetti's theorem only applies to infinitely exchangeable sequences. However, Theorem 3.1 by Kallenberg (2005) gives an asymptotic analog of this statement for the finitely exchangeable case.

Clearly, exchangeability allows for nontrivial dependence across units: For example, consider the random sequence $Y_i = M + SZ_i$ where $M, S$ are random variables, and $Z_i | M, S \overset{iid}{\sim} N(0, 1)$. The variables $Y_1, Y_2, \ldots$ are then not independent unconditionally, or weakly dependent according to any topology on the index set, but i.i.d. conditional on $M, S$. To illustrate the relation to de Finetti's theorem, note that $(M, S)$ are also sufficient parameters for the (random) marginal distribution $h_{Y_1}(y) = \varphi \left( \frac{y-M}{S} \right)$, where $\varphi(\cdot)$ is the p.d.f. of the standard normal distribution.

Applied to network data where the indexed units correspond to economic agents (nodes), this property corresponds to a model in which the indices or labels of nodes have no economic significance. In particular, if link preferences depend only on (exogenous and endogenous) node-level and edge-level characteristics and taste shocks, and all payoff-relevant exogenous variables are independent or exchangeable draws, then the resulting set of distributions over network outcomes is invariant to permutations of node identifiers. Note that this formulation is symmetric only unconditionally, i.e. before conditioning on realized node attributes. It furthermore allows for spatial dependence in outcomes, where we treat node location in the relevant space as part of the exogenous attribute $x_i$.[10]

An important potential source of stochastic dependence is from multiple equilibria, where a random mechanism for selecting among pairwise stable networks may coordinate players' decisions "globally" in the network in a manner that is not generally consistent with weak dependence. In a representation of the form (8.2), randomized selection among equilibria only enters through the mixture distribution $\mu$, which suggests using the realized empirical distribution of node-level outcomes as a sufficient statistic for the pairwise stable network selected in the data for inference that is robust with respect to the equilibrium selection mechanism.[11] Note that the equilibrium selection rule may itself depend on individual node labels, but in the absence of other restrictions on the set of equilibrium mechanisms the model as a whole remains symmetric in that it also includes the same equilibrium selection rule acting on any permutation of node identifiers.

---

[10] This is in contrast to spatial approaches that rely on weak dependence and are typically conditional on node location. This difference is also reflected in the structure of the limiting argument, where we consider "infill" asymptotics where additional nodes are drawn from a fixed attribute space rather than "increasing domain" asymptotics where the support of at least one relevant attributes expands as the network grows.

[11] Addressing multiplicity of equilibria using conditional inference given a sufficient statistic for the realized equilibrium has already been proposed in other contexts; see e.g. Brock and Durlauf (2001), Moro (2003), and Bajari et al. (2007).

### 8.3.3 Asymptotic independence of $\eta_{ij}$ and $W_i(\mathbf{D}^*)$

When link formation decisions are subject to strategic effects, node $i$'s link formation opportunities $W_i(\mathbf{D})$ may generally depend on her own decisions on which link proposals to accept or reject. A first important step in analyzing the asymptotic properties of pairwise stable networks is to determine whether statistical dependence between the different payoff inequalities in Definition 8.1 remains sufficiently strong to affect the limiting distribution of links as the network grows in size. Lemma 4.1 in Menzel (2015b) establishes that in any pairwise stable network, the taste shifters $\eta_{ij}$ are asymptotically independent of potential values of other nodes' network attributes, and the composition of agent $i$'s link opportunity set $W_i(\mathbf{D}^*)$. We next give an outline of the argument behind this result:

Let $\mathbf{D}^*$ be the pairwise stable network resulting from the tâtonnement process described in section 8.2.6 from an arbitrarily chosen initial condition $\mathbf{D}^{(0)}$. Note that availability of $j$ to $i$ given different values of $s_i$ depends on the structure of a network $\mathbf{D}$ only through the potential values of the network attributes $s_j(\mathbf{D}) = s(\mathbf{D}+\{ij\}, \mathbf{X}; j)$ and $t_{ij}(\mathbf{D}) = T(\mathbf{D}+\{ij\}, \mathbf{X}; i, j)$. Hence we can characterize the initial condition and the resulting pairwise stable network in terms of the joint distribution of $\eta_{i1}, \ldots, \eta_{in}$ with $(s_1(\mathbf{D}), t_{i1}(\mathbf{D})), \ldots, (s_i(\mathbf{D}), t_{in}(\mathbf{D}))$ for $\mathbf{D} = \mathbf{D}^{(0)}$ and $\mathbf{D} = \mathbf{D}^*$, respectively.

In order to analyze how the distribution of network statistics and link availability depends on taste shifters, consider the outcome of tâtonnement after we replace $\eta_{i1}, \ldots, \eta_{in}$ with an independent copy from the same distribution. In the presence of link externalities, such a change will generally change the values of other nodes' endogenous network attributes at subsequent iterations of the myopic adjustment process, and may even alter their distribution in the network as a whole in a non-stationary manner. However, in a sufficiently large network such a change is equally likely to alter the network position of a node $j$ that is available to $i$ at any stage of the tâtonnement process, as to alter that of a node available to a different node $k$ that is similar to $i$ in terms of exogenous attributes $x_k$ and network characteristics under the initial condition, $(s_k(\mathbf{D}^{(0)}), t_{kj}(\mathbf{D}^{(0)}))$. Fig. 8.1 gives a conceptual illustration of this idea.

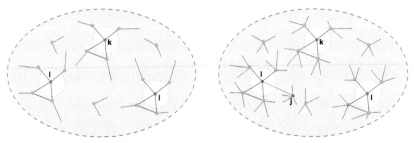

**FIGURE 8.1** Conceptual illustration of symmetric dependence: a change to node $i$'s taste shifters leads to a new link to node $j$ and alters the degree distribution in the entire network.

Most importantly, the taste shifters for that alternative node were left unchanged in this thought experiment, so that conditional on the marginal distribution of $s_1(\mathbf{D}^*)$, $t_{i1}(\mathbf{D}^*)$ in the resulting pairwise stable network, the transition rates from $W_i(\mathbf{D}^{(0)})$ to $W_i(\mathbf{D}^*)$ do not depend on the taste shifters $\eta_{i1}, \ldots, \eta_{in}$. The proof of Lemma 4.1 in Menzel (2015b) then shows that this property is in fact sufficient to conclude that, for any pairwise stable network $\mathbf{D}^*$, the conditional distribution of $\eta_{i1}, \ldots, \eta_{in}$ given $W_i(\mathbf{D}^*)$ can be approximated by the unconditional distribution $g(\eta_{i1}, \ldots, \eta_{in}) = \prod_{j \neq i} g(\eta_{ij})$ as $n$ grows large.

### 8.3.4 Limiting approximations to model components

We now turn to specific components of the model, and illustrate how to use many-player approximations identify state variables that can serve as sufficient statistics for these, and thereby drastically reduce the complexity of the state space for the network formation model. These approximations rely broadly speaking on two types of limiting results: for choice from a large set of statistically independent alternatives, the indirect (i.e. maximized) random utility is subject to statistical laws governing the distribution of extremes. On the other hand, the composition of alternative sets and distribution of network characteristics across all nodes can be described in terms of sample averages, to which laws of large numbers apply.

#### 8.3.4.1 Approximations for discrete choice from large sets of alternatives

Given the set $W_i(\mathbf{D})$ of available alternatives, Lemma 8.1 states that we can cast the pairwise stability conditions as (non-exclusive) choice out of $W_i(\mathbf{D})$. Noting that the set $W_i(\mathbf{D})$ is node-specific, endogenous to the pairwise stable network, and unobserved in typical applications, reformulating pairwise stability in this fashion does not result in any immediate simplification of the finite-network problem. Furthermore, under the relevant limiting sequence for the network, the number of alternatives $J_W := |W_i(\mathbf{D})|$ turns out to grow at a rate proportional to the parameter $J$ in the specification of marginal costs, whereas the number of proposals in $W_i(\mathbf{D})$ accepted by $i$, as denoted by the network degree $s_{1i}$, remains stochastically bounded.[12] However, in the following we show that the large size of the alternative set can be turned into an advantage under large-network asymptotics, where we can combine extreme-value theory and the structure of the (limiting) conditional Logit model to arrive at an approximate representation of conditional link formation probabilities.[13]

Consider the probability that, given the network $\mathbf{D}$ and link opportunity set $W_i(\mathbf{D})$, node $i$ has pairwise stable links with $s_{1i} = r$ nodes $j_1, \ldots, j_r \in W_i(\mathbf{D})$,

---

[12] A random sequence $X_n \in \mathbb{R}$ is stochastically bounded if for any $\varepsilon$ there exists a finite number $B < \infty$ such that $\lim_n P(|X_n| > B) < \varepsilon$.

[13] This argument was first developed in Menzel (2015a) for the two-sided matching case, and then extended by Menzel (2015b) for general models of network formation.

and rejects all other link proposals. In terms of node $i$'s link preferences, this event corresponds to choosing $r$ out of $J_W$ link proposals,

$$U_{ij_1}, \ldots, U_{ij_r} \geq MC_i > U_{ij} \text{ for all other } j \in W_i(\mathbf{D}).$$

In particular, $MC_i$ is the $(r+1)$st highest order statistic of the sample of random utilities $\mathcal{U}_i(\mathbf{D}) := \{U_{ij}(\mathbf{D}) : j \in W_i(\mathbf{D})\} \cup \{MC_i\}$. Under the relevant limiting sequence, $J_W$ grows to infinity at the same rate as $J$, so that $r$ remains stochastically bounded. We therefore generally have $r \ll J_W$, so that the accepted links correspond to random utilities that are extreme order statistics of $\mathcal{U}_i(\mathbf{D})$ whose distribution can be approximated using extreme-value theory.[14]

Assumption 8.2 ensures that extrema of the taste shocks $\eta_{ij}$ converge to the type-I extreme-value distribution, resulting in conditional link acceptance probabilities that generalize conditional choice probabilities for the multinomial Logit model. In particular, the probability that $i$ is available to a specific node $j \notin W_i(\mathbf{D})$ conditional on being connected to $r$ nodes in $W_i(\mathbf{D})$ converges according to

$$\lim_J \left| J P(i \in W_j(\mathbf{D}) | W_i(\mathbf{D}), j \notin W_i(\mathbf{D}), s_i = r) - \frac{r \exp\{U(z_{ij})\}}{1 + \gamma \sum_{z \in \mathcal{Z}} \exp\{U(z)\} p_z} \right|$$
$$\to 0 \tag{8.3}$$

as $J$ and $J_W$ grow large. We illustrate this result with a simple example for the discrete case in Appendix 8.B.

### 8.3.4.2  Inclusive values

From the expression in (8.B.1), we can see that in the many-alternatives approximation the probability of the most attractive link in $W_i(\mathbf{D})$ being of type $z$ depends on the set $W_i(\mathbf{D})$ only through the expression in the denominator,

$$I_i := \frac{J_W}{J} \sum_{z \in \mathcal{Z}} \exp\{U(z)\} p_z = \frac{1}{J} \sum_{j \neq i} \mathbb{1}\{j \in W_i(\mathbf{D})\} \exp\{U(z_{ij})\} \tag{8.4}$$

In the context of the Logit model for discrete choice, the quantity $I_i$ is commonly referred to as the *inclusive value* for the alternative set $W_i(\mathbf{D})$. Hence, $I_i$ can serve as a sufficient statistic for the set $W_i(\mathbf{D})$ with respect to conditional link formation probabilities.

A further simplification arises from the fact that although the inclusive values $I_i$ are individual-specific, under the conditions of our model the average in the right-hand side of (8.4) can be shown to satisfy a law of large numbers, so that

$$I_i \approx \mathbb{E}_n[I_i | x_i, s_i] =: \hat{\mathsf{H}}_n^*(x_i; s_i) \tag{8.5}$$

---

[14] See Resnick (1987) for a general reference.

as $n$ grows large, where $\mathbb{E}_n[\cdot]$ denotes the expectation with respect to taste shocks $MC_j, \eta_{ji}$ in the $n$-agent network, while holding the empirical distribution of $x_j, s_j$ fixed. In other words, nodes with the same attributes $x_i, s_i$ face linking opportunities that become more similar to each other as measured by the inclusive value of the set $W_i(\mathbf{D})$. Since the inclusive value is asymptotically sufficient for the set of alternatives, it does not matter for our purposes that the link opportunity sets for two agents with the same attributes differ with respect to the identities of nodes in that set, or its composition in terms of node attributes. We denote the conditional expectation under the selected pairwise stable network with $\hat{\mathsf{H}}_n^*(x; s)$ and will refer to it as the *inclusive value function* in the following.

The fact that the probability of $j \in W_i(\mathbf{D})$ given in (8.3) also depends on the inclusive value for $I_j = \frac{1}{J} \sum_{i \neq j} \mathbb{1}\{i \in W_j(\mathbf{D})\} \exp\{U(z_{ji})\}$, suggest equilibrium conditions for $\hat{\mathsf{H}}_n^*(x; s)$ that are of the form

$$
\begin{aligned}
\hat{\mathsf{H}}_n^*(x; s) &\approx \mathbb{E}_n \left[ s_{1j} \frac{\exp\{U(x, x_j; s, s_j, t_0) + U(x_j, x; s_j, s, t_0)\}}{1 + \hat{\mathsf{H}}_n^*(x_j, s_j)} \right] \\
&=: \hat{\Psi}_n[\hat{\mathsf{H}}_n^*, \hat{M}_n^*](x; s)
\end{aligned}
\tag{8.6}
$$

where $\hat{M}_n^*$ denotes the empirical distribution of $s_j$ given $x_j$ in the cross-section of network nodes. We also define the population analog of the mapping $\hat{\Psi}_n$ as

$$
\begin{aligned}
&\Psi_0[\mathsf{H}, M](x; s) \\
&:= \int s_{1j} \frac{\exp\{U(x, x_j; s, s_j, t_0) + U(x_j, x; s_j, s, t_0)\}}{1 + \mathsf{H}(x_j, s_j)} M(s_j | x_j) w(x_j) ds_j dx_j.
\end{aligned}
$$

Notice there are two potential challenges to establishing convergence in the previous step: for one, the expression inside the expectation evaluated payoffs at $t_0$ rather than $t_{ij}$. This step is a consequence of Assumption 8.5 (c) and established in the proof of Lemma 4.4 in Menzel (2015b).

A second challenge arises from the fact that the expectation assumes that the endogenous network attributes $s_j^*$ are i.i.d. draws from the cross-sectional distribution $\hat{M}_n^*$, whereas with multiple equilibria in the network, the selection rule may not treat nodes of the same type symmetrically. Specifically, for two nodes $i, k$ with identical attributes $x_i = x_k$ the composition of $W_i(\mathbf{D})$ may differ sharply from that of $W_k(\mathbf{D})$, leading to a gap between $I_i$ and $I_k$ that does not vanish as $n$ increases.

For example, if for a nontrivial number of nodes $j$ there are pairwise stable networks supporting two distinct outcomes $s_j = s_1$ and $s_j = s_2$, say, it may be possible to construct an equilibrium selection rule under which most nodes available to $i$ select the larger value, whereas most nodes available to a different node $k$ with $x_k = x_i$ and $s_i = s_k$ select the lower value. The proof of Lemma 4.3 in Menzel (2015b) establishes that this possibility does not affect convergence in (8.6) for a randomly selected node, regardless of the form of equilibrium selection mechanism. For an intuition for that result, note that in order to maintain large departures of $I_i$ from $H^*(x_i; s_i)$ for each $i$ in some set $\mathcal{N}^\circ \subset \mathcal{N}$, we would need to partition $\mathcal{N}$ into a subset $\mathcal{N}_1$ for which we select the high value $s_1$ whenever possible, and another set $\mathcal{N}_2$ for which $s_2$ is selected. Clearly, conditional on attributes, each node in $\mathcal{N}_1$ is equally likely to be available to any specific node in the set $\mathcal{N}^\circ$ as to another node in its complement. Now, according to (8.3), each node $j$ is available to a fraction of the remaining nodes that is of the order $1/\sqrt{n}$, where availability is independent across dyads. Hence any assignment of a node to the "high-equilibrium" group $\mathcal{N}_1$ is going to raise the inclusive value for a roughly equal share of nodes in $\mathcal{N}^\circ$ as in its complement, therefore reducing the scope for spreading the distribution of the inclusive values as $n$ increases.

### 8.3.4.3   Distribution of network variables

The payoff-relevant network variables $z_{ij} := (s_i, s_j, t_{ij})$ are endogenous variables in the network formation model that are determined simultaneously across dyads. In order to describe their distribution, consider first the subnetwork on $\mathcal{N}_{ij}$, the set of nodes that are mutually acceptable to either $i$ or $j$ for some value of $z_{ij}$. For such a node $l \in \mathcal{N}_{ij}$, we can define the *potential values* of statistics $s_l, t_{il}, t_{jl}$ for any configuration on the subnetwork on $\mathcal{N}_{ij}$ as the values of those network attributes taking the network structure on $\mathcal{N} \setminus \mathcal{N}_{ij}$ as given. For a pairwise stable network, any such subnetwork must satisfy the pairwise stability conditions in Definition 8.1 given the potential values.

By the previous arguments, taste shifters $\eta_{il}$ are independent of potential values for the network statistics for the node $l$ in a large network, so that the set $\mathcal{N}_{ij}$ represents a random sample from the distribution of $s_l, t_{il}, t_{jl}$ over the cross-section of nodes $\mathcal{N} \setminus \{i, j\}$. Under the assumption of independent equilibrium selection in Assumption 8.4, these draws are independent.[15] In the following, we will refer to that cross-sectional distribution the *reference distribution* of the payoff-relevant endogenous network characteristics and denote it with $\hat{M}_n^*(s_l, t_{il}, t_{jl}|x_i, x_j, x_l)$. Note that as $n$ grows large, the difference between the "take-two-out" distribution for the potential values among nodes other than $\{i, j\}$ and the distribution over the full cross-section becomes negligible, so that we can take the nodes in $\mathcal{N}_{ij}$ as draws from the distribution $\hat{M}_n^*(\cdot|x_i, x_j, x_l)w_n(x_l)/(1 + \hat{H}_n^*(x_l; s_l))$, where $w_n(x_l)$ is the p.d.f. of empirical distribution of $x_1, \ldots, x_n$.

Since all potential outcomes have to be supported by a pairwise stable network, the reference distribution is itself an equilibrium object. Specifically, for a given choice of $M(\cdot)$ and $H(\cdot)$, we can compute the probability $\hat{\Omega}_n[H, M](s_l, t_{il}, t_{ij}|x_i, x_j, x_l)$ that the potential values $s_l, t_{il}, t_{ij}$ are supported

---

[15] Without restrictions on equilibrium selection, the limiting representation of the model may be more complex in general; see Menzel (2015b).

by a pairwise stable subnetwork on a random network neighborhoods of the type described above. It is immediate that this probability gives an upper bound for the probability that a PSN corresponding to those values is in fact selected. Similarly, for any set of values $S_3 \times T_{13} \times T_{23} \subset \mathcal{S} \times \mathcal{T}^2$ we can compute the probability $\hat{\Omega}_n[\hat{H}_n^*, \hat{M}_n^*](x_1, x_2, x_3; S_3, T_{13}, T_{23})$ that at least one potential value in that set is supported.

Then the reference distribution has to satisfy the constraints

$$\int \hat{M}_n^*(s_3, t_{13}, t_{23} | x_1, x_2, x_3) ds_3 dt_{13} dt_{23} \leq \hat{\Omega}_n[\hat{H}_n^*, \hat{M}_n^*](x_1, x_2, x_3; S_3, T_{13}, T_{23})$$

for all values of its arguments.[16] The fixed-point mapping $\hat{\Omega}_n[H, M]$ depends on the sampling distribution of exogenous node attributes and its population analog $\Omega_0[H, M]$ can be defined in a similar manner by taking probabilities over the population distribution $w(x)$ of exogenous attributes. We make the following assumptions on the sample and population fixed-point mappings.

**Assumption 8.6.** (a) The mapping $\Omega_0$ is compact and upper hemi-continuous in H, $M$ for all $x \in \mathcal{X}$ and $S \subset \mathcal{R}$, and (b) the core of $\Omega_0[H, M]$ is nonempty. (c) The fixed-point mapping converges

$$\sup_{x, Z \subset \mathcal{R}} \left| \hat{\Omega}_n[H, M](Z) - \Omega_0[H, M](Z) \right| \to 0$$

uniformly in $H \geq 0$ and $M$.

It can be shown that these assumptions are sufficient to guarantee the existence of a fixed point $(H, M) \in (\Psi_0[H, M], \Omega[H, M])$; see Theorem 4.1 in Menzel (2015b).

### 8.3.4.4 Fixed-point convergence

The previous arguments introduced the two functions $\hat{H}_n^*$ and $\hat{M}_n^*$ as aggregate state variables for an asymptotic representation of the network model. Furthermore, when $x_i, s_i, t_{il}$ are all discrete, we can represent $\hat{H}_n^*, \hat{M}_n^*$ as Euclidean (finite-dimensional) vectors, so that these constraints become a finite-dimensional system of fixed-point conditions. In close analogy with generalized method of moments (GMM) estimation, we can treat these aggregate state variables as auxiliary parameters that satisfy a system of moment conditions.

Specifically, for a pairwise stable network, these state variables have to satisfy the fixed point conditions

$$\hat{H}_n^*(x_1; s_1) = \hat{\Psi}_n[\hat{H}_n^*, \hat{M}_n^*](x_1; s_2),$$

---

[16] If multiple outcomes are supported on the subnetwork, the $\hat{\Omega}_n[H, M](s_l, t_{il}, t_{ij} | \cdot)$ is subadditive, so that non-singleton events in potential values add nontrivial constraints on the reference distribution. The set of distributions satisfying these inequality constraints for all events in $(s_l, t_{il}, t_{ij})$ is called the *core* of the capacity $\hat{\Omega}_n[H, M]$.

$$\int \hat{M}_n^*(s_3, t_{13}, t_{23} | x_1, x_2, x_3) ds_3 dt_{13} dt_{23}$$

$$\leq \hat{\Omega}_n[\hat{H}_n^*, \hat{M}_n^*](x_1, x_2, x_3; S_3, T_{13}, T_{23}),$$

for $n$ sufficiently large. Under the assumptions made above, we furthermore find that the mappings on the right-hand side converge uniformly to their population analogs, $[\hat{\Psi}_n, \hat{\Omega}_n] \to [\Psi_0, \Omega_0]$, which, under regularity conditions, implies convergence of $\hat{H}_n^*, \hat{M}_n^*$ to the set of solutions of

$$H^*(x_1; s_1) = \Psi_0[H^*, M^*](x_1; s_2),$$

$$\int M^*(s_3, t_{13}, t_{23} | x_1, x_2, x_3) ds_3 dt_{13} dt_{23}$$

$$\leq \Omega_0[H^*, M^*](x_1, x_2, x_3; S_3, T_{13}, T_{23}).$$

The regularity conditions and convergence argument follow closely the standard proof for consistency of GMM; see e.g. Newey and McFadden (1994), and they can be extended to the (infinite-dimensional) case of continuous attributes.

## 8.4 Limiting model

We can now put together the approximation steps from the previous section to state the limiting distribution of the network formation model. In that limit, the local features of the network are determined by conditional link acceptance probabilities of the Logit form (8.3), whereas global features of the network are captured by the inclusive value function $H^*$ and reference distribution $M^*$, which were introduced in (8.6) and Assumption 8.6.

The limiting representation allows us to consider the link formation decision of a node pair $(i, j)$ separately on a **network neighborhood** of that pair. Specifically we define $\mathcal{N}_{ij}$ as the set of all nodes $k \in \{1, \ldots, n\}$ which may form a pairwise stable link with either $i$ or $j$ given some value of the endogenous network variables $(s_i, s_j, s_k)$ and $(t_{ij}, t_{ik}, t_{jk})$; see also Menzel (2015b) for a more precise definition.

The limiting model is then described in terms of three components:

- The **reference distribution** $M^*$ is a cross-sectional distribution of potential values for endogenous network variables for a node selected uniformly at random from $\mathcal{N}$.
- The **inclusive value function** is a nonnegative function $H^*$ of node-level attributes that summarizes the effect of size and composition of agents' link opportunity sets on conditional link acceptance probabilities.
- The **edge-level response** for a pair of nodes $i, j$ is the set of joint distributions for $d_{ij}, s_i, s_j, t_{ij}$ consistent with pairwise stability on the subnetwork among $i, j$ and their direct network neighbors.

These components jointly determine the link frequency distribution, where the edge-level response depends on the inclusive value function and the reference distribution through the distribution of size and composition of the network neighborhood of an edge $ij$. Conversely, the reference distribution and inclusive value function result from "local" link decisions that have to be consistent with the edge-level response, and are therefore determined by aggregate equilibrium conditions that also derive from conditional link acceptance probabilities. In the following, we also define the pseudo-surplus function

$$V(x_1, x_2; s_1, s_2, t_{12}) := U(x_1, x_2; s_1, s_2, t_{12}) + U(x_2, x_1; s_2, s_1, t_{12}).$$

### 8.4.1 Link frequency distribution

We characterize the limiting model $\mathcal{F}_0^*$ as a set of distributions over edge-level network variables. Specifically, we define the **link frequency distribution** as

$$F_n(x_1, x_2; s_1, s_2, t_{12})$$

$$:= \frac{1}{n} \sum_{i=1}^{n} \sum_{j \neq i} P\left(d_{ij} = 1, x_i \leq x_1, x_j \leq x_2, s_i \leq s_1, s_j \leq s_2, t_{ij} \leq t_{12}\right).$$

This object is not a proper probability distribution but corresponds to a measure which integrates to the average network degree rather than unity. Since the asymptotic sequence results in sparse networks with stochastically bounded network degrees, we normalize this sequence of distributions by the number of nodes $n$ rather than the number of edges, $n(n-1)/2$, in order to obtain a well-defined limit. With a minor abuse of standard terminology we also refer to the Radon–Nikodym derivative of $F_n$ as the p.d.f. of the link frequency distribution and denote it with $f_n(x_1, x_2; s_1, s_2, t_{12})$.

It is an important question whether any important information is lost by reducing the information on the network on this distribution. Notice first that we can equivalently represent any adjacency matrix $\mathbf{D}$ as an unordered list of node pairs corresponding to nonzero edges. In fact such a representation drastically reduces the amount of memory needed to store a sparse network graph. Furthermore, the focus of this chapter is primarily on estimation of, and inference regarding payoff parameters in a model which treats the network nodes as exchangeable units. Hence, we could replace the node identifiers in such a list with any known—exogenous or endogenous—attributes of the edge or either node which may be relevant to the likelihood of forming a direct link. However, we cannot rule out some loss of information about the "deeper" network structure in this step, so that this heuristic argument does not formally establish sufficiency of the link frequency distribution for the network formation model. Finally, since this list is unordered, we can equivalently summarize it by the average network degree and the empirical distribution of pair attributes among the nonzero edges.

## 8.4.2 Unique edge-level response

We distinguish between the case of a unique edge-level response for which the p.d.f. is available in closed form, and that of a set-valued edge-level response for which we can provide sharp bounds. In the case of a unique edge-level response, the event that a given outcome satisfies the pairwise stability conditions is equivalent to it being the realized (observed) outcome. With multiple pairwise stable outcomes in local subnetworks, this is generally not true since only one of the alternative outcomes supported by the realized payoffs is selected in the data. We discuss that more general case in the next subsection below.

By conditional independence, the probability of a link $d_{ij} = 1$ given potential values $s_i, s_j, t_{ij}$ in the presence of such a link, is given by the product of the link acceptance probabilities for nodes $i$ and $j$. Hence, using the Logit limiting approximation for the conditional link acceptance probabilities we obtain the limiting p.d.f. for the link frequency distribution

$$
\begin{aligned}
f_0^*(x_1, x_2; s_1, s_2) &= \frac{s_{11}s_{12}\exp\{U(x_1, x_2; s_1, s_2) + U(x_2, x_1; s_2, s_1)\}}{(1 + H^*(x_1, s_1))(1 + H^*(x_2, s_2))} \\
&\quad \times M^*(s_1|x_1, x_2)M^*(s_2|x_2, x_1)w(x_1)w(x_2) \\
&= \frac{s_{11}s_{12}\exp\{V(x_1, x_2; s_1, s_2)\}}{(1 + H^*(x_1, s_1))(1 + H^*(x_2, s_2))} \\
&\quad \times M^*(s_1|x_1, x_2)M^*(s_2|x_2, x_1)w(x_1)w(x_2)
\end{aligned}
\tag{8.7}
$$

where we define the pseudo-surplus function

$$
V(x_1, x_2; s_1, s_2) := U(x_1, x_2; s_1, s_2) + U(x_2, x_1; s_2, s_1). \tag{8.8}
$$

The fixed-point condition for the inclusive value function $H^*(x_1, s_1)$ was given by

$$
H^*(x; s) = \Psi_0[H^*, M^*](x; s) \tag{8.9}
$$

with the fixed-point operator $\Psi_0$ is defined as

$$
\Psi_0[H, M](x; s) := \int \frac{s_{12}\exp\{V(x, x_2; s, s_2)\}}{1 + H(x_2; s_2)} M^*(s_2|x_2, x_1)w(x_2)ds_2dx_2.
$$

The equilibrium condition for the reference distribution $M^*(s_1|x_1, x_2)$ is

$$
M^*(s_1|x_1, x_2) = \Omega_0[H^*, M^*](x_1, x_2; s_1) \tag{8.10}
$$

where the mapping $\Omega_0$ results from aggregating the edge-level response in the cross section. Since the edge-level response was assumed to be unique, the mapping $\Omega_0$ is therefore singleton-valued in the present case. However, this does not imply that the limiting distribution $F_0^*$ is unique since the fixed-point condition (8.10) may admit multiple solutions.

### 8.4.3 Equilibrium selection

In the case of a non-unique edge-level response, the model typically only yields bounds on the link frequency distribution, which are discussed in greater detail in Appendix 8.A. In this section we consider the case in which pairwise stable subnetworks need not be unique, but the researcher assumes a specific equilibrium selection mechanism. For example, we may assume that the network is a result of tâtonnement from the empty graph, so that with strategic complementarities the smallest pairwise stable network is selected. Alternatively, we may assume a model of tâtonnement with search frictions from a fixed initial state. In both cases, the model is reduced to a single distribution.

For a given selection rule, we can define $\pi(s_1, s_2, t_{12}|x_1, x_2)$ as the conditional probability that $s_i = s_1, s_j = s_2, t_{ij} = t_{12}$ given that $x_i = x_1, x_j = x_2$ and that these values are supported by a pairwise stable network. For example, if the equilibrium selection mechanism always selects the pairwise stable network with the smallest values of $s_i, s_j, t_{ij}$, and $d_{ij}$ then $\pi(s_1, s_2, t_{12})$ equals the conditional probability that, given $s_i = s_1, s_j = s_2, t_{ij} = t_{12}$ no smaller values of these variables are supported by a pairwise stable network. We show how to compute $\pi(s_1, s_2)$ for an example with preferences depending on network degree below.

Given the selection rule, the link frequency distribution has p.d.f.

$$
f_0^*(x_1, x_2; s_1, s_2) = \frac{s_{11}s_{12}\exp\{V(x_1, x_2; s_1, s_2)\}}{(1 + H^*(x_1, s_1))(1 + H^*(x_2, s_2))}
$$
$$
\times M^*(s_1|x_1, x_2)M^*(s_2|x_2, x_1)\pi(s_1, s_2|x_1, x_2)w(x_1)w(x_2)
$$
(8.11)

where the fixed-point mapping $\Psi_0$ is

$$
\Psi_0[H, M](x; s)
$$
$$
:= \int \frac{s_{12}\exp\{V(x, x_2; s, s_2)\}}{1 + H(x_2; s_2)} M^*(s_2|x_2, x_1)\pi(s_2|x_2)w(x_2)ds_2dx_2
$$

and the mapping $\Omega_0$ is also adjusted accordingly.

### 8.4.4 Convergence results

We can now combine the asymptotic arguments from the previous section to establish $\mathcal{F}_0^*$ as the limiting model for the network formation game. In the formal statements, $\mathcal{F}_0^*$ refers to the most general formulation of the model for the set-valued case; see Menzel (2015b) for a rigourous characterization. Models with a single-valued edge-level response or a specified selection mechanism can be seen as special cases of this setup for which the representation simplifies considerably.

**Theorem 8.1** (Convergence). *Suppose that Assumptions 8.1–8.6 hold, and let $\mathcal{F}_0^*$ be the set of distributions described before. Then for any pairwise or cyclically stable network there exists a distribution $F_0^*(x_1, x_2; s_1, s_2) \in \mathcal{F}_0^*$ such that the link frequency distribution*

$$\sup_{x_1, x_2, s_1, s_2, t_{12}} |\hat{F}_n(x_1, x_2; s_1, s_2, t_{12}) - F_0^*(x_1, x_2; s_1, s_2, t_{12})| = o_p(1).$$

*Furthermore, convergence is uniform with respect to selection among pairwise stable networks.*

This result is proven as Theorem 4.2 from Menzel (2015b). The main argument follows our exposition in the previous section, where we first show that linking probabilities in the finite network can be approximated by a model in which the inclusive value function $H^*$ and reference distribution $M^*$ are sufficient statistics for the global network structure. The next series of steps derives finite-$n$ and asymptotic fixed-point conditions for these state variables. We finally conclude by showing that the solutions of the finite-$n$ fixed-point problem converge to solutions of the asymptotic analog, which establishes the main conclusion of this theorem.

Menzel (2015b) furthermore gives conditions under which the bounds corresponding to $\mathcal{F}_0^*$ are sharp, that is, every distribution in that set can be achieved by a sequence of distributions over finite pairwise stable networks.

## 8.5 Identification and estimation

This section illustrates potential uses of the limiting model for identification analysis and estimation. It is very challenging to perform either task for the exact finite-$n$ model, so we propose more practical alternatives that treat the observable data as if it was generated from the limiting model. Given the main convergence result in Theorem 8.1, this general approach can be justified if we are mainly interested in asymptotic properties of estimators or inference procedures in the many-player limit.

Identification and strategies for estimation crucially depend on how data is sampled from the $n$-agent network. In typical applications, the researcher may only have information for a subset of nodes or edges in the network, where sampling need not even be independent across units.[17] For the purposes of this discussion, we assume that the researcher observes the matrix $\mathbf{X}$ of exogenous attributes and the adjacency matrix $\mathbf{D}^*$ for the entire network. Note that, given such a sample, it is also possible to construct the endogenous network attributes $s_i := S(\mathbf{D}^*, \mathbf{X}; i)$ and $t_{ij} := T(\mathbf{D}^*, \mathbf{X}; i, j)$. Since many-agent asymptotics is

---

[17] For example, a survey may only record the star subgraph induced by a set $\mathcal{N}_M^* = \{i_1, \dots, i_M\} \subset \{1, \dots, n\}$ of randomly drawn nodes, i.e. a random sample of nodes together with the relevant information on the nodes that have a direct connection to any node in that sample. In that case it may still be possible to reconstruct the endogenous network attributes for each node in $\mathcal{N}_M^*$ and edge on the induced star subgraph.

only used to provide approximations to the solutions of the network formation model, our convergence results can also be applied to identification analysis and estimation under other sampling protocols. However, for expositional purposes, we only present results for the case in which the full network is observed.

### 8.5.1 Identification

Identification from the limiting model is generally different from its finite-$n$ version. For the purposes of this section, we view identification analysis as a first step in devising estimators or inference procedures that are consistent as the number of players in the network grows large. In contrast, identification based on the finite-player model would be the relevant concept if we were interested in asymptotic properties given an increasing number of independent draws from one or several finite networks whose size is held fixed.

We now give a constructive argument for nonparametric identification of certain components of the model for the case of a single-valued edge-level response. First, the link frequency distribution $\hat{F}_n$ is nonparametrically identified from either the full network, or a random sample of edges in the network as long as the relevant endogenous network attributes $s_i, s_j, t_{ij}$ are recorded for every edge $ij$ in that sample.

### Identification of the reference distribution

The reference distribution $M^*$ was defined as the *joint* distribution for potential values of the network statistics $s_k, t_{ki}, t_{kj}$ for all possible configurations of the subnetwork in a neighborhood of nodes $i$ and $j$, $\mathcal{N}_{ij}$. Since by definition only one of these potential values is observed for any triad $ijk$, that joint distribution cannot be observed directly. However, under Assumption 8.4—imposing independent equilibrium selection across nodes—it is for our purposes sufficient to identify *marginal* distributions of potential values for each relevant subnetwork configuration. We can easily verify that under Assumption 8.4, these marginals of $M^*$ are equal to the conditional distribution of $s_l, t_{il}, t_{jl}$ given subnetwork configurations on $\mathcal{N}_{ij}$, and are therefore nonparametrically identified from the cross-section of the network.

For the cases we consider in more detail, potential values $s_l, t_{il}, t_{jl}$ vary with the subnetwork on $\mathcal{N}_{ij}$ only depending on $d_{ij}$, i.e. whether there is an edge directly connecting $i$ and $j$. In these cases computation of the link frequency distribution furthermore only requires knowledge of the marginal distribution of the potential value corresponding to $d_{ij} = 1$, which is equal to $\hat{F}_n(s_k, t_{ik}, t_{jk}|d_{ij} = 1)$ and can therefore be obtained directly from the link frequency distribution.

### Identification of payoff functions

We next consider identification of payoff functions for the case of a unique edge-level response with no edge-specific interaction effects. By inspection, we can rewrite the full characterization for the limiting model $\mathcal{F}_0^*$ in (8.7)–(8.10) in terms of the *pseudo-surplus function* $V(x_1, x_2; s_1, s_2)$ defined in (8.8) instead of the systematic part of payoff functions, $U(x_1, x_2; s_1, s_2)$. From this reparametrization it follows immediately that $U(x_1, x_2; s_1, s_2)$ is only identified from the limiting distribution if it can be recovered from the pseudo-surplus function.[18]

For the case of no endogenous interaction effects, $U(x_1, x_2, s_1, s_2) = U(x_1, x_2)$, we can re-state the limiting model (8.7)–(8.10) as

$$f_0^*(x_1, x_2; s_1, s_2)$$
$$= \frac{s_{11}s_{12}\exp\{V(x_1, x_2)\}M^*(s_{11}|x_1, x_2)M^*(s_{12}|x_2, x_1)w(x_1)w(x_2)}{(1 + H^*(x_1))(1 + H^*(x_2))}$$

where the inclusive value function $H^*(x)$ satisfies the fixed-point condition

$$H^*(x) = \Psi_0[H^*, M^*](x) := \int_{\mathcal{X} \times \mathcal{S}} s \frac{\exp\{V(x, x_2)\}}{1 + H^*(x_2)} M^*(s|x_2, x)w(x_2)ds dx_2$$

and the degree distribution $M^*(s|x)$ is given by

$$M^*(s_1|x_1) \equiv P(s_{1i} = s_1|x_i = x) = \frac{H^*(x_1)^{s_1}}{(1 + H^*(x_1))^{s_1+1}}$$

and does not depend on $x_2$.

Summing over values for $s_{1i}$, we can compute

$$P(s_{1i} \geq r|x_i = x) = \sum_{s=r}^{\infty} \frac{H^*(x)^s}{(1 + H^*(x))^{s+1}} = \left(\frac{H^*(x)}{1 + H^*(x)}\right)^r$$

so that we can express the inclusive value function $H^*(x)$ in terms of the ratio

$$\frac{P(s_{1i} = r|x_i = x)}{P(s_{1i} \geq r|x_i = x)} = \frac{1}{1 + H^*(x)}$$

for any $r \geq 0$.

We can now combine these components to recover the pseudo-surplus function from log differences of link frequencies,

$$V(x_1, x_2) = \log \frac{f_0^*(x_1, x_2; s_1, s_2)}{s_{11}s_{12}M^*(s_1|x_1)M^*(s_2|x_2)w(x_1)w(x_2)}$$

---

[18] It is worth noting that despite the fact that utilities were assumed to be non-transferable, the observable implications of the model depend entirely on a measure of joint "surplus" among the agents forming an edge. Formally this is a consequence of the two-sided nature of link formation and the (asymptotic) Logit form of conditional acceptance probabilities. In economic terms, a fundamental difference with models of transferable utility (see e.g. Choo and Siow, 2006 and Graham, 2014) is that the respective scales of $U(x_1, x_2; s_1, s_2)$ and $U(x_2, x_1; s_2, s_1)$ depend on the relative importance of observable relative to unobserved heterogeneity in preferences rather than a transferable "numéraire," see also Menzel (2015a) for a discussion in the context of matching models.

$$-\log \frac{P(s_{1i} = r|x_i = x_1)}{P(s_{1i} \geq r|x_i = x_1)} - \log \frac{P(s_{1j} = r|x_j = x_2)}{P(s_{1j} \geq r|x_j = x_2)}.$$

As shown before, all components in the expression on the right-hand side are nonparametrically identified from the observed network, so that this argument establishes nonparametric identification of the pseudo-surplus function for the model without endogenous interaction effects.

### 8.5.2 Maximum likelihood estimation

While the argument for nonparametric identification given above is entirely constructive, it does not provide a very useful approach to estimation if the model for payoff functions is parametric. As a more practical alternative, we next discuss maximum likelihood estimation based on the limiting model $\mathcal{F}_0^*$.

For the remainder of this section, we assume that systematic utilities are specified as

$$U(x_i, x_j; s_i, s_j, t_{ij}) = U(x_i, x_j; s_i, s_j, t_{ij}|\theta)$$

for a finite-dimensional parameter $\theta$. We also define the resulting pseudo-surplus function

$$V(x_i, x_j; s_i, s_j, t_{ij}|\theta) = U(x_i, x_j; s_i, s_j, t_{ij}|\theta) + U(x_j, x_i; s_j, s_i, t_{ij}|\theta).$$

For the case of a non-unique edge-level response, we also maintain the assumption of independent equilibrium selection, Assumption 8.4.

For the general approach, note first that, for given values of the aggregate state variables $H^*, M^*$, links are mutually independent with likelihood given by (8.11). While the fixed-point condition (8.10) may have multiple solutions, the marginals for the reference distribution $M^*$ selected in the observed network are nonparametrically identified and can be estimated consistently from the observed data as $n$ grows large. Following the general approach in Menzel (2016), we therefore propose conditional estimation given the realized reference distribution, which obviates the need to solve the fixed-point problem in (8.10) explicitly.

Below we give several examples for deriving the log-likelihood contribution for node $i$,

$$\ell_i(\theta, H) := \sum_{j=1}^{n} d_{ij} \log f^*(x_i, x_j; s_i, s_j|\theta, H)$$

from the limiting model. If the researcher observes the full network with $n$ nodes, the log-likelihood function corresponding to the limiting distribution is

$$\mathcal{L}_n(\theta, H) := \sum_{i=1}^{n} \ell_i(\theta, H).$$

The inclusive value function H* is not directly observed from the data, but we can estimate the fixed-point mapping $\Psi_0[H, M^*]$ by replacing expectations with sample averages with respect to $x_j, s_j$ across the observed nodes. We can therefore treat $H^*(x; s)$ as an auxiliary parameter in maximum likelihood estimation of the surplus function $V^*(x_1, x_2; s_1, s_2|\theta)$ satisfying the fixed-point condition (8.9). Noting that the fixed-point mapping $\Psi_0$ is an expectation over the distribution of node-level attributes, it can be estimated using the sample analog

$$\hat{\Psi}_n(\cdot) := \frac{1}{n} \sum_{i=1}^{n} \psi_i(\theta, H)$$

where the node-level contributions $\psi_i(\theta, H)$ are again derived from the limiting representation.

The resulting maximum likelihood estimator $\hat{\theta}_n$ can then be obtained by solving the constrained maximization problem

$$\max_{\theta, H} \mathcal{L}_n(\theta, H) \quad \text{s.t. } H = \hat{\Psi}_n(H) \tag{8.12}$$

Optimization problems including high-dimensional nuisance parameters that are defined by fixed-point conditions are common in structural estimation, where popular algorithms include the nested fixed point (see Rust, 1987; Ishakov et al., 2016) and MPEC algorithms (see e.g. Su and Judd, 2012). If the attributes $(x_i', s_i')'$ are discrete, then the function $H(x; s)$ can be represented as a finite-dimensional vector, so that the problem (8.12) can be solved by standard constrained optimization routines as `fmincon` in MATLAB®.

In order to illustrate this general approach, we conclude by re-stating several relevant examples developed in Menzel (2015b). Specifically, we state the log-likelihood function and fixed-point condition for the inclusive value function H* in each case. In each case the likelihood function is derived from the corresponding limiting model $\mathcal{F}_0^*$, assuming that the researcher observes the relevant exogenous characteristics for all nodes, $x_1, \dots, x_n$, and the full adjacency matrix **D**. The general approach can also be extended to random sampling from the complete network graph using inverse sampling weights.

**Example 8.1** (No endogenous interaction effects). We first consider the case of no endogenous interaction effects, with systematic marginal utility functions of the form $U(x_1, x_2) = U(x_1, x_2; \theta)$. For this case, the only relevant network variable is the network degree $s_{1i} := \sum_{j=1}^{n} d_{ij}$, and the inclusive value function does not depend on endogenous network characteristics, so that $H(x; s) = H(x)$ for all $s \in \mathcal{S}$.

Then the information in the sample can be summarized by the degree sequence $s_{11}, \dots, s_{1n}$ together with the nonzero link indicators, and the limiting model implies that the log-likelihood contribution of the $i$th node is given by

$$\ell_i(\theta, H) = \frac{1}{2}\sum_{j=1}^{n} d_{ij}\left(V(x_i, x_j|\theta) - \log(1 + H(x_i)) - \log(1 + H(x_j))\right)$$
$$+ \log s_{1i} - \log(1 + H(x_i)).$$

Note that the log of the last factor of the likelihood only receives weight one half to offset the double-counting of nonzero link indicators as we sum the log-likelihood contributions over the nodes $i = 1, \ldots, n$. The constrained maximum likelihood estimator maximizes the network log-likelihood $\mathcal{L}_n(\theta, H) := \sum_{i=1}^{n} \ell_i(\theta, H)$ subject to the fixed-point condition $H(x) = \frac{1}{n}\sum_{i=1}^{n} \psi_i(\theta, H)$ with

$$\psi_i(\theta, H) = w_i s_{1i} \frac{\exp\{V(x, x_i|\theta)\}}{1 + H(x_i)}$$

where $w_i := \frac{\mathbb{1}\{s_{1i}>0\}}{\frac{1}{n}\sum_{k=1}^{n} \mathbb{1}\{s_{1k}>0\}}$. The importance weights $w_i$ are used to obtain an unbiased estimator for the operator $\Psi_0$ in (8.9), noting that the reference distribution for the potential value of $s_{1i}$ from setting $d_{ij} = 1$ is equal to the conditional distribution of $s_{1i}$ given $s_{1i} > 0$ in the cross-section over nodes in the network.

**Example 8.2** (Many-to-many matching and capacity constraints). Next, we state the likelihood for a many-to-many matching model that assumes the same preferences as in the previous case, but allows each node to form at most $\bar{s}$ direct links, i.e. capping the network degree at $\bar{s}$. Furthermore, in accordance with classical matching models, we modify the notion of pairwise stability for networks (PSN, Definition 8.1) to allow for deviations in which a node simultaneously severs one link and forms another. Specifically, we assume that $d_{ij}^* = 1$ if

$$U_{ij}(\mathbf{D}^*) \geq \max\{MC_i, U_{ik}(\mathbf{D}^* - \{ij\})\}, \quad \text{and}$$
$$U_{ji}(\mathbf{D}^*) \geq \max\{MC_j, U_{jl}(\mathbf{D}^* - \{ij\})\}$$

and $d_{ij}^* = 0$ if

$$U_{ij}(\mathbf{D}^*) < \min\{MC_i, U_{ik}(\mathbf{D}^* - \{ij\})\}, \quad \text{or}$$
$$U_{ji}(\mathbf{D}^*) < \min\{MC_j, U_{jl}(\mathbf{D}^* - \{ij\})\}$$

for any $k$ such that $U_{ki}(\mathbf{D}^*) \geq MC_k$ and $l$ such that $U_{lj}(\mathbf{D}^*) \geq MC_l$. For $\bar{s} = 1$, this model corresponds to the stable roommate problem.[19]

---

[19] See also Pęski (2014) for an independent derivation of limiting results for the stable roommate problem under many-agent asymptotics.

The log-likelihood contribution of the $i$th node resulting from the limiting model is then obtained as

$$\ell_i(\theta, \mathrm{H}) \;=\; \frac{1}{2}\sum_{j=1}^{n} d_{ij}\left(V(x_i, x_j|\theta) - \log(1 + \mathrm{H}(x_i)) - \log(1 + \mathrm{H}(x_j))\right)$$

$$+ \log s_{1i} - \mathbb{1}\{s_{1i} < \bar{s}\}\log(1 + \mathrm{H}(x_i))$$

and the fixed-point mapping for the inclusive value function is the average of contributions

$$\psi_i(\theta, \mathrm{H}) := w_i s_{1i} \frac{\exp\{V(x, x_i|\theta)\}}{1 + \mathrm{H}(x_i)}$$

where $w_i := \dfrac{\mathbb{1}\{s_{1i} > 0\}}{\frac{1}{n}\sum_{k=1}^{n}\mathbb{1}\{s_{1k} > 0\}}$ as in the previous case.

**Example 8.3** (Strategic complementarities in network degree). Finally, we consider the case in which link preferences depend on the respective network degrees of nodes $i$ and $j$, $s_i = \sum_{k=1}^{n} d_{ik} \equiv s_{1i}$ and $s_j = \sum_{k=1}^{n} d_{jk} \equiv s_{1j}$. For simplicity, we assume that $s_i, s_j$ are strategic complements with $d_{ij}$, that is, the systematic part $U(x_i, x_j; s_i, s_j|\theta)$ is nondecreasing in $s_i$ and $s_j$.

With preferences of this form, the edge-level response is generally not unique, and in what follows we assume that, for any realization of payoffs, the observed network is selected as the maximal pairwise stable network under the partial order: $\mathbf{D} \geq \mathbf{D}'$ if $d_{ij} \geq d_{ij}'$ for all $i, j$. It follows from standard arguments for monotone comparative statics (see Milgrom and Roberts, 1990) that the maximal stable network is well-defined and can be obtained from myopic best-response dynamics starting at the complete graph $d_{ij} = 1$ for all $i \neq j$.

Under these assumptions the probability that a given network $L$ is generated by this selection mechanism is equal to the probability that $\mathbf{D}$ is pairwise stable times the conditional probability that payoffs do not support any larger network $\mathbf{D}' > \mathbf{D}$ given that $\mathbf{D}$ is pairwise stable. After some standard calculations, we find that under $\mathcal{F}_0^*$, the probability that the values $\bar{s} < s_1, \cdots < s_r$ for $s_{1i}$ are jointly supported is equal to

$$p(\bar{s}, \ldots, s_r|x; \mathrm{H}^*) = \frac{\mathrm{H}^*(x; \bar{s})^{\bar{s}} \prod_{q=1}^{r}(\mathrm{H}^*(x; s_q) - \mathrm{H}^*(x; s_{q-1}))^{(s_q - s_{q-1})}}{(1 + \mathrm{H}^*(x; s_r))^{r+1}}.$$

Hence, if we define

$$\tau(\bar{s}; r|x; \mathrm{H})$$

$$:= \sum_{\bar{s} < .. < s_r} \frac{p(\bar{s}, s_1 \ldots, s_r|x; \mathrm{H})}{p(\bar{s}|x; \mathrm{H})}$$

$$= 1 - \sum_{\bar{s} < s_1 < .. < s_r} \frac{(1 + \mathrm{H}(x; \bar{s}))^{\bar{s}+1} \prod_{q=1}^{r}(\mathrm{H}(x; s_q) - \mathrm{H}(x; s_{q-1}))^{(s_q - s_{q-1})}}{(1 + \mathrm{H}(x; s_r))^{r+1}}$$

the conditional probability that $s_0$ is the largest network degree for node $i$ given that $\bar{s}$ is supported by a pairwise stable network is given by

$$\pi^*(\bar{s}|x; \mathrm{H}) = 1 + \sum_{r=1}^{\infty}(-1)^r \tau(\bar{s}; r|x; \mathrm{H}).$$

For an implementation of the MLE it is possible to partially vectorize computation of $\pi^*(\bar{s}|x; \mathrm{H})$. Specifically, if $\mathrm{H}(x; s)$ only changes its value at a finite number $r$ of values for $s$, then $\pi^*(\bar{s}|x; \mathrm{H})$ can be computed by a double loop with a total of $2r$ iterations.

The log-likelihood contribution of the $i$th observation can then be written as

$$
\begin{aligned}
\ell_i(\theta, \mathrm{H}) \quad = \quad & \frac{1}{2}\sum_{j=1}^{n} d_{ij}\big(V(x_i, x_j; s_i, s_j|\theta) - \log(1 + \mathrm{H}(x_i; s_i)) \\
& - \log(1 + \mathrm{H}(x_j; s_j))\big) \\
& + \log s_{1i} - \log(1 + \mathrm{H}(x_i; s_i)) + \log \pi^*(s_i|x_i; \mathrm{H})
\end{aligned}
$$

and the fixed-point condition for the inclusive value function is obtained from the sample average of

$$\psi_i(\theta, \mathrm{H}) := w_i s_{1i} \frac{\exp\{V(x, x_i; s, s_i|\theta)\}}{1 + \mathrm{H}(x_i; s_i)}$$

where $w_i := \frac{\mathbb{1}\{s_{1i}>0\}}{\frac{1}{n}\sum_{k=1}^{n}\mathbb{1}\{s_{1k}>0\}}$ as in the previous case.

These full-network likelihoods can be adjusted for other sampling protocols by using the implied sampling weights for both the likelihood contributions and the fixed-point condition for $\mathrm{H}^*$. For Monte-Carlo simulations illustrating estimation for some of these examples; see also Menzel (2015b).

## 8.6 Conclusion

In this chapter we lay out a conceptual framework for many-player asymptotics as a practical tool for solving and estimating models of strategic network formation. We illustrate how to apply limiting arguments to the different components of that model to obtain tractable approximations and arrive at a limit distribution for the network that is substantially easier to analyze and interpret than the exact finite-player model. We then illustrate how to apply these results to estimation of link preferences in large networks for some representative cases.

The larger research program of using many-player asymptotics for estimation and inference is still a work in progress at this point, and a large-sample distribution theory for estimators is understood only for certain special cases.

# Appendix 8.A  Bounds for set-valued edge-level response

This appendix gives a characterization for the limiting model for the general case in which the edge-level response need not be unique, and the limit distribution only implies bounds on the link frequency distribution. We then discuss how these bounds can be used for estimation of the identified set for the payoff parameters.

## 8.A.1  Set-valued edge-level response

If the pairwise stable network on $\mathcal{N}_{ij}$ is not unique, the model allows for several distinct outcomes even holding the aggregate state variables $H^*$, $M^*$ fixed. Hence the link frequency distribution depends on a (potentially randomized) rule of selecting among locally pairwise stable outcomes, so that the limiting model $\mathcal{F}_0^*$ is the set of distributions generated by the set of possible selection mechanisms.

We can characterize that set $\mathcal{F}_0^*$ in terms of upper bounds on the conditional probabilities for events in the endogenous network variables $y_{ij} := (d_{ij}, s_i, s_j, t_{ij})'$ given exogenous attributes $(x_i, x_j)$. The upper bound for the event $y_{ij} \in Y_1 \subset \{0, 1\} \times \mathcal{S}^2 \times \mathcal{T}$ corresponds to the conditional probability that there exists at least one outcome $y_1 \in Y_1$ that is supported by a pairwise stable network on $\mathcal{N}_{ij}$, that is, we can bound the probability

$$P(y_{ij} = y_1 \text{ realized in data}|x_i, x_j) \leq P(y_{ij} = y_1 \text{ supported } |x_i, x_j).$$

In general, bounds for singleton events of the form $Y_1 = \{y_1\}$ alone are not sharp. For instance considering events consisting of two distinct outcomes $y_1, y_2$, we have

$$P(y_{ij} = y_1 \text{ or } y_{ij} = y_2 \text{ supported}|x_i, x_j)$$
$$= P(y_{ij} = y_1 \text{ supported}|x_i, x_j) + P(y_{ij} = y_2 \text{ supported}|x_i, x_j)$$
$$- P(y_{ij} = y_1 \text{ and } y_{ij} = y_2 \text{ supported}|x_i, x_j).$$

Hence, if the probability that $y_1, y_2$ are both supported is strictly greater than zero, a bound corresponding to the composite event $y_{ij} \in \{y_1, y_2\}$ imposes a nontrivial additional constraint on the set of possible distributions of $y_{ij}$. Formally, the mapping from sets $Y$ to the corresponding probability bounds defines a **Choquet capacity** (see Beresteanu et al., 2011 and Galichon and Henry, 2011 for a definition and its use to describe distributions for discrete games), a functional that represents the convex set of distributions satisfying these bounds.

We can then apply the limiting approximations to bounds for elementary outcomes of this kind to determine the edge-level response and the fixed point mapping for the reference distribution, $\Omega_0$. In the general case, either object will be set-valued. Specifically, sharp bounds for the link frequency distribution under $\mathcal{F}_0^*$ are given by the set of edge-level responses given any $M^*$ and $H^*$ satisfying the equilibrium conditions for the aggregate state variables,

$$H^* = \Psi_0[H^*, M^*], \qquad M^* \in \Omega_0[H^*, M^*]$$

Here, $\Psi_0$ is of the same form as before, and $\Omega_0$ maps values of $H^*, M^*$ to sets of conditional distributions for potential values of $s_k, t_{ik}$. It is important to note that the assumption of independent equilibrium selection (Assumption 8.4) is crucial for all network neighborhoods to be drawn from the same reference distribution.[20]

We discuss construction of $\Omega_0$ for two examples below. A full formal characterization of the sharp bounds for $\mathcal{F}_0^*$ is beyond the scope of this chapter; see Menzel (2015b) for a detailed description of the limiting model for the general case.

## 8.A.2 Set estimation and bounds

We now turn to set estimation of parametric models for the case of a non-unique edge-level response. As for the point-identified cases, we assume a parametric model for payoffs,

$$U(x_i, x_j; s_i, s_j, t_{ij}) = U(x_i, x_j; s_i, s_j, t_{ij}|\theta_0).$$

However, in the present case, the limiting model $\mathcal{F}_0^*$ is a non-singleton set of probability distributions. Without auxiliary assumptions on a mechanism for selecting among multiple pairwise stable networks, we can therefore only find bounds on the conditional probability for an event $A_{ij}$ in the variables $d_{ij}, s_i, s_j, t_{ij}$ for a dyad $ij$ in the $n$-player network, which we denote with $P_n(A_{ij}|x_i, x_j)$. Specifically, the limiting model can be used to construct functions $Q_L(\cdot), Q_U(\cdot)$ such that

$$Q_L(A_{ij}|x_i, x_j; \theta_0, H^*) \leq \lim_n P_n(A_{ij}|x_i, x_j) \leq Q_U(A_{ij}|x_i, x_k; \theta_0, H^*).$$

As for the single-valued case, these asymptotic bounds generally depend on the inclusive value function satisfying $H^* = \Psi_0[H^*, M^*](\theta)$ for the fixed-point mapping $\Psi_0[\cdot](\theta)$ defined as before. Also, we continue to assume that the marginals of the reference distribution $M^*$ are nonparametrically point-identified.

Following the classical econometric approach to estimating games with multiple equilibria,[21] we can use these bounds to construct moment functions of the

---

[20] See Menzel (2015b) for the general case with arbitrarily dependent selection mechanisms.
[21] See Tamer (2003), Ciliberto and Tamer (2009), Galichon and Henry (2011), and Beresteanu et al. (2011)

form

$$\mathbf{m}(A^{(r)}|\theta, \mathrm{H}) := \begin{pmatrix} \mathbb{1}\{A_{ij}^{(r)}\} - Q_L(A^{(r)}|x_i, x_j; \theta, \mathrm{H}) \\ Q_U(A^{(r)}|x_i, x_j; \theta, \mathrm{H}) - \mathbb{1}\{A_{ij}^{(r)}\} \end{pmatrix}$$

for any event $A^{(r)}$ in terms of $d_{ij}, s_i, s_j, t_{ij}$, where $\mathbb{1}\{A\}$ is an indicator function whether the event $A$ is true. From the definition of the asymptotic probability bounds, we then have the asymptotic conditional moment restriction

$$\lim_n \mathbb{E}[\mathbf{m}(A^{(r)}; \theta_0)|x_i, x_j] \geq 0 \text{ a.s.}$$

We can construct moment inequalities of this type for any collection of events $A^{(1)}, \ldots, A^{(R)}$. This approach can also be extended to events involving three or more nodes for which we construct probability bounds $Q_L(\cdot)$ and $Q_U(\cdot)$ from the limiting model.

Given these inequality restrictions, we can estimate the identified set

$$\Theta_I \ := \ \Big\{\theta \in \Theta : \lim_n \mathbb{E}[\mathbf{m}(A^{(r)}; \theta, \mathrm{H})|x_i, x_j] \geq 0 \text{ a.s. for each } r = 1, \ldots, R$$
$$\text{for some } \mathrm{H} = \Psi_0[\mathrm{H}, M^*](\theta)\Big\}$$

based on sample analogs for conditional expectations and the fixed-point mapping $\Psi_0$. This can be implemented using now standard techniques for moment inequalities; see e.g. Beresteanu et al. (2011) for a description. Since these bounds are only satisfied as $n \to \infty$, set estimation and inference can only be consistent (asymptotically valid, respectively) under the many-player limit.

We next give an example to illustrate how to obtain the probability bounds $Q_L(\cdot)$, $Q_U(\cdot)$ from the limiting model $\mathcal{F}_0^*$.

**Example 8.4** (Completion of transitive triads). Consider the model with payoffs

$$U_{ij}(\mathbf{D}, \mathbf{X}) = U^*(x_i, x_j) + \beta_{T,n} t_{ij} + \sigma \eta_{ij}$$

where $t_{ij} = t(\mathbf{D}, \mathbf{X}; i, j) := \max_{k \neq i, j} d_{ik} d_{jk}$ is an indicator of $i$ and $j$ having a common network neighbor. In order to obtain a potentially non-degenerate clustering coefficient in the limiting model, we assume the sequence $\beta_{T,n} := \frac{1}{6} \log n + \beta_T \geq 0$, which can be shown to satisfy Assumption 8.5 (c). We also let $t_{ij}(d_1, d_2, d_3)$ denote the potential values for $t_{ij}$ given the structure of the network after fixing $d_{ij} = d_1$, $d_{ik} = d_2$, $d_{jk} = d_3$ for $d_1, d_2, d_3 \in \{0, 1\}$. In particular, $t_{ij}(1, d_{ij}, d_{jk}) = 1$ only if $i, j$ are part of a transitive triad for $d_{ij} = 1$.

We consider probability bounds for outcomes in the subgraph on the triad consisting of nodes $i, j, k$, where either of the link indicators $d_{ij}, d_{ik}, d_{jk}$ may be one or zero. We do not assign specific roles to the nodes $i, j, k$, so it is without loss of generality sufficient to consider events with $d_{ij} \geq d_{ik} \geq d_{jk}$. For orders of magnitude, under the asymptotic sequence in Assumption 8.5 we can verify that the number of triads supporting $l = 0, 1, 2, 3$ stable links grows at the order $a_{ln}$, where $a_{0n} = n^3$, $a_{1n} = n^2$, $a_{2n} = n$, and $a_{3n} = n$, and their respective shares at rates $a_{ln}/n^3$. In particular, the dyad $ij$ is part of $n - 3$ distinct triads outside $ijk$, so that the probability for $t_{ij}(1, 0, 0) = 1$ is of the order $na_{3n}/n^3 = 1/n$.

Next we notice that the structure of the complementarity restricts multiplicity in subnetwork outcomes: Since $\beta_{T,n} \geq 0$, we can verify that, for any payoffs supporting $d_{ij} = d_{ik} = 1$ and $d_{jk} = 0$, there exists no other pairwise stable subnetwork on the triad. Also, payoffs under which a subnetwork with one or zero links is pairwise stable, may only support the complete subgraph $d_{ij} = d_{ik} = d_{jk} = 1$ as an additional pairwise stable subnetwork.

To compute the probability bounds $Q_L(d_{ij}, d_{ik}, d_{jk}|x_i, x_j, x_k; \cdot)$ and $Q_U(d_{ij}, d_{ik}, d_{jk}|x_i, x_j, x_k; \cdot)$, let $d_{ij}(t)$ denote the potential value for $d_{ij}$ from setting $T_{ij} = 1$. Then define $p_{ik}(t) := P(d_{ik}(t) - 1|x_i, x_j)$ so that, from our previous results,

$$\lim_n n p_{ik}(t) = \frac{s_{1i}s_{1k}\exp\{U^*(x_i, x_k) + U^*(x_k, x_i) + 2\beta_T t\}}{(1 + H^*(x_i))(1 + H^*(x_k))}.$$

For any event $A_{ijk}$ in the variables $d_{ij}, d_{ik}, d_{jk}$, the upper bound $Q_U(A_{ijk}|x_i, x_j, x_k)$ corresponds to the probability that an outcome in $A_{ijk}$ is supported by random payoffs. Hence we have

$$Q_U(0, 0, 0|x_i, x_j, x_k; \theta, H) = \lim_n (1 - p_{ij}(0))(1 - p_{ik}(0))(1 - p_{jk}(0)) = 1,$$

$$Q_U(1, 0, 0|x_i, x_j, x_k; \theta, H) = \lim_n n p_{ij}(0)(1 - p_{ik}(0))(1 - p_{jk}(0)),$$

$$Q_U(1, 1, 0|x_i, x_j, x_k; \theta, H) = \lim_n n^2 p_{ij}(0) p_{ik}(0)(1 - p_{jk}(0)),$$

$$Q_U(1, 1, 1|x_i, x_j, x_k; \theta, H) = \lim_n n^2 p_{ij}(1) p_{ik}(1) p_{jk}(1)),$$

noting that, as argued before, the contribution of triads outside $ijk$ to link probabilities is asymptotically negligible. The limits on the right-hand side are then obtained by plugging in component-wise limits for $p_{kl}(t)$ as functions of $\theta$ and H.

For the lower bounds, note first that the upper bound on the probability of transitive triads is of a smaller asymptotic order than that for a triad with zero or one link, so that

$$Q_L(0, 0, 0|x_i, x_j, x_k; \theta, H) = Q_U(0, 0, 0|x_i, x_j, x_k; \theta, H),$$

$$Q_L(1, 0, 0|x_i, x_j, x_k; \theta, H) = Q_U(1, 0, 0|x_i, x_j, x_k; \theta, H).$$

Furthermore, for any payoffs resulting in a triad with two links, the pairwise stable subnetwork on that triad is unique for $t_{ij}(1, 1, 0) = t_{ik}(1, 1, 0) - t_{jk}(1, 1, 0) = 0$, so that $Q_L(1, 1, 0|x_i, x_j, x_k; \theta, H) = Q_U(1, 1, 0|x_i, x_j, x_k; \theta, H)$. Finally, the transitive triad is the unique pairwise stable subnetwork if and only if all three links are dominant,

$$Q_L(1, 1, 1|x_i, x_j, x_k; \theta, H) = \lim_n n^2 p_{ij}(0) p_{ik}(0) p_{jk}(0) = 0.$$

We can also verify that bounds for composite events of distinct values of $d_{ij}, d_{ik}, d_{jk}$ do not impose additional restrictions on the limiting distribution. We can then form moment inequality conditions by comparing these bounds to appropriately normalized subgraph counts for triads in the observed network,

$$\hat{\mathbf{m}}_n^{(1)}(\theta, H)$$

$$:= \frac{1}{n^2} \sum_{ijk} \left( \mathbb{1}\{d_{ij} = 1, d_{ik} = 0, d_{jk} = 0\} - Q_L(1, 0, 0|x_i, x_j, x_k; \theta, H) \right)$$

$$\times \psi(x_i, x_j, x_k),$$

$$\hat{\mathbf{m}}_n^{(2)}(\theta, H)$$

$$:= \frac{1}{n} \sum_{ijk} \left( \mathbb{1}\{d_{ij} = d_{ik} = 1, d_{jk} = 0\} - Q_L(1, 1, 0|x_i, x_j, x_k; \theta, H) \right)$$

$$\times \psi(x_i, x_j, x_k),$$

$$\hat{\mathbf{m}}_n^{(3)}(\theta, H)$$

$$:= \frac{1}{n} \sum_{ijk} \left( Q_U(1, 1, 1|x_i, x_j, x_k; \theta, H) - \mathbb{1}\{d_{ij} = d_{ik} = d_{jk} = 1\} \right)$$

$$\times \psi(x_i, x_j, x_k),$$

for a vector-valued function $\psi(x_1, x_2, x_3) \geq 0$ that only takes nonnegative values. By the law of iterated expectations, the limit of the expectations for $\hat{\mathbf{m}}_n^{(k)}(\theta_0, H_0^*)$ is equal to zero for $k = 1, 2$, and greater or equal to zero for $k = 3$, so that we can use the resulting moment equalities and inequalities for testing and estimation.

**Example 8.5** (Strategic complementarities in network degree). Consider the payoffs from Example 8.3 with payoffs $U_{ij}(\mathbf{D})$ depending on $s_i := \sum_{j=1}^n d_{ij}$ and $s_j := \sum_{i=1}^n d_{ji}$. We now show how to construct probability bounds for dyad-level outcomes in $(d_{ij}, s_i, s_j)$ which do not assume a particular selection mechanism.

Similar to the discussion for the case of a specific selection mechanism, let

$$p(s_1, \ldots, s_r|x) := \frac{H(x; s_1)^{s_1} \prod_{q=1}^r (H(x; s_q) - H(x; s_{q-1}))^{(s_q - s_{q-1})}}{(1 + H(x; s_r))^{r+1}}$$

for any $s_1 < \cdots < s_r$, and define

$$\tau^*(\bar{s}; r|x) := \sum_{s_1 <..<\bar{s}<..<s_r} \frac{p(s_1, \ldots, \bar{s}, \ldots, s_r|x)}{p(\bar{s}|x)}$$

where the summation is over any ordered tuple of $r$ values for $s_{1i}$, one component of which equals $\bar{s}$. Then the conditional probability that $\bar{s}$ is the unique pairwise stable value of $s_i$ given that it is supported by a pairwise stable subnetwork is

$$\pi^*(\bar{s}|x) = 1 + \sum_{r=1}^{\infty} (-1)^r \tau^*(\bar{s}; r|x).$$

Since the sharp upper bound for the probability of the outcome $d_{ij}, s_i, s_j$ corresponds to the probability that these values are supported by some pairwise stable subnetwork, we obtain

$$\begin{aligned}
&Q_U(d_{ij} = 1, s_i, s_j | x_i, x_j; \theta, \mathrm{H}) \\
&:= \lim_n n P(d_{ij} = 1, s_i, s_j \text{ supported } | x_i, x_j) \\
&= \frac{s_i s_j \exp\{V(x_i, x_j; s_i, s_j)\} \mathrm{H}(x_i; s_i)^{s_i} \mathrm{H}(x_j; s_j)^{s_j}}{(1 + \mathrm{H}(x_i; s_i))^{s_i+1}(1 + \mathrm{H}(x_j; s_j))^{s_j}}.
\end{aligned}$$

Sharp lower bounds for specific values of these network outcomes correspond to the event that no other values of $d_{ij}, s_i, s_j$ are supported by payoffs, and can be obtained by multiplying the upper bound with the conditional probability that the given pairwise stable outcome is unique. Specifically, we let

$$\begin{aligned}
&Q_U(d_{ij} = 1, s_i, s_j | x_i, x_j; \theta, \mathrm{H}) \\
&:= Q_U(d_{ij} = 1, s_i, s_j | x_i, x_j; \theta, \mathrm{H}) \pi^*(s_i | x_i) \pi^*(s_j | x_j).
\end{aligned}$$

These bounds for singleton events are not sharp, but following Beresteanu et al. (2011) and Galichon and Henry (2011), we can obtain additional constraints by considering composite events consisting of several distinct values of these network variables.

## Appendix 8.B  Convergence of link formation probabilities to logit

In this appendix, we give a brief example to illustrate convergence of conditional link acceptance probabilities to their Logit analogs, as stated more generally in (8.3). For simplicity, we only consider the largest order statistic of the sample $\{U_{ij}(\mathbf{D}) : k \in W_i(\mathbf{D})\} \cup \{MC_i\}$, and we also restrict attention to the discrete-covariate case where $z_{ij} := (x_i', x_j', s_i', s_j', t_{ij}')'$ takes values in a finite set $\mathcal{Z}$. As a notational convention, we associate $0 \in \mathcal{Z}$ with the outside option of not forming a link. We also denote the proportion of nodes in $W_i(\mathbf{D})$ with $z_{ij} = z$ with $p_z > 0$ for all $z \in \mathcal{Z}$, so that the number of type-$z$ nodes in $W_i(\mathbf{D})$ is given by $J_W p_z$. For a given value $z \in \mathcal{Z}$, the highest random utility among the nodes in $W_i(\mathbf{D})$ with $z_{ij} = z$ is given by

$$\max_{j \in W_i(\mathbf{D}), z_j = z} \left\{ U_{ij}(\mathbf{D}) \right\} = U(z) + \sigma \max_{j \in W_i(\mathbf{D}), z_j = z} \left\{ \eta_{ij} \right\}$$

where, with some abuse of notation, we let $U(z)$ denote the systematic part of the marginal benefits with attributes $z_{ij} = z$. By independence of taste shifters, and since by Assumption 8.2 the distribution of $\eta_{ij}$ has tails of type I,

$$\max_{j \in W_i(\mathbf{D}), z_j = z} \left\{ U_{ij}(\mathbf{D}) - \log J_W - \log p_z \right\} \xrightarrow{d} \xi_{iz}, \text{ for all } z \in \mathcal{Z}$$

as $J_W \to \infty$, where "$\xrightarrow{d}$" denotes convergence in distribution, and $\xi_{iz}$ are i.i.d. draws from the extreme-value type-I distribution. Similarly,

$$MC_i - \log J = \max_{j=1,\dots,J} \sigma \eta_{ij,0} - \log J \xrightarrow{d} \xi_{i0}$$

where $\xi_{i0}$ is extreme-value type-I and independent of $(\xi_{iz})_{z \in \mathcal{Z}}$ and $(z_{ij})_{j \in W_i(\mathbf{D})}$.

Now the event that the link corresponding to the highest value in $\mathcal{U}_i(L)$ is achieved at some $j$ with $z_{ij} = \bar{z}$ corresponds to the event that $\max_{j \in W_i(\mathbf{D}), z_j = \bar{z}} U_{ij}(\mathbf{D}) \geq \max \left\{ \max_{j \in W_i(\mathbf{D}), z_j = z'} U_{ij}(\mathbf{D}), MC_i \right\}$ for all $z' \in \mathcal{Z}$. As $J, J_W$ grow large, the probability of that event can be approximated by

$$P\left( U(\bar{z}) + \log p_{\bar{z}} + \log J_W + \xi_{i\bar{z}} \right.$$
$$\geq \max \left\{ \max_{z \in \mathcal{Z}} \{ U(z) + \log p_z + \log J_W + \xi_{iz} \}, \xi_{i0} \right\} \bigg)$$
$$= \frac{\exp\{U(\bar{z})\} p_{\bar{z}}}{1 + \gamma \sum_{z \in \mathcal{Z}} \exp\{U(z)\} p_z} \qquad \qquad , \qquad \text{(8.B.1)}$$

for $\gamma := \lim_n J_W / J$, where the right-hand side expression follows from the usual Logit formula for exclusive choice from the finite set $\{\arg\max_{j: z_j = z} U_{ij}(\mathbf{D}) : z \in \mathcal{Z}\}$ and the outside option of remaining an isolated node.

This line of reasoning does not immediately carry over to the case of continuous types where $\mathcal{Z}$ is infinite, and the joint distribution of several extreme order statistics. However, the "Logit-type" approximation extends to the fully general case by applying extreme-value approximations directly to the conditional link acceptance probabilities, and is established as Lemma 4.2 in Menzel (2015b).

# References

Badev, A., 2016. Discrete Games in Endogenous Networks: Theory and Policy. Working paper. Federal Reserve Board of Governors.

Bajari, P., Benkard, L., Levin, J., 2007. Estimating dynamic models of imperfect competition. Econometrica 75 (5), 1331–1370.

Beresteanu, A., Molchanov, I., Molinari, F., 2011. Sharp identification regions in models with convex moment predictions. Econometrica 79 (6), 1785–1821.

Bickel, P., Chen, A., Levina, E., 2011. The method of moments and degree distributions for network models. The Annals of Statistics 39 (5), 2280–2301.

Boucher, V., Mourifié, I., 2012. My Friend Far Far Away: Asymptotic Properties of Pairwise Stable Networks. Working paper. University of Toronto.

Brock, W., Durlauf, S., 2001. Discrete choice with social interactions. The Review of Economic Studies 68.

Choo, E., Siow, A., 2006. Who marries whom and why. Journal of Political Economy 114 (1), 175–201.

Ciliberto, F., Tamer, E., 2009. Market structure and multiple equilibria in airline markets. Econometrica 77 (6), 1791–1828.

de Paula, A., 2013. Econometric analysis of games with multiple equilibria. Annual Review of Economics 5, 107–131.

de Paula, A., Richards-Shubik, S., Tamer, E., 2014. Identification of Preferences in Network Formation Games. Working paper. UCL, CMU, and Harvard.

Dzemski, A., 2014. An Empirical Model of Dyadic Link Formation in a Network with Unobserved Heterogeneity. Working paper. University of Gothenburg.

Galichon, A., Henry, M., 2011. Set identification in models with multiple equilibria. The Review of Economic Studies 78, 1264–1298.

Goldsmith-Pinkham, P., Imbens, G., 2012. Social networks and the identification of peer effects. Journal of Business and Economic Statistics 31, 253–264.

Graham, B., 2014. An Econometric Model of Link Formation with Degree Heterogeneity. Working paper. UC Berkeley.

Hellmann, T., 2012. On the existence and uniqueness of pairwise stable networks. International Journal of Game Theory 42 (1), 211–237.

Ishakov, F., Lee, J., Rust, J., Schjerning, B., Seo, K., 2016. Comment on "Constrained optimization approaches to estimation of structural models". Econometrica 84 (1), 365–370.

Jackson, M., 2008. Social and Economic Networks. Princeton University Press.

Jackson, M., Watts, A., 2002. The evolution of social and economic networks. Journal of Economic Theory 106, 265–295.

Jackson, M., Wolinsky, A., 1996. A strategic model of social and economic networks. Journal of Economic Theory 71, 44–74.

Kallenberg, O., 2005. Probabilistic Symmetries and Invariance Principles. Springer.

Kallenberg, O., 2016. A Weak Law for Moments of Pairwise-Stable Networks. Working paper. USC.

Leung, M., 2015. A Random-Field Approach to Inference in Large Models of Network Formation. Working paper. USC.

Lovasz, L., 2012. Large Networks and Graph Limits. AMS Colloquium Publications, vol. 60. American Mathematical Society, Providence, RI.

Mele, A., 2012. A Structural Model of Segregation in Social Networks. Working paper. Johns Hopkins University.

Menzel, K., 2015a. Large matching markets as two-sided demand systems. Econometrica 83 (3), 897–941.

Menzel, K., 2015b. Strategic Network Formation with Many Agents. Working paper. New York University.

Menzel, K., 2016. Inference for games with many players. The Review of Economic Studies 83, 306–337.

Milgrom, P., Roberts, J., 1990. Rationalizability, learning, and equilibrium in games with strategic complementarities. Econometrica 58 (6), 1255–1277.

Miyauchi, Y., 2012. Structural Estimation of a Pairwise Stable Network with Nonnegative Externality. Working paper. MIT.

Moro, A., 2003. The effect of statistical discrimination on black-white wage inequality: estimating a model with multiple equilibria. International Economic Review 44 (2), 457–500.

Newey, W., McFadden, D., 1994. Large Sample Estimation and Hypothesis Testing. Chapter 36. In: Handbook of Econometrics, vol. IV.

Pęski, M., 2014. Large Roommate Problem with Non-Transferable Utility. Working paper. University of Toronto.

Resnick, S., 1987. Extreme Values, Regular Variation, and Point Processes. Springer.

Rust, J., 1987. Optimal replacement of GMC bus engines: an empirical model of Harold Zurcher. Econometrica 55 (5), 999–1033.

Sheng, S., 2014. A Structural Econometric Analysis of Network Formation Games. Working paper. UCLA.

Su, C., Judd, K., 2012. Constrained optimization approaches to estimation of structural models. Econometrica 80 (5), 2213–2230.

Tamer, E., 2003. Incomplete simultaneous discrete response model with multiple equilibria. The Review of Economic Studies 70, 147–165.

# Index

Printed in the United States
By Bookmasters